IN THEIR OWN WORDS

*Writings of war correspondent Don Martin
and his 11-year-old daughter Dorothy*

An intimate view of WW1

Title: In Their Own Words
Subtitle: Writings of war correspondent Don Martin and his
11-year-old daughter Dorothy — An intimate view of WW1

Edited by: James Larrimore

ISBN: 978-0-6450923-1-8

Cover design by Thomas Shaddock

DEDICATION

This book is dedicated to my grandfather Don Martin and his daughter—my mother, Dorothy. It has been prepared as a contribution to the commemoration of the 100th anniversary of World War I.

ACKNOWLEDGEMENTS

The material compiled in this book includes hundred–year–old surviving writings by Don Martin, his 11–year–old daughter Dorothy and his mother Rose Martin, many handwritten.

Dispatches published in the New York Herald were retrieved from the website of Thomas M. Tryniski of Fulton, New York 13069, www.fultonhistory.com, on which scanned copies of all the New York State newspapers are available. This includes the 1917–1918 New York Herald newspapers, in which Don Martin's war dispatches appeared. Dispatches published in the Paris Edition of the Herald were made available from the newspaper archives.

Making this project come to fruition would not have been possible without the creative and careful editing assistance of Phillipa Butler, and the support and suggestions from the family—Irene Larrimore, son Mark Larrimore, daughter Corinne Larrimore Shaddock, and cover design by grandson Thomas Shaddock.

CONTENTS

War correspondents and additional names mentioned in diaries

Adams, Franklin P.	Capt., Stars & Stripes	Kenamore, Clair	St Louis Post-Dispatch
Bailey, Herbert R.	Daily Mail, London	Kerney, Jim	Trenton Times
Ball, Walter S.	Providence Journal	Kloeber, Charles E.	Associated Press
Battersby, Henri Prevost	Reuters London	Mackenzie, Cameron	London Chronicle
Bazin, Henri	Philadelphia Public Ledger	McFall, Burge	Associated Press
Bliss, William T.	Chicago Tribune	McKenna	Canada
Blumenfeld, Ralph	London Express	McNutt, Carroll	Collier's
Blythe, Sam	Saturday Evening Post	Miller, Webb	United Press
Bryans, Mortimer	Associated American Newspapers	Muir	Herald/Paris
Burke, John	New York Herald night editor	Murphy, M.F.	Chicago Tribune
Carroll, Ray G.	Philadelphia Public Ledger	Noel, Percy	Chicago Daily News
Cobb, Jeremy	New York Evening World	Ohl, Josiah Kingsley	New York Herald Editor-in-Chief
Cobb, Irvin S.	New York World	Orr, Ernest	International News Service
Collier, Robert	Collier's	Parkerson, John T.	Associated Press
Conger, Lt Arthur L.	chief of staff, Intelligence, 2nd Division	Pattullo, George	Saturday Evening Post
		Phelps, Frank	Theater manager
Cooper, George	New York Herald management	Pipp, Edwin G.	Detroit News
Corey, Herbert	Everybody's Magazine	Prenosil, Stanley W	Associated Press
Daley, George W.	New York Herald managing editor	Price, Burn	Herald/Paris, Manager
		Roberts, Elmer	Associated Press
Draper, Mel	New York Tribune	Ruhl, Arthur	Collier's
Eyre, Lincoln	New York World	Russell, Ben	Businessman
Ferguson, Fred	United Press	Sinnott, Arthur	Newark Evening News
Flaherty, Frank	New York Herald general manager	Smith, Fred A.	Chicago Tribune
Ford, Bert	International News Service	Snyder, Milton	Sun, New York
Forrest, Wilbur S.	New York Herald Tribune	Sproul, Arthur Elliot	New York Times
Foster, Maximilian	Committee on Public Information	Taylor, Frank J.	United Press
Gibbons, Floyd	Chicago Tribune	Tuohey, James	World
Gibbon, Perceval	London Chronicle	Underwood, Russell	Businessman
Green, Martin	New York Evening World	Wales, Henry G	International News Service
Greenwall, Harry G.	London Daily Express	Wallace	Telegram
Gregg, Joseph	World, St. Louis	Weaver, Charles	
Griggs, J.W. (Joe)	New York World	Welliver, Judd	Sun, New York
Hall, Henry Noble	The Times, London	Wheeler, Charles N.	Chicago Tribune
Hedin, Naboth	Brooklyn Eagle	Wheeler, John N. "Jack"	newspaper publisher
Holmes	New York Times	Williams, Myrtle	Collier's
Hopper, James (Jimmy)	Collier's	Williams, Skipper (Wythe)	New York Times
James, Edwin L.	New York Times	Wilson	International News Service
Johnson, Sam		Wood, Junius	Chicago Daily News

PREFACE

In 1917 Don Martin, my grandfather, was a well-known newspaperman around the United States, reporting on local, state and national politics for the New York Herald. In 1918 he became an American war correspondent covering the US expeditionary forces in the Great War. Don Martin died in France of Spanish influenza in October 1918, on the day his daughter Dorothy turned twelve. I never met him; I was born sixteen years after his death. Growing up, I did not hear much about my grandfather.

After my mother, Dorothy, died in 2001, I came into possession of many things from her early years when her father, my grandfather, was alive. Included were Don Martin's diaries for 1916, 1917 and 1918, and packets of letters—those sent to her by her father, and those which she and other members of her family sent to him while he was serving as war correspondent for the New York Herald.

Interested to learn more about my grandfather's reporting on the Great War, I came across the remarkable work of Thomas M. Tryniski of Fulton, New York 13069, who has developed the website www.fultonhistory.com on which scanned copies of all the New York State newspapers are available. This includes the 1917–1918 New York Herald newspapers, in which Don Martin's war dispatches appeared. The Herald also had an English-language Paris edition to which Don Martin sent almost daily dispatches once he was in France and reporting on the war, and these also became available.

As a contribution to the centennial celebration of America's contribution to the Great War, starting on December 7, 2017, up through October 2018, I posted on a daily blog all the available material that Don had written, taken from his diaries and his dispatches published in the New York and Paris Herald, as well as excerpts from his letters. After his sudden, untimely death on October 6, 1918, in Paris, tributes were published about Don Martin which were also posted. The blog presents quite a story.

Don's relationship with his "girl", daughter Dorothy, was described in a vivid and touching way in the tribute written by fellow war correspondent Martin Green. That led me to delve into the correspondence written to Don by his 11-year-old daughter. That turned out to be something special and led to preparation of this book.

This book tells the story of Don Martin and his "girl", his daughter Dorothy. Don Martin had been a widower since 1908 when his young wife died of diphtheria. Their only child, daughter Dorothy, was eighteen months old when her mother died. Dorothy was brought up by her grandmother in the small town of Silver Creek near Buffalo in upstate New York, while her father was based in New York City. Don Martin had a great affection for his daughter, and visited her as often as he could. Letter writing was an important bond between them and started early. The earliest surviving letter by Dorothy to her father was written at age seven in 1914.

This book gives an intimate picture of this father-daughter relationship and of life in small-town America in the midst of the Great War. This book is "in their own words". The material is taken from surviving documents, many handwritten. Don Martin was a conscientious diarist and the entries in his personal diaries for 1917 and 1918 provide the timeline for the other material in the book. Fifty-three of Don Martin's letters to Dorothy and his mother that survived are included. Dorothy, who numbered her weekly letters at her grandmother's bidding, wrote thirty-eight letters over the nine-month period, nineteen of which have survived and are included, as are ten of Don's mother's letters. These letters are incorporated at the times they were written. Also, a few of Don Martin's multitude of published war dispatches are included to give the flavor of his remarkable reporting style.

A list of the other war correspondents who Don Martin noted in his diary as having met and interacted with, and their news organizations, is given on page vi.

INTRODUCTION

"She's some girl," said Don Martin to me. "Only eleven years old and look at the French she springs on me!"

Don Martin's girl was his only daughter and he used to read to me in France the sparkling communications he received from her most regularly, and I can bear witness that … the first letters he read were those from a little girl in Silver Creek, New York. The correspondence between Don Martin and his eleven-year-old daughter, in mixed English and French, was a beautiful exemplar of the household tie between France and the United States, which this war has created. I think of him now crouched back in the seat of an automobile, whizzing along a poplar lined road in France, reaching into his pocket for a letter and saying: 'I want to read you something my girl told me in her last letter.'

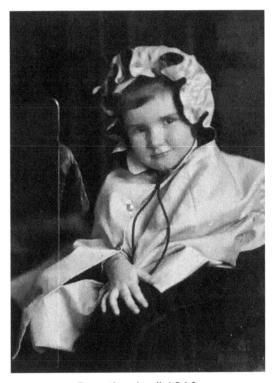

Dorothy, April 1910

And he was never too busy or tired to write to his girl. He was always picking up remembrances for her. I shall never forget what a row he raised when, on a trip with a unit of our forces, he lost a pair of little wooden shoes he had bought for her, with her name artistically cut into the sole of each shoe. He almost tore up the United States army in France."

So wrote Martin Green, the New York Evening World's leading war correspondent, in his tribute after Don Martin's untimely death from Spanish influenza on October 6, 1918, in Paris. The tribute was published in the New York Herald, Don Martin's newspaper, in its Sunday edition of October 13, 1918. The Herald's headline read:

'My Girl in the United States' Was Don Martin's Little Daughter.
Martin Green Tells of His Comrade's Devotion to Daughter, Twelve Years Old, as an Indication of His Character — Tribute to His Honor as a Journalist'

In this book that "sparkling communication" Green refers to between Don Martin and his daughter is brought to life after one hundred years through the surviving letters.

The last spark of that communication was a telegram Dorothy received from her father. Don Martin died in Paris on October 7, 1918, Dorothy's twelfth birthday. As perhaps his last act, Don must have asked a friend to send this cable to Dorothy shortly before he died.

This tale starts in the latter part of 1917 when the assignment of Don Martin to cover the American Expeditionary Forces in Europe was under consideration by James Gordon Bennett, the owner of the New York Herald. With that decision taken in late December 1917, Don traveled first to London, England, to head the Herald's office there, and then on to Paris, France, in March 1918. He joined the American war correspondents, who were first based in Neufchateau, then in Meaux, in Nancy and in Bar le Duc. Within a short time, Don Martin became recognized as one of the leading American war correspondents along with Floyd Gibbons of the Chicago Tribune, Martin Green of the New York Evening World and Ray Carroll of the Philadelphia Public Ledger.

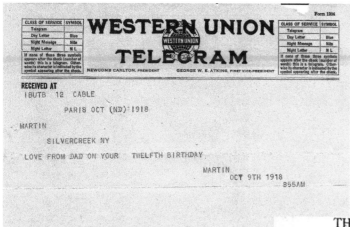

The cable received by Dorothy.

THREE COMRADES SEPARATED.

Left to Right.—
FLOYD GIBBONS,
DON MARTIN and
MARTIN GREEN.

Photograph from the New York Herald tribute shows Don Martin in the center of Floyd Gibbons and Martin Green.

"Martin was one of the best and the truest men with whom I have had a close relationship in my experience with the active working men in the newspaper business. I am truly, very truly, sorry to hear of this. He was of that sort that makes it quite worth while for a real man to do his best, efficiently, honestly and thoroughly."

— That was former President Theodore Roosevelt's reaction when he heard of Don Martin's death on Tuesday, October 8, 1918.

General John J. Pershing, Commander-in-Chief of the American Expeditionary Forces, wrote a letter of condolence to Don Martin's mother dated October 31, 1918.

AMERICAN EXPEDITIONARY FORCES
OFFICE OF THE COMMANDER-IN-CHIEF

France, October 31, 1918.

Dear Mrs. Martin:

May I offer you my sincere sympathy on the loss of your son and couple with it the hope that you will derive consolation from the manner and circumstance of his death? As well and as faithfully as any soldier he was serving his country on the battlefields of France, and his sacrifice, and yours, are for the land we love.

He shared the danger and exposure of the troops and did so in fine courage and spirit. His work was of the greatest value to the army which holds him in memory as a comrade. I am proud that he was my friend as I know you are that he was your son.

Please convey for me to his daughter, your grandchild, a message of gentle sympathy.

Sincerely yours,

John J. Pershing,

General Pershing's letter

Shortly thereafter Minna Irving of Tarrytown, New York, published a poem about Don Martin, calling him a "Soldier of the Pen".*

A SOLDIER OF THE PEN

He took the simple words we use
  And shaped them with his art
In wondrous imag'ry to show
  Poor France's bleeding heart.
He made us hear beyond the sea
  The roar of flaming guns,

And feel the nameless agonies,
  Inflicted by the Huns.
Enfold him with the starry flag:
  He died in uniform,
A stormy petrel of the press
  Who loved the battle storm.

Salute him with your lifted swords,
  Ye Allied fighting men,
Don Martin was a soldier, too—
  A soldier of the pen.
                    —MINNA IRVING

What made Don Martin so beloved? Private Leland R. B. Gilbert, field representative of the official government newspaper, Stars and Stripes, described it in the New York Herald shortly after Don Martin's death:

> *"As an American soldier and newspaper man, permit me to express along with hundreds of others my sincere regret at the untimely death of Don Martin. His interesting and well phrased pen pictures of our army were always eagerly awaited and appreciated to the fullest extent by many thousands of American soldiers in France. He possessed an individual and graphic style. At the same time he always was in the thick of the fighting and was prompt to chronicle events for Herald readers. He will be ranked with Joyce, Kilmer and other writers who have given their lives in the performance of their duties over here."*

Don Martin's newspaper was the New York Herald. The paper was founded in 1835 by the inventive editor James Gordon Bennett. Under Bennett's direction the Herald developed a style of reporting that was sensational in emphasis and high-spirited in tone, which influenced the entire American press. The Herald had a larger staff and published more news than any other New York City newspaper of its day.

Bennett's son, James Gordon Bennett, Jr., took over as editor in 1867. He was also a gifted editor and promoter—it was he who sent Henry Morton Stanley to Africa to find the long-lost explorer and missionary David Livingstone. He founded a Paris edition and contributed much to the paper's strengths.

Shortly after the Great War began in August 1914, the New York Herald signed up the renowned Percival Phillips as its war correspondent to report on the British troops engaged in the war. Bennett featured his articles on the front page of the New York Herald, with byline as 'Special Correspondent of the Herald with the British Forces in France'. That was a break from Bennett's rule of never bylining a reporter by name. He would continue that with Don Martin.

America entered the war in April 1917 and when American soldiers began to reach Europe to join the Allies, Bennett recognized that the Herald needed a reporter covering the American forces in France. He made a decision in October 1917 to send a correspondent to head the Herald office in London and cover the war from there. He selected his leading political reporter in New York, Don Martin. After Martin had established himself in France, his articles carried the byline 'Special Correspondent of the Herald with the American Expeditionary Forces in France'.

Don Martin left for Europe as an urbane, politically savvy, theater-going New Yorker. Initially, he viewed the war perhaps with a romantic air. But six months later, as he saw the war up close in France, his understanding changed dramatically. This is illustrated by the surviving *'subject for mail story'* note that he scribbled on a piece of paper in July 1918:

> *"This war where valor, bravery, heroism doesn't count. Gas, long range artillery robs war of all romance, glamor; makes it drab, grim, savage game of human slaughter."*

How much of this Don Martin conveyed to his daughter and family back home we shall see from his letters.

DON MARTIN AND DOROTHY
BIOGRAPHICAL BACKGROUND

Don Bermont Martin was born on October 2, 1873, in Silver Creek, NY, in Chautauqua County, near Buffalo. His father, Joseph B. Martin, was born in Cleveland, Ohio in 1845; his mother, Rosalie (Rose) Ann Bermont, was born in Escorse, Michigan, in 1853.

Don had three siblings, an older sister, Alta R. Martin, born in 1872; a brother, Roscoe (Rock), born in 1881, who married Inez; and a second sister, Julia B. Martin, born in 1883, who married Charles Howson. They appear in Dorothy's letters as Grandmother, Aunt Alta, Uncle Rock and Aunt Inez, and Aunt Julia (Jule) and Uncle Charlie (and their son Joseph, Dorothy's first cousin).

Don Martin met Ida May Masseth, from Canandaigua, NY, in New York City, and they married on December 27, 1905. Ida May bore a daughter, Dorothy Elisabeth, on October 7, 1906. Don Martin's mother, wife Ida May and baby Dorothy are shown in the photo taken in New York City in 1907.

Ida May Masseth Martin died of diphtheria in New York City on April 18, 1908. Don Martin became a widower with a daughter of less than two years age. With Don busy working in New York City, his family took charge of Dorothy. She was settled in the home of her grandmother in Silver Creek, where she grew up and lived when she wrote the letters to her Dad.

Don Martin began his newspaper career with the Buffalo Express, NY, where he developed a taste for political writing. When President McKinley was assassinated in September 1901 while visiting the Exposition in Buffalo, the journalist's graphic description attracted attention and resulted in his being brought to New York, first joining The New York American, and in 1904 the New York Herald.

At the Herald, Don served for a time as city editor, devoted chiefly to the political field. He worked in Albany during the sessions of the New York Legislature. From 1912 he was in charge of the political department of the Herald. His work in charge of the political straw vote of his paper for ten years attracted wide attention. One of his greatest personal triumphs was in the closely contested 1916 presidential election, when he predicted the re-election of President Wilson because the Herald's straw vote, which he personally conducted, indicated that result.

Don Martin numbered among his friends Theodore Roosevelt, William H. Taft, President Woodrow Wilson and Charles Evans Hughes. Hughes presided at the going-away affair at the New York Herald at the time of Don's departure for Europe. President Wilson sent a personal letter on his arrival in Europe.

Don Martin's wife Ida May (left), his mother Rose, and his baby daughter Dorothy.

Dorothy (18 months) and Ida May, New York City 1907

PART 1

Going to Europe
– August to December 1917

Dorothy began writing letters to her father when she was seven in 1914.

The first letter still existing is dated July 13, 1914, and was addressed to Don at The Herald, New York City, NY.

July 13, 1914

Dear Father

I am down to Buffalo. Grandmother has gone to do some shopping and I am staying with Aunt Alta. Mr Romer gave me a quarter to spend. The last time I came down to Buffalo Mr Romer gave me a dime. Yesterday afternoon I had an awfuly nice automobile ride. I got the bracelet and thought it was very, very pretty.

I'm very well and I hope you are too. Joseph is a very nice boy and today he did not want me to go to Buffalo. Aunt Alta said that she has got to use the machine now so I can not write any more.

With love,
From
Dorothy

I used the typewriter all myself and no one helped me.

In early August 1917, Dorothy handwrote the following two letters to her father, who was staying at the Hotel Ten Eyck in Albany, New York, on assignment.

Silver Creek, N.Y.
August 9th, 1917

Dear Daddy

It is about time I wrote to you. I feel very silly to-day and I am so excited that I don't hardly know where I'm at. Here is the reason – The other day some men decorated the park and half way up Oak hill, way down to Frank Erbin's store up to the Park Theater and way down to the foot bridge, with flags. A few are American – American army and American navy, but the rest are yellow + white + green + white and all colors like that. Some have two colors and some four or five. Then I didn't go down town again until this morning and my goodness. Every store + everything is all decorated up with red, white + blue flags.

Peddlers are all over town with hand-organs and strangers are all over town. You know these three days – to-day, tomorrow + next day is the Fireman's Convention. They are going to have a big parade to-morrow and a lot of races. They have got all sorts of Ice cream booths and men's games and fortune tellers and every crazy thing. Well, I guess you know all about that.

Joseph and his mother + father came a week ago Monday night. We have lots of fun playing. It is about all I do.

It has been awfully hot here but last night we had a storm and to-day it is real cool and it looks quite a bit as if we were going to

10

have another rain. I am invited down to Mrs Berry's at Dahn's Beach this afternoon with two other girls to go in bathing.

Will have to close now. Lots of Love + hugs + kisses

Dorothy

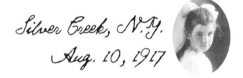

Silver Creek, N.Y.
Aug. 10, 1917

Dear Dad

Yesterday I wrote a letter and just as I was going to mail it the postman gave me a letter from you from the Ten Eyck. I addressed my letter for you to New York and Grandmother wrote one to you the other day and addressed it to New York too but maybe they will be forwarded.

To-day is a big day. Fireman's Convention. There are 15 bands here and about that many hose Co's. There are really just about 4,000 people in Silver Creek but to-day there are going to be 10,000. It is beautiful out to-day. Not hot – really very cool.

I got all the pictures. There [are] some really good ones of you I think too. I gave some to Aunt Josephine and I am going to give some to Marguerite Shumaker too.

Guess I will have to close and get ready to see the races downtown. There is a mid-way and all sorts of things.

Lots of Love + hugs + kisses

Dorothy

Don Martin in 1905

At work, 1917

For Don Martin, the start-stop story of his leaving for Europe to cover the Great War for the Herald was nerve-racking and seemingly neverending. He wrote a lot about it in his 1917 Diary. The first mention was in his entry of Sunday August 26, 1917. At that time he was engaged in overseeing the Herald's electoral poll for the mayoralty race in New York City.

Diary: Sunday August 26, 1917

Took 4:51 train from Albany to N.Y. On way in office met Ohl, Editor-in- Chief, who wanted to know if I would consent to go to London as chief correspondent there. Told him I would if the office would take care of all my financial obligations and gives me enough to live well on in London. Ohl said he would cable Bennett in Paris. I doubt if the old man will be willing to give me enough to make the place possible. I should be glad to go.

Diary: Thursday August 30, 1917

Guess nothing will come of the London offer. Saw Ohl at dinner and he didn't mention it. I didn't either. Not so anxious to be separated from Dorothy. Furthermore Herald probably wouldn't pay what I demand.

Diary: Sunday October 7, 1917

Ohl got cable from Bennett asking when I could go to London. They want me to go but the office wants me here until after the election. I'd just as soon go to London if the office will send $40 to $50 a week home and give me enough to live on in addition. I can't save anything anyhow so maybe this would be a good arrangement.

Diary: Tuesday October 9, 1917

Ohl said Bennett cabled for me to stay here till after election. From this the office infers I am to go to London right after election. I am willing. Hate to be separated in that way from Dorothy. However, I probably won't be away a great while, if, in fact, at all.

Daley says he doesn't like the London business because he wants me here. However, he says if Bennett will send me to the front, it will be worthwhile for me and Herald both.

And here I am! With a possible chance to be a war correspondent and have an experience as a newspaperman abroad! Once, such a thing would have caused great excitement in me but now not much. I haven't lost my romantic interest but I don't exactly care so much about going so far away from Dorothy.

Diary: Sunday October 14, 1917

Had quite a talk with George Cooper. He says Commodore Bennett has his mind made up for me to go to Europe, but that he wants me to finish up the Mayoralty campaign. However I shan't say anything about it till I get definitive word. Don't imagine Dorothy will like it but she is a philosopher. I won't go unless I can spend a week or so with her first.

With the prospect of leaving New York for England, here is what Don Martin recorded in his diary about the dangers of crossing the Atlantic.

Diary: Friday October 19, 1917

American transport Antilles, on way back from France, sunk in mid-ocean by German submarine—70 dead.

Diary: Saturday October 20, 1917

German raiders sunk 9 British, Danish + Norwegian merchant ships and 2 British torpedo boats. The world is beginning to wonder what's the matter with the British navy.

The uncertainty of whether he would go or not weighed on his mind, as shown in these diary entries.

Diary: Sunday October 21, 1917

John Burke asked me when I'm going to Europe. The more I think of it the more I hate to get so far away from Dorothy. Although I don't see a great deal of her, I realize how much she means to me. It's a rather different feeling than I've ever had before except for her Mother.

Diary: Tuesday October 23, 1917

Early this morning—about 2am—I had a talk with Flaherty, general manager, who said he thinks it unwise of Bennett to take me away from N.Y. He says he has advised the editors here that it's foolish to send me to London. So maybe I won't go at all. Doesn't make much difference. I shan't give it any thought at all till I hear definitely one way or the other.

Don Martin had not mentioned his Europe possibility in Silver Creek. Meanwhile, changes were brewing at the New York Herald.

Diary: Wednesday October 24, 1917

Flaherty told me he thinks there will be a big editorial change in the paper and that he hopes they will keep the "good men here", meaning me, he says. Probably nothing will come of the European matter after all. Probably I'm glad. I'm glad I have not mentioned it at home anyhow. The office here is running along on one leg or less.

Martin continued to get mixed messages about his going to London.

Diary: Sunday November 4, 1917

Cooper told me today to get my passports to be prepared for orders to go to Europe. However I am doing nothing. I have a strong "hunch" that I'll stay right here. Wrote a long letter to Dorothy.

The last "straw man" vote was published on Sunday, November 4, and the election took place on Tuesday November 6. Don Martin, the "Straw Man", was right once again, in an unusual election with many political currents flowing. He noted his success, and then started to turn to the possibility of going to London to take over the Herald's London office.

Diary: Wednesday November 7, 1917

About everyone I know called up or came in today to congratulate me on the Straw Man's accurate prophecy. I spoke to Daley about going home for a few days and he said to take a week off but first to leave order for passport so there would be no delay when word came from Bennett to go to Europe. Don't know just what to think but suspect no word will come from Bennett. Whether it does or not I will spend a week with Dorothy.

Diary: Thursday November 8, 1917

Went to the passport office with Voute of the Telegram and made application for France and England. Had photos made by Henry of our photograph dept. Had to use 4 for passport applications. Office hasn't heard definitely from Bennett that I am to go to Europe but Daley, Ohl and Cooper thought I better get passports so as to be ready. Funny office! I shall go to Silver Creek tomorrow or Saturday to have a rest + to wait definite news about London. Am anxious to see Dorothy.

Don Martin took off for his home in Silver Creek and had a grand week with his daughter, his mother and other folks.

Diary: Friday November 16, 1917

Got a letter from the office asking me to go around the state getting up a big story on the political effect of the woman suffrage amendment. No word about London. Guess that is off.

His next assignment took him around New York State and especially to the capital in Albany, where on November 22 he thought it was no-go for Europe.

Returning to the Herald office in New York the next day, he found there had been major management changes, but his assignment to London seemed to firm up.

Diary: Friday November 23, 1917

George Cooper now managing editor of the Herald says I am to go to Europe as soon as word comes from the Commodore. I don't take any stock in this.

But Don Martin was sent off to Albany to handle the copying of the names of all German aliens in New York City for publication in the Herald, which he described several times as "quite a job". While in Albany, his assignment to London finally did solidify.

Diary: Wednesday November 28, 1917

Well it looks as if I might go to Europe after all. Got a wire from Cooper this afternoon saying Bennett had cabled asking when I could come. Cooper said I could go on the St. Paul of the American line on Saturday, December 8th. So it looks as if everything is fixed now. I am wondering now how I can arrange to see Dorothy, Mother and the rest of the folks before I start. I certainly shall see them.

Diary: Thursday November 29, 1917

Got a telegram from Cooper saying the Commodore cabled for me to go to London. Said reservation had been made for me on the St. Paul of the American Line. Looks as if I am going at last but I'll have major doubts till I'm on the ship. Will go home for a day or two anyhow.

Diary: Monday December 3, 1917

Nothing new on the European matter but it is apparently settled that I shall go on the St. Paul Saturday. Wired Dorothy I will be up to see her. Left for Buffalo and Silver Creek at midnight.

Don left Albany for Silver Creek for what would be his last days with his daughter, his mother and his family. In Silver Creek he talked with Dorothy about his going far away to Europe.

Diary: Tuesday December 4, 1917

Put in a fine day in Silver Creek with Dorothy. She says she is perfectly willing I should go to Europe but it is very evident she regrets it. The poor youngster! But she is game. She says I was away once for six months and that she will be perfectly contented. We went down town in the afternoon and in the evening went down to call on Jule, Charlie + Joseph. Joe seems much interested in me all of a sudden too. He is a fine boy and smart as the dickens. Dorothy + I frolicked around the house till 9 when she went to bed. I carried her upstairs and had to throw her on the bed a half dozen times. She says she wishes she might always stay 11 years old, and she also says if she were a boy she would dress up this year as Santa Claus: take all the things she could spare and distribute them among poor children. She is a wonderful child but no longer a child. Her hair is long now and very beautiful too.

Diary: Wednesday December 5, 1917

Dorothy and I were together today every minute. She has her own notions apparently about my going away but she won't give any indication that she is worried, but I know she doesn't exactly like to have me go. When I asked her if she would worry, she said, "I don't know how to worry." She and I went down to see John Knox: went up to see his wife, and called on Mary Ann and Mrs. Merkshad. I found that almost everyone had heard that I am probably going to Europe.

At six o'clock Charlie, Jule, Dorothy, Joseph and I went in Charlie's car to a fire on the old Curson's place. An Italian's house burned to the ground. We had a good view of it. Later had dinner at Mother's and after bidding the family good-bye, I went to the trolley station with Dorothy to take the 8:15 car for Buffalo. Dorothy was right there at the finish. Arrived in Buffalo at 10 and met Alta at the Iroquois. She went to the station with me at midnight.

Back in New York, Don Martin began organising to leave but it still took weeks of preparation.

Diary: Thursday December 6, 1917

Arrived in N.Y. at 9:30 a.m. having slept all the way from Rochester to Peekskill. Find no absolute word has come from the Commodore for me to start for Europe, but Cooper says I am going just the same. At his request I engaged a $225 stateroom on the Philadelphia, which is to sail on Dec 16. There is no sailing of the St. Paul on Saturday, as Cooper said. I also got my passports in their final form. Everyone around the office taking it for granted I am going to Europe. I should like to be told with finality. I have from the start, despite assurances, passports and everything else, felt that something would upset the whole thing.

Diary: Saturday December 8, 1917

Everyone around the office bidding me good-bye in anticipation of the London trip which is still in a state of uncertainty despite the fact that Cooper says I am sure to go. I certainly am getting disgusted with the delay.

Diary: Friday December 14, 1917

Cooper still says I will go to Europe. He had some of the officers of the St. Louis at the office so I could meet them. Philadelphia sailing postponed. Next ship is the St. Louis on the 19th. Have made a reservation on that.

Diary: Sunday December 16, 1917

At last it seems that the European trip will materialize. Cooper called me up at noon—I was sound asleep—to tell me that word had come from the Commodore and that I shall get ready to go on the St. Louis on Wednesday. Now I shall get ready to go. Had dinner at Cooper's apartment on East 36th St. and talked over the European trip.

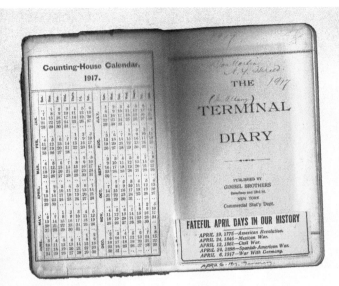

Don Martin's 1917 diary

Diary: Monday December 17, 1917

This was indeed a busy day. Got up at 8: bought a half hundred things for my trip across. Got my ticket—a stateroom on the St. Louis. Had talk with Cooper. I am to be in full charge of the London bureau and have privilege to send a lot of cable matter.

Spent the afternoon shopping, and getting finishing touches put on the trip. Everything is all "set" now for me to go to Europe on Wednesday. Have not the slightest fear.

Dorothy wrote to her father on December 17, 1918, after a telegram was received in Silver Creek saying he was departing New York by steamer. She addressed the letter Care American Line Steamer St. Louis, New York, NY. The letter was returned with the notation: *"Not on Board. Return to Sender"*

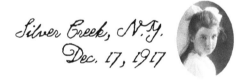

Silver Creek, N.Y.
Dec. 17, 1917

Dear Dad

I am just going to write you a teensy note because I am going to a party after school and we all have to stay for Geography and I have to finish my practicing and about a million other things, so I guess you can see what sort of state I'm in.

We got your telegram this morning and I'll say it certainly ought to be settled by this time, it has been postponed so many times. We have Santa Claus after you with some-thing and I do hope he will reach you before you go because he will not be able to fly across the ocean after you. I'll be glad to see the letter you are going to write.

Well, now Merry merry, merry a million times Christmas and the same with Happy New Year and Bon Voyage. Good-bye Goodbye, I won't worry so don't worry.

Lots of millions of hugs and kisses,

Dorothy

P.S. So many Hugs + kisses they will last till you get back.

[Scribble of hugs and kisses]

P.P.S.S. When you write from Over There don't forget to tell me when to write or cable.

Diary: Tuesday December 18, 1917

Well here I am getting ready in earnest to go to Europe. Much shopping and had quite a job. Trunks packed. Had quite a surprise this evening. Cooper took me into the Council room where the whole staff and a lot of friends from outside were waiting to present me with a farewell testimonial. Mr. Hughes* made the speech and spoke rather highly of me, I should say. He presented me with a very handsome watch—a gift from the staff—and then I got an expensive fob from Flaherty, general manager: a cigarette case from the staff and a leather passport holder from Cooper. It was a grand send-off. I didn't know I had so many friends. Sent night letters to the folks and then, at midnight, went to the York and packed a trunk etc.

The New York Herald building in 1895, the year it was built. It was demolished about 1940.

* Charles Evans Hughes, a leading man of the nation.

That surprise send-off got a big write-up on Wednesday December 19, 1917, in The Herald.

Mr. Hughes Aids in Giving Send-Off to Don Martin

Presents gift to Political Reporter on the Herald in Behalf of Latter's Associates

Don Martin, friend and associate of many of the leading men of the nation, and for many years political reporter of the New York Herald, who starts for Europe soon as a correspondent for the Herald, was thrust suddenly into the darkened council room in the Herald Building last evening by an escorting editor. When the lights were turned on Mr. Martin found himself surrounded by his cheering associates on the Herald staff.

Then followed the presentation of a series of gifts, some of which were camouflage and others persiflage, and at the proper time, in other words, the psychological moment, the assemblage parted and Charles Evans Hughes stepped into the room. On behalf of the staff Mr. Hughes presented to Mr. Martin a watch and fob, saying:

"Mr. Martin, my presence here attests to your success and accuracy as a Straw man. Again am I called upon, with great pleasure, to speak of your character, as I was on that chill evening on one of my superfluous journeys, when from the tail end of a railroad train I addressed your fellow townsmen in Silver Creek, Chautauqua county. You have attained the highest goal man may attain by having many friends who wish to honor you, among whom I have the pleasure of being counted as one. Your attainments and your success here have called you to higher honors abroad, and in presenting this watch and fob on behalf of your associates I only regret that it will be necessary to turn the hours ahead, but we rejoice that those lost hours will be restored to you when you return."

Mr. Martin expressed regret that his accuracy as editor of the straw vote, taken before each election by the Herald, had made it necessary for him to forecast the defeat of Mr. Hughes as republican nominee for President of the United States. *"And I don't know what all you people are doing here unless you want to see me drop dead, because I can't stand this for long."*

Don Martin wrote a long letter to his mother on December 18, 1917, which shows his uncertainty about the voyage and his perhaps romantic idea, at that moment, that he would get a "taste of war, but not in the danger zone, or near enough to it in fact to be in the slightest danger." That would change, as we shall see.

The New York Herald
New York, Dec. 18, 1917

Mother

I guess I am going to Europe sure enough now. I have a ticket for a stateroom on the upper deck of the St. Louis of the American Line and passports for England and France. The ship is scheduled to leave here at noon on Wednesday but there is always a possibility that there will be a delay of a day or two. However I daresay I will be well out to sea Friday evening when Dorothy is having her nightly romp. I would like to be there to help her have it and to throw her into bed. Maybe she will be too old for that sort of thing by the time I get back. That doesn't mean that I will be gone a great long while but that she is almost a big girl now and in a year or so will begin to be a young lady. She says though that she hopes she never will grow up and in spirit I hope she never will.

I will make arrangements with the office to mail a check to you each week. Out of that I wish you would give Rock $5 a week to keep up my loan association dues and to pay for Dorothy's lessons as well as Jule's expenses to Buffalo with her. I think there will be enough. If you don't get a check for a while don't worry over it because I have drawn considerable money ahead for expenses and there may be a little delay in adjusting things, but it will all straighten out.

I have mailed a little present for Alta to Silver Creek and have sent her some money with which to get things for Dorothy and Joseph. That is about all the Christmas I intend to give. Liberty bonds and the high cost of living give everyone an excuse for holding out on Christmas this year.

I have written Alta how I am to be reached. I will be in London probably about January 1 and will send a cable at once. Don't worry however if you don't hear for several weeks because the ships go slow and cables are slower. There will be no danger about my reaching England all right. The St. Louis is a big ship which has been transformed into a regular warship and even if she were hit by a torpedo, which is quite unlikely, there would be every facility on board for saving everyone. I have a heavy sweater, sleeping socks which they say are desirable; a police whistle to blow if I find myself adrift in a small boat and a flashlight to attract attention; heavy socks, underclothes, cap and everything one could need. In addition I am to be the Captain's special guest and he says I will own the ship; eat at his private table and share his quarters with him if I choose. However, I have a nice stateroom all to myself with a bath and every convenience and it is high up where one would have every chance in the world to get out if an accident happened. However it would be foolish to worry at all. No passenger ship has been torpedoed in a year—in fact in two years—and in stormy weather there is practically no danger. So far as stormy weather goes, I don't mind that. I like it cold and a heavy sea never bothers me at all.

When I land I will mail a letter to you and Dorothy and will hope to receive a letter from you too some time in January. The mails leave here about once a week and letters go through all right. My address will be the New York Herald, London, England. I shall be registered as the Herald's London correspondent in full charge of the London headquarters. I shall cable important news and send special articles by mail. It sounds like a big job but it won't bother me any. I am sure I can do it well but whether or not I can do it satisfactorily to James Gordon Bennett depends. It doesn't matter. I can't lose either way. I can make other connections if I wish to stay in London and break away from the Herald—which I don't expect to though—or I can come back here and get a good job in any one of a dozen places. So you see there is no way of losing out. Anyhow I shall see London and other parts of England; will see France I expect and possibly different regions along the front and will have a taste of war, but not in the danger zone, or near enough to it in fact to be in the slightest danger. I am in the best of condition to start with and there is no reason in the world why I should not remain so. Living will be very high but my expenses will be paid and you may be sure that I shall get enough to eat and have an excellent place to live.

I have about 50 letters of introduction from people of prominence here. The letters are directed to the statesmen, government officials, theatrical managers, playwrights, writers and travelers. I could have many more but I have now more than I shall ever present. I know a great many people who have headquarters in London and will, I am quite sure, within a few months, feel almost as much at home around Trafalgar Square, Piccadilly, Fleet Street and the Strand as I do on Broadway and I know Broadway pretty well.

I shall not worry about Dorothy because I know there is no need of it. Neither shall I worry about any of the rest of you. Dorothy is a very wonderful girl and I can already see a splendid future for her in every way. She has traits which she certainly never got from me which make her a most lovable youngster and I can see things about her which she no doubt does get from me, which will be helpful to her in after years. She thinks the world of you and even two weeks ago said she would never go to London or New York either unless you went too. I guess what the people of Silver Creek tell me is true—that you have brought her up in splendid shape and I think it has been a good thing for both of you.

Joseph and she are great comrades and they are certainly fine children. They don't grow any better. Joseph has some very remarkable characteristics and in addition has a brain which will make him a very superior man if it is directed properly as I know it will be. Maybe he doesn't get spanked often enough but he will find himself regardless of that when he gets a little older. I think an awful lot of him and I fancy he likes me pretty well too.

I have been doing nothing for a week but wait for word from Paris and for the ship to sail. On Saturday word came from Mr. Bennett for me to sail when I was ready and the St. Louis is the first ship out. I think it is a good opportunity for me. I have done all the kinds of newspaper work there is here and now a peep at Europe will be a good thing to broaden me out, but I don't know what I will do when I get broadened out.

By the way, that article to appear in the American magazine, about which I told Alta, will not appear until next September. The publishers notified me that they like it very much—I didn't write it but it is about me—but that it will be more timely next fall at the outset of a campaign. Maybe I will be back by that time.

I really don't know how long I will be away. It may be a few months. It may be till the end of the war. I will keep in touch with you by every mail and if anything goes wrong you will hear of it without delay; but nothing will go wrong. I will enjoy it no doubt. London is an interesting city and being the correspondent of the Herald there, having full charge of all the war news, gives one considerable prestige even in a city as big as London. I daresay I will have to wear evening clothes quite frequently.

Which reminds me I will have a hat box, a plain board box, a trunk and a small valise sent by express to Silver Creek to be held there. I have no place to keep them. The charges will be considerable but you can pay them and take the cost out of the money which will begin coming to you after a bit.

I may think of something else to say by tomorrow and will write if I do. I will write to Dorothy tomorrow anyhow. And I will send a night letter so that you will know Wednesday morning definitely that I am to sail or not to sail. Tell Rock and Jule that this letter is intended for them as well as for you. It is a long one and tells everything there is to tell. I have about a hundred things to do and about a dozen invitations to dinner both tonight and tomorrow night. Give my love to Dorothy and all the others and expect to hear from me by cable about January 1st or maybe the 10th.

With love
Don

Letter to Dorothy, December 18, 1917, New York, talking about Christmas and her life while he was away.

The New York Herald
New York, Dec. 18 -- 1917

My dear little girl

Just about the time you get this Dad will be on his way down the Bay enroute to Europe/ And you may know that he'll be thinking of you and wishing you were with him/. But my goodness! I can't get lonesome. There are a lot of people on the ship whom I know and besides that I am to be sort of a special guest of the captain and the steamship company. I have the greatest collection of things you ever saw—sleeping socks, flannel pajamas, a cap with earlaps, hot water bag, a heavy sweater, flannel underclothes, socks—and I don't know what else.

Today I have been rather busier than when you and I are together in Silver Creek, though no busier I guess than when bedtime comes and you turn loose that dynamic energy of yours. People have been coming in all the time; the phone has been ringing and on top of it all I have been trying to write some letters. This is one I shall write before I do anything else. The next one you get from your Dad will be from the other side and I will have a great deal to tell you.

I may be able to tell you where Bay Rum is—you know the poem we had about it—and then maybe I'll run across the Dingle family. I hope I do. I'll bet they're funny.

Now about that Santa Claus letter my dear young lady. I could have forwarded it to him, as I did last year, but you see it can't reach me in time now. So you better not write one this year. I think Santa Claus will keep you in mind. I told him quite a bit about you last year and he said then that he remembered you. He intimated to me one day a couple of weeks ago (I saw him by the merest accident in Albany) that he might find a doll's bed for you and just between us I think he had one all picked out then. He will talk to Aunt Alta about it. You'll come out all right I imagine. Your Dad won't send anything direct but there is just a possibility that something will come along. I sent you a pair of scout shoes the other day but they are not a Christmas present. And when I come back from Europe I shall bring you some nice things. I daresay you know that well enough.

My ship, the St. Louis, will leave here at noon tomorrow and on Christmas Day I will be out in the middle of the ocean. Probably I will arrive in London about Jan. 1 and then you will get word—or very soon after that. You must write to me Dorothy.

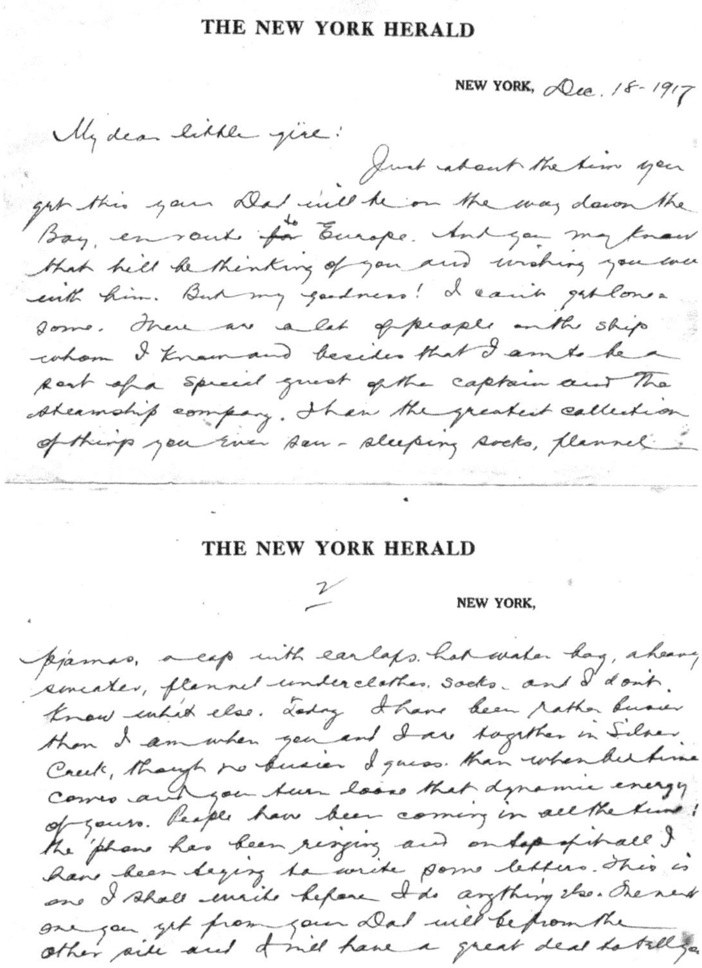
THE NEW YORK HERALD

NEW YORK, Dec. 18-1917

My dear little girl:

Just about the time you get this your Dad will be on the way down the Bay, en route to Europe. And you may know that he'll be thinking of you and wishing you were with him. But my goodness! I can't get lonesome. There are a lot of people on the ship whom I know and besides that I am to be a part of a special guest of the captain and the steamship company. I have the greatest collection of things you ever saw - sleeping socks, flannel

THE NEW YORK HERALD

2

NEW YORK,

pajamas, a cap with earlaps, hot water bag, a heavy sweater, flannel underclothes, socks, and I don't know what else. Today I have been rather busier than I am when you and I are together in Silver Creek, though no busier I guess than when bedtime comes and you turn loose that dynamic energy of yours. People have been coming in all the time! the 'phone has been ringing and on top of it all I have been trying to write some letters. This is one I shall write before I do anything else. The next one you get from your Dad will be from the other side and I will have a great deal to tell you

Extract from original letter to Dorothy of December 18, 1917.

It isn't necessary for me to urge you to keep at your music. I know you will do so. Aunt Alta tells me you are willing to do even more than the teacher asks. I guess you're a pretty good girl after all and so you probably won't have to work in a laundry at all. I hardly thought that would be necessary. In a year or two you will find you can play very nicely and you know your Dad is anxious to have you be a good musician. And you'll keep up your French too, won't you Dorothy? That will be a wonderful thing when you get older and then you will be glad your father was insistent and your grandmother French and patient. You go right ahead with all your outdoor playing too because that will be a splendid thing for you. Of course you are bound to grow up, even though you would like to be a Peter Pan but have all the fun you can right now. Sometimes I think you are a Peter Pan and that I'm one too. A fine pair of Peter Pans we make when I'm in Silver Creek.

Don't you forget what I told you about having the things you want, Dorothy. You just insist on it. I probably won't be here this spring to take you down to Betty's shop but Grandmother or Aunt Alta or Julie will, and maybe in the fall you and I will make another raid on the place.

My but this is a long letter! You will get tired reading it. You must see Uncle Rock, Aunt Alta, Uncle Charlie and Aunt Julie and tell them that this letter and the long one I wrote to Mother, are family or community letters, and that I will write to them all from London. I want you to see John Knox right away too Dorothy and tell him that I want to be remembered to him, his wife and daughters, and then you must say goodby to Aunt Josephine and Les for me too. Here's a good big hug and kiss for you Dorothy, and the best love,

From your Daddy

Finally, the departure!

Diary: Wednesday December 19, 1917

Started for London.

Left for London on the St. Louis (American Line) at 4 p.m. Got a lot of presents for use on the voyage and telegrams and letters. Herald printed story about last night's affair with Hughes picture and mine. Was at the pier at 11. Have got a stateroom with bath all to myself. Now (10 p.m.) the boat is pitching considerably but there is no storm. Weather is mild. Ship is lighted in the smoking rooms, library etc. but not a ray of light can be seen from without. Walking on the deck at night almost out of the question on account of the darkness.

About 2/3 of the passengers are American officers on the way to France, and a fine looking lot of men they are. I spent most of the time until pitch darkness on the deck. Hardly seems I am on my way to London + war correspondent but I am. Drew $500 expenses and arranged with office to send $50 a week home to Mother. I'm going to miss Dorothy.

Letter to Dorothy, December 19, 1917, On Board
(Handwritten)

U.S.M.S. "ST. LOUIS"
Dec 19 – 1917

My Dear Dorothy

Steamships these days never leave on time. We were scheduled to start at noon but it is 3 now and the work of loading is just going on. We may not get away till evening.

I have a very nice room and private bath—with a writing desk, easy chair, sofa and bed. I shall be very comfortable. There are a lot of persons on board whom I know and about 100 army officers of high rank. The ship would reach about from the Mill Lane to Dr. Coles (or it seems so) and there is no more danger than in going to Chicago. Because of the large number of army men aboard, we will be escorted away across by warships. Probably we shall arrive in England about Jan 30 *[sic]*.

I was quite flabbergasted last night at the office. I was asked to come into the big council room in front, and was fairly hurled amid about 150 of the editors, reporters, artists and other employees—as well as some men of prominence from outside—and was quickly informed that the gathering was for me. I won't attempt to tell you what was said. I am too modest. There were several speeches and then who appeared but Gov. Hughes, who presented me with a splendid solid gold watch about as thick as paper, with my initials on the back and engraving on the inside of the case showing that it was a gift from all the employees. It must have cost 4 or 5 hundred dollars. Then there was a very costly gold pot from the general manager; an initialed cigarette case from the managing editor; a fine leather passport case from the staff; several small things from various members of the staff, and a half dozen funny things. I gave the funny ones away but sent a toy piano to you. One present was a fancy wooden H about 3 feet high. It was explained that I would probably need it in England.

Hughes made quite a speech and I replied briefly, saying that the aggregation was not so friendly as would seem, because not one had been amiable enough to tip me off so I could prepare a speech. It was all quite complimentary. There was a short article about it in the Herald today, with my picture and Gov. Hughes. I didn't have time to mail papers to you, but I asked one of the girls in the office to do so, so you will probably see it. I also left an order to have the Herald sent to you every day. Tell Aunt Alta I got her fine box and have it in my stateroom. It is very acceptable.

I will say adieu now Dorothy for a short time. You will soon get a cable from London and a little later a long letter. Give my love to all the family, especially Joseph and keep a lot for yourself.

Your Dad

And then the adventure of an Atlantic crossing in the middle of a naval war.

Diary: Thursday December 20, 1917

At sea. 277 miles.

Slept too late to get breakfast but made up for it at 1 o'clock. Spent early part of afternoon walking on deck. Sea pretty rough and a good many persons sick. I haven't noticed any discomfort yet. Quite a musicale this afternoon. A young artillery lieutenant sang and played very beautifully. Ship has 600 passengers, more that ½ of them being U.S. officers going to France, and a fine looking lot they are. Decks are dark and tonight it was not allowable for people to walk outside on account of the sea. Sat in the smoker a while; then stood on deck a while and went to bed at midnight. No one seems much worried about submarines though everyone realizes there is danger.

Weather rough + windy.

Diary: Friday December 21, 1917

At sea. 373 miles

This has been a beautiful day. Got up at 9. Walked and sat on the deck nearly all the forenoon. At 11 a.m. everyone put on a life preserver and had a lifeboat drill. Good idea! At lunchtime everyone was kept off the decks and the gun crews fired at a target designed as a periscope. They scored 5 hits. At 5 o'clock Mr. Russell of Morris Beef Co.* + I went up on the bridge and then had dinner with the officers on the boat deck. It was a good dinner and I was hungry. Talked about submarines. The officers frankly say they would not be surprised if a submarine "got" the St. Louis but they insist they could get the passengers off. It doesn't worry me. I'm willing to take chances.

Weather mild + nice. Little sea.

Diary: Saturday December 22, 1917

At sea. 375 miles.

This was a pleasant day till late afternoon when wind shifted to South West, beating up a nasty sea. I played stud poker in smoking room with Mr. Russell, Kloeber of A.P., Lieut. Commander White + an English writer named Polland. Lost about $2. Played both afternoon and evening. Quite late wandered around the ship with young chap named Keegshon, on his way to Holland. He is a kid + very nice fellow. Am not meeting up with too many. Would rather not. At 12:30 a.m., after writing long letter on my typewriter to Dorothy, I lay in bed and read. Ship pitched and rolled furiously. Many people sick but so far I have enjoyed it. We are nearing submarine zone but no one seems worried. Learned that gun crew in practice last Thursday found two defective shells.

Weather nice but windy + foggy at night.

* Morris Meat Company, an American firm long established on the London meat market, held contracts for the supply of meat to the military.

25

Letter to Dorothy, December 22, 1917

At sea, Dec. 22, 1917

My dear Dorothy,

Here I am, away off the Newfoundland Banks, going at 19 miles an hour through a sea almost as smooth as Lake Erie in August. No submarines yet. Probably there will be none. No one seems to be worrying although everyone realizes the possibility that one might show up at any moment and shoot a torpedo at us. Still everyone would have a good chance to be rescued. There are plenty of lifeboats. Everyone has two life preservers in his room; every passenger has a card telling him which lifeboat he shall go to in case of trouble and we all have rehearsed the proceeding so as to be ready. I have a room of fair size and every comfort except heat. The boat is somewhat cold but no one minds it. Everyone wears warm clothes.

On the first day we made 277 miles. The second day 373 and the third 375. We are now on the Banks of Newfoundland, well out to sea, and will head due East, going either north around the Scottish coast or south around the Irish shore. It makes little difference which. We expect to land in Liverpool on Friday or Saturday and the first thing I shall do will be to mail this letter and additions to it which I shall probably write during the next few days. The censor will have to read it before it leaves England but I daresay there is nothing in it which will offend him and that you will get it about as I am now writing it on my own typewriter in my stateroom.

We left New York at four o'clock Wednesday afternoon. It was raw and cold all the evening. The next day—Thursday—the wind blew rather hard and there was considerable of a sea. The bow plunged into the swells several times and water raced down the promenade decks but not enough to do any harm. However, it was unpleasant on deck and most people remained inside. In the afternoon and evening perhaps 50 persons gathered in the library or lounge and there was quite a musicale. Several American officers on their way to France played the piano splendidly and sang all the songs well known on Broadway. It made things very enjoyable.

Yesterday was a nice day. Only a light sea and delightful air. We had entered the Gulf Stream ... It is much warmer than the surrounding water and warms the atmosphere. I walked up and down the deck nearly all the afternoon. In the evening it was not pleasant to be out. In the first place you know the ships have to be absolutely dark. Not a single ray of light is permitted to escape to the decks, so that a ship, no matter how large it is, cannot be seen unless an enemy is very close by. People are allowed to go on the decks at night but it is so black that few do so. The smoking room, where the men gather to play cards, etc. sits on the stern of the ship about 40 feet back of the main cabin and it is necessary for the company to run a rope from one house to the other so that, in the darkness, the men can see to get back and forth.

It all seems rather uncanny. A great big ship, plunging along swiftly through the night, with the white caps surging away on both sides, and not a light showing to warn a ship which might be coming from the opposite direction. However there is little danger of collision. The steamers going East are compelled to keep within a track well defined to them and vice versa. However the risks they run these days are very grave compared with the risks of normal times, but the officials of the ships and the passengers don't seem to mind it. In the evening every curtain is drawn tight and the spaces between the cabins and the dining rooms are darkened. Inside the ship, except for the lighted library and smoking rooms, one is reminded of a coal mine.

There are 600 passengers. Half of them are officers on their way to France and a fine looking lot of men they are. Most of the other passengers are British. At my table sits a youthful Scotchman who has been a Chaplain in the British Army in India. Also an Englishman who is returning home after 25 years in India. Then there is an English army officer, the wife of a Duke who lives in Canada and a few others of lesser prominence. The meals are very good but probably would grow tiresome after a bit. About half the passengers have not been to many of the meals on account of sea sickness. I have felt perfectly well... Thursday would have finished me I daresay if I were going to be sea sick at all.

I am writing this Saturday afternoon. It is now just 4:20 by the ship's time. In Silver Creek it is 2:40. I keep my old watch the way it was and the one I got from the staff set to ship's time. Each night the officers post a sign up saying that the clock will be set ahead 32, 34 or 36 minutes—whatever it may be. You see we are going East and when we get to London it will be five hours behind New York time, or ahead I should say.

Last night I had dinner up on the boat deck with the officers. They have a nice little dining room with their own chef and he gets nice things for them to eat. Tonight I shall do the same thing again. They expect to have a sort of banquet, and I am among five passengers invited. I have had a good appetite ever since we started and will no doubt continue to have. I go to bed about midnight and get up at nine. We can get breakfast up to 10 a.m.; have luncheon at 1 and dinner at 7:15. It is easy to sleep. Last evening—or about 5 o'clock—I was sitting on the deck in a chair, with steamer rugs, etc. wrapped around me and I fell asleep and stayed so for an hour. Many do the same thing. Tomorrow we shall have some sort of religious service for those who wish to go. On Tuesday we will enter the submarine zone and then everyone is on the watch. While there is always a possibility that a torpedo will strike us from one of the German submarines there seems little prospect that one will strike this ship. It is too fast for them. However if it does there are boats enough to take care of everyone...

I have heavy woolen underwear; a thick woolen sweater, woolen socks and a heavy overcoat so I am prepared for anything. In addition I have the boxes of candy which came from Alta, for all of you, and eat some every day. The nuts are good too. Then someone sent me a big basket of assorted fruit from Park and Tilford's and a fancy box of candies, figs, fancy fruits and all sorts of things. I have plenty to eat.

For this time I will close. Perhaps tomorrow or Monday—or maybe still later than that—I will write another chapter but there will probably be little more to tell. The ship pitches all the time on account of the big swells which are always found off the Banks but there has been not much roll. When I get to Liverpool I shall take a train direct to London—it is a four or five hour ride and will then go to the Savoy Hotel for a short time. I can't tell what I will do then. Maybe I shall have to go direct to France to see Mr. Bennett or I may have to stay quite a while in London. I will make sure to get a letter off to you on every mail.

The presents Alta wrote about did not reach me, Dorothy. It might be well to write to the post office department and ask to have the package returned, as it will never reach me now. I shall spend Christmas on the ship. We will enter the war zone then. I am sure you will have a cheerful and pleasant day and wish I could be there to share it with you.

With love,
Dad

27

Diary: Sunday December 23, 1917

At Sea. 407 miles.

Handts, my steward, called me at 9. Shaved and had breakfast. Then walked around on deck till lunchtime. Is a nice sun-shiny day. Sea a bit choppy but not unpleasant. People beginning to keep an eye out for submarines. No suggestion of any yet. Have seen no ships at all since first day. Missed church service. Nothing on board to suggest that this is Sunday. Wrote a letter to Dorothy. Sent considerable time with Mr. Russell who seems to be quite a fellow.

Weather unpleasant but warm.

Letter to Dorothy, December 23, 1917

At sea, Sunday, Dec. 23, 1917

Dorothy

We are 400 miles nearer Europe than we were when I finished writing to you yesterday. We passed from the Newfoundland Banks during the night and now are running straight East in the Gulf Stream, toward England — but it is a long way off yet. It is Sunday but there is nothing to suggest it. There was a religious atmosphere this morning but I missed it. In the big dining room they had the Episcopal service and I really intended to hear it but I decided to sleep late for a change and when I arrived at the dining room the service was over.

Just about this time, Dorothy, you are getting ready for bed — or you would be if your time was the same as it is here. The time in this longitude is twenty-five minutes after eight while in Silver Creek it is a quarter after six. I keep the ocean time on the new watch I got from the office and leave my old watch just as it was, so I have both the ocean and the land time at the same time.

There are three children on the boat. They are in the second cabin with their mother and are on their way to England. The youngest is about two and the oldest is about seven. They run about the deck almost all day and many of the big army officers pick them up and carry them around. They seem to enjoy it greatly.

Last night was beautiful. Early there was a heavy fog but as we drew back toward the Gulf Stream it disappeared and at eleven o'clock the moon was bright; that evening star you and I saw one night — remember? — was up and the sky was just packed with stars. They seemed very close by. Another man and I sat and walked about the deck till after midnight. It was not so dark as other nights because of the moonlight. The air was about as one would expect to find it in April or early May and not a suggestion of winter about it. Today is much the same. The sea has been reasonably calm all day but late this afternoon a South wind came up and now it is blowing pretty hard. The sea is choppy and this added to the long, deep swell which always is found on the ocean, makes the ship rock and pitch quite a bit. A good many people are sick. The places at the dining table are about half filled I should say. Some folks have not been out of their cabins since we started. I have been feeling first rate and do not look forward to any sea sickness at all. I guess my stomach must be pretty good. Last night I had dinner with the officers and it certainly was a fine dinner. After nine o'clock I was in the music room where there was an impromptu concert, anyone taking part who would volunteer. Some are good and some very bad. Several young men going abroad for the Y.M.C.A. took part and they seemed quite talented. I have become quite friendly with a man named Russell from Chicago. He represents the big packing interests of Chicago and is going to London to stay a year or more. He has been there a good many times before and will be a valuable acquaintance. He lives, while in London, at the Savoy Hotel and I shall go there too. There is no trouble meeting people. There is danger of meeting too many.

This afternoon I walked on the deck for a couple of hours and then sat in the smoking room and played cards till seven o'clock when I went to dinner in the regular dining room. I had soup; roast lamb, browned potatoes, celery, green peas, lettuce and chicory salad, pudding, ice cream, fancy pastry, coffee and fruit. One eats about twice as much at sea as any other place. I guess a sea trip is quite beneficial as a matter of fact. I have a salt water bath in my own bath room every morning and spend nearly all the time out on deck. I find that my room is one of the two best ones on the boat. An English officer has the other one. I have my wardrobe trunk, a valise and a suitcase in it and have plenty of room. There is a reading lamp at the head of my bed and I lie in bed and read a short time every night. Some of the persons on board sleep in their clothes, with life preserver right next to them and everything ready for a hurried escape in case a submarine attacks the ship. I haven't done that and don't intend to. I could get up and dressed in a few minutes and no torpedo could sink the ship in less than an hour.

At the table with me are some rather interesting people but they are terribly English. A young Scottish clergyman whom I mentioned yesterday has been ill for two days and an English woman, wife of a hotel proprietor in London, showed up today for the first time since we left New York. She said she had been ill.

Since I finished the foregoing I have been at dinner and up in the smoker playing cards and now there is a fine howling wind blowing. The ship is tossing around. It rolls sideways and pitches away up and down. The wind has swung around into the southeast and the indications are that there will be some mighty high seas before morning. I am sitting in my room and the chair almost tips over now and then. The things on the dresser move around and the whole ship squeaks and groans. Most of the passengers have gone to their berths and the chances are that before morning all who are not immune from illness, will be filled with sea sickness. The waves sweep over the bow of the boat and race down the promenade decks. It is a good blow but nothing like some of the storms the sailors have been through. Here in my room I can hear the wind whistle and roar against the sides of the vessel and occasionally can hear the propellers racing out of water. I don't mind it at all. In fact I am going up in the front where it is safe and have a good look at the sea when it is in a fury. There is one good thing about rough weather in days like these. Submarines can't do any business then. It is amusing to see people try to get along the passageways leading from the after part of the ship to the forward cabins. They grope their way along and stagger. Going down stairs is quite a job.

It is a good thing perhaps that I have my typewriter with me. It would be impossible to write with a pen tonight and I rather thought it would be a good idea to write to you every day so that when you get my letter you will have a pretty full account of my entire journey. Maybe on Tuesday and Wednesday I will write more briefly because then we will be in the submarine zone and I will no doubt be out on deck with most of the other passengers keeping an eye open for danger. We enter the danger zone on Christmas morning. I have been wondering if you intend to have your Christmas tree for your dolls as you said you probably would. It is a very good idea Dorothy.

They will have a special Christmas dinner on the ship but if the weather continues as it has started tonight there will not be a great many people able to enjoy it.

I will close now for this time. Tomorrow I will tell you how the ship fared during the night.

With love,

Dad

Diary: Monday December 24, 1917

At Sea. 389 miles.

Got up at 9. Visited for an hour at breakfast with a Mrs. Wells of London who is pleasant but very English. The 5 others at my table are English or Scotch and I pass them a specimen of American humor + sarcasm now and then. Sea had calmed down. Everyone hoping it will get stormy as we enter the war zone as storms seem a safeguard against submarines. Played poker in afternoon. Lost $5 [about $80 in 2021].

Visited most of evening with an English woman Mrs. Rose. Then went to smoking room. Met Russell who wanted me to play checkers with an English pilot who had beaten nearly everyone. I beat him 6 straight + Russell was happy.

Everyone beginning to fret a little as we near the war zone. Good many persons slept in their clothes. I didn't but Russell + I sat up till 3 a.m.

Weather quite calm + warm.

Letter to Dorothy, December 24, 1917

At sea, Sunday, Dec. 24, 1917
Christmas Eve

Dorothy

It is not a bad night at sea for Santa Claus but I doubt that he will come on board the ship. They say he has not been around much in this part of the world since the submarines began to sink vessels. I don't blame him. It would be a shame if he should be caught by a torpedo and killed. What would all the little girls and boys all over the world do then? No one will hang up their stockings tonight but I am quite sure you will do so, and Joseph too. I guess Santa Claus will fill them up with things you will both like. I have the sweet part of my

Christmas right here on my desk—the boxes of candy and nuts. I have been munching away at them every day and they have been very acceptable.

The storm last night kept up till early morning but did no harm. You would have laughed if you could have seen me getting ready for bed. I would start to take off a shoe and would pitch half way across the cabin. After a while though I got in bed and it was all right then although I was bumped about quite a bit. I read for an hour and it was terrifying but to me rather pleasant (for I knew there was no danger) to hear the wind roar around the windows and hear the waves sweep over the bow. My room is up in the bow on the promenade deck. This morning the old steward, Handts his name is, came in at nine o'clock and called me for breakfast. I asked him how the weather was and he said it had all cleared up and that the day was fine.

And it has been fine. Of course the ocean is never smooth like Lake Erie down at Dahn's Beach in the summer but it was smooth nevertheless. There were very few, if any, whitecaps, and no swell big enough to give any motion to the ship. I spent practically all the afternoon on the deck, walking about or standing in sunny places and talking to other passengers. Everyone talks to everyone on a ship you know and after a week all are pretty well acquainted. I just came up from dinner a few minutes ago and shall write a short addition to the letters I have already prepared for you. I daresay you will have more than you can read but you may take it in installments; read a little one day and save some for the next.

The voyage from now on will be more exciting. I have noticed the tension already. Tomorrow, Christmas, we will be in the war zone, which means that part of the ocean in which the Germans long ago set apart as unsafe for ships to sail. We will be in it along about noon—a fine Christmas present—and it is hoped that in the evening two torpedo destroyers will meet us and escort us the rest of the way in. They cannot prevent a submarine from sending torpedoes but they are at hand to give immediate help in case of a tragedy and that is very important. The water in the ocean is not very cold—the temperature today of the water was 60—and one could keep afloat in it for quite a while.

About all the passengers talk about now, as we approach the danger zone, is submarines. All say they are not worried but quite a few sleep with their clothes on and several women intend tonight to take blankets and sleep in the library. They do that because their rooms are two stairways below the boat deck and a torpedo might hit them in their berths. I don't know that I blame them. My room is on the boat deck. From my bed to the row boat to which I have been assigned in case of accident is but thirty steps so I can go to bed with a feeling of reasonable security. Many of the men are a little uneasy. While they are all courageous, they cannot help feeling that, after all, we are away out in the middle of the ocean and that, if the ship should be struck, she would sink in an hour or so and everyone would have a tough time getting into the life boats. I think about it now and then but I certainly do not let it worry me. I remind myself of what you said one day, "I don't know how to worry." I have my life preserver handy; know how to put it on; have a flashlight and a police whistle where I can reach them quickly and have my clothes placed so I could easily and quickly get into them. That is about all one can do. Of course no one knows anything about the submarines. They may appear in the middle of the night or may rise up from the bottom of the sea any time. It is all guess work. We have to trust to luck. However, I have no doubt we shall reach Liverpool without seeing one at all.

The weather is most remarkable. One hardly needs an overcoat. People sit on the decks (in the dark of course) till early in the morning with nothing extra on but their overcoats. It is the most comfortable weather for this time of year the steamship men have known in a long time. The indications now are for calm weather all day Christmas. Everyone is hoping for a big storm, inasmuch as submarines cannot work well in stormy weather and the ship can stand any sort of a sea. Tomorrow I shall write to you about the incidents aboard ship on the first day in the danger zone. Everyone will be on deck, keeping an eye open. On the bridge of the ship, day and night, there are six men with glasses to detect anything unusual, and all along the decks, night and day, are sailors, keeping their eyes open also. Should a submarine be sighted the passengers would instantly be ordered to the dining room and there they would have to stay till the affair was disposed of one way or another. I shall make it a point to be with the officers if anything happens, as I am anxious to see any engagement the gunners might be called upon to take part in. But you may be sure I shall not run any unnecessary risk. I am too anxious to get back to see you, young lady.

In the music room just in front of my cabin, and in the big dining room, one flight down, the soldiers are practicing for a concert tomorrow night. There is considerable talent among them and the concert will bring a pleasant end to what will probably be a dull, though possibly very exciting, day. I will say good night now Dorothy.

With love,
Dad

Diary: Tuesday December 25, 1917

At sea—383 miles. Christmas.

Indications that the passengers are at high tension appear as we keep approaching the war zone. Many of the officers of the army + Navy are pessimistic. Everyone is hoping for stormy weather, as they prefer any kind of tempest to submarines. Passengers are most of the time scanning the horizon. We are not yet in war zone but as the subs are likely to appear anywhere—people are nervous. I'm a bit concerned myself because of the large number of uniformed officers aboard. The Germans would probably shell any boats they might put off in and every lifeboat would have some. The passengers filled 12 stockings and presented them to children in 2 + 3 cabins. A soldier impersonated Santa Claus.

Tomorrow at 10 a.m. 2 torpedo destroyers will take us in charge. Stayed up late. Everyone did. Weather is calm. Moon out like a silver ball. We can be seen for miles. Few people went to bed. All want to be ready to get out quick. Russell + I sat up till 4. Then I had a nap.

Weather calm.

Letter to Dorothy, December 25, 1917. At Sea

Christmas, 1917
2300 miles from New York

Dorothy

We had a Santa Claus at sea after all. Last night he appeared from somewhere and left eleven stockings filled with all kinds of things hanging up in the music room. With each one also was a doll and such odd looking dolls. On each stocking was the name of some little child either in the second or third cabin. There are only eleven on the ship so you see Santa Claus overlooks nobody. At eleven o'clock this morning, just after there had been a divine service in the big dining room (I attended too), Santa Claus appeared on deck, dressed in a red coat and fur hat, with big boots and a white beard. He had a pack on his back and over his arms were many things. He went up on the top deck to speak to the captain, to whom he gave something. Then he wished a happy New Year to all the officers of the ship and after that strolled leisurely around the main deck, bowing and smiling. It's a pretty close view to have of Santa Claus. He went down two companion ways to the second class cabin and gave to each of the children there a doll and a stocking. Then he went down to the steerage or third cabin and did the same thing. Some of the children are as big as Joseph but most are smaller. One little girl asked him if "Santa Claus came in a submarine."

All of a sudden Santa Claus disappeared. Some people on board thought they were smart, said Santa Claus was one of the army officers dressed up but I didn't recognize him as any such thing. You must tell Joseph about this. He will be interested.

That wasn't the only suggestion of Christmas Dorothy. Last night after midnight the English cooks, stewards, waiters, etc. marched around the cabin entrances singing Christmas carols. It is an English custom you know. They sang them pretty well too. About 1 o'clock another man and I were walking to the aft deck when we heard singing from another source. We traced it to the stairway leading to the steerage. There were about 100 American sailors—on their way to join their crews in England and France—singing the Star Spangled Banner, Old Kentucky Home, Suwanee River, Down in Tennessee and many other American songs. They were having a great old time. So you see that, even if we are in the region where a German submarine is liable to blow us up, people are not melancholy. Quite a few persons stayed up all night because they were told that we would enter the submarine zone during the night. I cannot exactly say I blame them because many of them have berths below the water line and a torpedo might blow out their berths.

It is rather astonishing to see how indifferent 600 people can be in the presence of momentary danger. Everyone knows that a submarine could sink our ship if it should happen to be in our neighborhood. Nearly all the passengers say they are not alarmed but it is obvious that they are all at high tension nevertheless. Few persons are sleeping around the deck as they were two or three days ago. They are all alert. Their eyes are wide open to catch the first view of one of those terrifying periscopes. Up in the crow's nest there are four bluejackets* with strong glasses, scanning every inch of the horizon. In the extreme bow are two sailors doing the same thing. On the bridge are the captain and four of his officers. Along the decks on both sides are sailors on watch and standing beside the big six-inch gun astern, the two four inch guns forward and the two four inchers amidships are gun crews ready to fire at an instant's notice. The ship's captain does not expect to leave the bridge from now till we reach Liverpool—58 hours hence. We have not quite reached the real danger zone. We will strike it this evening about 8 o'clock and will be in it then until we reach Liverpool. It would be consoling if we had a convoy but we will not get one till tomorrow morning. Two torpedo boat destroyers will cavort around us like porpoises from the time we reach them till we get into Liverpool harbor. The passengers say they wish they were here now. They cannot prevent a submarine from shooting a torpedo but their presence scares the submarines and furthermore the destroyers can pick up passengers who fall into the ocean.

The surface of the sea now—3 p.m. here now but just noon in Silver Creek—is very smooth. There is a long very low swell but one could keep afloat in a canoe. It is seldom like that in the winter. It is propitious for submarines. Last night was moonlight in the early hours and the people were worried because, although we are painted up to look like the sea, at night we must stand out against the horizon like a mountain, and could be seen by any lurking underwater craft. At ten o'clock clouds appeared and it was fairly dark after that. No one can tell yet how it will be tonight, but inasmuch as it is the most nerve-racking night we will have, people are hoping for clouds and a storm. Although the passengers insist for the most part that they are not afraid, it is quite noticeable that the only subject they take interest in is submarines.

When I finish writing to you Dorothy I shall go on deck and walk around with the other people, keeping my eyes open too. It is not very pleasant in my cabin, notwithstanding it is roomy. The air is not warm and the atmosphere is always more or less damp. I wish you could see my quarters. I have two pictures of you on the desk at which I am writing. They are the two you saw last winter in Albany, those I had framed. I hope there is snow in Silver Creek and that you and Joseph are having a great old time. We have not had a flake of snow at sea. It is more like April than December. As we near Ireland it probably will get colder and when we get to London there will unquestionably be rain and fog. There is certain to be bad weather in London at this time of year.

Several people have asked me what I am writing. They hear my typewriter going. I tell them I am writing a daily record of the voyage for my daughter. They all think that is a splendid idea. Some of them are trying to do the same thing with a pen but it is almost impossible to write legibly when the ship is rocking heavily and then it is so much more difficult that one would not write at the length I do on the

* Junior enlisted sailor

typewriter. I daresay you will have reading enough to last you a couple of weeks. However, you may pass it along to the folks and they will know about as much of winter travel across the Atlantic as I do.

There will be a special Christmas dinner tonight. They will have turkey. They have almost too much to eat all the time. Still we all have good appetites. I shall finish this series of letters about Thursday and will then have it mailed at once in a Herald envelope. Maybe if it goes by the same ship I am now on it will carry U.S. stamps but you will get it all right and no doubt you will know it came from England. If I can arrange to have it mailed by the same ship you should get it about January 10, but prior to that you will have received a cable from me.

Merry Christmas to you and Joseph, even if I am not there to help you have it. I'll bet Santa Claus was pretty good to both of you. He ought to be. Did you ever write your letter to Santa this year?

With love,
Dad

Diary: Wednesday December 26, 1917

At sea—415 miles.

This has been (at 5 p.m.) the most thrilling day in my career. Two torpedo destroyers appeared over the horizon at 7:30 a.m. I was asleep but Russell woke me and we went out and saw two destroyers (American) approach. Came within 1,000 feet of us, and began their patrol. Most of the passengers were out to see them. Many had not been to bed at all. Great relief now that convoy is with us. No question but passengers were very nervous. Though most of them pretend indifference. Am somewhat disturbed myself. Sea smooth at dawn but at noon stiff gale sprung up and now there is a heavy sea, almost too heavy for safety if we should have to take to the small boats. Destroyers hover about with spray flying all over them, but at times almost out of sight. Passengers are comforted somewhat but all know we are now right in the war zone. Wrote long letter to Dorothy on my typewriter, telling all about last night.

Letter to Dorothy, December 26, 1917

At Sea, Monday, Dec. 26, 1917

Dorothy

Our most exciting night has passed and it is interesting to see the relief of the passengers. Two torpedo boat destroyers flying the American flag appeared over the horizon at half past seven this morning and in a very few minutes passengers were crowding out on the decks to see them and wave a welcome. A few of the persons had been in bed sound asleep. Most of them had either remained fully dressed in the dining room or the cabins, or had sat or walked the deck. The night was ideal for a submarine attack—a glassy sea with a full moon. The St. Louis, tearing along at 21 miles an hour, must have looked like a mountain etched against the moonlight. We were in the danger zone and it has been assumed from the start that German submarines are out on the Atlantic somewhere waiting for a convoy of 47 cargo ships which left New York a day ahead of us but which are three or four days behind us now, we having speed and they having none.

The scene on the ship last night was the most remarkable I have ever known. People had been gradually approaching a climax and it came last night when it was known that finally we were in the war zone and when the hope of a big blow and a dark or foggy night was gone. Either a fog or a storm would add to the security of the ship but instead of either we got one of the most perfect, if not beautiful nights, ever known at sea. For ten miles astern we could see the moonlight glistening on the water and for that distance at least we must have been visible to any submarine which was lurking about. Had one been approaching it would have been in the dark foreground and no matter how alert our watchers and gunners were, it could have slunk along, hurled a torpedo at us, and submerged without so much as giving us a tiny peep at it. About twenty men, naval cadets and gunners, were at their posts steadily all night. They stood around like statues with their gaze focused on the horizon. They never speak and passengers who ventured to ask them questions might as well have talked to a sphinx. It was all business and very tense business too. It was known that two torpedo boat destroyers were speeding out from the Irish coast to accompany us in. With them at hand the danger is lessened but by no means eliminated. A submarine can easily enough rise to the surface for an instant, get its range and discharge a torpedo and escape, but when the destroyers are around the submarines are disinclined to take any chance. The destroyers can go 40 miles an hour and occasionally rush upon a submarine and crush it before it can get far below the surface. Furthermore, the destroyers are always there to pick up passengers and to prevent the submarines from coming to the surface and shelling a vessel. The hope of everyone last evening was that the destroyers would arrive with daylight. It was obvious that nearly everyone was more or less nervous and it is easy to understand why everyone should be; after all a plunge in the ocean is an unpleasant prospect. The moon was hidden by clouds for half an hour about nine o'clock but then the clouds drifted away and from that time on the moon stood out as brilliant as silver in a cloudless sky. The weather experts said there would be no breeze before daylight.

In the smoking room men were playing cards, chess or checkers— incidentally I played six games with the ship's champion, an English pilot who had defeated all the naval men on board, and beat him six straight, showing I daresay that I was not overcome with nervousness—and in the big dining saloon a concert was going on. There was singing and various other forms of amateur entertainment and it really was pretty bad. Henry L. Stimson of New York, formerly Secretary of War and candidate for Governor against Dix in 1910, presided. I know him quite well. He is a lieutenant colonel of artillery, volunteer, and is going straight to France. He is quite a favorite on board. He made a hit with the crowd, numbering about 500, in the dining room when he spoke of the willingness of everyone these days to take any risk to aid in the battle against German barbarism. Then he said he would quote from a Christmas letter which he had opened yesterday. "It is a letter I hold very sacred," he said (meaning of course that it was from his wife) and it says, "No matter where you may go, or however your career may end, I shall always be glad you went because it was the right thing to do."

A couple of Englishmen sang and I wouldn't have blamed the Germans just then if they had torpedoed the ship. They were abominable. A half dozen American officers sang and played and were a noticeable improvement. The concert began at nine o'clock and lasted until eleven. Then people drifted out to the decks and went to the two lounging rooms—the music room and the library. The cabin doors—that is the doors to the sleeping apartments, were open all night and many persons walked or sat on the deck with life preservers on. The life boats were swung out from the davits and hung over the side of the ship so they could be quickly lowered. That was a somewhat disquieting situation. It accentuated the danger everyone knew he or she was in. The ship quivered constantly and groaned, indicating that the captain was putting on all his power to hasten toward the torpedo destroyers which were flying out to escort us to shore. It was the first time the vessel was being forced. Some of us who had talked with the officers of the ship understood what it all meant. The smooth sea and the moonlight disturbed the sailors. They knew that at any moment a torpedo might slip through the water, leaving no trail that could be detected and giving no clue to the presence of a foe. Consequently, they were eager to get to the rendezvous, to fall under the protection of the torpedo boats, or hornets of the sea as they are called. Ten o'clock in the morning was the time set for meeting with the protectors. The extra speed we took on anticipated this time nearly three hours.

I sat around with others till one o'clock. Then I sat in the dining room for an hour. Next I sat in Mr. Russell's room, across the aisle from mine, for a short time and at three o'clock lay down with part of my clothes on, to get some rest. I quickly fell asleep and the next I knew Mr. Russell who had not lain down at all, came in and shook me. I was sound asleep but was up in an instant, in such a daze that I wasn't sure whether he said a torpedo or a torpedo boat destroyer had arrived.

In two minutes I was on the deck. It was eight o'clock. The wind had started and a fairly good sea was running. On the deck were perhaps 200 persons. They were all looking in one direction. I noticed that their expression had changed overnight. Everyone was speaking to everyone else. Officers with binoculars were gazing at the horizon, and women, with slippers on, as well as men with bath robes, were swarming out of the cabins to see what it was all about.

Far to the East we could see a speck. A wreath of smoke floated from it. An English pilot gazed at it with glasses and almost shouted, "It's an American destroyer—she's two masts." People hurried around to find someone to tell it all to. Women who had risen from the library and music room settees, fatigued, cross and irritable, put their arms around one another and even the sailors themselves, stolid as they always seem, smiled and took an interest. Presently a second speck appeared a mile south of the first one. Another destroyer. They grew larger steadily. The officers said they were about ten miles off. It seemed hardly five minutes before they loomed big against the sky and their smoke screens looked warlike against a sky tinted with a rising sun.

All the passengers crowded to the forward decks and pressed as far against the gun ropes as they dared. In a very few minutes the larger of the two destroyers swung around and we had a full view of her. The crew was standing against the deck house, waving. A signal officer was standing on the highest point of the deck house signaling to our ship. He told us to put on all speed and to head toward a certain point.

The people on this ship waved handkerchiefs, hats and neck scarfs and shouted to the men on the destroyer. It was but a moment before the other protector, a much smaller craft, swung around on the other side and her crew waved good morning to us. The people on the St. Louis ran around talking to one another with excitement and joy. If there had at any time been any doubt that the passengers—and this applies to the army and navy officers too—had been greatly alarmed, the relief and happiness they felt as the destroyers came alongside proved that they had indeed been worried if not frightened.

The narrow porpoise-like destroyers—you know they draw but a few feet of water and cut the waves like a knife—are now zigzagging along beside us, probably not more than 1,000 feet away. They are signaling constantly with flags and the passengers of course do not know what the messages are. The less the passengers know, in fact, the better off they are. Both destroyers are painted to look like the ocean (camouflage) and the waves split and break over them in great clouds of spray. I do not think I have ever seen a spectacle quite so thrilling. The little hulls are almost out of sight at times, being completely submerged. But they are ready at a second's notice to give battle to submarines and presumably will convoy us safely in to Liverpool.

Last night was the most nerve-racking of all, I expect, although there will be plenty of excitement tonight. This will be our last at sea. We will wake up in sight of the coast of Ireland and at eight o'clock, it is expected, will be at the dock in Liverpool. I shall spend the night, if I am permitted to leave the ship, at the Adelphi Hotel in Liverpool, which is said to be the best hotel in England. If we are compelled to stay on the ship till Friday morning, I will probably stay at the Adelphi Saturday night and go to London Sunday. I want to have a look at Liverpool and, as a matter of fact, will welcome one night in a soft, good sized bed, with no danger of being attacked by a submarine.

No one of course knows what may happen between now and tomorrow evening, but the supposition is that the destroyers will be able to get everybody to safety in case a submarine manages to shoot a torpedo into us. Everyone feels more secure at least but I imagine it will be a worn and weary company which will land in Liverpool. The women especially are affected. A woman in third class, with three children, looks as if she hasn't slept in three days and I imagine she hasn't. I cannot say that I have not felt uneasy but I have not been scared. I have not felt that I would not have a fair chance to escape, without crowding out anyone else, and that is all one can expect. But it is very evident, to one who crosses at this time, that the dangers are much greater than one is led to believe. In fact no one has any business to cross the Atlantic now unless it is absolutely necessary. I wouldn't have you on here for a million dollars. I would be worried then. It is odd how the human point of view changes. Many of the passengers say quite nonchalantly that they expect at least half the passengers will be saved if we are struck—not a word about the other half! All the men sort of agree informally that in case of an accident they will make it a point to see that the women with children are taken care of first. Danger seemingly breeds a sort of heroic gallantry and I have no doubt that if a torpedo should strike the St. Louis and sink her there would be found a very chivalrous body of men.

Do you know Dorothy that I have already written what would be almost a two column story about last night—I mean this letter would make that much. Still it is not often that one gets an opportunity to write at first hand an article about a night ride through the danger zone on a steamship which is being hunted by submarines—a steam-ship which, with cargo and all, is worth fifteen million dollars. If something should still happen and I should be fortunate enough to get to a cable office the chances are that I would take this letter and cable most of it to the Herald, not as a letter but as a story of the night. I haven't written it exactly for a girl of eleven or twelve but you will understand it all and if you don't Mother will read it so you will.

I don't know what has been going on during the last hour, but probably nothing much. I came directly to my room from breakfast and now I shall put on a sweater and overcoat and go on the deck and join the rest of the ship's company in watching the boats glide and circle around us, burying their noses in the waves and sending up clouds of greenish, silvery spray which rise a hundred feet in the air. I will very likely spend most all of the day on the decks and tonight will sleep with my clothes on. It sounds foolish but it is a nice precaution. If the ship should be struck the lights would go out immediately and one would have difficulty in dressing. Safety in a rowboat would depend largely upon the way a person is dressed and so it is well enough to be dressed and ready. It is only one night more anyhow and the beds are so uncomfortable that a little more discomfort makes no difference.

I may write you a short addition to this letter later in the day. If anything worthwhile occurs I certainly will. Tomorrow I will write briefly because I will have a lot to do then and will mail the whole literary output from Liverpool.

> With love,
> Dad

Here is a record on the voyage so far —

> *Dec 20 – 277 miles*
>
> *Dec 21 – 373*
>
> *Dec 22 – 375*
>
> *Dec 23 – 407*
>
> *Dec 24 – 387*
>
> *Dec 25 – 383*
>
> *Dec 26 – 415*

Total to noon Dec 26 — 2617 miles.

Back in Silver Creek, Don's mother, Rose Martin, wrote him a letter on December 26, 1917, addressed *c/o New York Herald Bureau, [Fleet Str,] London, England*. The envelope is marked *'Opened By Censor.'*

Dec 26th

Dear Don

If you were in N.Y. I should say, I will write you a few lines. But being so far away, I will write more than a few lines—will every day think of you, in fact we all do, but just now I am thinking more then ever, just as you are getting nearer and nearer your destination and I shall be very glad when you get over. I hope it has been a pleasant journey and that you have enjoyed it very much. You certainly had a wonderful Send-off, which must have made you feel very good—to start with. We all felt good over it, and proud too, and Rock was quite excited.

And now Christmas is over. We had quite a busy time before Xmas writing cards and doing up bundles, and right here I will say Dorothy got everything she wanted, and was so happy she just could not keep still a minute. Just now she is trimming her tree over. Yesterday we went to Julie's to Dinner and today Roscoe sent (or brought) a whole lot of turkey for our Dinner. I didn't give so freely for Christmas this year, but it did not make any difference with the rest of them, and yourself included. That is a beautiful Ring you gave me. I shall prize it very much, more then I can tell you, just what I really liked, and sometimes wanted very much. I guess you must be a mind-reader. About a year ago when I was in J.K. Adam's I bought one, and paid $1.00 for it, but was ashamed of it, and so I dropped it somewhere. With me it's something good or nothing, and now I have a good one, and I am so glad. I think as we get older, we get more and more like children. And Inez and Roscoe gave me a lovely Satin Dress, the color is dark lavender. That is just what I want too, and Alta got me a silk petticoat to go with my dress—and Dorothy got me some silk stockings. So you see I ought to be very happy and I am. Still there is something kind of sad about it. Julie gave me a subscription for the Cosmopolitan and a waist. Everyone has been so good to me, and I got so many cards too.

Well Don, you too know how it seems to get so many things, for you certainly got your share before you sailed. I hope you got Dorothy's and mine too, with all the rest. I was glad to read in that splendid letter you sent me, they all read it, how well equipped you were, but I hope half of the things you mention you would not have to use. And now Don I shall be very careful of those checks that come. I shall deposit them all and draw just what I need, and leave the rest in the Bank, of course, and will use checks to draw the money (or rather pay with checks).

Dorothy's shoes just came now. They are very nice. She put them right on, and will go down to mail this letter.

I am going to write to you on Saturday. Lots o' hugs an' kisses,

Dorothy.

Do you know anything about my Baby Grand piano?

And now I must wish you a very happy New year, and lots of love. You will notice I numbered this letter No. 1, and Dorothy will number hers also.

From Mother

Diary: Thursday December 27, 1917

At sea.

This was the most exciting day of the voyage. We passed Fastnet, well out to sea, during night and were in the most dangerous part of the war zone at daybreak. The destroyers were with us all night and all day, and they gave comfort + a feeling of security. The passengers were scared but pretended nonchalance. At noon the 6-inch gun fired 2 shots at what was believed to be the periscope of a submarine 2,000 yards back. I was near the bow and could see neither the alleged sub nor the striking of our shells. Many believed there was no submarine. Some of the ship's gunners said we hit the submarine. Others said not. In any event it gave us the one thrill needed as a climax to a rather nerve-racking voyage. No one seemed scared. It is remarkable how people will adjust themselves to almost anything. Russell + I had dinner "on top" with the officers. We got to the dock in Liverpool at 11 p.m. but couldn't land. We learned that, on Christmas Day, an American ship had been sunk by a sub almost at the identical spot where we fired at something. These are thrilling times.

Weather cold + clear. Sea calm.

Letter to Dorothy, December 27, 1917

In the Irish Sea, Dec. 27, 1917
About 100 miles from Liverpool

My dear Dorothy

We saw a submarine—at least many of those on board did. I did not. Many believe it was all a false alarm but it apparently was not as the members of the stern gun crew swear they saw a periscope and believe they sank it. The sailors always believe they made a "hit" but indications seem to be that in this case they did.

In any event it provided a very exciting few minutes. It happened two hours ago—just at noon, at the entrance to the Bristol Channel. I was standing in the bow when I heard a shot from the rear gun. Then there was scurrying about, indicating that perhaps the moment we had all looked for and many had feared, had come. I ran back toward the stern to see what was going on. I never thought about running for my room and a life preserver. Most people did that. There was a second shot. Immediately our boat swung quickly to the right—so swiftly in fact that she listed till it was hard to stand on the deck. But the picturesque features came from elsewhere.

The two torpedo destroyers which had been convoying us were on either side of us. They both wheeled around instantly almost in their own length and sped toward the spot where the two shots from the stern gun had struck. People came from their cabins with life preservers on. The stewards had gone around giving an alarm. A great airship—a dirigible they call it—had come from the Welsh coast early in the morning and was moving along just ahead of us, watching the surface of the ocean. It was about 500 feet in the air and moved along—in fact still moves along for it will stay with us till we reach the safety zone—without seemingly moving at all. It turned as quickly as it could when the shooting occurred and went back. One of the torpedo boat destroyers dropped a depth bomb. Both destroyers and the airship circled around for fifteen minutes while we zigzagged ahead as fast as all the power could shove us. The purser and other officers came out and called upon everyone to go inside. I had to laugh at the courtly ineffectiveness of the purser. He said:

"Everyone go inside please. Come; go inside as rapidly as possible. Why can't you hurry? I'm distressed. You must hurry."

I thought it would have been somewhat different if a New York City policeman had been doing it. Then stories began to circulate as to what had happened. The stern gun crew say they saw a periscope come up 2,000 yards astern; that she rose well above the water and started toward the ship. They immediately let go a shot which struck about thirty feet from the periscope. They fired a second shot which, they say, sent up a terrific splash, indicating to them that it had struck the submarine. However, nothing more was seen or heard of the underwater vessel. I have not yet verified the details of the incident but intend to do so when I see the officers at four o'clock. The story told by the Steward is that the dirigible and the gunners saw the periscope about the same time. The dirigible, which is 250 feet long and carries a crew of 7 men, flashed a wireless alarm to the torpedo destroyers who dashed to the spot indicated. Later, it is said, the dirigible sent a wireless to the ship St. Louis that it was certain the submarine had been struck and sunk.

I rather enjoyed it all. The sea is calm. The destroyers are close by and other ships are in the vicinity. The coast of Wales and Ireland both can be seen about 20 or 30 miles off and we are getting out of the zone of acute danger. Since daylight we have been in the most dangerous region of all. It is the submarine hunting ground. These horrible underwater things have reaped a harvest of more than 100 ships in the neighborhood of the Bristol Channel since the war started and here they keep on constant watch, sometimes just beneath the surface and more often lying on the bottom waiting for the whirr of a propeller to call them to the surface for a quick survey and discharge of a torpedo. Probably the one which we are supposed to have hit this morning was lying on the bottom. It is hazardous for them to come to the surface for more than a few moments because all over this part of the sea there are trawlers—scores of them—watching for periscopes; airships and dirigibles flying around like gulls looking far down beneath the surface and torpedo boat destroyers leaping and flashing here and there to fire at everything that remotely resembles a periscope. So you can see that this is also a danger zone for the submarines. They cannot come up even for a long breath without risking destruction and death. My hope is that the shots we fired this noon damaged the submarine just enough to condemn the sailors to a lingering death.

It is surely a weird picture—a big ship ripping along at top speed with the one big balloon keeping just ahead of her, another coming along a few miles behind; a score or more of little trawlers moving about and two destroyers cutting through the waves on either side of the big vessel. No one will ever know definitely whether we sank a submarine or not. I shall try to cable something about it to New York as soon as I get to London and will write an account of it this afternoon to send back by mail at once.

Last night was one excitement. People slept on deck, in the library and smoking rooms and in fact all over the ship. Very few ventured to undress and go below where they would have been in great danger if a torpedo struck the ship. We were in the real danger zone all night and the moon was out part of the time, this increasing our danger. About 100 men sat in the dining room playing cards or talking and all insist that they were not afraid but were merely staying up to see any excitement that might occur. That's camouflage. I slept from nine o'clock in the evening till midnight and then stayed up till five when I lay down again and slept till nine. I have had sleep enough for a trip like this but I can assure you I would not care to take any more. Everyone is glad it is about over. Now, when we are getting out of the danger spots, officers who, during the anxious nights gave assurance there was no danger, say that if a torpedo had struck the ship three or four or even two days ago, the loss of life would have been very great. Still we don't care. The dangers are all behind us—that is, nearly all. We are now proceeding rapidly toward Liverpool. Submarines have been seen all around here and we shall not be actually out of danger till after dark tonight. We shall reach Liverpool, we expect, about nine o'clock but cannot go ashore till tomorrow. We can see land and will be in the Mersey River soon after dark.

I may add a line or two to this letter Dorothy after we reach Liverpool but chances are I will not do so. I may have to pack my typewriter up during the evening. However you will have a pretty long account of the entire voyage—a more complete account I daresay, than anyone else will have. You might let John Knox see it if you wish and also Josephine and Lee. I think possibly they would be interested in knowing about some of the details of a trip through the submarine zone at such a critical time as this.

The most noticeable thing about today's incident, which was of course the most exciting of all, was the cool headedness of all the people on board. An elderly lady from Chicago was dressing when the steward told her to hurry out. She had her clothes about on. Before leaving her cabin she insisted on powdering her face and putting on a bit of rouge, to protect her skin, she said, from the salt water. The women were nonchalant. They went into the cabins reluctantly and came out as quickly as permitted to do so. They seemed eager to be on deck and determined to have a full measure of any excitement which might take place. The truth is everyone had been thinking and talking submarines for days and they were ready for almost anything. I think a good many would have been bitterly disappointed had not a submarine been sighted. Personally I have my doubts whether it was a submarine after all but inasmuch as the officers say it was, I guess it will have to be so recorded.

By tonight I expect there will be a hundred versions of the story and people who were in bed, or at luncheon or somewhere inside, will be giving graphic accounts of the incident witnessed by them. I am wondering if, by the time I get to London, I won't have a version of it myself, notwithstanding that now I am convinced I did not see the submarine, nor did I see the shot strike. These stories grow and are embellished with the telling.

The weather is colder today, but clear. The Irish sea is always cold at this time of year. The temperature for three days was in the neighborhood of 55. Today it is about 45 and a raw wind is blowing. I remarked that if we didn't get trouble in the Irish sea there could be no more hope.

I am going down to the purser's office to get about $100 changed to British money. Then I am going to watch for submarines a short time, pack my trunk, which must be ready for moving to the deck tonight and then see the Captain and chief officer who will tell me their interpretation of the submarine incident. I am anxious to get ashore to have a sleep in a real bed and will stay at the Adelphi Hotel, Liverpool, on Friday night. That is said to be better than any hotel in London and I am going to sleep from ten o'clock Friday night to 10 o'clock Saturday morning.

At noon I shall go to London where I will be in the evening. I will cable you from London and will also write so you will get a letter a couple of weeks after you have finished this long one. I imagine it will take almost two weeks for you to finish this one, but it will be interesting anyhow. You know few persons are able to give details of a trip through the submarine zone. The censors cut everything interesting out of the letters. Maybe they will do so with this one but I doubt it.

I have already seen enough of the English people, through association with those on the ship, to realize the complete truth of the statement that an Englishman never sees a joke till the next day. They are totally different from Americans. I am quite sure I shall not like them. One woman said to me the other day, "Oh, I could tell you are an American from your accent." I replied, "I would feel quite ashamed of myself if you couldn't." Another woman at the table, with true British conceit, said that Muller, the gallant German commander of the raider Emden, was a sportsman, but, she added, "Of course his mother was an Englishwoman." "Yes, and Kaiser William's wife is an English woman too," I replied.

With love
Daddy

It is now 15 minutes after 3 in the afternoon here and 15 minutes after ten in the forenoon in Silver Creek. Love to all. Da

Don Martin on his 44th birthday, 1917

And then disembarking in Liverpool and transfer to London.

Diary: Friday December 28, 1917

Left the ship at Liverpool.

Left the St. Louis at 10 a.m. with Russell + went to the Adelphi Hotel which seems about like the best class American hotels. Went at once to the police and registered. Then to the office of Morris & Co. with Russell. I left him and came to the hotel to read and take a nap.

Had our London office on the phone and gave someone details of the submarine incident to be cabled to N.Y.

Liverpool is nothing like I had expected. Streets are overrun with soldiers—many of them wounded—legs + arms off.

Had dinner at the Adelphi with Russell, Wente of Liverpool, James, Missitt + James' brother. James + Missitt officers on St. Louis. Missitt pretty loud. James fine chap. Wound up with too much Scotch whiskey. Am glad I don't touch it. Liverpool like a tomb at night. Lights in buildings all out. Curtains at every window. My room here is a beauty. Fireplace and fine bath room.

Weather normal. Cloudy + damp.

The New York Herald ran the story about the submarine encounter on the front page of Part 2 of the Saturday, December 29, 1917, edition, for the first time with a Don Martin byline.

The story he cabled is a bit different from what he wrote in his diary; the style gives a foretaste of the stories he would later send home on how he saw the war taking place.

ANOTHER U-BOAT SUNK BY AMERICAN SHIP AS PASSENGERS APPLAUD

Vessel at British Port; Crew Certain That Shot Destroyed Submarine

ENCOUNTER DESCRIBED BY HERALD REPORTER

Those Aboard Refused to Go Below While Naval Gunners "Potted" the Submarine

By Don Martin

Special Despatch to the Herald

London, Friday. – We have just arrived on board an American steamship. The voyage was uneventful until the vessel was nearing this side when we had an adventure with a German submarine, which we have every reason to believe we sank before it could attack us.

It was noon, with most of the passengers on deck, and while many were in the mid-day promenade there were scores of faces lining the rails and scanning the sea, as they had done for hours since we entered the barred zone. The sea was calm, with hardly a ripple, and the steamship was cutting along swiftly, the lookouts at the posts and telescopes pointed in every direction of the compass.

Submarine is Sighted

Soon there was a cry that an enemy submarine had been sighted. Direc- tions were hastily called from the crow's nest to the bridge and gun positions. For hours and days the gunners had been waiting this moment eagerly.

The quickness with which they sprang to the alarm was remarkable. There was a snap and click and we knew that the guns were pointing, and soon there would be a crash and a bang. Officers not actual- ly engaged in the encounter with the submarine hur- ried among the passengers and advised them to go to their staterooms, but to be prepared, with lifebelts on, to hurry to the decks and get into the lifeboats.

It was feared that if the U-boat fired shells at us passengers on the decks would be injured by shrapnel.

No One Goes Below Decks

But, so far as I could see, there was not a single passenger who would miss the opportunity of seeing the fight. Not one of them went below decks.

It must be said that whatever excitement there was, if any, was so well suppressed that it was not evident. There were no hys- terical women and the men leaned on the rails, shaded their eyes with their hands and even joked a bit. Among us were numerous passen- gers who had crossed the ocean many times since the war began and never saw a submarine. This was the chance for which they had been waiting, if not praying.

I do not know how they did it, but those gunners of ours had the range of that periscope, a mile away, so quickly that the first shot was fired before many of us reached advantageous places from which to see the encounter.

The First Shot Misses

The shell apparently mis-sed the moving target, but the explosion as the shell left the gun, and again as the shell "popped' in hitting the water, sounded good to everyone on board. Every shot of the gunners brought applause from the passengers.

Soon after another shot was fired and that was the one which we believe ended the existence of that submarine. It apparently hit very near the periscope. A volume of water spurted into the air, a cloud of smoke rose from the submarine and then the sea at that spot settled and became calm like the rest of the ocean.

Officers of the steamship believe that a good hit was made, that the submarine was severely damaged if not actually sunk.

Then the destroyers acting as our convoy hurried up to the scene and circled the spot where the submarine had been but found nothing.

A dirigible airship accompanying the convoy searched the sea near there but failed to see anything of the enemy.

The naval officers on board also are firmly of the belief that we sank the submarine. They say that certainly another submarine has been accounted for.

Dorothy sent her father a full report on her Christmas in her letter No. 2 dated December 29, 1917 (Letter 1 did not survive). It was addressed *c/o New York Herald Bureau, London [Fleet St] England,* and Don Martin wrote on the envelope: *'Recd Jan 23'.*

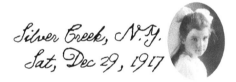

Silver Creek, N.Y.
Sat, Dec 29, 1917

Dear Dad

Well now I am going to write you letter No. 2. I did not number my last letter because I did not know about numbering them then. But I will number this one No. 2 and so the other letter was No. 1. Now do yuh understand that?

It is quarter past ten now and the mail man just went into Weeks so he will probably stop here in a minute with the Herald. The Herald comes every day now and probably before very long we will see something from London.

I have been lazy lately. Yesterday morning I didn't get up or wake up either until eight thirty. This morning I woke up at eight. But anyway, Christmas and the day after it I got up very early. The night before Christmas I could not sleep, I was so excited — and — so what do you suppose I did? why — I just didn't sleep, that's all. Heeeee! Haaaaaaa!

Well, the first thing is — I went to a party at our Sunday school at half-past five and got home at eight. Well I was anxious to get to bed so I could get up all the earlier. But when I got home, I had to carry a whole market basket full of presents over to Uncle Rock's and bring it back again full of different presents. Then I had to carry some over to Aunt Josephine and when I got back I had to answer about six million questions on the telephone and then I sat down and watched Aunt Alta knit (she's finally learned to knit) a minute and then she made me do it to see if I could, and then she showed me some presents she was going to give Grandmother an' then I saw two more presents on the table an' I asked her what they were and she put on that comical grin o' hers and said, "Oh, nothing you care about."

But by that grin of hers I could tell it was something I was supposed to keep out of. An' 'en Uncle Rock came over and we talked a minute and then — at last I started to get ready for bed. I hung up my stocking and when I got into my nightgown I ran after the end of it around the table and jumped on the couch and pounded on the piano and ran around like a wild cat all over the house and finally I stopped and went upstairs and then came back down and gave one grand leap into bed and – and – stayed there. You see I slept down stairs. Well, then nothing much more happened that I knew of. Aunt Alta went down to Aunt Julie's for a while and I went to sleep for a while. I don't know but I can imagine what Grandmother was doing.

Well, I woke up an' I didn't have the least idea what time it was an' as I came out and lighted two of the lights here in the dining room, got my stocking, looked at the tree and then looked at the clock and it was only twelve o'clock.

Well, I turned these lights out and lighted the light in my room so I could see what was in my stocking. There was a small Christmas tree in the top, then a card, then a lot of nuts and grapes, then two oranges and a big apple. (yes, I am very well thank-you) then I turned the light out again and put my stocking at the foot of my bed and went to sleep until three. Then till four, then till five, then I waited in bed until half-past five and then I got up and stayed up. I lighted some lights and looked at all the bundles and then I started opening them. The first one I opened was a monster and what do you suppose was in it – a Bee-aa-uu-tt-ii-ff-uu-ll ma-hogany colored four poster an' about everything else, doll bed! An' it was just grand – of course – and it fits every one of my dolls, it's so big! I just l-o-v-e it.

Well, next I opened a ((((Beautiful)))) doll's bureau! It is all white with some pink and white creton over the drawers (there are

47

three drawers) and around the edge of the dear little square mirror. It is just the right size to go with my bed and – ok – I have got to have bran' new bedclothes for my beautiful bed, so Aunt Alta is going to buy some creton just like that on my bureau for a spread and something to put over the pillows.

Then I opened some more packages an' got – a beautiful leather music case, two bea–utiful hair–ribbons, a two pound box of Huyler's candy, a dandy scrap book to keep the things you write in, from – you. O' course the doll's bed and bureau from you too. Then I found a big package from Uncle Rock an' Aunt Inez which said on the outside, Handle With Care, and I unwrapped about six million different pieces of paper very, very carefully and finally got to a little box about two inches square (at first the package must have been about a foot square) and I opened it up and it was a lovely gold thimble. And I had been so careful. Some joke, huh? Then I got – (of course these things should all have a "lovely" before them) a knitting bag with a skein of orange yarn in. But I am going to knit something for Hospital quilts so I won't have to use it to do "fig knitting" with. That was from Aunt Julie and Uncle Charlie. A string of pearls (Don't forget about that word "lovely") from Aunt Lou.

I am going to send you a card she sent me in this letter. Another knitting bag from Marguerite Schumaker, a book "Rebecca of Sunnybrook Farm" and a game from Joseph, one of those "Dollar" Boston pencil Sharpeners from Aunt

Josephine, some nice perfumery, an Account Book to keep when I send your letters and all that from Grandmother. Also, my stocking full was from her, and some silk stockings and two hair-ribbons from Aunt Alta, lots of cards, a silver spoon from Mr. + Mrs. Brooks and a few things like handkerchiefs from some of the girls in school. And Christmas night what do you suppose came from New York? Why, a teeny weeny piano for a baby and it was for me. It didn't tell who it was from or anything, but we imagine you sent it for a joke (Are we right?) Well, I guess that's about all about Christmas except that I am going to take the tree down today. 'Bout enough isn't it?

Grandmother got the check from the Herald again yesterday. That makes the second one. She has put them in the bank and has a check-book. We went to Buffalo again yesterday. It only takes 10 or 15 minutes at the dentist now as he only has to tighten things up a little.

It was awful weather in Buffalo yesterday. Cold as the I don't know what with a terrible wind blowing. It is awful cold here today. This morning it was zero and now it's only about six above.

Oh, I pretty near forgot to tell you — my scout shoes came the other day and they just fit and they are just dandy. This morning that brush for Aunt Alta came and we called her up and we are going to send it to her. Also your hat-box + trunk came the other day and we have them in the hall.

Grandmother wrote you a long letter Thursday but my letter and the one Granny wrote just cost three cents to send them so Granny is afraid you won't get them.

I was down at Aunt Julie's Wednesday and I helped the Red Cross. She had a sort of little club and they make all sorts of bandages. I helped by pulling out bastings, turning hems, and turning some bandages right side out.

Well, now I better close. I guess I had about six million things to tell you but I can't remember them now so I will tell them to you in my next letter.

Lots of Love an' hugs an' kisses,
Dorothy

Silver Creek, N.Y.,
Sat. Dec. 29, 1917

Dear Dad,

Well now I am going to write you letter No. 2. I did not number my last letter because I did not know about numbering them then. But I will number this one No. 2 and so the other letter was No. 1. Now do yuh understand that?

It is quarter past ten now and the mail-man just went into Weeks so he will probably stop here in a minute with the Herald. The Herald comes every day now and

Excerpts of Dorothy's letter No.2

make all sorts of bandages. I helped by pulling out bastings, turning hems, and turning some bandages right side out.

Well, now I letter close I guess. I had about six million things to tell you but I can't remember them now so I will tell them to you in my next letter.

Lots o' love an' hugs an' kisses
Dorothy

51

PART 2

Covering the War from London
– January to March 1918

Having arrived in London on December 29, just before New Year's Eve 1918, Don Martin was to spend his next three months watching and reporting on the war from there.

His thoughts were often with his 11–year–old daughter Dorothy, back home in Silver Creek, New York. He wrote frequently to her and noted in his diary receiving six letters from her while in London.

Diary: Saturday December 29, 1917
In London

Left Liverpool for London at 11 with Russell. My room in Adelphi cost 3/6—not bad. Shared carriage on train with Russell, an army and navy officer and a nurse returning to France. Arrived London 3:45. Darkness already fallen. Got trunks and other luggage to Savoy Hotel in taxi. Room awaiting. Is very fine one. Has all comforts of N.Y. hotel. Had dinner in Savoy alone. Then went to our office at 130 Fleet Street. Had some difficulty finding it. Saw Champion, in charge, and had visit with him. He seems a pleasant chap. Looks very much like Bennett.*

London a weird place at night. Fully half the persons on streets or anywhere else are soldiers or sailors. Quite a few Americans. Met Phelps, Frohman's** manager here. He seems to be a devoted follower of J. Barleycorn. Went to my room at 9 to rest up—fell asleep at once and so at 10:30 went to bed. Don't know whether I shall like London or not but think not. However there is much to see and I shall improve my time. Shall do nothing till I hear direct from Mr. Bennett who is in Beaulieu. Weather damp—of course.

*Herald owner James Gordon Bennett
** Charles Frohman, American theater owner/producer

Diary: Sunday December 30, 1917

Slept till 10 a.m. Had breakfast with Russell. Later went for a walk with him over to Buckingham Palace, Hyde Park etc. Streets were slimy. Sort of drizzle all day. Wrote to Dorothy.

In afternoon took short walk with young Kergstra of State Dept. Later went to Herald office, 130 Fleet St. Found it cold like all other places in London. Got wire from Bennett telling me to take full charge in London, and congratulating me on my cable dispatch about the St. Louis and the submarine.

Went to hotel at 11 p.m. after dining with Kergstra in Simpson's.

London is certainly a dreary place at night, with everything darkened so air raiders can't see it. Everything is cold and damp and comforts as we know them in New York are unknown. Fully half the men everywhere are in uniform, and many wounded. England believes she will win the war, but realizes it is a big task. Is relying on America for the men, the ships and the supplies needed. Weather wet and cold.

Don Martin wrote his first letter to Dorothy from London, on December 30, 1917.

Savoy Hotel
London, W. C. 2.
Sunday – Dec 30 – 1917

Dorothy

There is no telling when this letter will leave London—the censorship is so strict and the mail is so tremendous—but nevertheless I shall write a brief note so you will know that I am in London. And what a place it is! Dark at 4 o'clock and all the street and shop lamps darkened. In fact it is so black at night that one has almost to feel his way. I haven't had much of it yet.

I arrived here at a quarter to four yesterday afternoon from Liverpool and came directly to this hotel which is about like the Waldorf Astoria. I have a fine big room with a bath. There are drawbacks though. For instance heavy curtains hang in front of all windows and it is a violation of the law to part them when there is light in the room. The Savoy is the rendezvous of nearly everyone in London, especially Americans and I have already met quite a few persons I know. I went to the Herald office at 130 Fleet Street soon after I got here and had difficulty finding it because of the darkness. It is about 15 minutes walk from the Savoy.

I may look for a bachelor apartment if I stay here for any length of time. I like it well

The Savoy Hotel in London, where Don Martin stayed and where he wrote many of his letters, appears little changed today from its wartime days.

enough in this hotel but it is one of the most expensive places in London and in wartime that means a good deal. I shall within a day or two write you a letter on my typewriter and then will give you a few details of my arrival etc.

One thing very conspicuous is that England has been brought face to face with the war. About half the persons one sees on the streets, in the hotels or anywhere else are soldiers and a good many of them have crutches. Then the darkness, you know that it is to check the air raids at night. An airship passing over London now after 4 p.m. could not distinguish a single ray of light. That is fine for the security of the people but think what it means to the comfort of millions of people.

I got in bed last night at 10:30 and got up at 9:30 this morning (Sunday). I am now going to breakfast.

With love
Dad

December 31, 1917—New Year's Eve in London

Diary: Monday December 31, 1917

Slept till 10:30. Had breakfast in the Savoy. Saw Judd Welliver, Sun correspondent. He is depressed and wants to get back to N.Y. Nearly everyone is more or less discouraged. Is a good experience for me but I should prefer to be in N.Y. Sent cable to Dorothy. Not doing much work yet. Just looking around to get my bearings ...

Webb Miller,
United Press

Went to dinner with Welliver at the Wellington on Fleet St. Met [Mel] Draper of the Tribune, [Webb] Miller of the U.P. and a Mr. Moare, all Americans, and went with the crowd to Moare's lodgings where we had some of Welliver's homemade mince pies, some candy liquors etc. and a lot of conversation. Saw the new year in. Opinion of the correspondents is that Allies have a fierce task ahead licking Germany.

After we all finished, the crowd escorted me through a lot of lanes and alleys to Fleet St. Welliver then walked to the Savoy with me.

Weather cool and raw.

Don Martin wrote a short note to Dorothy on December 31, 1917, again on Savoy Hotel stationary, mentioning a cablegram he had sent her and what he had done that day.

Savoy Hotel
London, W.C.2.

Dorothy

I was looking through my suitcase today and I had a good laugh. It was like finding something in my shoe. It was a note written by you reading: "He Haw! I put this in your suitcase and you never knew it. Hope you have a good time in Europe. Lots of hugs and Kisses etc." I remember now you told me you had put something in my suitcase and I wondered what it was. Now I know.

London is a great place. No sunshine. Just half fog and mist. Streets wet. Complete darkness at night. I can see already that I shall not like it but if five million other people can stand it I guess I can. I sent you a brief cablegram today so you will know everything is all right with me at the beginning of the year.

I did not intend this as a letter, Dorothy, just a line to tell you about the note of yours in my suitcase.

Today I walked about a bit. Saw the King's palace, the London Bridge, St. Paul's Cathedral and some other buildings of historic interest. They are all screened against air raids. People talk a great deal of these raids, which occur about four or five times a year, but it is easy enough to get to protected spots when they come. You can bet I shall do that. Pretty soon I shall write a longer letter on my typewriter.

With love
Dad

Diary: Tuesday January 1, 1918

New Year's Day in London

One of the first things I did was to buy this diary. Then went to Herald office on Fleet St. Bothered by loss of cablegram which came last night and was mislaid by the hotel. Came to my room in Savoy at 10:30. Pretty lonesome business in London.

Weather raw and cold.

Don Martin's first "mail story", dated January 1, was published in the New York Herald, Sunday, January 20, 1918, without byline.

Germany Has No Chance Whatever to Win War,

English Firmly Believe

Sacrifices Only Increase Determination of People to Triumph

Even if Twenty Years of Fighting is Required

[Special to the Herald]

Herald Bureau, No. 130 Fleet Street, London, Jan. 1

Before leaving the United States, I heard many persons actually ask if there was any possibility that Germany might win the war.

In England, where the people are face to face with war conditions and in possession of much more information than drifts across the Atlantic, the answer is quickly and most emphatically given:

"There is no chance whatever that Germany will win. The Allies will win if it takes twenty years, and we've got the men and money to do it.

"The people have the fortitude and the patience, and Germany knows it."

One does not have to be in Great Britain long to realize that the old spirit—commonly called pluck and tenacity—which won so many wars has been roused now as never before. England is groping around in inky darkness at night. She is having much less food than she ought to have. She is paying high prices. She is sacrificing her amusements and her pleasures. She is staying indoors at night and constantly watching skyward for enemy aircraft.

Her pleasure automobiles are a thing of the past. Banquets are unknown. Bars are closed except during short periods at midday and in the evening. The army of workers goes to work in the darkness of early morning and returns home in the foggy blackness of early evening. Women are doing things they never before dreamed of doing. Children are being put in factories the moment they can leave school.

Hardships Increase Determination

In brief, London—and all of England as well—is putting up with discomforts which might well be expected to stagger, if not completely discourage, a nation. But England is neither staggered nor discouraged. It may be said quite truthfully that the more sacrifices she is called upon to make and the more privations imposed on her the more dogged becomes her determination to crush Germany, and to stick to the task till a complete job has been done.

Measured by the inconveniences and hardships London already is suffering, New York city knows nothing at all of the war. To begin with, daylight does not start till nearly eight o'clock in the morning, and daylight ends at four. In all the great city not a light gleams from a window. The streets are black. Street lamps burn at infrequent intervals. All are shaded so that only a small circle of light is thrown on the pavement.

Shops appear closed. Restaurants which compare with the gaudiest or finest on Broadway seem locked tightly from without, yet within there are lights and crowds. One might walk the entire length of the Strand, Piccadilly, Fleet Street or any of the other popular thoroughfares at night and not see the first suggestion of life behind the solid walls.

The first dispatch continued on.

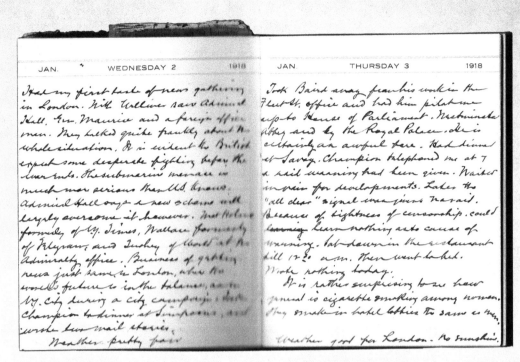

Diary pages, January 2–3, 1918

Diary: Wednesday January 2, 1918

Had my first taste of news gathering in London. With Welliver saw Admiral Reginald Hall [Director of Naval Intelligence], Gen. Maurice [Director of Military Operations at the War Office] and a foreign office man. They talked quite frankly about the whole situation. It is evident the British expect some desperate fighting before the war ends. The submarine menace is much more serious than U.S. knows. Admiral Hall says a new scheme will largely overcome it however.

Met Holmes formerly of NY Times, Wallace formerly of Telegram, and [James] Tuohey of World at the Admiralty office. Business of gathering news just same in London, where the world's future is in the balance, as in NY City during a city campaign. Took Champion to dinner at Simpson's and wrote two mail stories.

Weather pretty fair.

January 3, 1918 — Air raid warning, but no air raid.

Diary: Thursday January 3, 1918

Took Baird away from his work in the Fleet St office and had him pilot me up to House of Parliament, Westminster Abbey and by the Royal Palace. He is certainly an awful bore. Had dinner at Savoy. Champion telephoned me at 7 and said warning had been given. Waited in vain for developments. Later the "all clear" signal was given. No raid. Because of tightness of censorship, could learn nothing as to cause of warning. Sat down in the restaurant till 12:20 a.m. Then went to bed. Wrote nothing today.

It is rather surprising to see how general is cigarette smoking among women. They smoke in hotel lobbies the same as men.

Weather good for London. No sunshine.

Diary: Friday January 4, 1918

After breakfast at Savoy went to Fleet St. office and read the papers. At 3:45 met Baird at the hotel and went with him to the war office to have talk with Gen. [John] Buchan, mouthpiece for foreign office [Director of Information]. Reporters meet there once a week. Had dinner at Simpson's. Went to Fleet St. at night. Took Champion around to the Cheshire Cheese and bought him a drink. I was much interested in the famous place which figured so prominently in the life of Dr. [Samuel] Johnson [1709-1784] whose biography I have read in such detail. Went to bed about 1 a.m.

Weather fairly good.

January 5, 1918 — First time to London theater.

Diary: Saturday January 5, 1918

Went to our office at noon. Got wire from the Commodore* asking if I couldn't do something about London circulation. Poor old Commodore! He has skipped about two generations. I can see where I will get in trouble with him before long. Went for a walk on Black Friars Bridge: up in the Trafalgar Sq. region and then to the Savoy. Dropped into the Cock Tavern where Wordsworth used to hang out. Had dinner at Cheshire Cheese with Champion and then went to the London Gaiety Theater to see the "Beauty Spot," a musical comedy. Is a pretty dull show but beautifully staged. Champion thinks the Commodore is unfair in putting the circulation matter up to me. "I should worry?"

Rather nice day.

January 6, 1918 — First published dispatch, on the Italian and Palestine war scenes.

Diary: Sunday January 6, 1918

Went for quite a walk alone. Went away down to Throgmorton St., Stock Exchange, Bank of England; across Black Friars Bridge, up other side of Thames and across Waterloo Bridge to Savoy. Pleasant when I started but began to rain. Dinner at Simpson's after I had written about 3 cols. for mailing. Went to Fleet St. office and dictated a long letter to Commodore about his circulation telegram. Returned to hotel at 11 and came to my room which I find will cost me $3.75 a day. Not so much as I expected. Lloyd George stated England's war aims. Will insist on France getting Alsace and Lorraine.

Weather pleasant till 2 p.m. Then rain.

Martin's daily room charge at the Savoy of $3.75 would be $70 today, using the ratio of the Consumer Price Index—August 2020/ January 1918 = 259.9/14.0 = 18.6.

January 7, 1918—Don Martin settles in to reporting from London.

Diary: Monday January 7, 1918

Went to Fleet St. and wrote a couple of stories for mailing. Walked up to Piccadilly and about a half-mile on Regent St. London is certainly a great city. The magnitude of business is very impressive. Met Martin Green of the Evening World at the Savoy. Had dinner at Simpson's with Kloeber of the A.P. and a N.Y. lawyer named Nash. Then went to Herald office and talked with the office boy for an hour. Returned to hotel and sat in the big restaurant till midnight. Wrote a long letter to Dorothy. Weather pleasant. Some sunshine

[Martin Green and Don Martin would become known as two of the leading American war correspondents.]

* Herald owner J G Bennett had been Commodore of the New York Yacht Club

The letter Don wrote to his daughter Dorothy on Monday, January 7, was newsy, telling her about what he had found in London. And there is mention of his going to France, but not in winter. He made a copy of the letter and sent it with a friend leaving for New York; both copies survive.

 Dorothy,

I have just come from a walk through Piccadilly, Regent Street (the Fifth Avenue of London) and Trafalgar Sq. and will now write you a more or less brief letter. Writing seems unsatisfactory because there is no telling when the ships leave and then there is no certainty that one's letters will be on the first ship that starts. You see Dorothy every letter that leaves England has to be read by the government and it takes time. This is done because spies might send important information to America and in that way get it to Germany. All letters leaving America have to be read by the government too so there is delay at both ends. I have an idea I will get a letter from some of you in a few days, inasmuch as an American ship came in on Saturday.

I wrote to Alta last night just before I went to bed. She will no doubt show the letter to you so there is no need in repeating what I said to her. Unless the vessel which carried my former letters was sunk you will have learned all about my voyage over before this reaches you. I shall no doubt stay in England for quite a while. There is no use trying to do any war correspondence at the front in the winter. The weather is cold, the ground frozen and the killing has ceased till spring. It is likely that in the spring I will go over to France for a while. I can't exactly say I like it here. London is a wonderful city. There are miles and miles of business and millions of people. Even though all the younger men are in the army and navy,

> **Pasted on first page of letter:**
>
> ## LIGHTING TIMES TONIGHT
> **Lamps to be lighted, 4.36 p.m.**
> **Blinds to be drawn in London, 5.30 p.m.**
> **Sun sets 4.6 p.m.; rises to-morrow, 8.6 a.m.**
> **Moon rises 2.3 a.m.; sets 12 p.m.**
> **New Moon on Saturday**
> 'Recd Jan 23, 1918. Del'd by John Knox from Dan Reid'.

London streets are crowded and from the appearance of the stores, restaurants, etc. one would not know there is any war on. Still the streets are filled with men in uniform. I daresay if I should go down to the lobby of this hotel now I could count at least fifty officers standing about. The streets are filled with them. Some are home on leave, as they call it; some are wounded; some are on sick leave and a great many are passing through London on the way to France. There are evidences of war everywhere.

I see Americans everywhere. At least twenty are staying in this hotel now. Dan Reid, who used to go to school in Silver Creek is at the Savoy Hotel with some other men I know. A New York newspaperman named Martin Green, of the New York World, arrived today also. I haven't seen him yet but he is looking for me and I am waiting to hear from him.

The city seemed terribly cold during my first few days here but it is better now. I got some heavy underwear and have become used to the raw air. I took a little cold but got quickly over it. I get plenty to eat and am hungry about all the time. I guess it is the atmosphere and the exercise I get. I walk many miles every day just to look the city over. For breakfast I get two soft boiled eggs. They are as fresh as any eggs to be had anywhere. Then I have a cup of coffee—no cream but hot milk—with two tiny pieces of sugar; two small slices of bread or toast (that is all the law allows during war time) and some jam, jelly or marmalade.

Everyone eats jelly and jam here and I rather like it. You see young lady it is not possible to get supplies here because of the large number of ships sunk and people are curtailing. Still no one goes hungry. I get dinner usually at a famous restaurant called Simpson's. They have staples of beef and mutton. A carver wheels a table around with the roast and cuts off a slice of whatever you order. Now they can serve only so many ounces. Ordinarily one can have two or three servings if he wishes. However one helping is a great plenty. For about a dollar [$20 today] a person can get plenty to eat at Simpson's. There are many small, cheaper restaurants and they are all good. London is filled with restaurants but they all are at a disadvantage now. There is practically no fruit. Grapefruit is unheard of. Oranges cost 25 cents each [$5] . Apples cost as high as 30 cents [$6]. That is because little fruit is raised in England and all the room on the available ships is used for transporting supplies more necessary than fruit.

Regent Street is like one continuous jewelry store. I never saw such displays of diamonds and jewelry of all sorts. The stores for women's dresses, coats, etc. look about as they do in New York or any other city and the shoe stores—of which there are a great many—have about the same kind of displays as other cities.

I spent New Year's Eve with some New York newspapermen and a couple of London writers. We had some American mince pie which had been sent to one of the Americans from his home in Maryland. The apartment we were in is in a building 300 years old yet it was comfortable. I am invited on Friday to a luncheon at this hotel by the American Luncheon Club, and I expect will meet quite a few persons of whom I have heard. The Savoy is a very large and very fine hotel but as it is the headquarters of practically everyone of note in London—I mean persons travelling—I thought it wise to stay here for a while at least. I should say it is about like the Waldorf Astoria in New York.

I don't expect to get homesick, Dorothy. It would be funny if I should because I never have yet. Just the same I would like to see you once in a while. Goodness, if I stay away a year you will be almost a young woman. I daresay your hair is getting long already. Don't you fail to let the folks know if there is something you want. When shoe time comes again perhaps you better send to Best's and get some there. Their shoes seem to fit you pretty well.

I am going to write a story for the Herald now and then I shall go to Simpson's for dinner. After that I shall go to our office on Fleet Street—about fifteen minutes' walk from here—and return about eleven o'clock to read an hour and go to bed. There has been no air raid yet by the Germans but I expect some day I will see one. I will take good care of myself though, so you needn't worry. When you have a little time you might write me a short note. Address it to No. 130 Fleet Street. Have a good time and remember me to Joseph and all the folks.

With love and a kiss,

Dorothy: I am mailing you a letter today in London. I am giving this copy to Dan Reid who leaves here in a couple days. He will mail it in N.Y. You can let me know which reaches you first. *[Handwritten]*

Dad

January 8, 1918—Visit from Silver Creek friend.

Diary: Tuesday January 8, 1918

Had a pleasant visit with Dan Reid, once of Silver Creek. Had dinner with him in Savoy. Talked about everyone in Silver Creek, particularly of John Knox and his family. Afterward I went to Dan's room and met other members of the Am. comm. of which he is a member. Wrote letter to Dorothy + sent it by Dan.

Dan told me some interesting things about his observations in France and I shall write a story about them. Early in the day I saw Colonel [John] Buchan, intelligence man for the Foreign Service.

Got lot of letters from N.Y. One from Joe Tumulty, Secretary to President Wilson.

Weather wintry. Coldest day of year. Snow.

Letter from Rose Martin (No. 3)

Dated Jan 8, 1918; postmarked London Jan 28 'Opened By Censor' c/o New York Herald Bureau, London [Fleet Street] England

Jan 8th, 1918

Dear Don,

Will just write you a few lines this time to tell you we are all real well. Every thing is just the same as it always is, excepting that we are having terrible cold weather. I am wondering if you are getting our letters. This is No. 3 from me and Dorothy has written 3 or 4 and she will write you again Saturday. We will all be glad when some of your letters come.

Have discovered some of your writings in the Herald and was glad to see it as then I knew you were all right. This week Julia will take Dorothy to Buffalo in my place.

I sent that letter you wrote on the ship to Alta. We all had to see it. I shall be so glad to get a letter from you from over there.

I know you must be very busy writing and now I hope you have every thing to make you comfortable. Will stop now as I don't seem to be able to write decent. I almost want to tear it up. But I must not as I could not write another any better.

With lots of love,
From Mother

January 8: in Washington, President Wilson addressed a joint session of Congress in a major speech laying out America's aims for the Great War in 14 points, which became known as *Wilson's Fourteen Points*. Martin noted the event in his diary the next day.

Diary: Wednesday January 9, 1918

Dictated a couple stories to Baird who is a prize bone head. Saw Gen. [Frederick] Maurice, [Director of Military Operations] of the [Imperial] General Staff. He reviewed Haig's report and quite immodestly claims credit for everything that has been done on the Western front.

Dinner at Simpson's and then the Fleet St. office till midnight. Martin Green left for France tonight.

Wilson's speech on war aims printed today in England.

Weather cold but fair.

Diary: Thursday January 10, 1918

Went to the office at noon and dictated three stories to Baird. Saw the Admiralty spokesman. He says German submarines are now more successful in bad weather than good. 18 ships sunk this week. That's bad. It is very evident that the submarine menace is getting worse.

Had dinner at Simpson's again. In afternoon walked down to 64 Mark Lane and called on Mr. Cilly, Barbiano agent in London.

English papers pleased with all of Wilson's speech except part about Freedom of the Seas.

Weather clear, mild and sun shining!

Letter from Dorothy (No.4)

Dated January 10, 1918; postmarked Jan 12, 4PM
c/o New York Herald Bureau, [Fleet Street] London, England

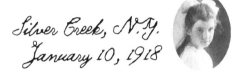

Silver Creek, N.Y.
January 10, 1918

Dear Dad

I feel very silly this afternoon as you can probably or – will soon see. I am also in a <u>terrible</u> hurry. Mrs. Draezert is here cleaning + she just told me about the ice-skating. I knew that it was just grand under the bridge yesterday + that there was a crowd up there but I couldn't go up. You know it's up where I used to throw stones in the water. But she said that there has been skating for the last few days, and Dr. Balmer goes up there + does all sorts of fancy things + all of the teachers are up there + picks + bushels + barrels of children + even a lot of grown up men + women. And children 4 + 5 yrs. old are up there skating. And they have bonfires to get your feet warm. Even at night they have candles + lanterns, so they skate until nine P.M. This is not going to be a very long letter and I guess you know why. But I will write you another note in the [~] of the week. Do you know what that funny thing means? (middle)

I had a little club that I belong to last week + I had a awful good supper. Ha! Haw! Ha! Ho! We do Red Cross work. Mostly knittin'. For supper I had Ham, + jelly + peanut butter sandwiches + cocoa with marshmallow in + then we had some orange + lemon jello + little cakes for desert. Grandmother made all but the cakes which Aunt Julie made for me. They were little sponge cakes. Some had chocolate frosting with a nut on top + the others had white frosting with red candied cherries on top.

Well I guess this is about all there is to say. You see, Christmas + everythin' like that is all over. Now I will close down + mail this letter + chase over + get Iola + then we will chase back here + then, oh, then we will chase up for a joyous afternoon skate. Last time it was for a joyous afternoon slide but this time nixy on slide but skate. Oh! I bet we would have bushels + barrels etc of fun if you were here.

Oh, we see articles in the Herald from you now and are glad to see them.

Lots o' love an' hugs an' kisses,
Dorothy

January 11, 1918 — Winston Churchill speaks to the American Luncheon Club

Diary: Friday January 11, 1918

Went to luncheon of the American Luncheon Club at the Savoy, as guest of Mr. Underwood of N.Y. Winston Churchill made speech saying that winning of war depends on America, who must act quickly. [Viscount] Northcliffe [British publishing magnate], Ambassador [Walter] Page [US Ambassador to Great Britain], Admiral Simms [Commander of US Naval Forces in Europe] and a lot of other distinguished men were present. Later went to the War office and saw Sir Edward Carson [Irish politician, Member of War Cabinet] who says he doubts if the League of Nations dream can ever be realized. Had dinner at Simpson's. Then went to Fleet St. after getting ready a letter to Mr. Bennett telling him what I think ought to be done here.

Am amazed at the pessimism everywhere regarding the outcome of the war. Everyone now seems to think that the Allies have their hardest fighting ahead to whip Germany and may not do so. America has a different notion of things than we have here but no information can get by censor.

Weather fair but cool.

Diary: Saturday January 12, 1918

Talked to Baird about a telegram I got from Bennett last night. Bennett is a "nut" all right. He says he wants "not political generalities but fresh news, interviews, arrivals at hotels, etc." Fresh news by mail in these times of uncertain mails! I can see where I have a fine row with the old imbecile. However I shall humor him along. Baird will have to get the hotel news and I will get some real interviews.

Met Judd Welliver and went with him to tea at the home of Casson sisters — 4 of them and nice girls too — at Herne Hill. They tried to play old American songs and how they murdered them!

Their singing is almost as bad as Welliver's and he ought to be arrested. Got my first letter from Dorothy and it is a splendid one.

Weather pleasant.

Diary: Sunday January 13, 1918

Began day with walk to Leicester Sq. with Russell. Went with him as far as Hanover Gate apartments. Left him and walked about 2 miles back to Oxford Circus where I took the subway to Whitechapel. Just wandered around to see region I had always heard about. Looks nothing like N.Y.'s Ghetto. Returned to hotel. Wrote story of London's comforts and fortitude and also "Sidelights on the War," for N.Y. edition. Some flub-dub for Paris*. Went to Fleet St. and gossiped with Champion till midnight. Sent letter to Mr. Bennett telling what I think ought to be done here for the Herald. Imagine he will take exception to nearly all I suggest.

Really a fine day.

Diary: Monday January 14, 1918

Got busy trying to systematize things. Got letters from Mr. Bennett telling me to reorganize any way I wish, and to live either at the Ritz, Claridge or the Savoy. He seems to think I ought to get in touch with everyone of importance in England. Had a talk with Baird and told him what to do. He was so completely shocked that he was unconscious (?) for a couple of hours. It looks to me as if none of the men in the office ever did anything.

Dinner at Simpson's. Wrote to Cooper, McEwan and Jim Hagerty. At Fleet Street till midnight.

Read till 1 a.m. Am astounded more and more at the pessimism of the English.

Weather pleasant.

---

* The Paris edition of the Herald. Martin will write frequently for the Paris Herald once he is in France.

Besides the letters to the people he mentioned in his diary entry, Don Martin also wrote a letter to Dorothy Monday night, January 14. In it he projected correctly how the war could end in 1918.

My dear Dorothy,

That was a splendid letter you wrote—the first letter I have received from you in London. I got it Saturday, January 12 and it left Silver Creek on Dec. 22. It had not been opened by the censor. I guess he knew it was from you and therefore was all right.

You were certainly a busy girl just before Christmas, weren't you? Rock wrote about the birthday cake. I am anxious now to hear all about your Christmas. Isn't it a shame that the things Santa Claus had for me failed to reach me at the office or on the St. Louis? I told Alta about it in a letter and I suppose you have taken steps to get the package back. I wish I had it. You remembered all your cousins and that was very nice.

I couldn't imagine what was the matter when I opened your letter. I suppose you used the red ink just to make it different. It looked very good. That picture of me using spy glasses was not any worse than other pictures you have drawn. How do you do that?

Formal portrait of Don Martin

I have nothing very great to tell you. I go to the offices of the government and learn all they know about the war. Then I write part of it. The censorship is very strict you know but that doesn't mean, by any means, that the Germans are getting the best of the war. They will get licked all right. I heard Winston Churchill make a speech the other day at the American Luncheon Club meeting. I was a guest. He is one of England's leading statesmen. I also saw General Maurice, a member of the British military staff. He is on a par with General Haig only he does the battle planning from here. It is very interesting to talk with him.

The eating here is a little different from that at home. Sugar and butter are very scarce and it is costly to buy fruit. However everyone gets enough to eat. I am still living at the Savoy and probably will remain here. It is warm and that is a good deal in London. Steam heat as I believe I told you is almost unheard of in England. Everyone uses fireplaces. The floors are cold and one side of you freezes while the other toasts. Still that is the way in all the homes, rich and poor. The Savoy has heat and until spring comes I shall stay here.

I may go over to France when the winter breaks up, at least for a little trip. There is no sense in going over there now because the armies are snowed and frozen in. The expectation everywhere is that as soon as it is thawed out a little, the Germans will make a great offensive in France with the intention of defeating England and France before America can get in the war. She will no doubt make a great attack but from all I can learn the Allies are prepared to resist it. If Germany makes her great offensive and fails to break the Allies' line the chances are that the war will end this year, with Germany beaten. If Germany breaks the Allies' line and wins a victory, the war will not end but the defeat of Germany will be delayed considerably and will depend upon the Allies holding together and avoiding trouble at home. All this I imagine you better have Uncle Rock translate for you.

Yesterday it was sunshiny and I took advantage of it by walking for three hours. I went through a section of the residence district and then walked all over Whitechapel which corresponds to the lower East Side of New York, yet looks nothing like it. It is the poor section and is populated with Jews.

I went to No. 64 Mark Lane. I walked there from our office. It is about a mile and a half. The office is on the fourth floor of a five story building and seems comfortable. There were pictures of the Barbeau family all over and a very recent picture of Lex. I had a very pleasant visit with Mr. Cilly.

London is a five story city, Dorothy. The highest building is ten stories and nine out of ten are five stories and very old. A really modern building is quite a novelty. But it is a wonderful city. You can walk for five hours and never get out of a lively business district. Everyone seems to have money and the store windows look just about the same as those in Buffalo or New York. It is said that there are 800,000 British soldiers in England all the time, most of them on leave from the front. The streets of London are filled with them and in the hotels there are thousands of officers to be seen all the time.

You must tell me the date when some of my letters reach you Dorothy so I will have an idea about the mails. I know they are very slow. I wondered if you got the letter I wrote you on board the St. Louis while we were waiting to start.

Your Christmas card was a pretty one, young lady. You certainly wished me a merry, merry, merry, merry Christmas. You know all about the Christmas I had now. It was a rather new experience.

Here's a kiss and a hug for you Dorothy and love for all the family, both on Main and Dunkirk streets.

With love
Dad

Diary: Tuesday January 15, 1918

Called on Mr. [Ralph] Blumenfeld, owner of the London Express and presented letter from Mr. Bennett. Blumenfeld was very pleasant. We visited for an hour and he assured me he will be very glad to do everything he can for me.

Visited Col. Buchan with the other correspondents. He says America will not have much of a fighting force before the latter part of the year and that he thinks the English and French can hold the line till U.S. is ready. Looks to me like studied pessimism.

Dinner at Simpson's again. Rained all day. The very worst day I ever saw. Dictated to Baird a couple of stories for N.Y. and letters to London hotels about news we ought to get from them.

Rain—rain—rain—Not cold though.

Don Martin handwrote a short note to Dorothy the night of January 15, including news about James Gordon Bennett and the Herald London office. It was "Opened by Censor".

Savoy Hotel. London W. C. 2
Tuesday night, January 15-1918

Miss Full-of-Mischief

That's what you said you were and I have no doubt it is true. I have been in the hotel all the evening—most of the time in my room writing and reading and I shall write just a wee bit of a note on this little stationary before I go to bed.

The reason I haven't been out is the weather. It has been half raining and half snowing all day and now at midnight I can hear the dripping of the rain. London is a dismal city on a rainy night but it is particularly so in these times when there are no lights in the streets.

I have had several letters from Mr. Bennett and he wants me to reorganize the London bureau from top to bottom. It needs it too, so I guess the old Commodore is not so crazy as most people think. Everyone does things in an old fashioned way in London and I have rather startled the old fogies in the office here by the programme I have outlined to them.

Tell Julie that I intend to write to her after a bit—and tell Rock that I shall write to him too. I have been rather busy during the last few days but I can hardly say I haven't time to write. I guess if you have read all I have written to you so far you have been pretty busy. I wonder if you got your share of the blizzard which started in Chicago. I read about that in the London papers. They never have snow in London, except slight flurries, and the thermometer seldom goes lower than 20 and seldom that. The days are getting longer now. By June the nights will be short. Daylight starts at 3:30 a.m. and lasts till nearly 10 pm. You know England is rather far north. I'll go to bed now young lady.

With love,
Dad

Diary: Wednesday January 16, 1918

Saw Mr. [William] Sutherland, Secretary to Lloyd George relative to interviews with the Premier. He thinks he may be able to arrange one. Pretty difficult to get things done quickly in England. Called on Louis Nethersole at Lyric Theatre to arrange interview with Doris Keane, American actress who has been playing [Mme. Margherita Cavallini in] "Romance" here for 3 years. He said he would like to have me at luncheon with her next Thursday. Had dinner at Simpson's with Mr. Whaley, the man whom I met on the ship. Then went to Fleet St.

Judd Welliver came into office and Champion and I went to his office to see photographs of his family which just came. A fine family he has.

Weather rainy + foggy.

Diary: Thursday January 17, 1918

Went to office early and dictated a couple of stories to Baird, whose stupidity is enough to drive one frantic.

Met Canadian officer who for three hours in my room told me the harrowing story of his escape from a German prison in Saxony. Only trouble is the story is 2 years old. Met Welliver and Mrs. Lerney in the evening and went with them to the James' Theatre to see "Charley's Aunt." Later went to Fleet St. and dictated a story to Champion. The whole Herald office certainly ought to be reorganized or closed altogether.

Wrote a letter to Mrs. Welliver telling her about Judd's joy at showing pictures of her family.

Weather very bad. Rain.

Letter from Rose Martin

Dated Jan 17, 1918, 'Opened By Censor', Notation 'Recd Feb 9'. C/o New York Herald Bureau, London [Fleet Street] England

Jan 17, 1918

Dear Don,

Dorothy and I have been writing regular once a week, which makes two letters a week. And I hope you have received some of them. O Don, when I began writing this letter I was a little blue at not having received news from you, and just a few minutes ago the Postman brought two letters from you, one great long one, and another one, and I will say that changed everything. I waved them at Dorothy. She said from DaDa, Oh. I told her we would all have to read them. Julia was here when they came, the large one was almost ready to drop out, and we were both so anxious to read it that we took it out, but it being 11:30 Julia did not have time, neither did I, so when Dorothy came home she read half of it. She hated to stop but she had to. The last thing she said, don't lose my place.

Well after dinner I sat by the fire and read it, and it took one hour, and it was so interesting that I could have read it over again, and will later, but wanted to write these few lines first. Well Don, what an experience you did have, and still you did have a very good time too. I can just imagine what anxiety there was among some of those people, and I thought of you on that boat many times and was mighty glad when you got over, and now I hope you will get our letters. I don't think your letters were opened or looked over excepting the end of the long envelope. That was badly torn and I am very glad that we heard from you. Julia will take Dorothy to Buffalo tomorrow instead of me, and she will take those letters to Alta, and she will bring them back. Then I will take care of them (my, but that is a good letter).

With lots of love. Mother

Dorothy will be home soon from school, and perhaps she will write a little more to put in this envelope, which I will let her address. She certainly can do it better than me. Again good bye and good luck, Mother

—Last Page—

Have just finished rereading your letters and I begin to realize that you were all in great danger, and that it is dangerous to cross the Ocean at present. It is said that an Ocean trip is the best thing in the world for the health but I don't see how one like that could be. That was a terrible journey. That was the end I was afraid of.

Heigh! – Leigh! Look out there!

 Dad,

What does that sound like huh? Skatin'? Yep, yuh betcha. Sure 'nough thing. After school some of us stayed for an hour an' a half down in the gym' and did all the imaginable stunts alive. Standing on head then turning head alone around, wheelbarrow walk + frog + elephant walk – (I'll describe those some other time.) and – as I said – everythin' 'maginable. After we'd been there 'bout as – oh good gracious I don't know why I always am putting sad for said – oh jickerty, now look at the mess I have made, will you!

Well as I were a sayin' – 'bout as I said an hour + a half, Miss Butler said it was 'bout time for us to have some outdoor exercise. So most of us came up this way an' got our skates (Miss Butler lives right across the road from us.) an' went up to the ice pond on the creek + just got back. Loads o' fun. Had a big fire to get warm by. Well so long till as soon as I can get up on the skates again to the creek.

Got your book o' letters this noon + it's just like reading a story book. Just read two so far. O'rful interestin'. Well, so long till Saturday.

Lots o' love an' hugs an' kisses
Dorothy or Dot or Dotty

Diary: Friday January 18, 1918

Went to luncheon of American Luncheon Club with Russell. Then to office. Nothing much to do. Mr. Miller of United Press called for me and we went to dinner at Simpson's. Went to office in the rain. At 12:30 at hotel met American sailors from S.I. [New York] who told me how they were fired at by submarine. Dictated cable and wrote story for Paris. War news quiet. Submarine sinkings low after 2 very bad weeks. Food situation here getting bad.

Allies are worried about the threatened spring drive of Germany. Whole issue rests upon the submarines—whether the Allies can overcome it either by building enough new ships or destroying the subs.

Weather sloppy but warm.

Diary: Saturday January 19, 1918

Got up at 9 and went to Claridge to see Paul D. [Cravath] of N.Y., advisor for U.S. to Inter-Allied Council. He introduced me to Oscar T. Crosby*, Pres. of Council with whom I had long confidential talk. He says German attack soon to come will be biggest blow ever struck by any army. He says French and English pull and haul and Germany knows it and is making the most of it. Submarine menace serious he says.

Went to office for while. Then walked a roundabout way to hotel where I wrote two columns "sidelights" for mailing. Dinner at Simpson's again. Went to Fleet St. office in evening for a short time. Bought Locke's "Beloved Vagabond" and began reading it.

Weather nasty but warm.

* Oscar Crosby, President of Inter-Allied Council for War Purchases and Finance, later became Assistant Secretary of the Treasury.

Letter from Dorothy (No. 5)

Dated January 19, 1918; postmarked Jan 19, 1:30PM; Notation 'Arrived Feb 9'. C/o New York Herald Bureau, London, England

Silver Creek, N.Y.
January 19, 1918

Dear Dad

Here goes for letter No. 5. I am not sure whether I numbered my last letter or not. Grandmother forgot to put the number on her last one, but it was No. 4. I always put the number of my letters down on one of the lower corners on the side where it is sealed. Now you will know where to look for the number.

I just finished eating my breakfast and now I will write this letter and take it down town and mail it. While I am down-town I will also buy some sort of a birthday present for Elizabeth Hammond as I am going to her birthday party this afternoon. I got your long, long – or I mean 6 short letters Wednesday morning, also the one you wrote in Liverpool. Wednesday was the 16th.

Your bunch of letters was just like a book. It is very terribly interesting. It certainly was a – oh, I don't know what to call it – trip. One thing is – an <u>interesting</u> trip. Wasn't it? Grandmother has read it. Aunt Julie, Uncle Charlie and Aunt Atta so far.

We went to Buffalo yesterday and I had my music lesson and had my teeth or rather the braces on my teeth tightened up. Aunt

Alta did not have time to read all of the letter so she kept it and sent it up by special delivery last night. Uncle Rock will take it to read next. It is very cold today, just 4 above 0. I am sitting at the little white stand right near the stove writing this letter. The gas is lower than usual. You probably know that everything is shut down on account of coal for five days. The whistles don't blow and even grocery stores open half day. I wonder how the weather is where you are.

Well I must close now.

Lots of Love an' hugs an' kisses, Dorothy

Enclosed with Letter 5 were these drawings titled "Winter sports with <u>girls</u> too you bet!" and subtitled "Hoppin' on [sled] and a lot more than this; ice skating, snowballing; sled sports—going down, a spill".

Diary: Sunday January 20, 1918

Slept rather late. Walked through a new part (for

Judson
Welliver,
New York Sun

me) of London, Soho Square section. London is certainly an interesting city. Judd Welliver came up to my room at 7 and we went to Simpson's for dinner. Then I went to the office for an hour or so. Am pretty well convinced that no one does any work in the Herald Bureau so will shake it up a bit. Wrote about 4 columns for mailing. Also wrote to Dorothy.

Weather rainy part of day but warm. Moonlight.

Diary: Monday January 21, 1918

Started cleaning up the Fleet St. office, physically and establishing a little system. Both the office and the staff are dying of dry rot.

In Simpson's at dinner I met Charlie Wheeler of the Chicago Tribune who has come here to do about the same thing I am doing. Spent couple hours with him. He thinks the war will end this year with an economic collapse in Germany. He thinks Germany is bluffing about the big offensive. Went to Fleet St. office and talked to Champion about readjustments. He is certainly, as Bennett says, wedded to routine.

Weather beautiful. Quite astonishing.

Diary: Tuesday January 22, 1918

Had luncheon (breakfast) with Louis Nethersole [director of Lyric theater] at an Italian restaurant on Dean St. Then met Charlie Weaver at Savoy. Went to Fleet St office with him; showed him the Cheshire Cheese and Temple Court and walked to War Office with him in the rain. Saw Sutherland at 10 Downing St. (Lloyd George's Secretary) but not able to get interview. Took a Mr. Brownell to Lyric theater to see Doris Keane in "Romance". It is the big hit of London but I can't see much art in it. After show went to Miss Keane's dressing room and had interview with her. She is no wonder. She invited me to her home for luncheon Thursday.

Sat up till 2 a.m. writing a letter to Mr. Bennett about reorganization of the office. Beautiful day but rain beginning at 4:30.

January 23, 1918—Don Martin fully in the saddle as London war correspondent.

Diary: Wednesday January 23, 1918

Had breakfast in Lyon's Corner House—scones, marmalade and coffee—1 shilling [equivalent to $8 in Oct 2017]. Very good too. Then went to Fleet St. Dictated some letters to Baird, to Carson and Duchess of Marlborough relative to interviews. Walked down and back with Lingwood who pointed out the Rothschild's bank. Also walked out on London Bridge.

Went to hotel at 5:30 and wrote a 2 column story on my visit to Doris Keane the actress. Dinner at Simpson's. Then went to Fleet St. Have my office looking pretty good. Got long, fine letter from Dorothy telling all about Christmas. She writes exactly the kind of letters I have always wanted to get.

Weather nice but rain at night.

Sketch of James Gordon Bennett, eccentric owner of the New York Herald and Don Martin's boss.

Diary: Thursday January 24, 1918

Went to the office early and read the papers. Then went to Doris Keane's house to luncheon. Met her husband (not much), a couple of Lady Somethings and had an American meal of fried chicken, corn fritters and lemon pie. It was a splendid luncheon. Miss Keane showed me through her home which is very beautiful and I read her part of a story I have written about her as the "rage of London". I didn't think much of the outfit.

Saw Admiral [Sir William Reginald, "Blinker"] Hall [Director of Naval Intelligence] at 4:30. Then went to office and to St. James' Theatre to see opening performance of "Valentine," a musical comedy. Some pretty music. Lack of men is big handicap to stage in London now.

Weather beautiful.

Diary: Friday January 25, 1918

Drew $50 from the office—1st expense money. [equivalent to $930, August 2020]

Breakfast at Lyon's. Went to the office and spent couple hours. Wrote a 2 column story on the submarine situation as it really is. Got several letters from N.Y. Met Mr. Miller of the U.P. at 6: went to dinner with him at Simpson's and them to Wyndham Theatre to see Barrie's "Dear Brutus". Is a good satire. Went to Fleet Street for a half hour, then to the Savoy and wrote a letter or two. Warning for an air raid but none happened.

Germany's reply to Lloyd George and President Wilson [Fourteen Points]. Practically tells them both to go to the devil. Whatever else may be said, Germany plays her part. Instead of fighting like a gentlemen she fights like a thug which is the way to fight—for only thugs should fight.

Another beautiful day.

Diary: Saturday January 26, 1918

Became a regular sightseer and spent 2 hours in the Tower of London. Went all through it—from the Crown Jewels tower to the place where murders were committed 40 years ago. It was like living through my English history.

Diary: Sunday January 27, 1918

Got up before 10. Had breakfast in the hotel. Took bus out to Richmond, through Hammersmith. Beautiful day and I enjoyed it. Walked around a while and took a bus back. Stopped in Lyon's Corner House and had some lunch. Then to my room and wrote for about 2 ½ hours. Wrote a story about President Wilson as Man of the Hour—world's big figure. Also wrote a very long letter to Mother, telling her about almost everything. Dinner at Simpson's and then to Fleet St. for an hour. Came to hotel about 11:30 to read and go to bed.

Moonlight nights and everyone expecting air raids. Germany's peace answer gets cool reception everywhere. Speaks like a conqueror.

Weather delightful.

Don Martin wrote a four-page letter at the Savoy Hotel to his mother on Sunday evening, dated January 27, 1918. He wrote about the war and especially about the expected London air raids.

New York Herald, London Bureau
130, Fleet Street, E.C.4.
January 27, 1918

Mother

All my letters so far have been to Dorothy but they were of course meant for you all. There isn't really much to tell that I haven't already written to her. I am well and contented. You probably read of the scarcity of food here but people get enough to eat. I just this minute came from Simpson's—quite a famous place in London—where I had as fine a piece of mutton as I ever ate and plenty of it. I also had boiled potatoes and celery and an apple pudding. That is almost too much for anyone.

I have been in the place a good deal and the tips I ordinarily give in New York seem to be rather princely here so I am quite well known in Simpson's and consequently get very good service. For instance, with the exception of Tuesdays and Fridays which are meatless, they have roast beef and roast mutton. Men with great big trays come to your table with whichever you wish. You can readily see the advantage of knowing the carvers. Then, when you are about finished the waiter brings a large hunk of cheese to your plate and permits you to slice off what you want. A good meal in Simpson's costs about $1.

Of course everything is shillings and pence here. A shilling is 24 cents. A penny equals our two cents. The silver pieces are half pennies, pennies, six-pences (12 cents), shillings, two shillings, two-shillings-six-pences and then bills; first a ten shilling bill, which is equal to $2.50 or to be exact $2.40, and twenty shillings, or one pound, which approximates our $5 bill but which really amounts to $4.84. One learns how to count and handle (and spend too) the money very quickly. Notwithstanding the scarcity of things it does not cost any more to live here than it does in New York and the restaurant prices are less.

I live at the Savoy Hotel which is one of the three leading hotels in London. My room costs me $4 a day [$74, Aug 2020] but I have an expense allowance. I could go elsewhere at less cost but it pays, in my business, to be where the people are. The Savoy is the gathering place of the Americans and almost everyone else. There are a dozen people living in the hotel whom I know and almost every day I meet someone else from New York, Chicago or some other place.

My room is a large one with a great big, very fine bed, which when not in use, has a watered silk pink spread on it. I have a dresser with side mirrors; three big circular windows, because the room is semi-circular; a little hallway leading into a large bath room, a big easy chair, two or three other chairs; a reading lamp at the head of my bed and a big clothes press or wardrobe. I couldn't be fixed any nicer. I keep my typewriter in my room and while I am at the office quite a bit I do a good deal of writing here. I have a couple of photographs of Dorothy in the room. They are framed. She has seen them both. I should like a newer picture though. I wrote her about it.

I have had a good deal to do in the way of reorganizing the London office. It was terribly run down. The men in it have been here for many years and are old fogies. I am getting things in pretty good shape though. There is no use going to France yet. In fact it is almost impossible for anyone to get where he can see anything of the fighting. I probably shall take a trip over there after a while—maybe when the spring campaign starts. It is expected that there will be some terrible fighting there on the Western front as soon as spring has come. If Germany loses heavily it may mean the end of the war. If she has successes it will mean only that the war will be prolonged until American troops can get on the scene. Germany is still powerful but it is only because her people are willing to stand any amount of privations at home and her rulers are willing to have her people slaughtered like cattle. If the Allies would give up its camouflage and fight as Germany does—like a thug and a ruffian—Germany would not last so long. This pretending to be a gentleman yet fighting a thug is bad business according to my way of looking at things.

I cannot say that I would rather be here than in New York. London is a wonderful city but I imagine I will have seen all I want to of it in a few months. I have walked over a good part of it and have taken busses out to the outskirts. Today I took a bus and rode out to a suburb called Richmond. I should say it is about fifteen miles. Except for a space of about four miles, we were on streets which looked like the average city street—hotels, apartment houses, all five, six and seven stories high; and rows, or miles and miles, of little private houses two stories in height. The city looks nothing like New York. There are no vacant lots anywhere—though of course there aren't in New York either—but the structures are low. It reminds me of West Philadelphia.

Yesterday I decided to do no work so I went to the Tower of London. It is the most historic place in the city and sets on the banks of the Thames. The Thames, by the way, is quite a river. The Tower stands just as it was built by William the Conqueror. The Bloody Tower where crown princes were murdered and Kings and Queens were imprisoned is still just as it was. The room where Walter Raleigh was imprisoned, and the stone walk where he used to take exercise, remain precisely as they were.

The chapel where Mary Queen of Scots was betrothed to a Spanish King by proxy is unchanged. In the armories guns and armor are kept from the 11th, 12th and 13th centuries. Then the Crown jewels are to be seen. The whole outfit is said to be worth about one hundred million dollars in actual value and it looks it. I spent three hours in the place. People who always live in London never go to see it. It is too easy. So I decided I would do it while it still seemed a novelty.

I have been in St. Paul's Cathedral, Westminster Abbey and in the House of Parliament. I have seen a good many of the big men in England. I have got along pretty well so far. I am taking advantage of the spare time I have to see the leading shows of London also. Tickets for the openings are sent to the Herald office so I use them. I have seen thus far the Beauty Spot at the London Gaiety; Charlie's Aunt, an old show; Valentine, a new musical comedy; Dear Caesar, a satire by James M. Barrie; Romance, with Doris Keane whom I interviewed; and last night, Love in a Cottage, one of the best shows I have ever seen. There are about a dozen more I expect to see and there is no reason why I should not. There are something like thirty or forty theaters in London and they are always filled. People have to have some diversion. The audiences are made up of soldiers largely too. You see there are always about a half million soldiers in London. Some are on leave from the front and a good many are on duty here or passing through the city.

Fully half the men to be seen any time in any restaurant, high or medium class, are men in uniform. On the streets one sees hundreds of them everywhere. I have probably seen fifteen or twenty who are blind and a hundred or more with a leg off and I couldn't begin to tell how many wearing crutches. They are all young men too. Still no one seems down-cast. People here are taking it all in a most philosophical way, just as if it is a job that somebody must do. That is precisely what it is, by the way, and United States is the one who must do it. The people there may as well get ready for a big casualty list because one is bound to come unless Germany should yield to peace agitation this summer, and I doubt if she will.

It looks to most people as if the war will end sometime in 1919 although there are plenty who think it will last two years after that. The submarines are the terrible thing. If the Allies could only overcome them they could win a military decision in France but as things are now there are not enough ships to transport the American soldiers and Germany of course knows it and hoped to smash the Allies before our men can get to France. Of course a few hundred thousand men would help but anything short of a million as things go now doesn't count for so much. There has been no air raid since I arrived in London. One has been looked for every night now for a week because it is moonlight. Twice during that time a warning has been sent from the coast but neither time did the Germans get as far as London. No one except the authorities ever knows just how far they got, or why they didn't get farther. People have plenty of time to get under cover. The trouble is the people in the outlying sections have no safe cover to go to. No small private house is substantial enough to resist a bomb. One would go straight through it. One would also go straight through a building like the Eureka shop or the Stewart block. Any old fashioned four or five-story brick building would probably be wrecked if a bomb landed on it. The larger buildings of steel and concrete and a great many such buildings are to be found in the business parts of London would be safe enough. This hotel I am in is safe. The only trouble is it is very close to a hotel, now used by the government, which the Germans are eager to hit. However, there is no danger downstairs.

When enemy planes appear off the coast of France, on their way toward England, word is sent to England. It is passed straight to London. Then the police go through every street whistling and giving other signals which mean, and everyone understands, "Take Cover". There is a half hour or more in which people may find places of safety, I am told, and by the time the airplanes appear over the city the streets are deserted except for the police and such daring people as want to see the excitement.

The airmen fly over together and look very much like a flock of geese. English fliers immediately start after them and big guns mounted on buildings all over the city begin firing at them. I am told it is a thrilling spectacle. Usually two or three Germans are killed and their airplanes smash on the city. Bombs drop in various parts of the city and succeed in killing people who were in the street. Generally it is women or children.

If a raid comes at night the clerks in this hotel call up every person in the place and ask them to come downstairs if they wish to do so. There is absolutely no danger away down stairs. This hotel is nine stories high and of very strong construction. No bomb could destroy more than one or two of the top floors. I am on the third floor from the basement—really the second floor up. So when you read about air raids in London, as you no doubt will very soon, don't be worried about me. Last night every one expected a raid. It was a clear moonlight night and no low-lying clouds. The raids are much more serious than people generally believe. They are the one thing which people more or less talk and think about all the time.

I am glad you all had such a good Christmas. I am sorry your Christmas parcel to me did not get to the ship in time. I suppose Alta wrote to the post office authorities and got it back. I hope she did. You know all about my trip over. I guess I wrote enough to tire you all out about it. Tell Alta that check from Bauman came all right. I deposited it with the Guaranty Trust Company of New York, which has a branch here. It is just as safe there as anywhere. Maybe you better arrange to pay the dentist out of the money which accumulates in the bank, if there is enough. I believe he was to have a $50 payment every few months or so. Also, how about painting the house? I should think the family ought to get together on that proposition. Alta is willing I am sure. It wouldn't cost anyone much if we all got together on it. Talk this over with the others.

I should very much like to see Dorothy and Joseph. Dorothy writes most remarkable letters. She can write as well as her Dad now. I imagine she will be quite a literary girl by the time she is eighteen. Be sure she has such things as she wants.

This is a terribly long letter but it is Sunday night and I have time. I am going down to our office on Fleet Street now. We are only a few hundred feet from the Cheshire Cheese restaurant and right back of that up a queer old alley, is the house where Dr. Johnson lived. The whole city is packed with things of historical interest and fortunately I am quite familiar both with the literary and political history of the country so that I enjoy them all. I shall enclose a menu from the Old Cheshire Cheese. I have become quite well acquainted in there with the old waiters and I go in once in a while and occupy the seat where (they say) Charles Dickens, Oliver Goldsmith, Dr. Johnson and David Garrick sat. One can buy the cups they drank out of too. People have been buying them for a hundred years so I guess it must keep some factory busy all the time making them.

Tell Dorothy I will write to her in a little while. She wrote me all about her Christmas. The watch given to me is a beauty and the fob to go with it is also very handsome.

With love
Don

Diary: Monday January 28, 1918

My first air raid. Warning at 8, over 1:15 a.m.

The air raid I have been fearing and yet hoping for came. I was in Simpson's eating when warning was given. When I finished walked to the Savoy. People were hurrying to shelter. Guns boomed about 9. They were London's barrage. I looked from windows of my room but could see nothing. Hung around lobby. Firing continued for a half hour. Then quiet for an hour or two when word sent that another squadron Germans coming. Then things happened. I heard all I care to. Was standing in lobby about 12:30 when there was a terrific crash. A second later another much nearer. The Savoy rocked; windows smashed; women screamed and fainted. Everyone thought hotel was struck.

I had just finished a letter to Dorothy saying raid was over and I am safe. The bomb which shook us hit Savoy Mansions directly back of hotel and ripped out whole front. Another hit Covent Garden (now a market) and wrecked it. Another wrecked a 4 story bldg on Longacre and killed about 40 persons who had taken shelter there. Charlie Wheeler of the Chicago Tribune and I walked around to see damage. Then I went to Fleet St. returning at 3 a.m. and going to sleep.

I can't exactly say I like air raids.

Don Martin wrote a letter to Dorothy at the Savoy on January 28 telling her about the air raid. This would be the biggest event of his three-month stay in London. He stopped writing when it was announced that the air raid was continuing and finished the letter the next day.

[Handwritten]

January 28, 1918

Dorothy

The air raid everyone has been expecting came tonight. Just now I am sitting downstairs in the Savoy waiting till the "All's Clear" signal is given so I can go down to the office. The noise of the guns, fired at the aeroplanes, makes a din about like the noise down in front of John Knox's when, on the night before the Fourth, the boys have put thousands of small torpedoes on the track when a car comes along.

I was in a restaurant next door at 8 o'clock when the police whistles were heard outside. No one seemed excited where I was. I was finished so I came over here and here I have been ever since. The lobby is pretty well filled, and the big restaurant down one flight is packed, because this is about as safe a place as there is. The signal was given at 8 and guns have been going off ever since—and it is now 11 o'clock. There is no way of knowing tonight whether bombs did any damage. You will probably know from the papers almost as soon as I do. The probability is that a good many people somewhere have been killed. I went out in the Strand—and looked up but could see nothing but the moon and stars. I didn't stay long because it is foolhardiness. One might lose an arm or a leg or his eyesight and then spend the rest of his lifetime wondering why he hadn't had sense enough to stay inside.

There are all kinds of reports around the lobby. A man nearby says one fleet of aeroplanes was driven off by English fliers and that two more fleets are on the way over the city now.

The streets were first filled with people hurrying into buildings and toward the subway stations. Policemen were hurrying them along, and everyone was offering suggestions to everyone else. I had but a short way to go, and was perfectly safe, yet two or three persons stopped and said—"Come on in here." A lot of elderly men and women are sitting about the lobby looking thoroughly frightened and a good many officers in uniform are standing about "en camouflage." Ask Grandmother what that means. Everyone pretends to be indifferent but everyone is a bit restless just the same, because a bomb is a serious thing and sometimes the aeroplanes are invisible but directly over here.

The guns which we hear are on embankments and substantial buildings, and a good many are in the parks. They send up a constant barrage in the hope that the aeroplanes will be destroyed. I was tempted to go up on the roof of the hotel where I might see all there was to be seen but I should rather be safe than sorry or dead and I fancy you approve that bit of philosophy.

The battle in the air may last for two or three hours yet. Maybe no one will be hurt and there may be hundreds killed. It is usually the people in the poor sections, where the buildings are frail, who suffer.

Just now the firing has stopped and some people are going out and getting in automobiles, apparently eager to get to their homes before another flock of the air machines arrives. Some Canadians who live here and whom I know just came in. They were out during the early part of the raid. They say they could see the fliers and see the shells break all around them. Still the Canadians are not going out again—and neither am I till the "Clear" signal is given.

The moment the air is clear the police shout "All's clear" and in all the hotels and other public places announcement is made. There is some satisfaction in having come safely through one of the raids but still as only about one person in a hundred is hit or hurt, it seems nothing much to brag about.

The last information about the situation was just passed around by the hotel management. It is that 30 machines are within 20 miles of the city. So I guess there is more excitement to come. The lobby is filling up again and the hotel attendants advise people not to go out. Tomorrow or next day I will write again and tell you how it all wound up. If tomorrow I learn that the raid was a very serious one I may send you a cablegram telling you "You shouldn't worry."

With love and a kiss,
Dad

Your letter written at Josephine's came today.

Diary: Tuesday January 29, 1918

Everyone talking of yesterday's air raid. Was worst ever known. Official figures say 47 killed and 160 injured. These figures are away under. About 30 planes started the raid and 4 or 5 dropped bombs. One big one was destroyed. About 15 bombs did damage but no one but officials knows how much, as English authorities give out only meager news and papers print only what gov't wants. I went around and saw the results of bombs. The Longacre building just converted in heap of wreckage. A big chunk of Savoy Mansions scooped out.

Another warning at 9 o'clock tonight. Heard no bombs but barrage made a fierce racket. Machines came over Southeast part of city but were driven away after dropping few bombs. About 6 killed and 30 injured. People sat around hotel lobby till 2 a.m. I was at Herald office when maroons* sounded but went to Savoy.

Pleasant day. Moonlight tonight.

The next day, another letter to Dorothy, telling more about the air raid. Many of the details are the same as recorded in his diary.

January 29, 1918

Dorothy

Well maybe things didn't happen rapidly last night after I finished writing that long letter to you. A bomb just missed the hotel. I had just finished your letter and had put it in the box when there was a terrific explosion. We all knew it was close. A few seconds later there was another, much more deafening and the hotel rocked like a rowboat, it seemed. I was talking with a man at the time. There was a noise like about a dozen claps of thunder all merged into one; then the sound of things smashing mingled with crashing glass in the restaurant, the screaming of women and the cries apparently of persons who had been injured. People all around the lobby turned pale and I imagine most of them expected the hotel to collapse. I wouldn't have been greatly surprised. And then on top of it flames could be seen from windows in the back of the hotel.

It was undoubtedly the most exciting experience I had ever gone through with. A big apartment building, unoccupied fortunately, had been hit. It almost adjoins the hotel. It is four stories high and a chunk about 20 feet thick and four stories in height was just cleaved, or scooped out, by a bomb. Another bomb—the one we heard first—had struck a famous old London building now used as a market and wrecked that, strewing glass and fragments of stone all over the streets for blocks. I should say there were two inches of crushed glass in the street. I went up to see it. A little further off another bomb had struck a five story building in which two or three hundred people had hurriedly gone for shelter. This building was pulverized. It just disappeared. The casualties occurred mostly here. Another bomb struck in the Thames which is not far away. Others landed in various parts of the city but the public doesn't know where because the authorities do not give out the facts. I shall mail you a couple of London afternoon papers and you can get an idea of the raid yourself, from them.

I didn't see any aeroplanes although early in the evening I went out to have a look and peered from my window. They fly so high up and are painted in such a way that it is impossible to see them, although occasionally one may see a puff of flame or smoke when a shell from the London guns explode. Anyone

* A type of warning gun

who wants to go out and look for such spectacles is welcome. I shall not do so. No one does unless he is crazy. Suppose for instance a bomb would drop where the bandstand is at home. It would leave a hole about 30 or 40 feet deep where that stands, would blow to bits anyone who might be standing anywhere in the square. That is how powerful the bombs are. However the hotel where I am is safe because there are a lot of floors above the lobby and the building is very solid construction. There I shall stay when the raid warnings are given. We had a long time last night to get to cover. The lobby and restaurant—or part of the restaurant where the windows weren't broken—were filled with people until two o'clock this morning. Then the police began blowing whistles meaning "Clear" and people went out. I went around to see where the bombs had fallen. The streets were packed. Policemen were along the street at short intervals and more than 50 Red Cross ambulances and first aid automobiles were moving to and fro. It was impossible to get near the Long Acre building because a fire had started in a big building next door. This burned for an hour. A fire also started right behind my hotel but the firemen extinguished it in five minutes.

Twenty-five or thirty enemy aeroplanes are supposed to have started in the raid and about 100 English aeroplanes went up after them. Anyhow I have been in a raid and I am not at all anxious to have another. I might as well get accustomed to them though. The indications are that there may be others this week—maybe tonight. It will be moonlight all the week and the sky is clear of clouds and those are the conditions favorable to successful raids. Everyone is waiting tonight for another warning. I am sitting in my room—it is just 8 o'clock—but if I hear the warning whistles and the maroons—or warning guns—I will go down stairs where it is entirely safe. I didn't send a cable to you today. You know of course that if anything happened to me in a raid you would hear of it very quickly through the Herald but I will be very careful and you don't need to worry. Tomorrow or later in the week I will write to you and let you know what happened after I finished this letter. I shall remain in the hotel.

No one had talked of much else than the raid all day. People speak to strangers in restaurants and on the street about it. There is no question that London worries over them but still they take it all with philosophical resignation and say "Oh well, it's about 100,000 chances to one you won't get hurt." Then most Londoners believe it doesn't matter where one goes—if he is marked to be hit he will be hit anyhow. I don't believe that. Give me a safe place.

I don't know whether newspapers containing accounts of the raid will be permitted to go through the mails or not. I will mail a couple anyhow. They are the two leading evening papers in London. You will see that they don't look much like the Evening News at home.

I shall write a story or two now Miss Dorothy and then go down stairs and wait to see what happens.

With love,
Dad

In Don Martin's first month in London, The New York Herald published 34 of his dispatches, amounting to about 20,000 words.

Diary: Wednesday January 30, 1918

Went to office at noon and read papers. Then to hotel and wrote two long stories about air reprisals, and the threatened German attack on Western front. Had dinner at Simpson's. Then Skipper Williams of the Times, N.Y. called and took me to the Apollo Theatre to see "Inside the Lines," a stupid play—a travesty on Americans. To see the English burlesque Americans seems so foolish, because the English are a joke. One American is worth a dozen Englishmen at anything.

Went to office in a taxi for a few minutes. Then sat around lobby with Charlie Wheeler till 1 a.m. Air raid threatened again but no warning given. Report Germans were driven back.

Weather foggy but clear later in day.

Diary: Thursday January 31, 1918

Another day and night of air raid suspense. Was heightened by stories of big raid on Paris. Spent most of afternoon in office. Was writing story of personal experience in raid when Skipper Williams of Times called up and asked me to go to Princess Theatre to see "Carminetta", a musical comedy. Was artistic show but somewhat coarse. Alice Delysia, the Star, is very clever. Is a French woman. [C.B.] Cochran, manager [and English impresario], took Williams and myself to her dressing room where we chatted with her. Sir Charles something was there too.

Went to hotel and finished air raid story. Took it to Fleet St. office for mailing. Air raids expected but none came. Now stated that 200 were killed and 500 hurt in Monday's affair. Children were buried alive in the John Bail building where mothers had taken them for shelter.

Unpleasant weather. Fog afternoon + night.

Diary: Friday February 1, 1918

Spent most of the afternoon in the office. Saw Colonel Buchan and Lord Robert Cecil, foreign secretary. Both had tea while they were talking to the correspondents. In the evening Milton Snyder of the Sun, who has come to London to relieve Welliver, came in the office. Sat around lobby till 1 a.m. with Ben Russell and a chap named Mortimer Bryans of Chicago. Still find the British pessimistic over war outlook. They seem to think next 3 months will be the crucial period of the war.

Got letter from Commodore saying my expenses will be paid, with my salary through N.Y. office.

Weather raw and cloudy. No raid weather.

Diary: Saturday February 2, 1918

Spent all the afternoon in the office. Arthur Elliot Sproul of N.Y. came in and told me all about Russia. He left there 2 weeks ago. Had dinner at Simpson's with some Canadians. Met a captain who told us about battles of Vimy and Lens; also a young private, who is now a lieutenant who is going back home with his right arm useless.

Went to office for a short time in evening and returned early to the hotel. Got Herald of Jan 18 which contained the first of my stories. It was signed.

Weather damp, foggy + streets muddy.

Diary: Sunday February 3, 1918

Had breakfast with Buchanan, an old newspaper friend, but now a captain in the Aviation Corps. Later went for jaunt around with him to Cheshire Cheese, Whitechapel; then taxi drive by Parliament, Buckingham Palace, etc. Had tea with him and then to hotel where I wrote several articles for mailing. Dinner at Simpson's and then to Fleet St. for an hour or two. Sat around lobby of hotel talking till 1 a.m. with Major General Swift.

Food situation getting unpleasant here. Must have sugar and butter cards tomorrow. Hotel left ½ lb sugar in my room. Each guest gets the same to last a week.

Submarine sunk and crew captured by American destroyer.

Weather very foggy. Not cold.

Diary: Monday February 4, 1918

Spent most of the afternoon at the office. Had dinner at Simpson's—no meat though it wasn't a meatless day—and in the evening went to the Strand Theatre and saw an American play "Cheating Cheaters," which I had already seen in N.Y. It went very well.

Went to office later and wrote two letters to go by a friend who sails on the St. Louis tomorrow.

Weather nasty.

Diary: Tuesday February 5, 1918

American transport Tuscania torpedoed—This is first one.

Went to office about 12:30. Ordered a suit of clothes and an overcoat. Saw Colonel Buchan at 5. He says England will carry out a reprisal system against the Germans. It is about time. Went to see "Nothing but the Truth" at the opening—Savoy Theatre. Is an American farce. I saw Millie Collier in it at home. Went to the office later. Visited with Charlie Wheeler till 1 a.m. Am getting very few letters.

Ordered a suit of clothes and an overcoat, both loud. I want everyone to know they are English and everyone certainly will.

Weather warm but nasty.

Don Martin hand-wrote a letter to Dorothy the night of February 5, with commentary on the uncertainty about how the war would proceed.

February 5, 1918

Dorothy

I have just a few minutes to write a note to be carried to U.S. by a friend who leaves on the St. Louis today—late this afternoon. He will post it when he gets in New York [Note: postmarked Feb 21] and you will probably get it before you receive my letters of last Monday and Tuesday [Jan 28 and 29] telling all about the air raids. There isn't much to say that I haven't already written but I thought it would be nice to send a short note anyhow. I haven't received much mail lately. I have an idea that a ship carrying European mail from America has been lost. One carrying mail from here to United States was sunk on Jan 27 and no doubt some of my letters were on it.

Tell your Uncle Rock that the war is pretty serious business yet and that there is no chance of the Allies winning anything like a crushing military victory this year. Neither can the Germans defeat the Allies although they intend to make a great attempt to drive through the line to Calais which would give them an opening on the English Channel. They probably can't do it. The thing or things which will probably end or very greatly hasten the end of the war will be economic troubles. England is facing a very serious labor situation and the food problem is getting serious too. No one in England now can order what he wants. He must take what he can get—what the government has decided he must have.

Germany is worse off than England but the people there have no spirit of rebellion—yet—as the British have and there is just a possibility that the English may face a condition which will compel them to negotiate a peace.

The submarine is the big factor. It is vastly more of a menace than the world knows, and it is not overcome or growing less. Without the submarine to combat the Allies could win the war without any doubt, but until the submarine is overcome there is doubt about the outcome. Everyone is pessimistic here. The optimism of U.S. is not paralleled here. The original purpose to sweep out the Hohenzollerns has been abandoned. It probably can't be done. The trouble is the Allies are fighting against a nation which knows no scruples. It is really and truly a struggle between chivalry (Christianity) and barbarism. This is all, Dorothy, for Uncle Rock and Charlie to talk about. Perhaps it may give them a new insight into the situation.

Now I shall end this letter because there is not much more to say and because it is getting late. I have decided that you needn't figure on working in a laundry. That ought to please you.

With love and a kiss,

Dad

Diary: Wednesday February 6, 1918

Got up a little earlier today to get breakfast before the crowded lunch hour. Went to office and wrote a labor story I had told Baird to do. He is the prize bonehead surely enough. How he has managed to keep out of a home for undeveloped creatures is a mystery to me. Wrote a letter to Mr. Bennett in Beaulieu about expenses.

Charlie Wheeler has gone to Darling to commute. Good idea to get out of air raid zone. Had dinner at Simpson's. Saw Gen. Maurice [Director of Military Operations at the War Office] in p.m. Also saw war relics and photos in Royal Academy. They make our Civil War remnants look pretty insignificant. At office for hour or two this evening.

Sat in Savoy restaurant with Kelly and Brownell and listened to the orchestra play "Over There," which is now the popular war song.

Weather pleasant till evening—then rain.

Diary: Thursday, February 7, 1918

Had a rather busy day. Did a lot of work in the office. Then went to Admiralty office to inquire about sinking of Tuscania, American transport. Had previously seen Irvin S. Cobb at the hotel. He was on Baltic in same convoy with Tuscania. Told me good story which I cabled quite fully to N.Y. Also wrote story for Paris.

Had dinner at Cheshire Cheese with Champion. Met Nuptal, Burke's friend there. Went to office and then to bed. Got letter from Mother and enclosure from Dorothy.

All talk now is of threatened German offensive on which she will stake everything. Admiral Hall says submarine situation and food very serious.

Weather pleasant. Warm.

Don Martin hand-wrote a short letter to his mother the evening of February 7, 1918, in London, in which the war ending in late 1918—as happened—is mentioned.

Savoy Hotel
London, E. C. 4.

Mother

Your letter dated Jan 17 with the inclosure from Dorothy reached me today. The mails are pretty slow. I have an idea that some of my letters both going and coming have been on ships which didn't reach port. We don't hear about sinkings right away. Today we heard of one which no doubt has caused excitement at home—the Tuscania. I got a good story about it from Irvin S. Cobb who was on XXXXXX [RMS Baltic] which saw the submarine attack. It is pretty serious business.

The submarines are very active and no ship is safe. We were in very great danger during the last two days of our voyage but I didn't let it worry me. It is foolish to worry over something that can't be helped.

I imagine my long letter kept you all pretty busy for a while. And very soon you will have another long one I wrote you last week. There have been no more air raids since I wrote to Dorothy and I wouldn't be surprised if there were no more.

The food situation is not good at all here. The world shortage seems to center here because of the dearth of ships. A glass of good rich milk is never seen. Cream is not used at all and good butter and plenty of it belongs to a past age in England. Still everyone gets along. There is no doubting that the world is tired of war and the feeling now seems to be that the war will end late this year after both sides have done everything possible to make sure of a good show when peace conferences begin.

There have been some nice days lately but there is a drizzle nearly every night. Here in the Savoy Hotel it seems almost like being in New York—there are so many Americans.

Are you receiving a check each week from the office? Also do you see anything in the Herald from me? I imagine they sign my name to a story now and then.

That was a crazy note Dorothy wrote. I guess that is what she wanted it to be. I will write to her in a few days. I hope she is learning to skate well. There is no skating here.

With love,
Don

Diary: Friday February 8, 1918

Had a somewhat varied day. Met Irvin S. Cobb at the hotel and went with him and Captain Sifton

Irvin S Cobb

of Canada to the Cane tea room. In the evening went to a dinner of the Rotary Club with Russell at Connaught rooms. Heard very good speech by Minister of Labor.

At hotel at midnight met Major General [Eben] Swift and Colonel [Alfred J.] Booth and sat in restaurant with them for a half hour. Then took Colonel Booth around and showed him where the bombs fell. He is just back from French front. Says no cause for pessimism. He talks like a real American.

Reports now say only 100 men lost on Tuscania, American transport sunk off Irish coast. First reports 210 lost.

Fine day.

Diary: Saturday February 9, 1918

Went to office at noon and did considerable writing. Went for long walk through Holborn section. Got letter from Dorothy. Dorothy is certainly getting to be a great girl. She writes fine letters. Met Robert Hanna a Canadian Lieutenant from Vancouver who told me how he won the Victoria Cross at Vimy Ridge. It is a wonderful story of how he saved practically a whole battalion. Went to office a short time tonight.

Weather very nice. Drizzle at night.

Diary: Sunday February 10, 1918

Went for a long walk by myself—across Westminster Bridge; then around by Buckingham Palace and to the Savoy.

Went to the office at 4 p.m. and wrote several stories—about the speculation regarding end of the war, etc. Had dinner at Simpson's and then went to the office again. Wrote a short letter to Dorothy. Am beginning to realize how much Dorothy means to me.

Eating in London is getting rather monotonous. Not much meat, little butter, practically no sugar and no fruit except at high prices. Think I must have lost 7 or 8 pounds.

Weather delightful.

Don Martin's short letter to Dorothy on Sunday, February 10, commented on her letters.

Sunday, February 10, 1918

Dorothy

You are a funny girl. Those pictures in your letter No. 5—dated Jan. 19—were very good. I guess you have been having a great time during the snowy days. We haven't had any here. Your picture of yourself and your long hair answers a question I asked recently. Probably you braid your hair now. Where in the world did you get on to the English pronunciation? "Hee, haw" looks funny with the h's left off. I just wrote a long letter to Julie. You needn't think I can write all my letters to you. However I guess I ought to write a lot to you because you are a pretty nice girl to write to me so often.

This isn't intended for a letter. I am just about to leave the office to go to the hotel and thought I would write a line or two to tell you that two of your letters came at once—yesterday—and I couldn't tell from the writing that they were from the same Dorothy. One you write backhanded and the other the usual way. Are you revising your handwriting style? In a few days I will write you a long letter—not too long— and tell you whatever there is to tell. I suppose by this time you have my air raid letter. By "by this time" I mean when this reaches you. It takes about 20 or 21 days for a letter to go from here to Silver Creek. I suppose the censors have to laugh at your letters if they have any time at all for laughter. They certainly make me laugh.

Be careful in the house when the gas is low and don't get the croup. Wait till summer to get that. It isn't so bad then. Give my love to Joseph and tell Mother I got her letter the other day. Is she going to have the house painted this spring? It needs it I am quite sure. Do you have any spending money young lady? If not tell Grandmother to give you some. You can't get along without spending money.

A kiss and a hug for funny Dorothy.

Lovingly, Dad

Diary: Monday February 11, 1918

Spent practically all day at the office. Had dinner at the Savoy—a pretty good one—appetizers, sole, pheasant and potatoes as well as apple dumplings and grapes. Went to the office at night. Welliver and Snyder came in about 11. I walked up to Judd's hotel, the Bedford, with him and sat in his room till 2 a.m. trying to cheer him up. He is going back to N.Y. in a few days and seems to feel that his London experience has been unsatisfactory.

Weather pleasant.

On February 12, 1918, Martin heard speeches by the King and Lloyd George at the House of Lords.

Diary: Tuesday February 12, 1918

Saw the House of Lords and Commons in session. King and Queen, Crown Prince and all the rest of the useless outfit in the Lords. King made (or read) a speech. Spoke clearly and well. Ceremony here brief and shorn of its pomp and gold decorations because of war. Heard Asquith [former Premier] and Lloyd George the Premier in lively argument. Was my first view of both; also of the King. Lloyd George made one of the best speeches of his career. All on war— the Versailles conference. Refused to tell details as would amount to treason, he said. Is a very forceful actor. Used only few notes—America cheered; also every reference to President's answer to Heartling and Czronin published today. King and everyone says war must go on till Germany is willing to talk a decent peace. Cabled something to N.Y.

Weather delightful.

Diary: Wednesday February 13, 1918

Saw the place I have always wanted to see— Shakespeare's birthplace etc. at Stratford on Avon. Spent two hours in the old house which looks older than I thought. The old lady, Mary Rose, who tells tourists all about it, seemed to be determined to convince us that Shakespeare really lived there, although I had taken it for granted. Saw the church where he is buried and everything else to be seen in the beautiful old town.

Bought serving spoon for Mother and a pin for Dorothy. Also addressed about 30 postal cards. Altogether it was the most interesting day I have ever had. Left at 10:30 with Judd Welliver and got back at 11:15 p.m. Went to office for an hour. Then to hotel.

Had pleasant weather. Was amused at fact that everyone spotted Judd and me for Americans. Practically no one visits Stratford now with the war on.

Pleasant day.

Letter from Rose Martin (No. 6)

Dated Feb 13, 1918; postmarked Feb 14, 8:30AM, Notation 'Arrived Paris, Mch 13'. New York Herald Bureau, London England [38 Rue du Louvre, Paris]

Feb 13th Wednesday, 1918

Dear Don

Will write a little letter just to say we are all right and well. The weather is a little more moderate—but we had a regular flood yesterday. The ice piled up high in the Creeks and could not get out, so all the cellars on Parkway filled up, and on Dunkirk St. too. Marguerite Schumaker came here last evening. Her Father is away, and her mother is not feeling well, and she got nervous about the flood. She said it was in their back yard, and in all the back yards along there. I told her she could stay here all night if she wanted to, but on account of her mother she didn't. So, it began to work a little on Dorothy too, but it didn't last long. Still she had to sleep with me though, and she got to cutting up, as she does once in a while. She is too funny for anything when she gets to going. Margaret got to laughing. I guess she forgot the flood and everything else too, so she went home feeling pretty good. This morning every thing is frozen, with ice piled high around the Mill and even in Brunds back yard.

I was glad when you said in your letter that you would remain at the Savoy Hotel, as it is warm there, when you told of the Rain dripping and the Bigness of London, and being dark so early. Makes me think of Dickens' stories. He tells so many things like that.

Well Don, you are very far from home but I don't think as (you say) that you will be homesick. You see, you are away from home most of the time, so that will help, but there are a lot of them there that, I am sure, will be, those that have not been away from home before. I hope you will keep well and not want for any thing.

People are beginning to live a little different here too, but not like over there yet. One nice thing we have plenty of fruit. Wish you could have some as it is so healthy, but if you can get the (Dried cooked) there are peaches—Apricots—prunes—apples. They are all very good for one. Am glad you have marmalade—that is good too. England I guess is where it originates from, especially Orange-Marmalade. And now be careful of yourself.

With Love,
Mother

Diary: Thursday February 14, 1918

Irvin S. Cobb called me before I was awake. We had breakfast together. Then I went to the office where I spent most of the afternoon. Saw Admiral Hall at 4:30. He is worried about the submarines. England is very sadly in need of wheat. Had dinner at Simpson's. Then went to office. Wrote a few articles. Hotel at midnight. People beginning to talk about air raids again. New moon.

Weather cloudy and raw.

Diary: Friday February 15, 1918

Got up at noon. Went to the office and read the papers. Saw Colonel Buchan and Lord Robert Cecil. Latter intimated there will be no concrete economic discrimination against Germany after the war, but that the Allies will inevitably favor each other. Walked over from Whitehall with Draper of the Tribune. He understandably has a sneaky feeling of friendliness for Germany. I told him what my views are about the international murderers and highwaymen. Had dinner at Simpson's. Went to office and wrote a lot of business letters.

Submarine menace getting worse. Threatened Hun drive on West front not started. I think it is largely bluff. Feeling growing there can be no military decision. Submarines are the vital factor. No disguising that. World helpless before them.

Weather very nice.

The evening of February 15 Don Martin wrote a long letter to his sister Alta. Besides recounting much of what he wrote in other letters, he had a lot to say about the situation in England and the war.

New York Herald, London Bureau
130, Fleet Street, E. C. 4.
Feb. 15, 1918

Alta

At a rough guess I would say that this letter will probably reach you about the 15th of March. Some times I get a letter dated fifteen days prior to its delivery and then sometimes it is 25 days after. The mails have been very tardy lately. I haven't had a letter from the other side in ten days. I received your letter. The check I received from Bauman was lost going back. The Guaranty Trust Co. where I deposited it wrote the other day that it went down with the Andania and asked me to send for a duplicate. I shall have to do so.

You would laugh yourself sick if you could see Dorothy's letters. She draws pictures with each one. She is by no means an artist but she is determined to draw. Josephine Brand sent me about a dozen little pictures Dorothy made over at Brand's one day when no one knew anything about it. They are very funny. Dorothy's letters are excellent though. Mother writes now and then; Rock sends along a business like note occasionally and I hear from New York quite often. I wrote a long letter to Jule the other day and I write very frequently to Dorothy. That letter I wrote on the ship was a terribly long affair and I guess it was asking a good deal of anyone to read it all. However I had more time than I knew what to do with on the trip over. You sized the situation up correctly. Everyone was chipper the first few days out but after that the tension increased until the last 36 hours the snapping of a match would make everyone jump. It's the same way now when an air raid is on. If someone slams a door people whirl around and jump. In about ten days the air raid period will be here again. The Germans presumably will bombard London again. Despite the hundreds of fliers who go up to oppose them they are able to fly over the city. The sky is a big place. It is no doubt thrilling to go out and watch the combats in the air but it is far wiser to stay inside and that is what I intend to do. Anyone with sense will do the same thing. You see when airships, or aeroplanes, appear, three or four hundred guns all over London send up shrapnel which bursts well up in the air and a piece of it in its descent is sufficient to fracture a skull. (My typewriter is giving me trouble right along) No building is absolutely safe but the chances are about 100,000 to one a person won't get hit, so we are all willing to take a chance. However the air raids are genuinely serious affairs. A bomb weighs all the way from 100 to 500 pounds and is composed of T.N.T. It would go straight to the cellar of an ordinary five or six story building.

I had an interesting time Tuesday. I went to the House of Lords to see the opening and to hear the King. I heard him and saw him. He spoke in a splendid voice and read his speech as though he understood every word of it. The Queen sat beside him on an ermine-clad chair and beside the King was the Prince of Wales, a very nervous looking youngster who was home from the Italian front for the occasion. The King is a very human person. Of course he has nothing whatever to do with the war. He is merely a symbol of unity. It was a very pompous ceremony and was worth seeing. Then I went to the Commons and saw the opening there. I was very fortunate because Asquith, former Premier, and Lloyd George, present Premier, had a very sensational clash over the Versailles conference. They are not the best of friends. Asquith was removed as Premier and Lloyd George was selected as a sort of compromise. Asquith is a brilliant man and he baited George till there was a very spectacular tilt back and forth. It lasted three hours. I was fortunate enough to hear about a dozen of the leading members of the Commons talk.

Tomorrow (Saturday) morning I am going to the Bow Street court to hear the case of Colonel Repington*, who is to be examined for violation of the Defense of the Realm Act. He criticized the government for "bungling the war". This may turn out to be a very noted case. The things going on here are nearly all big and I have been lucky enough to get in to see and hear them all. I have been spending the last three or four days with Irvin Cobb who is staying at the Savoy where I am living. He is quite an interesting person. I used to know him when I first went to New York.

On Wednesday I went to Stratford-on-Avon and spent the day there. A man named Judd Welliver of the New York Sun wanted me to go out with him as he, Welliver, was returning to New York the following day. It is the most interesting place I ever saw. We saw Shakespeare's birthplace, the church where he is buried and everything else connected with his life and death. I asked the sexton of the church if the church looked the same in Shakespeare's time as it did when we were looking at it. "Oh yes," he said, "Shakespeare used to sit in that seat right there. The part of the church where he is buried is comparatively new. It was built in 1460. The original part, which is still just as it was, was erected in the 12th century." The whole town of Stratford looks about as it did 300 years ago. The old atmosphere is preserved for business as well as sentimental reasons. Ordinarily 1,000 Americans visit the place each month. No one has been going there since the war. The town itself has a population of 8,000. I bought a couple of spoons and a small pin and Mr. Welliver is taking them home to be given to Dorothy, Mother and Mrs. Brooks. Mrs. Brooks you know is Dorothy's God mother and I like to remember her now and then.

*Charles Repington's articles appeared in the Morning Post (London), owned by Howell Arthur Gwynne.

I shall probably be here for some time. There is nothing much to be done in France. The war news centers here. Maybe I shall get over to the front for a spell, later. The indications now are that by the time you get this the Germans will be launching the biggest offensive of the war but unless they have developed some new form of fiendishness, they will not penetrate the Allied line. The war is a sad affair. It would seem as if neither side could possibly score what the world would regard as a military victory, no matter how long the thing runs. The side will win which can keep gaining in air strength and still keep peace back home.

The world is getting pretty weary of the war but the Allies want to lick Germany. Still the German people are ready to live on water and black bread while the other people will not accept this. There will never be a German peace unless the submarine completely wipes out the commerce of the world. My own idea of the situation is that there will be a sort of compromise peace which will be compelled because of the attitude of British labor and the food scarcity of the world; but that the peace will leave Germany hated the world over. She will pay her penalty in the years to come and I hope that is true. Personally I hope that the Allies will be able to stick together and avoid domestic troubles until Germany is completely crushed but that is not likely to happen. England is up against it because of the submarines which are worse now than ever and will probably continue to get worse. Still England is a terrible foe when she gets up against it and if she is able to get food enough to keep her going she may stick till she hands Germany what Germany ought to get.

It all depends on what America can do. If enough ships are launched and kept afloat to transport a million or two men and the supplies necessary to maintain them, Germany will be whipped good. It is all a question again, as you can see, of the submarine. That is the frightful factor in the war. I am frank enough to say that I would prefer to stay here until the danger is over and I can't exactly say that I am stuck on England. London is a wonderful city though. It is easily enough the center of the world. One learns that very quickly. I have been all over London and am getting to know it well. It is filled with places of interest.

I am quite close to the war here. The streets are filled with soldiers. I daresay that every afternoon during a walk of an hour, I pass 20 soldiers each with a leg off and two or three blind ones. One must not think they predominate though. Except for the presence of tens of thousands of khaki clad men in the streets one would not know anything was wrong with England. Business goes on just as usual apparently. Manufacturing is at a standstill though. Only "essentials" are made now. All other factories are making munitions and kindred things. Food is hard to get. Everyone is on a ration. Meat, sugar and butter are very scarce but vegetables are plentiful. Tobacco costs quite a bit and saloons are open only five hours a day.

The streets are pitch dark at night and women work as street cleaners, bus conductors, postwomen and as elevator operators. Young men, except those who use crutches or wear service badges, are seldom seen yet the streets are crowded all the time. I am living at the Savoy which is one of the big hotels. It is the hangout for Americans.

I guess this is about letter enough for this time. It is getting late anyhow and my typewriter is acting very contrary. One can't buy a typewriter for love or money in London. I could get $250 for this one but of course I wouldn't take it. However I must have someone look it over. I carried it over on the boat with me.

Don

Diary: Saturday February 16, 1918

(Another air raid, 9:30 till 12 p.m.)

Got up early and went to Bow St. Court where Col. Repington and Arthur Gwynne were on trial for violation of Defense of Realm Act —furnishing information to the enemy through one of Repington's articles in Post which Gwynne owns. Adjournment taken. Went to office for couple hours.

Had dinner at the Berkeley with Mrs. Sproul of N.Y. Went to Fleet Street and a few minutes later—at 9:30—got air raid warning. I grabbed a bus and went to the Savoy. Sat around lobby with some of my Canadian friends till 1 a.m. All clear given at midnight. Heard no bombs so guess raiders were driven off. Came to my room at 1 a.m.

Germans sank 8 trawlers off Dover and fired 30 shells into Dover killing a child.

Weather fine.

Another short, handwritten letter to Dorothy on Saturday night, February 16, commented on how the air raids weighed on people's minds.

 Dorothy

This afternoon in writing to Rock I said the weather conditions favored an air raid tonight. You tell Rock I was a good prophet. I had been to a dinner at the Ritz and had gone to the Fleet Street office when I heard the "maroons"—guns fired to warn people to "take cover." I got on a bus and came to the hotel where I have been ever since. We heard firing for a half hour but heard no bombs.

At half past twelve the policemen blew bugles signifying that the danger was over. So now I am in my room ready for bed.

The lobby was filled with people till a short time ago. No one goes to bed till "All clear" signal is given. Downstairs women were sitting around with smelling salts. They take the raids pretty seriously. We have no way of knowing whether bombs were dropped or not. The chances are the English fliers, who always go up, drove the Germans away.

We have a new moon now. It will be full the early part of the week so if the sky is clear the chances are there will be raids every night. It isn't very pleasant but people make the best of it.

You are quite an artist Dorothy. I have laughed every time I have looked at the pictures sent with your last letter. I haven't had a letter now for some time and I understand no mails have left here for New York for two weeks. So you have had none either. I hear some American ships have come in during the last day or two though so I probably will find a letter from you on Monday. You certainly write splendid letters. Here's a good night kiss young long-haired lady.

With love,
Dad

Diary: Sunday February 17, 1918

(Another air raid—10 to 12:30 p.m.)

Went for long walk this afternoon through the poorer districts. Stopped in office to do some writing but didn't stay because I was unable to get a fire started. Had dinner in Simpson's with Hacker and Motherwell, Canadians, and a nephew of Hacker's who has been 4 Christmases in the trenches.

Went to the office and left there at 10:00 o'clock when another air raid warning was given. Went to Savoy where I stayed until 1 a.m. (that is in the lobby) when the all clear was given. A shrapnel shell struck in front of the hotel but didn't explode. Report that St. Pancras hotel and station struck by bomb. Outlook for this week pretty bad. People are very nervous. The bombing is very serious business.

Weather clear but raw.

Diary: Monday February 18, 1918

(Air raid again – 9:15 to 12:15 p.m.)

Breakfast in Savoy. Went to office and wrote "Sidelights" etc. Learned that bomb last night struck St. Pancras hotel and railway station and killed 20 or 30 persons. Newspapers print very little, giving no names or addresses. Went to hotel and read an hour; then had dinner at Simpson's and went to Fleet Street. As expected heard the sirens at 9:15. Got a taxi and came to the Savoy. Looked around the streets for awhile but saw nothing. Sat around the lobby with big crowd till "all clear" given after midnight. Then visited till 1 with a Mr. Larned and a Mr. Fitzgerald of Detroit who were on the Tuscania. Heard no bombs but plenty of barrage gunfire. The raids are by no means pleasant.

Got a letter from Cooper saying everything fine.

Weather fine but a little raw.

Diary: Tuesday February 19, 1918

Up early. Went to Sunderland House on Curzon St. to see the Duchess of Marlborough [Consuelo Vanderbilt] with whom I had an appointment. Had a pleasant ½ hour chat with her—the first interview she ever gave to a newspaper. Told her I would come back in a few days and read it to her. She talked about the war work she has done. She is really quite a charming woman, quite handsome yet though getting a bit grey. In the afternoon went to the Commons and heard a most interesting controversy between Lloyd George and Asquith. Much hostility to Premier because of charges that he lets Northcliffe run the government through his newspapers. Went to office; wrote the Marlborough story and waited for another air raid warning which didn't come. Got wire from Bennett to interview Repington and Gwynne. Couldn't get them tonight.

Very thick black fog.

After getting used to air raids, and pretty much exhausting the theater and sightseeing, Martin's desire to get on to the ground where the war was being waged increasingly manifested itself—now by a suggestion to Commodore Bennett.

Diary: Wednesday February 20, 1918

Had breakfast in Lyons. In the office most of afternoon. Saw Gen. Maurice. Then called at the Marshall Syndicate office with Steele. Had dinner at Simpson's and went to the office, spending the evening there.

Wrote to Mr. Bennett suggesting a trip to France. Also wrote to George Cooper and to Dorothy. Came up to hotel at 11:30 and sat around till 12:30 with Maj. McKenzie of Regina, Canada. No air raid—too cloudy.
Got a suit of clothes and an overcoat from my Gillett's tailors. The suit is pretty flashy, I'm afraid. Weather drizzly most of the day.

The letter of February 20 that Don Martin wrote to Dorothy contained some interesting news about his doings and more about air raids.

 Dorothy

No. 6 arrived today. Mother's letter dated Feb 5 came at the same time. I hadn't received a letter in quite a while so two seemed like a treat.* There is no way of telling anything about the mails. Sometimes a letter dated on the 1st of a month will be here sooner than one dated fifteen days later; but however, I imagine they all reach their destination some time. So John Knox came, or went, up and had a good visit with Mother and Julie did he? That's good. He is always very interesting to talk to. I suppose he and Dan Reed had a great old visit about the war. I am going to write to John some day. You tell him I said so will you young lady? Now don't you forget it. It won't take much time for you to stop in there on your way to school.

I couldn't make out the writing on that picture in the corner of your letter. I think it is " 'ave an"— I don't know what the rest of it is. That's a good idea—swimming at the Y.W.C.A. Maybe by next summer you'll be so proficient that you can live at Dahn's Beach and swim back and forth from Silver Creek every day. By the way if you are thinking of going to the Beach next summer you better speak for a cottage now. Why not engage one for the whole summer?

I don't know where I'll be. Probably here but one can never tell. Bennett might take it in his head any time to have me go back to New York though I doubt it very much. He seems quite satisfied with my work so far. Most of that stuff in the Sunday paper from London is mine. Now and then I notice they sign something. It doesn't matter to me whether they do or not. I am seeing a good deal and in a way having a pretty good time. I heard the Prime Minister and Mr. Asquith have their set-to in the House of Commons on Tuesday. It was a debate which will be talked about for a long time. It is rather difficult to get into the Commons or the Lords here, much harder than to get into Congress in Washington. Yesterday morning I had breakfast with the Duchess of Marlborough at her beautiful home, Sunderland House in London. I wanted to interview her about her war charities—you know she was Consuelo Vanderbilt—and I wrote and asked her about it. Although she has never consented to see a newspaper man before she asked me to come to her home and I had coffee at ten o'clock in the morning with her. She is a middle-aged woman now but is still very beautiful. Some time in the Herald you will see a story I am writing about her.

The weather here has been very fine for some time—until today and yesterday. Yesterday there was a black fog. It was so thick that lights were necessary all day. Today it has been drizzling. Everyone is glad though because air raids come only on moonlight nights with a clear sky. This is the new moon period. Next week there will be a full moon so if the weather is clear we may expect air raids every night. We had one Saturday night. A large hotel about two miles from mine was struck and part of it was knocked out. There was another raid Sunday night and a third on Monday night. Last night we had a rest and tonight there is peace.

London is a most picturesque place when the raid warnings are given at night. Busses rush around in a race for the barns. People run for the subway stations and substantial buildings. In the crowded sections tens of thousands of women rush into the subway stations with babies in their arms—sometimes three or four—and with pillows and blankets. You see the raids are on four or five hours. Bombs are not dropped all that time but people are uneasy.

* Neither letter survived.

The first signal is given when the air machines cross the coast 40 miles from London and the "All Clear" is not sounded till the last of the machines has vanished back across the coast. During the four or five hours the Germans are trying to get over the city and the English fliers are fighting with them. The Germans are over the city and able to drop bombs for only a very few minutes but it doesn't take many minutes to drop a bomb and one bomb can do a lot of damage. I look after myself all right. You needn't worry. Here's what you do Dorothy. Tell me the date my letters arrive and the date they were written, only those from now on. I am anxious to know about them. It isn't important but I would like to know. Have a good time but be careful of automobiles when you are in Buffalo. Be very, very careful. There are no automobiles here except taxis and trucks. No one is permitted to use one for pleasure. Gasoline is too scarce. England knows there is a war all right.

Don't think you must write every little while young lady, but write when you have a rainy or very bad day. Then you can't go out to play. I mailed a postal card to Mr. and Mrs. Brand from Stratford on Avon. Tell me if they get it. Some time the postal authorities won't let postal cards through. Here's a kiss and hug,

With love
Dad

Diary: Thursday February 21, 1918

Had a very busy day. Attended Repington and Gwynne hearing at Bow St. for violation of Defense of Realm Act. Were convicted and fined 100 pounds each [$9,000 August 2020]. Then to office. Wrote quite a bit of stuff. Got a very funny letter from Dorothy. Saw Gwynne, editor of the Post at 6:30. Got an interview with him on the hearing, etc. and cabled it to Paris and New York. Got dinner at Simpson's late. To the office again. Mr. Sproul came in and gave me another good interview on Russia. He says "Who wins Russia wins war." Mailed 1½ columns to Paris. Left the office at 12 and sat in Russell's room at the hotel till 1:30 a.m.

Wore for the first time new check suit, I had it made at Gillett's. Fits but is certainly a loud one. Think I am a bit ashamed of it. Gave little Jo, the office boy, an old suit which is good as new.

Weather clear but cool.

Diary: Friday February 22, 1918

Went to the office at noon. Wrote a 1½ column story on the airmen and their importance, chivalry, etc. Ordered a morning suit at Gillett's. Got my passport back at the Bow Street station and came to my room to dress for the Washington birthday dinner at Connaught rooms. [Grand Connaught Rooms was one of London's most impressive, stylish and opulent event venues, situated in Covent Garden]. To the dinner with Russell and Underwood. Had a meatless meal. Sims* of our Navy gave a very humorous speech. Went to Fleet St. for short time and returned to hotel at midnight.

Germans marching on Petrograd. Bolsheviks now preparing to resist. Looks to me as if Russia is the big prize of the war and Germany will have it unless the Allies (with Japan) are able to do something quickly.

Weather pretty good.

* Admiral William Sims was commander of all United States naval forces operating in Europe.

Diary: Saturday February 23, 1918

Spent the afternoon at the office doing nothing much. Came up to the hotel at 4 and spent a couple hours in my room reading. Went to the office in the evening but did nothing but sit around. Rather looked for an air raid but clouds obscured the moon. Sat up in Russell's room till about midnight.

Russia now the big point of interest. The Bolsheviks threaten to oppose the Germans next but they can do nothing. The big German drive on the French front has not started.

Weather pleasant.

On February 24, Don Martin wrote in his diary 'Unless I get to the front'.

Diary: Sunday February 24, 1918

Went to J.W. Griggs' (N.Y. World man) home in Liddrake Grove for tea. Had a pleasant visit. He has been on the Italian and French fronts. Went to the office in the evening. Read Heralds up to February 3. Find they run a lot of my matter in the Sunday paper but don't sign it. Can't say I like the way it is handled; nor do I like the idea of using the mail instead of cable. However, I don't care one way or another. I went to be in this new world atmosphere for a while. Then I shall kick and return unless I get to the front.

Seemed like good night for an air raid but there has not been one yet and it is now 1 a.m. Will write a letter to Dorothy.

Weather fine.

A long, hand-written letter to Dorothy on Sunday night.

Sunday night, February 24, 1918

Dorothy

You couldn't guess what I have been doing—eating some cookies and a couple of oranges in my room. Sometimes I feel a bit hungry late at night and in London the restaurants are not open all night the way many are in New York and other American cities. They don't have cookies here, or at least they don't call them cookies—they are called cakes and they are not very nice. You see butter is scarce and some other kind of stuff is used.

On my desk I have what is called a food card. I got it today. Tomorrow and thereafter no one can get meat or butter in a restaurant or a store without a card and he can get only a certain allowance. The card is punched by the restaurant owner or store keeper (if you are a householder) and then you can get no more anywhere that day because no one will honor a card already punched. It is just a precaution to provide for an equitable distribution of the meat and butter available. With so many ships being sunk food is rather scarce in England. However there is plenty of fish, eggs and vegetables and people get along.

This afternoon I went out to have tea at the home of Mr. Griggs of the New York World. I had a pleasant visit, some good tea and some real cake. Having tea is quite a fad in England. Everyone does it. I guess it is not because people are crazy over tea but simply because it is an excuse for inviting people out. Just now when things are so scarce people don't invite their friends to dinner.

Oh yes I must tell you how I get sugar. I am entitled under the rationing system to six ounces a week, so every Saturday the hotel management leaves a sack, sealed, containing the exact amount, in my room.

I noticed that you do about the same thing on a typewriter that I do. Aunt Alta tells me that about the first thing you do when you get in her office is to write your Dad. That is a splendid idea.

I wish you could see a new suit of clothes I bought. It is pretty loud I fear. I don't care. I wanted an English suit and I have one. I shall probably order some more, but of a somewhat more modest design. The one I refer to is a grey check and is a fine piece of woolen. You will laugh when you see it sometime. I imagine Mr. Welliver, a friend of mine, has arrived in New York about now, and if he doesn't forget it he will mail a package to you containing a little souvenir I bought in Shakespeare's town. There was also one for Mrs. Brooks. I believe I have already written to you about these things.

No air raid since last Monday night. Everyone expected one tonight because of the full moon, but there has been no warning yet, and it is one o'clock in the morning. Usually they come before midnight. Zaps as you call them don't come anymore. They are so slow that the English fliers always get after them too easily. The Germans come over in machines called Gothas—very large aeroplanes carrying two and three men and having a speed of 100 miles an hour. If there are no raids for three more nights there will be a comfortable feeling in London for three weeks—or until the next moonlight period.

I shall get in bed and read for a half hour before going to sleep. Your standing in school, Dorothy, was excellent. It is as high as anyone should want to stand. I understand too that you are showing very marked progress in your music. Don't neglect that will you?

A goodnight kiss from Dad.

Diary: Monday February 25, 1918

Rather a dull day. Did some work at the office. Had sort of a grouch for no apparent reason and "jumped on" the fogies at the office for not being "on their jobs".

Had dinner at Simpson's with Judge Neal of Chicago and at 7:30 walked over the Waterloo Bridge to see the women and children lining up to get into the subway in case of an air raid. Saw but few. Good night for an air raid but none given up to midnight (the hour now). Went to the office, got the Morning Telegraph proofs and came to the hotel.

Weather sharp but pleasant.

Diary: Tuesday February 26, 1918

Read the papers (New York too). Wrote to Newton, Oliver and the Commodore about Hearst getting permission to get English news, and that is about all, except to see Col. Buchan at 5 p.m.

Was at the office most of the evening. Wrote a long story on the war situation to date—an analysis of the developments etc. England is by no means sure of being able to lick Germany as she hoped to lick her. America seems to be the only optimist. Russia's elimination has rather staggered the Allies.

Weather sharp but pleasant.

Diary: Wednesday February 27, 1918

Finished the day helping "Save the King" in the grill room downstairs. Was with Brownell who is more or less a "nut" and a Miss Simmons of Shanghai. Was at the office part of the afternoon and evening. Wrote a long story about King George and his hobbies for mailing to N.Y.

Met Parkerson of the A.P. in the afternoon and went with him to the Press Bureau to see how it works. The newspaper gathering business here is much the same as in the U.S. Had dinner at the Savoy. Got letter from Jennings in N.Y. saying the London news is the best he has ever read. Sounds good but guess he had a brainstorm.

Submarine report shows 14 big ships sunk this last week.

Weather pleasant but showery.

Diary: Thursday February 28, 1918

Began the day at noon with an interview on the labor situation with Arthur Henderson, union leader. He was annoyed at directness of questions I had prepared but finally agreed to think them over and answer them. They are certainly very pointed. Spent an hour in Westminster Abbey. Saw Admiral Hall. He says food situation will get worse. Had dinner at Cheshire Cheese. All the evening at the office. Sent a long labor interview Baird got with my questions with Wilson of the Seamen's Union. Cabled 200 words to N.Y. Wrote several business letters. Also got a letter from Dorothy. She is unquestionably a humorist. Was making a snow woman because she can't make legs.

Sunshine, fog, snow, drizzle, clear, freeze—some day.

On March 1, 1918, Don Martin received word that Commodore Bennett wanted a correspondent at the front, and almost got a go-ahead for France from the Commodore.

Diary: Friday March 1, 1918

Quite a busy day. Lingwood woke me at 9:30 to read a couple of telegrams from the Commodore—one to see Mr. Whitehead of the Whitehead Aircraft Co, which I did this afternoon—his factory is in Richmond—and another, more important (to me) either to recommend someone to go to the front unless I think it preferable to go myself—providing I can get some "good" man to replace me while I'm away. Wired tonight I think it all right to go myself and to leave the London office as it is. Am anxious to know what the Commodore will say. Whitehead told me most interesting story how the Commodore lent him $1,000 years ago at Monte Carlo when he, Whitehead, had lost everything. A good news story to put in the Commodore's obituary, unless he lives forever.

Worked at the office until midnight. Then to the hotel. Irvin Cobb has left some things for me to keep till he gets back from the front.
Weather clear, windy + very cold.

A short, hand-written letter to Dorothy from the Savoy on Friday night, March 1, "just a line before I go to bed", mostly reacting to her letter writing and doings.

Friday night, March 1, 1918

Dorothy,

Here's another "teeny-weeny." It's a long time since I wrote the last one. This will be very "weeny" in every way—just a line before I go to bed. I went out to a suburb called Richmond today to go through a big aeroplane factory. Before going I had luncheon with a theatrical man whom I knew in New York. This evening I was at the office.

Joseph will no doubt show you a long typewritten letter I wrote to him yesterday. His father wrote to me and enclosed a nice little note from Joseph. The little chap said he hoped I would write to him some day and then it occurred to me that even though I had thought of him a good many times I had never written him even a note. So it was about time. Don't you think so? I hope Dorothy your snow woman was a success. I hope also you put a pretty dress on her. A snow woman ought to have fun, I suppose and yet if you put very warm clothes on her she wouldn't need any because she would disappear. Where did you get that expression "joy birds?" That is a new one to me. I'm glad you are all getting on without colds. It is instead Joseph must have one. Perhaps he's careless. I told him I suppose he is a wild Indian and I'll bet he is. You must tell me what Madame Blanev said about your music; I hear you are doing very nicely with it. I guess you have had the worst days at the dentist's. I have been finished now for just a year.

Goodness but my letters are slow in reaching you! It seems as if I have written twenty. Yours come quite promptly and you are a very sweet little girl to write so often. I am always very, very glad to hear from you because you write crazy letters—just like your Dad and your Dad's letters.

A goodnight kiss Dorothy,

From Dad

Diary: Saturday March 2, 1918

Took a long walk over Waterloo Bridge; up the other side of the river to Lambeth Bridge; then back by the Admiralty etc. to the hotel. Had been at the office for three hours. Had dinner at Simpson's—have a meat card now—and then went to the office and stayed till 11:30. Wrote several short stories; got up the statements on the war anniversary for April 5 and wrote a 1½ col. story to go with them.

Shall now eat a couple of oranges, some cakes I bought yesterday in Richmond—eating is different than it used to be—and go to bed. What wouldn't I give to run amuck in Mother's icebox after she had had a chicken dinner! Have lost 8 pounds but feel perfectly well. Everyone is losing some.

Weather windy + very cold.

And Saturday evening, March, 2 Don Martin wrote a long letter to his mother about the war and Germany.

New York Herald, London Bureau
130, Fleet Street, E.C.4
March 2, 1918

Mother

Goodness, it seems as if I write to almost everyone but you! I write so many letters though to one member of the family or another—and one is for all of course—that I am about written dry. It is Saturday night and I am at the office because I have no other place to go. I have been writing some articles for the New York and Paris editions and also some business letters and I see no reason why I shouldn't keep my typewriter humming a while longer and write to you.

I receive letters from everyone. They arrive here on an average of three weeks after they are written. The last one I got was from Dorothy and it was by far the craziest letter I ever received—and also the best. She is a human dynamo all right. She told about a snow woman she was building or going to build. She said it would have to be a woman because she couldn't make legs. The eyes would be stones because coal is too expensive to be used for foolish purposes. Then she had a hat she "togs" up in to put on the woman. Oh she went into a great rig-amarole. One of her letters is as good as a tonic. There is no doubt she is a humorist. And there is no doubt she knows how to write either. She can write better at eleven than I could at fifteen.

Then I got a letter from Charlie the same day and with it came a plaintive note from Joseph—just as cute as anything could be—asking if I would ever write to him. The poor little chap! I sat right down and wrote him a long letter. I had intended doing it all along but you know it is so easy to put things off. I am awfully sorry he has a cold. Dorothy says she has escaped one so far. I am hoping also that you are taking care of yourself and are escaping those stomach attacks.

You wouldn't have indigestion if you were here because you would not be able to overeat. The food is all right and there is plenty but it is altogether different from what Americans are accustomed to. The bread is only part wheat. I don't know what the other part is—sawdust I think. There is no taste to it. Yesterday I was out to a suburb called Richmond—really part of London—and on the way to the railway station out there I passed a little bakeshop. I bought a half pound of candy and ate it all, and a pound of small cakes which I have in my room. That is I have part of them in my room. I ate some last night and shall eat some more tonight. They aren't very good. I would like to be turned loose some night in that ice box of yours after a chicken dinner with home made bread and plenty of butter. However don't get the impression I am going hungry. I have all the money I want to spend for food and can get as good as anyone and no one needs to go hungry though no one can get exactly what he would like best.

I have opportunities to go out to the homes of some Americans anytime I want to. There are several American correspondents here whom I know and they are very nice people. I spent last Sunday afternoon with a man named Griggs and some friends of his. He has three children here and his wife worries to death when there is an air raid. You see a two or three story house would be no protection at all, and the best they can do is to trust to luck and hope that a bomb won't strike their house. Probably one never will and yet the only one dropped some night might. One is foolish to worry. There has been no raid now for two weeks. There has been a moon but the weather has not been good for flying. Now there will be no raids till the next new moon—two weeks hence and maybe not then. I look after myself.

I shall enclose a postal card I got out at Stratford-on-Avon, Shakespeare's town. It is a picture of a little tavern, hotel or saloon or whatever you wish to call it. It dates back to Shakespeare's time. Nearly everything there does in fact. I hope the spoons and pin I sent back by Mr. Welliver reached you all right. He is a New York Sun man and he returned recently to New York. He said he would mail the packages to you. One was addressed to Mrs. Brooks. She will appreciate it.

The war is going on about as usual. No one can tell what will happen. The Germans are bound to be licked but I imagine not very hard. That would take too long and the world is getting pretty weary of war. Charlie tells me the draft age may be increased to 40 and that he might have to be drafted. Rock would be eligible too wouldn't he? They are too old to be taken in active service though and maybe experience of one kind or another wouldn't do them any harm. The war has reached the stage where almost everyone must be willing to make whatever sacrifice there is to be made. If I were ten years younger I would get in the service in some capacity.

United States is likely very soon to read a long list of casualties among Americans. They are going to be in the fight and many of them will naturally be lost. They are a fine looking lot of men. I understand they are splendid fighters. The Kaiser is a fine specimen of humanity. He is responsible for the whole business and why in the world someone doesn't murder him and confer a blessing on the world is more than I can understand. The fact that someone doesn't is proof of the fact that the Germans are all the same. There never was a good German I don't think. I know I shall never wear, eat or have anything as long as I live that came from Germany and I will never patronize a German at home. That is what I think of them.

I have made a rather long letter out of what was started as a short one. It is now eleven thirty o'clock and I shall close up the office and walk up to the Savoy hotel. That is about as far as from our house to the railway station. It takes just fifteen minutes. The weather today and tonight is very sharp and windy. I rather like it though.

Give Dorothy a kiss for me and remember me to the neighbors, relatives etc.

With love
Don

And the next day the Commodore gave Martin a "Go"!

Diary: Sunday March 3, 1918

Looks as if I might get to the front after all! Got wire from Commodore telling me to make arrangements to go, leaving office as I suggested to Champion and Baird. Asked how soon I can go and if Washington must make authorization. Replied that Washington must act but I will get busy tomorrow. Also got wire to cable my Henderson interview. Sent 1000 words and it is a very good story.

In the afternoon went with Russell to have tea with him at the home of a woman acquaintance of his. She is rather more intelligent than most of his friends. Got up at 1 p.m. Spent all the evening at the office.

Weather rainy and cold.

Don Martin wrote a comprehensive summary of the war situation as seen from London. This mailed dispatch was published in the New York Herald on March 18, 1918, with a byline. By then, he was in Neufchateau, France. It was tagged Sunday — probably Sunday, March 3.

Allied Victory Certain by 1919, but Submarine Is Still a Great Peril

United States Now Setting the Pace and Other Nations May Support Whatever Attitude She Takes—Is Big Brother to Entente and Doom to the Hun

By DON MARTIN

[Special to the Herald]

Herald Bureau, No. 130 Fleet Street, London, Sunday

If the civil populations "stick" there will be a complete victory, but it probably won't come before 1919. That is the conclusion one is justified in reaching here in the thick of the war atmosphere. But for the Russian collapse, which is complete and hopeless, an end of the war in 1918 was in sight. That end was predicated on a great allied offensive.

With the German armies reinforced and literally hewn into the earth. the indications are that there will be no concerted offensive against the Hun before midsummer, and perhaps not then.

England's great problem does not lie on the western front, however. It lies with the submarine, which is still a grave menace.

The following statistics show the net result of the submarine activity, or the British shipping losses, for a year up to February 1 of this year.

Gravest Period to Come

The gravest period of all, so far as submarines are concerned, will be the next three months. If in that period the German snakes of the sea fail to fulfill the Von Tirpitz promises the danger of grievously injuring England from beneath the sea's surface will have passed. And meanwhile the United States is taking her place on the battle line, and the British, Colonials and the French are gazing upon them with admiration.

A strong peace offensive from Germany is now believed to be more probable than a sustained military offensive. With Russia practically at their mercy, the Germans, experts say, would make almost any kind of a western peace and still be big winners in net results of the war.

But it is well to bear in mind this seemingly established fact—Germany, with all her new divisions from the eastern front, cannot demolish the Allied line, though she may cripple it temporarily, and, therefore, for the next few months the world will see two military Titans glowering at each other over a barbed wire barrier almost humanly impossible to surmount.

German People Tired of War

If one is to judge from the editorials in the German newspapers, the people of Germany are tired of the war and would gladly accept the terms laid down by President Wilson if the militaristic group would relinquish its ambition for conquest. It is a fair deduction from the statements made in the German press also that but for the mailed fist of the militarists a large element of the population would demand peace.

The collapse of Russia heartened the Germans. Prospects of a commercial conquest of that domain and the persistent promises of Von Tirpitz that the submarine will yet force England to her knees are the food upon which the war weary masses of the Central Empires are being fed. A prominent Briton who reads German newspapers— and copies of all of them are obtained—tells me that Germany is not confident of winning against the Allies.

All the German calculations, it is asserted, are based on a termination of the war before the United States gets into full action. German prisoners—Saxons, many of them, who are hostile to the Prussian domination—have told allied officers that while Germany derides America, she knows in her heart that so long as America gives her resources to the allied cause Germany's hopes for a satisfactory peace are very slim.

Thorn in Hun's Side

The United States is unquestionably the thorn in Germany's side, and although there is a disposition here to hasten peace, the feeling is growing that the United States will continue to be the thorn in Germany's side until Wilson's peace has been effected.

The statement is quite

	Big ships	Small ships	Total	Unsuccessfully attacked	Total attacked
Feb 25	16	6	22	16	38
Weekly averages					
March (5 weeks	16.4	8.2	24.6	15.6	40.2
April (4 weeks)	29.0	9.5	38.5	21.0	59.5
May (5 weeks)	17.6	8.2	25.8	18.8	44.6
June (4 weeks)	21.5	6.5	28.0	22.5	50.5
July (4 weeks)	17.0	3.25	20.25	13.75	34.0
Aug (5 weeks)	17.6	3.2	20.8	9.8	30.6
Sept (4 weeks)	10.5	7.75	18.25	11.0	20.25
Oct (4 weeks	14.5	4.75	19.25	5.25	24.5
Nov (5 weeks)	9.6	4.7	14.4	6.4	20.8
Dec (4 weeks)	14.25	3.75	18.0	9.75	27.75
Jan (5 weeks)	9.6	3.2	12.8	8.2	21.0

frankly made now by public speakers that the anti-German forces could have obtained only ... without America's aid. France and Holland were both in the doldrums. Reports now coming from the highest sources say that France is more virile than ever and more enthusiastic than at any other period, and all because of the wholehearted support given by America. England is war weary. No secret is made of that fact. But she is at the maximum of her strength, and, despite mumblings now and then by certain labor elements and the earnest desire of the business element for peace, she will "carry on" till the men from over the seas are in the line.

Statesmen in England are constantly asking if the desire for peace will ... of a continuation of the war until the original idea of peace is carried out, viz. repudiation by the people of Germany, of the forces which plunged them and the world into war. There is no violation of confidence in saying that the mass of people of Great Britain do not feel that it is necessary to "go to the limit," as it is said, do not feel that the Hohennzollerns must be cast out before there can be peace negotiations.

America to Set the Pace

But the men who do the thinking for this nation are fairly of the opinion that the United States, with her whole heart and soul in the war of idealism, will negotiate only with a Germany, which is representative of the "People" and not representative of the present ruling class.

In other words, to paraphrase the sentiments of the Europeans, the United States will from this time on set the pace and the Allies will have to support her in whatever attitude she takes. She is the one upon which hangs the big situation. She is at once the big brother of the Allies and the doom of the Hun.

Writing in the Manchester Guardian, Mr. Edgar Wallace, one of the most eminent of the experts, said: "Supposing that Germany were able to get a peace based upon the surrender of Alsace and her colonies and the relinquishment of her authority in the Russian provinces, her plans would be fairly obvious.

No Need for Great Navy

"There would be no need for a great navy. She could protect herself by minefields and submarines. She would devote her attention to the building of U-boats and aircraft, and save a great deal of money which otherwise would be spent on the construction of larger guns and perfect her land forces for the conquest of France, Holland, Belgium and England. These secured, she would turn her attention to America.

"There is nothing fantastic about that theory; it is a common sense view of what would happen. If the present form of German government remains on top, the question of peace or war is at the discretion of a small coterie of princes. It is inevitable that a second war would follow, and just as inevitable that if the people of France, England and American stick with it, the world conquering dreams of Germany will be forever shattered.

"It may be that sticking it out for another two years is better, if we suffered a little for the next years than that our sons should be conscripted, that we should be burdened with enormous taxation than that our country should live under the menace of war more terrible than this present war has been."

Diary: Monday March 4, 1918

The busiest and most annoying day I have had. Got a note from the Censor that a letter he enclosed from Helene showed I had sent a letter back to U.S. by a boat passenger—which I had, but with no intention of dodging the censor. However he called my attention to the fact that I violated the law—which I did. I wrote a letter of apology and promise and then began worrying which I am still doing. Champion eased my mind (?) by telling me all the cases he knew where men had been ruined by clashing with the law in this way.

With Baird went to American and French consuls and got my passports vised. With Draper of Tribune went to Burberry's and ordered a war outfit and a fine trench coat—$110.00! [$2,000 August 2021] However I want to be ready if the French front thing goes through. Wired Commodore authorization must come from Washington but perhaps I better get to Paris to complete arrangements. Cabled Tumulty, President's secretary, to get busy for me.

Weather cool and windy.

In a letter from Don Martin to his daughter written on March 4, 1918, he showed growing excitement about going over to France and the war front.

London, March 4, 1918

Dorothy

It is just possible that you will have to address your letters to me in France after a bit. It may not come out that way but if it is possible to get permission to go with the American Army—that is at its headquarters—I shall go to Paris and then on to wherever the Americans may be in France. I got a telegram from Mr. Bennett yesterday telling me to prepare to go to the front and asking what arrangements would have to be made. I made inquiries today and learned that the only way one can get to the front is to get permission from the authorities in Washington. That is not easy to get, but only because there is room for but a few correspondents and the space is generally filled up. However I have started the thing going and if I succeed you will get a cable from me long before this reaches you. I went to the American and French consuls today and got my passports vised so if I get word that everything is all right I shall be able to start without delay.

Then again it may all fall through. I hope it doesn't though because I would of course like to get up as near the front as possible so I could write some stories of the battle scenes etc. You may be sure I will be too far back to be in any danger. I sent a cablegram to Joe Tumulty, President Wilson's secretary today, asking him to see if he could do anything in Washington. He is a very intimate friend of mine and no doubt will bring the matter to the attention of the President. Then if the war department has room I may get through all right. Mr. Bennett has no doubt cabled Washington also and there ought to be some developments of one kind or another before a great while.

During the next few weeks the front will be a lively place, if all the predictions come true. You have probably read in the newspapers about the great "offensive" the Germans intend to make. I have an idea—but it is of course just my own opinion—that there will be no offensive. I really hope there will because the Germans will probably lose a large part of their army and about the surest way to lick them good is to kill all their soldiers! The English never say much about what they intend to do or what they expect but when there is some hard fighting to do they are always on the job and come out in first place. That is what they will do this summer unless the Huns have devised some new kind of fiendishness like poison gas of a more deadly variety and I guess they have not done that.

From what I read in the papers here I guess your heavy snow has gone. Probably though there is enough left to make snow women out of. Why don't you take a photograph of the next snow woman you make and send it to me? And by the way have you ever done anything about getting some pictures taken of yourself? You know I haven't any very recent ones.

The weather here is rather bad. March is always bad in London I am told. It is cold and windy but that has one virtue—there are no air raids when the weather is bad. I almost think the Germans will quit this air raiding business. They thought it was fine as long as they were killing or injuring people in London and remained safe themselves. But things are different now. The Allies are giving them a good taste of their own medicine and maybe it will have some effect on the bullheadedness of the Germans.

I haven't done anything unusual since I last wrote you. I go out for a walk usually every day and spend most of the time in the office, writing things for the New York and Paris editions. If I go to France it will probably be with the understanding that I shall return here. I am getting so I like London. It is, as I have told you, a very wonderful city and after one has been here a while he finds that the stories about the English not having a sense of humor and not being friendly to Americans are not true. I have got along splendidly. The trouble has been I find that Americans have never seen the real Britishers and the Britishers have not seen what we think are the real Americans. The war is bringing them together.

I have been in the office all the evening—Monday—but will go to the hotel as soon as I finish this letter. If you should get a cablegram from me saying that I have gone to France, you can address me care the New York Herald, 38 Rue du Louvre, Paris. The letters will be forwarded from there. If there is another address preferable I will cable to you.

Remember me to Mother, Rock, Inez, Julie, Charlie, Joseph and Alta—and anyone else you think of. And keep a little love for yourself.

Dad

Diary: Tuesday March 5, 1918

Began the day by seeing the censor. He said there was no need of worrying over the notes I sent by boat but that it wasn't a good thing to do. I agreed with him and assured him I had no intention of doing anything irregular and certainly will give no further cause for criticism which I shan't.

Heard nothing from the Commodore about the arrangements for the front. It is too early to hear. Was at the office most of the day. In the evening took Metier of Vancouver to the office and wrote a story for him about the reception given for his Victoria Cross friend Hanna, in Kilkenny, Ireland. Metier wants to send it to a Vancouver paper. Wrote a good column story for him. Weather clear and reasonably pleasant.

Diary: Wednesday March 6, 1918

Went to Burberry's this forenoon and tried on my uniform. Some of the old timers may outshine me in brains and experience but certainly not in clothes. Hope I get a chance to wear them. The breeches, tunic and outer coat cost $115. Have heard nothing from Bennett further. Now, in conformity to my custom, I am worrying lest the thing fall through.

Spent part of the afternoon at the office, and most of the evening. Being good and hungry, I got a big dinner at the Savoy—fish, steak, pancake with jelly etc.—cost 2.50 but was worth it. Also got my hair cut. Doesn't take long to cut it now—there isn't enough left.

Weather ideal—mild + sunshine.

The clothing bill of $115 is equivalent to $2,100 today, using the Consumer Price Index ratio of 18.6. The dinner bill at the Savoy of $2.50 is equivalent to $47 in mid-2020.

On March 7, 1918, Commodore Bennett gave Don Martin the order to go to France.

Diary: Thursday March 7, 1918

(Another air raid—started 11:30, over 1:45.)

Looks as if I shall go to the front. Mr. Bennett wires to go to Paris and stay at the Crillon Hotel where he will engage a room. Things coming along very well so far.

Left at 10 a.m. to visit J. A. Whitehead of the Aircraft Co. Went through his big plant which turns out 150 aeroplanes a month. Attended a luncheon at his beautiful home on the Thames near Richmond after a pleasant automobile ride through the country. Made a speech which seemed to take pretty well. About 70 prominent men—editors among them—present. Got back at six.

Went to office and while talking to Champion about the orders to go to Paris heard sirens. No one expecting an air raid. He and I came up to the Savoy. I hung round the lobby after standing on Waterloo Bridge till the barrage started. Heard no bombs but saw place of big fire. Came to my room at 1:45 a.m.

Weather delightful.

©ALondonInheritance (Pictured c.1990)

In London Don Martin worked from this building at 130 Fleet Street which housed the New York Herald's London bureau.

Diary: Friday March 8, 1918

Well here I am at 1:30 a.m. in my room, ready practically to start for France. Hustled all day. Had luncheon at the Carlton, as the guest of Russell Underwood, Ben Russell and Frank Phelps. Underwood was host. Wrote a very long letter to Dorothy. Dictated to Baird a 1500 word story on Whitehead; dictated other letters, sent cables, got my outfit together packed up; had dinner as guest of T. J. Whaley, a big oil man. Stayed at the office till 11:30; then came to the hotel and went to Russell's room with some of his friends and am now about to take a bath. Have spent a lot of money! $30 for boats [equivalent to $550 today], $112 for uniform etc. and a lot besides for odds and ends. Arranged for ticket, got my police permits, passports, etc. Everything is all ready now for my journey.

Weather fine.

A six-page typed letter to Dorothy on March 8 from the Herald office on Herald stationary told what he thought would happen to him in France, and about his new clothing.

New York Herald, London Bureau
130, Fleet Street, E.C.4.
March 8, 1918

Dorothy

Well young lady your Dad is going to France. Just where he will go in France after he gets there he doesn't know but if the office has been able to get permission for me to go to the American front, I shall go to there. If not I shall go to the front anyhow, only not as regular and permanent resident of the general headquarters but as a visitor. In any event I shall see some of the war and probably when I get back to the United States I shall be able to tell you a good many stories of the fighting. I shall not be up there where there is danger so you mustn't worry. I know you aren't given to worrying anyhow, but if you are, you may feel certain there is no danger to your Father. The chances are that I shall go to some small French village not far from the firing line and live at some farmhouse or villager's place. It will be quite interesting. Strangely enough I shall very likely go to the very section of France from which Grandmother's folks came and wouldn't it be remarkable and fine if I should be able to get trace of some of the descendants?

Some of the older correspondents and literary stars may outshine me for experience but I can assure you that will not eclipse me for clothes. I went to the famous Burberry's in London and got a complete outfit. I guess I'll have to tell you about it. I have a regular officer's uniform—knee breeches and tunic with a green brassard (band) on the right arm and a red letter C. printed on it. That means correspondent. Then I have a pair of fine army lace boots (they cost $30); heavy socks or stockings, and brown shirts. In addition to all this I have a khaki colored trench coat with fleece lining and a belt around it. It comes just below my knees and is both waterproof and warm. The fleece is buttoned on the inside and can be taken out and worn separately. My hat I haven't got yet. I am to have an American field hat and I couldn't get one of American style in London but can in Paris. I haven't had the outfit on yet. I suppose when I first don it I will think that all the world is looking at me when, as a matter of fact, probably no one will notice me at all. You see military uniforms of all kinds are common everywhere but when one steps out in one for the first time he feels self conscious. I think when I get to Paris I shall put the whole regalia on and get my photograph taken. Then I will send you a print of it and you will know that your Dad was a war correspondent for a while anyhow. Some time when I am back home I will have to put it on again and let you have a good laugh.

I made preparations in a hurry. I got a telegram from Mr. Bennett first asking if I thought I could leave the London office in charge of the regular staff for a few weeks or months while I went to the American front. I told him I could. He then asked what arrangements had to be made and after telling him, I began to get ready. Yesterday I got a telegram telling me to start for Paris when I got ready and I am ready. I have all my things together. I got a big carryall and my uniform and other clothes will go in that. I shall leave here tomorrow afternoon and will be in Paris Sunday night. Mr. Bennett told me to go to the Crillon Hotel, which is a very good one. He said he would engage a room for me.

When I get there I shall wait till authority to go to the front comes from Washington. You will get another cablegram from me before you receive this. Then I shall write to you frequently from France.

111

You should address your letters, as I believe I said, to 38 Rue de Louvre, Paris, care the Herald. The cable address is just "Herald, Paris."

The object of my trip is to be with the American troops when the great German offensive takes place, if it ever does. The American troops are showing up very well. The Huns can't scare them. I am quite sure the Americans will give a good account of themselves wherever they are and there will be many interesting stories to be written about them. It is a splendid opportunity of course. It is the biggest operation in the biggest war in history and I ought to know something about war when I get back.

Today the Mr. Russell of whom you have heard me speak, Mr. Underwood, who represents the Erie Railway in London, and Mr. Phelps, who represents the Frohmans, gave me a very swell luncheon at the Carlton Hotel. There were about a dozen friends of mine there. I had a good luncheon and a good time. Yesterday I attended a luncheon given by a Mr. Whitehead, President of the Whitehead Aircraft Company. He is a friend of Mr. Bennett's and Mr. Bennett wired me to see him. The dinner was given to editors and publishers from all over Great Britain. I was asked to make a speech after all the others had spoken and I have reason to believe (that is the way we newspapermen write) that I made a reasonably fair hit with the crowd. I talked about America and told a few stories.

No one knew I was an American until I was introduced. You see I had on that loud suit of English clothes I told you about. It deceives everyone and shocks nearly everyone. I don't think I shall wear it much.

Your letter, written in Alta's office reached me today. It is the only letter I have received from United States in ten days. I had it in mind when I called you "Funny" in the cablegram I sent today. You are funny all right. The other letters you have written between that date and this will come to this office and will be forwarded to Paris. I will get them all.

And what do you think! I couldn't get away from London without being in another air raid. I was sitting here last night at half past eleven, not even dreaming of an air raid—there was no moon and the night didn't seem to be clear—when there was a bang of guns—the maroons. With Mr. Champion, manager of the office when I'm not here, I went to the Savoy Hotel. We walked up and stood for fifteen minutes on the Waterloo Bridge to see if we could see any operations in the air. We saw nothing but stars. When the barrage started we went into the hotel and I remained there. The "all clear" was not given till a quarter to two in the morning. About two Gothas out of seven or eight got by the English fliers and the barrage, and dropped bombs on the outlying sections. No bomb landed within four miles of the Savoy. The official reports tonight are that about 16 were killed and 50 injured. No big buildings were hit but several dwellings were destroyed and women and children were killed. This is a fine bit of warfare to wage! The Germans are sowing the seed for a hatred which will last a hundred years. It seems that the night was clear and the Aurora Borealis, or Northern Lights, provided light enough to guide the Gothas over the city. The Northern Lights are very beautiful at this latitude—you look at your geography Dorothy and you will find that London is almost as far north as Labrador. It is the Gulf Stream which gives enough warmth to make Great Britain habitable. It is warmer in winter than Silver Creek. I drove through about twenty miles of country yesterday to attend that luncheon and noticed farmers plowing and planting. Everything is green.

Now everyone is wondering if there will be another raid tonight. It is about the same kind of weather as last night. It is now ten o'clock and I shall be here till half past eleven. If there is a warning I shall walk slowly up to the hotel, to see the picturesque street scenes, and then stay in the lobby until it is over. I shall rather be glad to be out of the raid zone for a while. The raids are not pleasant. Someone has to be killed every time a bomb is dropped.

When spring weather comes Dorothy you must be fitted out with some nice clothes. You know what you and I would do if I were there. Betty's shop. That's a good place for you and Mother and Alta or Julie to go in about a month. Tell the folks to take some of the money that has accumulated—if any has—and spend part of it for a good outfit for Miss Funny. You can pick out the things you like. You won't need many shoes for summer. You can go barefooted. Why not, by the way, send to Best's for shoes? The firm has your name and so forth and if your feet have grown you can send them the new size.

This is a corking old letter for length. Oh yes, when I said "if any has accumulated," I didn't mean to imply that you or anyone else is careless. I was merely thinking of the high cost of everything. Goodness! My war outfit cost me more than $200, but the Herald will pay for it and I will have it.

By the time you get this I will have crossed the English Channel, which is the stormiest place I guess in the world. I will find out then whether I am immune from seasickness or not. There is just about one person in a hundred thousand who doesn't get sick crossing. The trip I shall take will be six or seven hours on the water. I can't see anything to worry over about that. If one were sick all the way over it wouldn't be anything terrible. On the St. Louis coming over people were sick for six days. I have been at sea quite a bit and in many rough seas too and I have never yet been the least bit sea sick. Probably I shall have a story to tell you when I get to France. There is no submarine danger in such a short trip.

This letter, like the rest, Dorothy, is for all. Give my love to all the folks and tell them I shall write to one of them or all—and certainly to you—very soon after I get to France. I see you are still aiming to be a great artist. Keep at it! You're improving.

With love and a kiss
Dad

On the night of March 9, 1918, Don Martin left England and crossed the English Channel into France.

Diary: Saturday March 9, 1918

(Left Southampton for France)

Got up at 10:30 this morning and finished packing. Went to the office. Old Baird, bonehead though faithful, came to the train to see me off. Ben Russell also spent the last hour in London with me. He is a very fine sort. I got a porter from the Savoy to put me on the train.

Am on the Channel boat "Hantonia"—8 p.m. waiting to start across the Channel to France. Travelling is not easy. Arriving at Southampton at 6 p.m. had to go through a regular gamut of officials. It certainly wouldn't be easy to get through if one were trying to conceal something.

It is a perfect night but the channel has a bad reputation. Tomorrow's entry will show whether I have broken any record of immunity from seasickness... This is a small boat and is filled. No one seems worried about submarines.

Weather perfect.

PART 3

First Step Towards the Front — Paris, March 1918

On March 10, 1918, Don Martin arrived in Paris to cover the American Expeditionary Forces.

Diary: Sunday March 10, 1918

(Arrived in Paris 10 p.m.)

Here I am in Paris after a very tiresome but interesting day. Arrived at Havre at 7 a.m. but heavy fog necessitated staying at anchor till 10 when we came in. Calm all the way over. I lay down for few hours but kept my clothes on. Long unpleasant wait to get passports vised and baggage passed at Havre. Had lunch at famous Tortoni's with couple Englishmen, one of them decent. Went for long walk all over the city.

Started for Paris at 5:19. Had no trouble with baggage. Slept most of the way to Paris. Met fine young aviator named Hodges of Albany, Ga., on the train and brought him with me in a taxi to the Crillon Hotel. Probably won't see him again. Bennett picked out a good hotel for me. Went to Herald office and met staff. Burn Price [Manager, Paris Herald Office] and I then went for an hour's walk up one side of Seine and down the other. Back to hotel at 1 a.m. ready for bed!

Weather ideal.

Arriving in Paris for the first time Don Martin was immediately taken by the city, calling it the "wonder city of the world."

Commodore Bennett had put him up at The Crillon, just about Paris's best hotel. And eating there and at the restaurant Prunier led Don to exclaim "the London people 'feed', here they feast".

In the fourth year of war and not far from the front line, he still found "steak and a dozen oysters".

(Pictured 2017)

The Hotel Crillon on the Place de la Concorde, facing the Seine and next to the U.S. embassy.

Diary: Monday March 11, 1918

Air Raid—Paris 9:45 to 12:25.

In afternoon wandered around by myself. Met Burn Price and with him visited Notre Dame, Magdalene, the Latin Quarter and various other places. Had dinner with him at Prunier's restaurant. Then came to the hotel, the Crillon, which is about the best in Paris. Newton D. Baker, Secretary of War, is here.

Met Kerney of Trenton, who is here on government business. Paris is certainly a magnificent city—entirely different from London. One is business; one art. Did no work. Waiting for word from Commodore.

Life is just one 'damned air raid after another.' One started in Paris at 9:45 p.m. and the bugles for "Finis" sounded at 12:25 a.m. I was in my room when it began. Had just finished a long letter to Dorothy. Went down in the lobby. People much more excited than in London. Heard two or three bombs. Went out to see excitement but got lost in Place de la Concorde and came back.

Weather warm. Heavy fog.

A handwritten letter to Dorothy from Paris dated March 11 told her that he had already begun to explore Paris.

Hotel de Crillon, Paris
Monday – March 11, 1918

Dorothy

Well here your Dad is in Paris! I just finished breakfast (It cost $2.75) in the hotel after having slept for nearly twelve hours. This hotel is one of the finest in Paris—about like the Plaza or St. Regis in New York. I got here at half past ten last night after a rather tiresome day. I spent six hours in Havre, and five hours on the train which got here on time.

The manager of our Paris office called here about the time I arrived and he and I took a walk for an hour on one side of the Seine and down the other. The lights are all out here because of air raid dangers but even in the dark one could see that Paris is beautiful. I went to bed at midnight and slept until noon. The night before I didn't take my clothes off though I lay down for a couple hours. I wasn't sick crossing the Channel. The water was almost as smooth as the old millpond used to be; good weather for submarines but we saw none.

Now I shall wait here till I get word from Mr. Bennett. I expect to go up to the front pretty soon but will write fully about it as soon as I learn all about it.

Now (1 p.m.) I am going out for a walk of two or three hours. Maybe I will write to you again tonight or tomorrow. Call the letter No. 1 Dorothy and write some time when it reached you.
I shall number all my French letters.

With love,
Dad

Returning to the Hotel Crillon from that walk, Don Martin typed a second letter to Dorothy dated March 11, with more about the glories of Paris.

Hotel de Crillon, Paris
March 11, 1918

Dorothy

I brought my typewriter along with me and so you are liable to get another long letter. It may be full of mistakes because the machine is half locked up and the table on which it stands is so high that it is very awkward for me. However I decided to tell you about my first visit to Paris and the trip from London here. I have been in Paris less than 24 hours but I have already seen enough to understand why it is called the most beautiful city in the world. Whenever I have been in other cities—say Chicago, Philadelphia or London—I have wondered why people there didn't move to New York. I don't have the disposition to ask people here such a question. The city is just dotted with beautiful buildings each of which is of historical interest. I walked around two or three hours this afternoon with the manager of the Paris office of the Herald and he was able to point out many of the places. We saw Notre Dame, the Hotel de Ville, the Chamber of Deputies, the Magdalene Church or Cathedral, and walked all through the famous Latin Quarter. I sat on the piazza of the Grand Hotel in the Rue de Capucines and drank a glass of lemonade, and walked through the Rue de la Paix, the street which has all the jewelry shops. I never saw anything like the displays. There has been a heavy fog all day so I have seen the city at a disadvantage but tomorrow probably the sun will be shining and I will walk around some more.

I started in by having the best breakfast I have had since I left New York. Here the restaurants serve you as if they were glad to do it. In London the managers and waiters serve you because, apparently, they have to do it. There is about the same difference between London and Paris as there is between a burdock and a lily of the valley. The waiters in this hotel saw that I was an American at once. They can always tell it and they are glad when they get one to wait on. I told him I wanted breakfast—although it was lunch time—and he suggested an orange, filet of sole, fried potatoes and chocolate. It was all fine. There is no sugar to be had here now. There is no milk served after 9 in the morning. The orange was good and the chocolate was sweetened in some way so it all tasted very good. But the cost is very high. My bill this morning was $2.75 [$51 August 2021].

For dinner I went with Mr. Price, the Paris manager, to the famous Prunier restaurant. Mr. Bennett occasionally goes there when he is in Paris. We telephoned to reserve a table. One has to do this because the applicants for tables are so numerous. We had Portuguese oysters, roast beef and potatoes, braised endive and a fancy chocolate pudding. The bill here for two was about 25 francs, or slightly more than $6 [$112 August 2020]. Everything is high everywhere in Paris because of the scarcity of everything.

After dinner Mr. Price went to the office and I came to my room where I am now. There is nothing to do in the evening in Paris. The theaters are open but I don't care to go to a show I can't understand. The restaurants all close at nine o'clock and the houses and streets are all dark. The Germans have been bombing Paris lately and people are keeping the City as dark as possible. I shall sit in my room till about half past ten when I shall get into the subway—right near the hotel—and go to the Herald office at 38 Rue du Louvre for a half hour or so.

This hotel, I find, is the very best hotel in Paris. Mr. Baker, Secretary of War, is staying here now. General Pershing stayed here and all the diplomats from most of the important countries stay here. It overlooks the Tuilleries and is a magnificent building. Mr. Bennett believes in doing things up right. I shan't know what my programme will be until I hear from him. I wired him last night—he stays in Beaulieu on the Mediterranean—that I was here and now shall sit around or go sightseeing till he tells me what he has in mind. I got a message from one of his lawyers telling me that Mr. Bennett had wired him to do anything he could to facilitate my journey to the front; but I thanked him and said I would see him after I had heard from Mr. Bennett. There is only one way to deal with Mr. Bennett and that is to deal directly with him and take orders from no one else. That is my system. I rather expect that in a few days I shall be on my way to the American front. Paris is filled with American soldiers. I must have seen a thousand today. I met two or three—yes four or five—men I knew in the United States.

There was no sea at all on the trip across the channel so I was not sick. I enjoyed the day in Havre. That is a very picturesque old city, with the principal business street facing the harbor and sailing ships moored just across the street from the stores. In a big park nearby there were about 50 women selling flowers. The French are great for flowers. I ate in the big restaurant—Tortoni's, which seats about 1,000 persons— and walked all over the principal parts of the city before leaving at five in the afternoon. The train on which I traveled from Havre stopped just once between Havre and Paris and that was at Rouen.

Before I leave here Dorothy I shall write you another letter but it very likely will not be a long one. You will show this letter to Mother and the rest of the folks and they will know all about my trip up to date.

With love, Dad

Diary: Tuesday March 12, 1918

Have been in Paris long enough to realize it is the wonder city of the world. London and New York are uncouth by comparison. Even the brick and stone yards along the Seine are artistic.

Breakfast in the Crillon. Dinner with Price at the Chatham Grill. Got wire from Commodore to go to front and report from there on what I think better be done. Then he will decide whether he wants me to remain indefinitely or return after a bit to London. Price says his (Bennett's) health bad and he is too sensitive about being seen to have me down to Nice to see him. Commodore also wired me to make arrangements first to go on trip with Secy. War Baker who leaves Paris today for front. Couldn't be arranged. Saw H.C. Caxe, one of C's fool hangers-on. He went with me to 16 Rue St. Ann to get front permit. Drove with Caxe through Champs Elysees, Bois Boulogne etc. past Bennett's house.

Last night's raid worst yet. Many killed by bombs and in subway panics. Paris much more excitable than London. Wrote to Dorothy. Called at office 38 rue du Louvre. Stayed in hotel at night.

Weather ideal.

Don Martin recounted to Dorothy his first air raid in Paris in his letter dated March 12, and more about his impressions of Paris.

Paris, March 12, 1918
Hotel Crillon

Dorothy

I guess your Dad is a hoodoo. Wherever he goes there seems to be an air raid. Last night when I finished the letter to you I started down to post it and the maid was talking like a streak and waving her hands. I thought she was having a fit of some new kind. But I discovered it was merely her French way of telling me that there was an air raid going on. They are not used to them in Paris as they are in London and moreover the people here are very, very excitable, especially on air raid nights. I had heard the "alert" signal given but didn't know what it was. In London it is called "Take cover." Here a siren blows. It is about like the whistle on the Eureka shop. It is attached to a steam engine which rushes about the streets. It was a dark night, but a few stars were shining, and a raid was hardly looked for. However it came and was a very fierce one—by far the worst Paris has known. The figures of persons killed have not been given out but it is said the fatalities were quite numerous.

I heard bombs strike in this vicinity. I went down in the lobby and stayed there from a quarter to ten till a quarter to one o'clock. A lot of most distinguished Frenchmen were sitting around and a good many prominent Americans too. I found a man from Trenton and another person from Iowa whom I knew. The lobby was darkened and the lights in all the rooms were shut off. During a lull in the raid I and two other men started across the Place de la Concorde to see where a bomb was supposed to have fallen but it was so dark we lost our way and returned. This hotel is right in the heart of the very exclusive section of Paris. It is close to the Tuileries Gardens, the Champs Elysees and a lot of other famous and beautiful spots. Paris is rather excited today over last night's performance and right now people are rather expecting another raid tonight. These raids are getting to be terrible things. People are getting very sick of them and I guess when the war is all over and everyone understands everything that has happened the world will know why people grow tired of them. The Germans have no consideration for women or children, hospitals, churches or anything else. They will have to pay dearly for their barbarism some day.

I have spent a good part of the day making arrangements to go to the front. Mr. Bennett wired me to make arrangements to go around France with Mr. Baker, Secretary of War, who is here, but it was too late to make the arrangements. Only the three news associations were allowed to send men. I got a telegram from Bennett to see his lawyer here and to have him make arrangements for me to go to the front. I shall probably get a pass for a month to start with.

Mr. Bennett wants me to go to the front, look it over and tell him what I think ought to be done. I imagine he is trying to make up his mind whether he wants to spend all the money it will cost to keep me at the front right along. You see automobile hire costs about $100 or $150 a week alone and there are other very large items. However, unless an air raid gets me, I shall probably be going far over in France within three or four days—maybe sooner—and you will get a letter from me where the glare of the bombardments may be seen. It is not so terribly far away. The nearest point in the battle line is only 60 miles from Paris but where I shall go is considerably further than that.

Yesterday I believe I told you that Paris is far more beautiful than all the other cities. Tonight I can emphasize that. Take the Rue Rivoli for instance, Dorothy. That runs along the Tuileries Gardens for almost a mile. The buildings are all six stories high, are all the same, and all have marble colonnades in front of them. There are no high buildings. This hotel, for instance, looks like a ruin on the very outside but it is beautiful just the same and inside is as fine as anything in New York. I sent you a postal card giving a picture of it. I took an open taxi this afternoon, it being warm and sunny, and drove out through the Champs Elysees and the Avenue Bois du Boulogne. They are magnificent. Everything seems to have been built and laid out with the aim of pleasing the eye.

For dinner I went to a place called the Chatham Grill and had a splendid dinner—porterhouse steak, fine fried potatoes, endive salad and a lot of fruit all mixed up. The cooks here certainly know how to get things up nicely. There is no sugar or butter though but the French are so clever one doesn't miss them. I have been over pretty much of the city and can get around all right without a guide. I wish I could speak French. Most of the waiters speak English. The chief clerk here today appeared in an officer's uniform. He had been on sick leave for five months and tomorrow starts again for the front. But people are tired of war just the same. I don't blame them. One sees plenty of one-legged men and women in mourning in Paris.

I must stop writing such long letters to you or you will have to stay out of school to read them. I wish I could get a letter or two myself but it will be a long time before I receive one I suppose.

Here's a hug and kiss, From
Dad

Diary: Wednesday March 13, 1918

Have become a regular sightseer. Went around alone this forenoon for a couple hours. Got a pass for a month at the American front. Can get it extended if necessary. Met [Burn] Price [Paris Herald Manager] at the Crillon at 3 and took a taxi ride through the poorer sections down to the Bastille and the quays along the Seine. Bought a captain's hat to go with my correspondent's uniform.

Had dinner with McKerney of Trenton (and his daughter) at Prunier's. Went with them to the Hotel Meurice to have a look and returned to the Crillon. Visited with them till about 11. Then I went down to the lobby for a short time. Was deserted. Came to my room about 11:30 to read and write a letter or two. Got lot of letters forwarded from London. Bennett wired again about working the trip with Baker. It can't be done. Looks now as if I shall go to the front next Monday.

Weather superb. About like June in Washington.

Drawings from Don in
Paris sent to Dorothy
March 1918

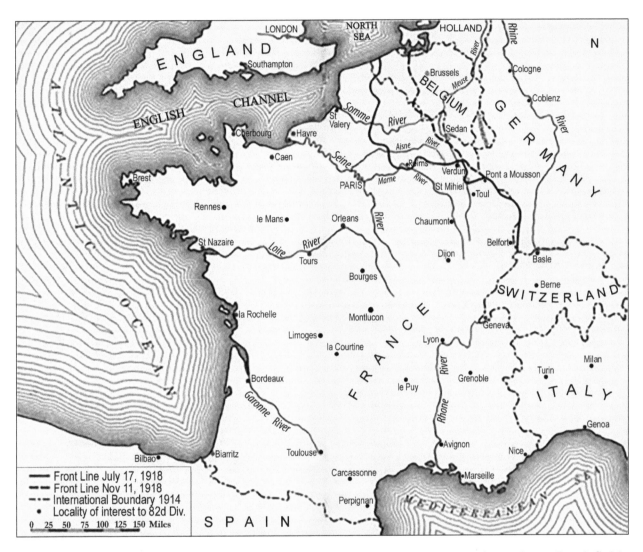

This map, taken from *American Armies and Battlefields in Europe* (American Battlefield Monuments Commission), gives an overview of the Western front in 1918. It shows Southampton and le Havre, where Don Martin has just come through, and Paris. Also indicated, in relation to the front line in July 1918 and November 1918, are Chaumont, site of AEF Headquarters, and Toul, St Mihiel, Verdun and Reims, places that Martin will be reporting from and about.

Diary: Thursday March 14, 1918

Am getting good food here but it costs a fortune. Breakfast in the Crillon costs about $2.50 and dinner slightly more—up to $4 [$47 and $74 August 2020]. Had dinner this evening with Price at the famous Boeuf a la Mode place. It was fine. In London people "feed"; here they feast. Walked around most of the day. Wrote an interview with Kerney. Went to the office in the evening and got Muir to put a letter to Dorothy in French. I sent it to her tonight and I'll bet it will keep her guessing. Met Kloeber of the A.P. on the street; also Pipp of the Detroit News. Walked along the Champs Elysees for an hour.

Spent the evening in the hotel. The streets are dark and I wouldn't want to be caught outside in an air raid. Paris is much more scared over them than London. The streets here are dotted with crippled soldiers and I see thousands of women in mourning. Business goes on though almost as if there was no war. Weather fine. Sunny and mild.

Diary: Friday March 15, 1918

Went to a theater tonight—the Folies Bergere—and saw a pretty good show. N.Y. would never permit the things that go on there.

Price and I went after having dinner at a well known Italian place on a walk all through the Montmartre section which is very picturesque. Went up on the highest hill in Paris and surveyed the city. Earlier in the day I had walked about for a couple of hours. Bought some nice Easter cards and mailed them to Dorothy. Great excitement in the afternoon. Terrific explosion which made everyone think we were having a daylight raid. Powder magazine in St. Denis blew up. The Crillon Hotel shook and windows broken in many parts of the city. See hundreds of American soldiers everywhere in Paris.

Weather splendid.

On March 14, Don Martin sent a letter to Dorothy written in French, to see if she would be able to read it. He explained about this letter to his mother in a letter to her dated March 15. In it he also commented on his limited ability in French, almost—but not quite—admitting regret that he did not as a boy take the opportunity to learn French from his French mother (who taught Dorothy French when she came under her care).

Hotel de Crillon, Paris

Mother

I just wrote a letter to Dorothy which I'll bet will make her laugh. If it takes you as long to read it as it took me to write it your housework will be neglected for a day. You needn't tell Dorothy for a while how I did it. I got one of the men in our office here to compose it for me after I had written in English what I wanted to say. I am very anxious to know how much of it Dorothy could read herself. I wish now I had learned French, although it isn't exactly necessary. Almost everyone here understands a little English and this combined with pocket money and a few words of French enables an American to get along.

I have been delayed getting arrangements made to get to the American front but delay in Paris is a holiday anytime. I have gone all over the city, walking and in a taxi cab and can find my way readily enough now. This hotel is a very beautiful one. It overlooks the Tuileries Gardens, and just beyond them is the Seine. The Louvre is but ten minutes walk and the Palace Royal, the Madeleine, the Royal Opera

House and the Champs Elysees but a stone's throw off. Mr. Bennett engaged a room for me here, and he is no "piker."

The food is the best in Paris. London is like corned beef and cabbage and Paris like a dainty salad. Eating is an art and an institution all over France, but it comes high. To get an ordinary dinner in this hotel costs from $4 to $7 [$74-130 August 2021]. For instance, a confiture on jelly costs 80 cents [$14] an order. Chocolate costs 50 cents [$9] for a small pot. But everything is the very best. The prices are not much higher than normal.

There is nothing to do in the evening. No restaurant can keep open after 9:30 p.m. and the street lamps are all darkened. I come in right after dinner if I eat outside which I usually do, and sit here in the writing room or go to my own room. I have been going to bed before midnight which is quite unusual for me. Then I get up fairly early and walk around anywhere. Paris at this time of year is delightful. The weather is about like our May. The trees are bare yet but the grass is green and some flowers in the parks are beginning to bloom. The streets are crowded and the displays in the hundreds of jewelry and modiste's shops are wonderful. I now see where New York gets its ideas. The people are tired of the war but they cannot quit. I see thousands of women in mourning everywhere. French officers are everywhere and the French soldiers are a fine looking class of men. They look exactly like the pictures you have seen of Napoleon's times. American soldiers are almost as numerous as at home.

Your two letters, one telling about the flood, Marguerite Schumaker, Dorothy's mild terror and her happiness, came yesterday. They were forwarded from London, along with a long typewritten one from Dorothy, and another from the young literary lady. They all made quite a treat for me. Dorothy writes a splendid letter. The one done on the typewriter was just as well written as if a grown up person had done it. She certainly has ability. I am glad she is making such good progress with her music and that her teeth are responding to the treatment.

I am just as careful during air raids as anyone can be. The one here the other night was a very bad one but I stayed in the hotel. The Secretary of War and many other very prominent persons were in the lobby. So if we had been hit, the Germans would have got a somewhat distinguished gathering. We have been looking for another raid tonight but there is no alarm yet (10:30 p.m.) so I guess there will be none. They are the same here as in London. About 60 women and children were killed in a stampede in the subway the other night. They had gone there for safety and a few fell off the platform, whereupon the stampede followed. There is danger to everyone whenever there is a raid but only one in many hundred thousand is killed so there is no need of worrying. It seems as if everyone these days must run some risk.

I am rather counting on going to the American front on Monday, March 18. I don't know how long I shall stay. If living conditions are as bad as some of the correspondents say, I think a few weeks will do me. I have permission—military passes etc—in my pocket now. I shall be close enough to see all the detail of battle but will be either far enough back from the actual firing line, or underground to be entirely safe. No correspondent has ever been hurt, nor even scared so far as I know. Tell Rock I shall make inquiries about Frances Chapman's husband. I already had his address, as accurately as it could be obtained. I shall write to you as soon as I get in the place where I shall be quartered.

By the way will you have Rock send me a list of those ancestral names and addresses? I have them somewhere but don't just know where to place my hands on them, and if they are not to be found, a duplicate list will probably reach me in time.

With love,
Don

A handwritten letter to Dorothy dated March 15 enclosed some Easter cards and told about a children's game.

Hotel de Crillon, Paris

Dorothy,

Here are a few Easter cards which I hope will reach you by Easter. The mails are so slow and uncertain though that they probably won't. Anyhow they will be nice to put in your room. Why not have them all put in one frame?

This is another beautiful day. There was great excitement this afternoon. An explosion, which shook nearly all Paris, made people think there was a daylight air raid. I was in my room at the time and I went down stairs. Everyone else did the same thing. People expect almost anything in these war times and Paris you know is only a few miles from the war zone. I shall go out to dinner in about an hour—it is now half past five—and may go to a theater tonight, providing there is no air raid. These raids upset everything.

I was out on the Champs Elysees this afternoon and saw more than a thousand children playing there. There were both poor and rich. Most of them spin tops and have a sort of whip which they cut or sweep under the top while it is spinning—that keeps it going. It is a very popular sport with the youngsters of Paris.

I am wondering how you made out with the French letter. If I could speak French as well as you can it would be a fine thing for me. I shall probably write to you tomorrow or Sunday.

With love and a kiss,
Dad

Diary: Saturday March 16, 1918

More sightseeing. Walked here + there. Paris is interesting all over. Met Price in the afternoon + wandered around with him. After a nap for an hour I tried a French barber. He half-shaved and half-skinned my face, plastering lather in my mouth, eyes and ears. There are no barbers like those in U.S.

Had dinner with Price in the Chatham Grill, one of the best and most expensive places in Paris.

Had a fine steak + a dozen oysters. London is starving compared to Paris. Went to the office 38 Rue du Louvre for an hour this evening and came back to the hotel in the subway. Am already to start for Gondrecourt Monday morning.

Sent about 20 postals to various people. No question that Paris is the best city of all for beauty of streets, architecture etc.

Weather delightful.

Watercolour depiction of coach leaving the New York Herald business office at 49 Ave de L'Opera, Paris, on July 12, 1892. The trip was partly funded by Herald owner J G Bennett who is one of the two men depicted behind the driver. (Titled *Paris-Trouville In 13 Stages – The Departure At The New York Herald Av. de L'opera, Paris,* by Manuel Luque.) The Herald also had another office at 38 Rue du Louvre.

Letter from Dorothy (No.13)

Dated March 16, 1918, postmarked Mar 16, 11AM; no 'received' notation; c/o New York Herald Bureau, 38 Rue Du Louvre, Paris

Silver Creek, N.Y.
March 16, 1918

Dear Dad

Here goes for letter No. 13. You will notice that I am writing on a different kind of paper to-day. The other day I was looking for something in the long closet and I ran across my black traveling bag, in which I found this paper, so I thought I would use it. The morning paper just got here (It is 8:26 now) and it said to stop sending things to the boys "over there", so <u>maybe</u> we can't send things to you, but I guess we can. I have my Indian suit on this morning, just for instance. I

Dorothy, age 11

will have to wear it to school this or rather <u>next</u> week, sometime, as I am in an Indian Dance down at school.

In school for lots of our work, we use slates now instead of scrap paper – it saves a lot of paper and we like it too.

Now about that letter business, I am going to start now and keep an account of when I get all your letters, because Grand-

126

mother and I are both mixed up in when we get them. Well, now let's say – I know I got the cablegram from you Monday. The Cablegram said – Starting France address Paris office – then – Love You – then there was a word that looked like fung but Uncle Rock found out that it was supposed to be funny, but what would that mean – Love you funny?

Martin. Huh? When you write to me after you get this letter, please 'splain, will you? And say – would your address in Paris be c/o New York Herald Bureau, Paris, France etc? You said Paris office, so I thought it would be the same as it was in London, only in Paris. Then the only difference would be that the Paris office is in Paris and the London office is in London. Now can yuh figger' out what I'm trying to tell yuh? Huh – or I mean 'uh? Ha (Ha) Then last Saturday (March 9) your letter dated Feb 20 came. I would have told you about it in last Saturday's letter but it did not come until after I had mailed my letter. Then I got 4 cards from you last or rather this (I'm always getting the weeks mixed up) week, all of which were dated Feb 13th. I got two of them Monday, the 11th, the day I got the Cablegram, and I guess I got the other two either Saturday or Tuesday. I am not sure.

We went to Buffalo again yesterday, and I took my music lesson, and Joseph his theory lesson. I also went to the dentists and he just tightened up the braces and compared my teeth with the way they were at first. He is spreading my jaw quite a bit.

We hope the candy we have been sending has reached you, and if it has, we hope you like it. Aunt Alta sent you a box yesterday. I almost forgot to ask you if you have maple sugar and cigarettes there – do you? Or don't you smoke cigarettes at all anymore? Do you like maple sugar? Ummmmmm – I do! If you do, I will send you some. Trees have been tapped in the last two or three weeks, and the weather is getting pretty spring like. To-day it is so windy that one can't hardly stand up. If it was just a little warmer, it would be the kind of day I love. The last few days it has been real sunshiny and nice. The first night that it got warmer the creek came way over in front of the schoolhouse – but it went back again – leaving ice and logs + lots of brush. But the water out of the faucets is black! We have to use pump water for everything!

I am knitting squares for soldiers or Belgian Blankets now, but I am going to learn to knit something else – but you can guess a while on that. Ha! Ha!

I told John Knox that you would write to him soon and that you were in France, etc. He sure done do make me laugh. Ha! Ha! He also said that you told him that you have wanted a good pipe for a long time, so he said he had just received a dandy, and he was going to send it to you. Hope you get it.

Yes – Aunt Josephine and Uncle Lee did get their postal you sent them and Mrs. Brooks her spoon and Mrs. Fairchild her card and – ok – everybody you sent something to got something – I

128

guess. I am sending something that was in the *Morning Express* about Silver Creek. We know about it. Well I must close now and mail this letter.

Lots of Love an' hugs an' kisses,
Dorothy

I call myself Mischievous, Giggling Dot. And my chum – Jean Fox – has the same as my first two. Ha! Ha!

P.S. We are all well and hope you are too.

Diary: Sunday March 17, 1918

Began the day with a walk on the Champs Elysees and the Bois du Boulogne with Price. Maybe in normal times it outshines N.Y. but now it is no more attractive than 5th Ave. or Riverside Drive. I came back to the hotel, wrote a 2 col story on Paris in wartime; sent a cable to Dorothy and packed up ready for a trip to the American front—Gondrecourt—tomorrow morning. Start at 8, so must get my baggage checked tonight. Looks now as if I am after all to see the actual war front. Understand the living conditions are very bad but if I get a clean place to sleep I shall be all right.

Had dinner with Price and then came to the hotel to write some letters and to get my baggage to the station.

Weather good.

Letter to Dorothy the evening of March 17 telling her about his preparations to leave Paris the next morning.

Hotel de Crillon, Paris
Sunday night, March 17, 1918

Dorothy

Packing up a "hold all" and stuffing other things in a suitcase to be left behind, and making sure that everything is all right is quite a job. I have been fussing around about half the afternoon and evening and now I am about ready to start.

I went to the station with my typewriter and the hold-all and left them—checked them as we say at home—and now I shall get up at 6 a.m. to get an eight o'clock train. I must allow an hour at the station to get my ticket, get my baggage and make the crazy Frenchmen at the station understand what I mean. I may miss the train anyhow; then I shall have to wait a day. Travelling is a hard job now. Passports have to be fixed up everywhere and the suspicion is that everyone is a spy or something of that sort. I shall get to a small place called Gondrecourt at one in the afternoon and will then take an automobile to some other place where I shall make my headquarters. If you want to reach me you can do so through the Paris office. One can't send addresses in the war zone through the mails but the office will always know where I am. Your letters will be forwarded from either Paris or London. It may be that I will be back in Paris or perhaps on my way to London again by the time this reaches you. If I find that there is nothing to be seen at the front, and no place to sleep but in some old shack, I probably will not stay more than a month. However, I can't tell about that. You will hear from me frequently.

I have enjoyed my stay here. I think I have seen Paris pretty well and can find my way around very easily. I bought a half dozen funny little soldier handkerchiefs for you Dorothy but I can't send them through the mail as there is a duty on them. I have put them in my suitcase and some day you shall have them. The shops here are just packed with pretty things but there is no use buying them because there is no way to get them back. I guess I'll save money—maybe—huh? Today I walked around quite a bit and had a fine dinner. The restaurants here certainly know to get up nice things to eat, but then they have been noted for that for 200 years.

How is your school coming on young lady? Your letters indicate that you are getting along pretty fast. I guess you have been deluged with letters and postal cards from me. You'll have to get a warehouse to keep them in.

There hasn't been an air raid since Monday night. Maybe the Germans are getting enough of them now that the French and British have been bombing their towns. There doesn't seem to be any chivalry in war since Germany ran amuck. It is just barbarism.

I shall go to bed now Dorothy to get 5 or 6 hours sleep in preparation for a long day tomorrow.

With love and a kiss,

Dad

Letter from Rose Martin

Dated March 17, 1918; postmarked Mar 18, 5PM, c/o New York Herald Bureau, Paris, France

March 17th

Dear Don,

Dorothy wrote yesterday, and I guess the rest of the family have all written. So, I guess I had better get busy and write too. I shall not attempt to tell just when I received your last letter, but it must be three weeks ago. Hereafter I shall make a note of it. Then I will know exactly without guessing. We got your Cable March 11 telling us you were leaving for France. It was a surprise, but I knew you would like it, so I was pleased, and now I should be anxious to hear from you, from there. I notice they have air raids there too. So, you be careful of yourself. Hope you are living in a safe place, just like in London. Did Mr. Bennett want you to go there? He may take quite a notion to you (I hope so).

We are having a very cold raw March, lots of wind. I have just got over a horrid cold in my head. Julie is getting over a sore throat cold. Joseph has had a cold for a month past. But Dorothy is as strong as a pine knot. She stays perfectly well, no cold, nor anything else. Every Saturday she writes you a letter. Then she plays every day after school outdoors. She practices real good, and is improving in her playing. The proofs of her pictures we were going to have taken are not good, so we will have to try again. Too bad, as I wanted you to have them about now.

She thinks a lot about that Shakespeare pin, and I do too. And I think a whole lot of my little Ann Hathaway spoon. I wish I could send you something too. We have been sending candy, hope you have received some of it. But if there is something that I could send that you would like, I would be glad to do it. Let me know.

Shall be glad when the war ends and you get back on this side again. I wish there was a Napoleon—or a Joan of Arc—for France. Perhaps they would win quick but they (the Allies) must win, without fail. They must, sure.

John Knox was here after he saw Dan Reed and told us all about everything he knew. It was very interesting. He is very nice, and he brought the letter that you gave Dan to bring us. I cut out Dan's speech and Julie said she would send it to you. It's very good too. There was a long article in the Herald, March 14th. It was about Admiral Sims. It was signed "By Don Martin," Special to the New York Herald. It looked nice. But how can I find your articles from Paris. I will first have to guess, that's all. Alta just came in from Buffalo unexpected. She went over to Roscoe's, so I will finish this off here.

Good bye and lots of love.
Mother

P.S. Monday 18th AM. We have just received your letter mailed London, February 24th. It was a very good and nice letter.

Thus ended Don's first one-week stay in Paris. He would return numerous times for brief periods in the next months.

131

PART 4

Closer to the Front Line
— Neufchateau, March to June 1918

Two-and-a half months into his assignment in Europe, Don Martin was to witness — and report on — the war, still from a distance.

Diary: Monday March 18, 1918

(Arrived in Neufchateau)

Some day! Left Paris at 8 this morning after exciting trip, or vexatious trip to station. The French are artistic but for providing conveniences they are antiquated. Rode on train 6 hours to get here. Had good meals on train and was met in Gondrecourt in government auto, which brought me here—about 20 miles. Am spending the night at Neufchateau, the American base headquarters. Have room in funny little hotel.

Am on the very edge of the war zone. Met Martin Green, Draper, Gibbons, Orr, Forrest, Johnson, Ferguson and other correspondents. Had dinner with some of them at the officers' club and spent the evening later there. Put on my uniform for the 1st time. Breeches are too tight. Neufchateau a picturesque place. War corresponding not what it once was. Censor is so strict it is almost impossible to send anything. To get the news one must cover about 200 miles a day in an auto. Is a big job. I got a gas mask and steel helmet tonight for trip to front tomorrow. Am writing this by candlelight.

Weather pleasant.

Martin was headquartered from March to June with the fifteen accredited correspondents*
in the town of Neufchateau, a middle-sized town 200 miles (321km) east from Paris and
south of the war front. During this period, he began to send daily dispatches from the war
areas which were featured in The New York Herald and in syndicated newspapers across
America. These began to establish Don Martin as a leading U.S. war correspondent.

Diary: Tuesday, March 19, 1918

Got up at 6 a.m. Started at 7 with Kloeber and
Orr for Luneville, headquarters of the Rainbow
Division. Had breakfast at Nancy. This town
has been bombed terribly. Most of the people
have moved away. Ride was very cold. Waited
three hours at Luneville for [Secretary of War,
Newton] Baker. Saw him in a hospital where
he was seeing American wounded men. Got
story of his experiences in the trenches from
Major [Frederick] Palmer**, but I also got a short
talk with him which I have cabled to N.Y. and
wired to Paris. I can see the censor is going to be
the troublemaker.

Returned to Nancy where we had luncheon and
then came back to Neufchateau which is the
headquarters. Had dinner at the Officers Club.
Met quite a few people I know. Town filled with
Americans. French getting as much money as
possible out of them.

Weather cool. Shower in afternoon.

Diary: Wednesday March 20, 1918

(Saw first shell fire)

Got my first view of shell fire. While I was in
village of Domjiron with Junius Wood of Chicago
News, Germans opened fire
on town—gas and shrapnel.
While Wood and I were having
dinner with Capt. Hammond,
shells were falling continually
about 300 yards away, around

Junius Wood

American batteries. Finally shells began to fall in
village and all around. Everyone hurried out and
stood in fields and along road for 2 hours while
Germans dropped 1,000 shells and big French
guns blazed away in return. Was very thrilling.
Americans never left their batteries. Four men
hurt. No one killed. Was my first glimpse of real
war. Wood and I returned by way of Luneville
and Toul. Got back at 10:30 p.m.

Shells made sound like a buzz saw or zither
string breaking. No chance of dodging them.
Can't see them of course. They do comparatively
small damage.

Weather wet and cold.

Diary: Thursday March 21, 1918

Didn't get out of Neufchateau today. Decided to
get a bit of rest. Went around with Wood; visited
a veterinary hospital with him and Bazin of the
Philadelphia Ledger; had luncheon at the club
and wrote a long letter to Dorothy.

Spent a short time at the club and went to bed
at 11 p.m. Kloeber and Orr went to Paris. Had
quite a visit with Henry P. Davison of N.Y., head
of the Red Cross.

Weather cool.

* Source: Chris Dubbs, 'American Journalists in the Great War', p210
** Major Fredrick Palmer, Director AEF Press

Don Martin wrote to Dorothy on March 21, 1918, from Neufchateau.

 Dorothy

Well your Dad has seen a realization of a good many of the war pictures we have all seen in the last three or four years. I have ridden probably 400 miles in automobiles since I arrived here Monday afternoon [March 18] and shall ride many hundreds miles more in the next few days. I don't know whether I shall stay or not. I am not sure that I want to stay. It is no easy job by any means. To get to the various points where information must come from it is necessary to keep on the go from early in the morning till evening and then to do such writing as is required after that. It is not $$$$$$$$$$$$ (there are some of the dollar marks you make once in a while Dorothy) allowable for me to mention the name of the place where I am staying nor where I have been but I can tell you that I am not a great way from the German border and am where war is very close at hand.

I have seen hundreds—I might say thousands—of farm houses and barns which have been burned down or torn to pieces by shell fire; I have passed thousands of soldiers' graves alongside the roadways and in the fields nearby (They are graves of soldiers who were buried where they died.) I have seen many towns which have been practically ruined by bombs dropped from airplanes; miles and miles of supply wagons and ammunition trains; soldiers on sentry duty, on the march, at mess, in camps and in hospitals. For the short time I have been in France I have done pretty well.

Yesterday I got rather closer to the war than I intended to get and I think it is quite true that I was a bit worried for a time. So was everyone else and they all had a perfect right to be worried. I went with a Chicago News reporter—an old friend of mine—to a head-quarters nearest to the German line. It is a town about as large as Forestville but, as you perhaps know, the towns here are nothing like ours. Here there is one street and the houses are all built of stone or brick and are one solid line. The barn and the sitting room front directly on the street and are side by side. Perhaps there are four or five cross streets with a couple of houses on each but the main street is the village.

Well I arrived at this town at noon and was the guest of the commanding officer, an American. From the back window of the second floor of his headquarters, which was an ordinary stone farmhouse, we could see shells from the German guns breaking about 300 yards away. It was as if you should stand on the roof of our house and see shells break just across the creek. They kept getting closer but we ate dinner and paid no attention to the bombardment. The shells make a great noise when they explode and send up a splash of dirt about 30 feet in the air. The German guns were presumably four or five miles away but had the range of our position and were trying to destroy some of our batteries.

Just after we had finished dinner and were starting out to see the batteries in action, word came that shells were falling in the village and we postponed the trip. Then for two hours and a half there was great excitement. More than a thousand shells fell in and around the village. Several buildings were shattered. I walked up the street with most of the other people—all soldiers—in the village and stood there in a light rain while the shells fell and exploded and a great battery of French big guns fired back. It was the first artillery duel I had ever seen and I was seeing it from very close range indeed. I was, we will say, about by our house and shells were falling about where Barbeau's is. We could hear the shells sing or whistle or buzz or whatever it is but before that we could see the big splash of earth where it struck. Then, a few seconds later, we would hear the sound of the shell explosion. All the time there would be the roar of our own guns and the distant rumble of the guns in the German line. I had a steel helmet on and a gas mask about my neck ready to adjust if word came that gas was being swept toward us. Many gas shells were used during the bombardment but the air was still and the gas just remained where the shells exploded.

I of course saw only a little incident in the war but it gave me an idea of how terrible a thing it all is. The Americans are fearless and the French are wonderful. They don't know what fear is either. While the fighting or shooting was going on, two army ambulances—not Red Cross ambulances—went right through the street that was being shelled. Any second a shell might have killed horses, men and all but the drivers and the stretcher bearers don't think anything of this. Also, while shells were bursting on both sides of a road which lay about a quarter of a mile from where I stood, a motorcyclist on an important errand shot right along indifferent to the dangers. He got through all right although shells struck every few seconds somewhere along the road.

Such things as this are going on all the time almost everywhere. The Chicago man and I were on the point of staying to see a possible night barrage at the same point but we had been away so long that we returned. We were about 70 miles from where we are staying so we did not get back till after ten o'clock. The government provides automobiles and drivers for the newspapermen but we have to pay $10 a day a piece.

Eating is very good here. At the officers' mess yesterday I had good butter—the first I have had in a long time—eggs, meat, marmalade, white bread, coffee and cheese. Here where I am I have good food also. I eat in an officers' club. It is reasonably expensive but good. The French people here mostly wear wooden shoes and the children dress in queer clothes. They are fine looking children though. The country itself is very beautiful. It is spring now. The day I arrived here it was warm. Yesterday it was rainy. Today it is sunshiny but cool. It will probably remain cool for two or three weeks but in two weeks everything will be green and flowering.

There are thousands of Americans around here. Nearly all the Americans can say a few things in French but the French cannot yet talk much American. The particular aim of the French seems to be to get as much money as possible out of the Americans and give them as little as possible for it.

I shall write to you again after a few days Dorothy, and meantime I will take no chances on getting hit by a shell. I expect I shall see some very interesting points in the line in the next week or ten days and probably will know more about war than I thought I ever would. Maybe after a while I'll be able to write you a letter in French again.

I have an idea that I'm somewhere near the very region where Grandmother's people came from. Here's a kiss for you young lady and love for all the family.

Dad

Diary: Friday March 22, 1918

Had an interesting trip with Bazin of the Philadelphia Ledger. Went to Azincourt, close to the line. Heard much cannonading. Talked, through Bazin, with interesting old French lady who refuses to leave her native village although it is close to the danger line. Also saw the Salvation Army at work close to the line. On way back stopped at Toul; saw the city pretty well; sent a postal to Dorothy and spent a half hour in the old Cathedral.

Got back to Neufchateau at 5 and wrote an interview with Henry P. Davison, head of the Red Cross. Finished the day at the club with Floyd Gibbons of the Chicago Tribune.

We get reports of beginning of big German offensive at Cambrai.

Weather delightful.

Diary: Saturday March 23, 1918

(Great German offensive begins)

Spent most of the day writing mail stories. Wrote a 2½ column story of my experience during shelling of Domjiron, and column story about the old lady of Azincourt. Had photographs taken of myself in my uniform to send to Dorothy. Went to post office to get mail but found none. Walked around Neufchateau quite a bit. Had dinner at club with Bryan + some other correspondents.

Big offensive on in earnest at Cambrai against the British. Air raid on Paris during entire day.

Weather very fine.

March 1918 – France
Correspondent N.Y. Herald

Letter from Dorothy (No.14)

Addressed c/o New York Herald Bureau, 38 Rue Du Louvre, Paris, France

Silver Creek, N.Y.
Mch 23, 1918

Dear Dad

Here goes for letter No. 14. It is not going to be a very long one, because yesterday I had an "air raid" in my stomach. But I am much better to-day, and by to-morrow, I will probably be all right.

We all went to Buffalo in the "Lizzie Limousine" yesterday, but all I did was to sleep in the auto and at the Y.W.C.A. I didn't eat a thing all day, until we got home, then I ate a little. Then I went to bed, and slept good all night, and ate a big breakfast this morning. Yesterday when we first got in Buffalo, Grandmother bought me a pair of shoes at Eastwoods. They have white tops, black bottoms – or whatever you call them – and they tie. They were five dollars. In last Saturday's letter, I told you I was enclosing something about the burgulars here, but I forgot to put it in my letter, so I will put it in to-day.

Anna Kelling is here sewing for Grandmother and Mr. Casbeam is out cleaning up the yard.

I wear my straw hat nearly all the time now, as you see it is Spring, and the weather has been spring weather too. The thermometer has been up to 66. Next Friday when we go to Buffalo, I am going to get an "Easter Bonnet".

Your cablegram, saying Going American Front Monday. Dad's love — arrived here Tuesday, Mch 19. Even if you aren't here with me all the time, I can be prouder than any of the girls if I want to — prouder than Jean Fox, even if her father is Deputy Sheriff, yes — even prouder than Iola Dickinson, even if her father was elected President of the village the other day, because none o' em have the chance to go out right on the front, where they fight, unless they fight too.

None of the women were elected for anything, but everybody says that the women defeated the women. Mrs. Bert Kofoed and Mrs. William Fuller were the ones that were nominated. Every one that was elected was a Republican. I'm glad of that.

In your letters you say you have received my letters — 5 and 6 — but have you received letters 1-2-3 and 4? Aunt Julie called me up a little while ago, saying that Joseph had received a nice letter from you. She said the letter said that you were going to write a letter to me in a few days — and — sure enough — one came this morning. They must have come on the same ship as Joseph got his this morning too. His was written Feb. 28 and mine the 4th of Mch., and they both got here on the 23rd of Mch. — to-day.

I told you about two weeks ago that I had my picture taken, but we got the proofs, and they're all very punk. So, we are going to wait another week or so, and have them taken either in Dunkirk or Buffalo.

I get an allowance of 25 cents every Saturday now. I bought a new pair of roller-skates the other day, and Joseph bought a new pair yesterday. He can skate pretty well now.

On my last Saturday's letter, I only put a three cent stamp, so it will probably not reach you, because Grandmother wrote a few days after, and Uncle Rock mailed it and found out a five cent stamp is needed for it to go to Paris. Uncle Rock also wrote you a letter, and sent you some maple sugar. We sent all three letters to – c/o New York Herald Bureau, so you may not get them, but we hope you do. We are glad you are going to the American front to "see the sights", and we are also glad to know that you are in hardly any danger as you said in my letter. But you better look out.

I better close now, and mail this letter. I said this was going to be a _short_ letter. Some short letter!

Lots o' love an' hugs an' kisses,
Dorothy

P.S. Do they talk funny in France? I mean in speaking the "Yankee" language. Parley vous Francais? Oui! Oui!
P.P.S.S. I better hurry up with my French or you'll beat me at it.

Diary: Sunday March 24, 1918

(Palm Sunday)

Hung around Neufchateau all day. Great excitement over report from Paris that Germans had bombarded the city with a gun from nearest point in Germany, 75 miles away. Frenchmen around the Lafayette Club much exercised. Went for walk about Neufchateau. Had dinner at the club with Floyd Gibbons of Chicago Tribune. Beat him half dozen games checkers. He was determined to go to Paris to get his wife out of the city. I almost went with him but concluded it would be unwise. Went to bed about midnight. No letters from home.

German offensive, talked about so long, has started in vicinity of Cambrai. Pessimistic reports tonight.

Weather excellent.

The massive German offensive, begun on March 21, against the French and British lines had initial success. Between March 21 and March 26, the British Expeditionary Forces suffered around 75,000 casualties.*

Diary: Monday March 25, 1918

Was awakened long before daylight by thundering of motor trucks past the hotel—the Agriculture. Reinforcement of French on way to help out British who are falling back under terrific assault of Germans. Left at 10 a.m. with Henry Wales of International News for Toul. Went close to the line. Heard firing nearby and also cannonading at Verdun where new German attack is to be made. Went to various headquarters near line, read communiqués from Berlin saying Germans winning great victory. Local developments subordinated to great offensive which is apparently the great feature of the war. Great gloom among Americans and French. On all the roads guns and men being rushed north. Looks like the vital stage of the war. Returned to Neufchateau at 6 p.m.

Weather ideal but cool late in the day.

Diary: Tuesday March 26, 1918

Everyone in Neufchateau waiting, almost breathless, to hear from front where Germans attacking. Solid line of trucks loaded with supplies—airplanes, machine guns, etc.—passing through Neufchateau all day. 1200 trucks thundered by between 8 a.m. and 3 p.m. Now at 6 p.m., great guns, hundreds in number, going through on motor trucks. Americans marveling at capacity and organization of French and deploring American inability to help out the Allies in this vital crisis of the war.

People gobbling up papers to get latest news. French confident they will be able to repel advance of the Boche. U.S. a rather pitiable spectacle, hanging around here where nothing is going on. My own opinion is the war will be won or lost in coming 6 days and I believe the French and British will turn the Germans back and make victory in another year assured.

Weather very cold and snappy. Slight snow flurries.

* Source: Peter Hart, The Great War, p.425

Diary: Wednesday March 27, 1918

Went around to the Toul front with [Edwin L.] James, the noisy young man from the Times who has just arrived.

Edwin James

[This young man was Don Martin's auto partner on many coming day trips to the front. Edwin James joined the New York Times in 1915 and become Managing Editor from 1932 to his death in 1951.]

Nothing going on. Am more and more convinced this whole outfit, with exception of some of the special men, are merely police reporters. James is as blasé as if he has been a war correspondent all his life. Riding was very cold. Got back at 7 and had dinner at the Club.

Interest here and everywhere centers in the big offensive against the British. Germans still advancing. Is a terrible thing. I believe they will be stopped though. Whole war hanging in balance now and Americans are getting into safe sectors while French going North to save Paris!

I passed over 2000 motor trucks today with French reinforcements. No letters from home yet.

Weather clear and pleasant but very cold.

Diary: Thursday March 28, 1918

Wrote a long letter to Mr. Bennett telling him the only way for the Herald to get real news from the front is for it to have its correspondent accredited. Am anxious to know what his reply will be. I don't care to stay here unless I have opportunities to visit the front every day. As a matter of fact the job of covering the war is a police reporters job anyhow, and most of the correspondents are of the police reporters class.

Interest centers yet in the big German drive. Reports are rather disquieting but I feel confident the French and British will turn the tables on the Germans within a day or two. Americans are having no part in this biggest of all battles.

Got a lot of mail, including letter from Dorothy.

Weather cool.

Don Martin's letter to James Gordon Bennett dated March 29, 1918, gives an interesting look into how the American war correspondents operated, and about his unique situation as a 'visiting correspondent'. He clearly wants to get into the major league.

 Dear Sir,

I have visited all the points where Americans are in the line and have been able to get material for several mail stories, which I have written, and for a few articles which I telegraphed to the European edition. Because of the activity elsewhere things have been quiet here but developments along our sector suggest that it may soon furnish important and interesting news.

Had I the facilities for getting around that the other correspondents have I feel confident I could get some good beats and could also get material for first class special articles. I could then go to the trenches or to any point on the line wherever I might wish and could get out with the men at the front

141

in such a way as to keep me in intimate touch with the situation. As a visiting correspondent I can get out from time to time and no doubt can continue to get some good stuff but so long as I am not accredited I am at a decided disadvantage and when the big developments come, cannot be assured of being in on the ground floor. There is no one place from which the news of Americans is distributed. It has to be gathered at the division headquarters, of which there are three now, and only those correspondents who have daily use of the automobiles, as the accredited men do, can visit the headquarters. Frequently it happens that a good piece of news breaks which I might get exclusively for Paris and perhaps New York as well, but as I am a visiting correspondent, I get it only when it comes here for general distribution. Occasionally the Chicago Tribune man, who goes around daily to the fronts, gets good items a day before a visiting man can possibly have them.

The Tribune, Sun, World and Times have accredited men here. The Times man arrived two days ago. He says he has orders to beat the Herald and World and, if necessary to do so, to cable at the highest commercial rate. From what I have seen of him, and know of him, he will not set the world afire. Besides these accredited men there are accredited correspondents for the Associated Press, the United Press, the International News, the Scripps McCrea outfit, the Chicago Tribune, Chicago News, Philadelphia Evening Ledger, Philadelphia Public Ledger, Boston Globe, Saturday Evening Post, the Newspaper Syndicate and the Evening Sun. I know most of the men personally and can ride about with them as their guest but it is not satisfactory and I know the Herald will not obligate itself to any newspaper. I am the only unaccredited correspondent here.

I am explaining all this to you so you may have a full understanding of the exact situation at the front. The government provides automobiles for the accredited men. Now and then when special visitors come a party is made up and all are sent out to such points as they wish to visit. If I were accredited—were placed on the same basis as the others—I should visit the various fronts every day; would live with the men at the front, would go into the trenches, all of which may be done with perfect safety, and would get some corking good stories. Many of the correspondents here are police reporters, sent by the associations and many good stories slip right by them.

So far, on the few occasions when I felt I had stories worth cabling to New York, I suggested to the Editor in charge in Paris that he relay the dispatch. This system might prove unsatisfactory if a big story came up, as one no doubt will. I am told that a story cabled direct to New York will reach there in from ten to twenty hours ordinarily, while one relayed through Paris frequently does not get through for 36 or 40 hours. The other correspondents have cards issued in Paris, giving them authority to send cables. Without them one cannot cable unless he pays for the dispatch himself. When the cable company in Paris issues a permit a correspondent's name is placed in a book here and after that he can cable whenever he wishes. Unless his name is in the book the Frenchman will accept nothing. However, as you wired, I shall send matter to Paris and will tell the Editor there to relay when I believe the story is worth while.

I have looked the situation over thoroughly and have given you my best views concerning it. I think that, during the next few weeks and certainly during the next few months, this sector, which is being steadily lengthened, will be productive of big news and I believe that if I am placed on an equal footing with the other men here, I can hold my own, and very probably considerably more, with anyone else.

Most respectfully,
Don Martin

Diary: Friday March 29, 1918

James and I went in auto almost to Verdun. Went to American head-quarters in the Verdun sector. Were in danger zone for couple hours but no shells fell. Picked up Bazin and brought him back by way of Bar le Duc and Gondrecourt. Got no news. Had no lunch but a big dinner at the officers' club in Neufchateau.

Indications are that German advance has been checked but situation is still critical.

Weather miserable—rainy + cold.

Diary: Saturday March 30 1918

Went to Chaumont and saw Baker, Secretary of War, and General Pershing. Had quite a talk with Pershing, but he wouldn't release it for publication. Hung around Chaumont for 4 hours with Junius Wood and James. Baker seems a weak person to be head of our war department. Doesn't know what is going on. Pershing is a "line one". He apparently knows situation on the front is serious. Says the 1st division of our army will start for the real front on Wednesday. I wired Mr. Bennett to make request for me to go with it.

The more I see here the more I realize how infinitesimal our part in the war is and how different the present story might be if Wilson had gone into the war, as he should have done, when the Lusitania sank. All our soldiers in France wouldn't last an hour in the furnace north and east of Paris. Meantime Germans are starting new attack.

Weather rainy and cold.

Letter to Dorothy on March 30 from Neufchateau, giving a report on what he was experiencing since the German offensive got under way.

Dorothy,

I'm not writing as frequently as I did. There are two reasons: I am frequently off in queer little places where it is impossible to write and here in the town where I am staying most of the time—it is near Alsace—the room is so cold and the light so poor (as it is now, by the way) that it is not easy to write.

Since your Dad left Paris he has been where there is a distinct war atmosphere. For instance right now, with the rain falling heavily, a steady stream of ponderous motor trucks is passing through here, right in front of the hotel. It seems as if everything is on the move, since the biggest battle of all started a week ago.

The autos you wrote about are nothing compared with what I have seen on the road and going through here—tens of thousands of them. As soon as things quiet down and the weather gets warm enough to throw a little of its glow into my room I shall write you a long letter on my typewriter. I have seen a good deal of France in a couple of weeks. I ride from 100 to 200 miles a day in an automobile. Today I was at General Pershing's Headquarters, which is a long way from the battlefront. I had quite a talk with him. I also saw Secretary Baker at a chateau nearby. Yesterday I was up at Verdun, of which you have read. I wasn't where the shells were falling but could hear the bombarding which goes on incessantly. I have passed through dozens of towns which have been battered to pieces and have seen a little of everything, including a peep into the trenches. I guess I will have quite a bit to tell you when I get back.

Just now everyone is worried over the German attack. I don't think it can be successful but there is just a chance that it will be. If it fails the world will have to tip its hat to the French again. We—the Americans—do not count and the British seem to lack the genius and valor we all thought they still had. Still no one but the men actually in charge of operations know what is being done so maybe the Germans will be licked good as they ought to be.

It took me two hours to read my mail yesterday. There was one letter from you, two (and a duplicate of a previous one) from Rock; one from Mother and two from Alta. I hadn't received any in a long time so they were very welcome. I shall answer them when I get my typewriter going. I hear, Dorothy, you are a splendid music scholar. I am very glad of it. I want you to play well, and I hope you will be able to speak French too. I am getting so I can get along pretty well at it.

I don't know how long I shall stay here. I may go up to the big battle but again I may not. It is very difficult to get authorization. A hundred want it and only 6 can go. I fear I shall not be one of the lucky ones. I shall write again in a few days anyhow.

With love and a kiss

Dad

Diary: Sunday March 31, 1918 Easter

Easter and nothing but suggestions of war everywhere. American troops moving through Neufchateau in the rain and mud all day and most of the night. They are relieving the French in quiet sectors so the French can go up to help in the big fight. Indications are that the French have checked the advance of the Germans but the situation is still serious. It is all up to the French again. The British didn't last. Gen. [Ferdinand] Foch, Frenchman, made commander in chief.

I stayed in Neufchateau all day. Wrote some mail stuff—also letter to Dorothy. Sat around the club till 11 with Floyd Gibbons and some Hearst men.

Weather rainy except for two hours of sunshine.

Diary: Monday April 1, 1918

Went to Menil la Tour and Ansauville with James. Visited several interesting spots en route and passed miles and miles of Americans, some moving from the big battle front and some to relieve others. Was within couple miles of the front, but saw no excitement as action temporarily is all on the big front. Information is a bit more encouraging.

Got back to Neufchateau at 5:30. Wrote two stories for Paris and N.Y. Got letter from Dorothy. Says one of her wisdom teeth has been pulled but she says not a word whether it hurt. Had dinner with Junius Wood, George Pattullo, Lincoln Eyre and Sam Johnson.

Weather miserable—rainy but not cold.

Source: National Archives photo no. 111-SC-11339, Neufchateau, April 25, 1918

The Allied expeditionary Force Press Office at Neufchateau provided automobiles each day to take the correspondents to where they wanted to go. This photo, taken on April 25, 1918, shows the lineup of autos in Neufchateau, with correspondents already in the first three cars ready to leave press headquarters for the front.

Diary: Tuesday April 2, 1918

Stayed around Neufchateau to do some little things. Attended to my income tax affidavit; wrote to McEwen, the Herald cashier, enclosing affidavit; and sent a couple more stories to Paris. Also wired the Commodore that I must be accredited.

Had dinner at the club and sat around there and read till 11 p.m.

Fighting around near British front stopped temporarily. Looks as if both sides are preparing for a new and bigger battle.

Weather rainy all day. Mud terrible.

Diary: Wednesday April 3, 1918

Went with James to Menil la Tour to see the 26th Division which has come there to replace the 1st. Watched an observation balloon crew operate. Went to Boucq where General [Clarence Ransom] Edwards [Commander, 26th Division] is quartered in a chateau about 800 years old. Gave a French interpreter named Maillot a ride back. Stopped for an hour on way back in a prison camp. Went all through it. Talked with prisoners who have been astonished at passing miles and miles of Americans. "Who will win the war?" I asked a young prisoner. "I am a German," he said.

Cabled couple stories to N.Y. and couple to Paris also to be relayed. Got no reply from Bennett regarding getting accredited. In evening at club sat for several hours with Ray Carroll, Floyd Gibbons, Jeremy Cobb, Martin Green* and several officers.

Armies quiet in Picardy.

Weather pleasant—1st one in some time.

Diary: Thursday April 4, 1918

Spent a very dull, rainy day in Neufchateau. Interest of all correspondents now centered on the First Division which is soon to leave for the Arras section to get in the big fight. Wrote some letters and hung around the club. Would write some mail stuff but my room is too cold and the light too poor. Am waiting to hear from Bennett before making a fight to be one of the few who will go with the 1st Division.

Had a slight touch of indigestion during the night but am all right now.

Weather miserable.

The New York Herald began to include the following notice in the newspaper at this time:

> "Don Martin is cabling fine despatches to the HERALD daily from the American front in France. Read them to-day—and every day."

Diary: Friday April 5, 1918

Went to Toul and Nancy with James. Looked around both towns quite a bit, particularly Nancy which is very beautiful and terribly battered from the Hun air raids.

Correspondents told that the 3 Association men may go with the First Division headquarters and that the other men may be accredited to the various regiments—must, in fact, be like staff officers subject to same rules as other officers. This sounds all right to me except I don't like idea of being limited to one regiment, and hardly see my way clear to go unless I get some word from Bennett.

Weather delightful but showery in p.m.

*Here the leading American war correspondents were together: Carroll, Philadelphia Public Ledger; Gibbons, Chicago Tribune; Cobb and Green, New York Evening World.

GENERAL HEADQUARTERS
AMERICAN EXPEDITIONARY FORCES
G. 2. D.

Press Division, P.O.731.

April 5, 1918.

Mr Don Martin   , Accredited Correspondent,   New York Herald

     You are attached to the   6th Artillery   and authorized
to accompany it until further notice. You will report to the Command-
Officer of that regiment and will be under his orders and exactly in
the same status as any other member of his regiment which you will not
be detached from until after the present emergency. You will not leave
the regimental sector except for the purpose of filing dispatches with
the censor at Division Headquarters. It is understood that circulation
other than as above indicated is forbidden.

                                      CAMPBELL KING,
                                      Lt. Col., Gen. Staff,
                                      Chief of Staff.

Don Martin's letter of attachment to the 6th Artillery.

Letter to Dorothy on April 5 from Neufchateau, mostly personal things, but also about his interaction with the war.

With the American Army in France
April 5, 1918

My dear Dorothy

I wish you came in and have a peek at me now. There is a candle on the table—the only light I have, as you know—beside me is a map of France, a gas mask, some of your letters, and a lot of telegrams and cablegrams. The room is small and I have to keep nearly everything on the table. I suppose I might write to you in the daytime when there is more light but I usually go out about 7 or 8 and don't return till 6 or 7. Then I have to write some telegrams for Paris and perhaps some cables for N.Y. and after that get dinner. We have pretty good meals at the officers' club. I have seen quite a bit of the smaller side of the war, but couldn't get up to the big battle as only two American correspondents were allowed there and they had been at the front for a long time. Maybe later I shall get to the British and French fronts.

I bought something for you the other day which will please you I'll bet—a pair of wooden shoes, or sabots as they are called here. I am going to have your name engraved or carved on them by some French soldier and will either send them to you or pack them away to carry back with me some time. They will make you laugh. Nearly everyone wears wooden shoes in this part of France—that is, to work in. I also bought a couple of souvenir handkerchiefs which I shall keep for you.

I have seen a lot of the most interesting places. There are no farmhouses in France. The farmers all live in little villages with one street, no yards and a big church, always very old. Every day, if I go to Nancy, as I frequently do, I pass a church 800 years old. Services are held in it every Sunday. I don't think a single of all the churches I have seen was built after 1700. I have seen some very cute children along the country roads where they sit while their mothers, grandfathers and grandmothers work at ploughing, planting or gathering dandelion greens. Their fathers are never around. They are all in the war or dead.

Yesterday I spent two hours in a prison for Germans. One of the Germans could speak English. They live well enough. In one of their long wooden buildings where they sleep, they have a small stage where they give comedies. You see Dorothy by using automobiles we can cover a great deal of country and we go somewhere every day where the American soldiers are guarding the line against the Germans. I certainly have learned a great deal I never dreamed of about the detail of war. You may be sure I shall have a great deal to tell you when I return. It is just possible that I may accompany some of the Americans when they go for the first big battle but I shall not unless I am sure I shall be pretty well out of real danger.

Isn't this funny paper? I bought it here in this old, old town. It was about all there was. Still there are good stores here. There is one department store where one can get almost anything and a lot of small stores where dainty things to eat may be purchased. The French are great for eating.

I went to a queer old photographer the other day and had some pictures taken. I think they are very poor but I shall send you one of each nevertheless. I am not half so sad as I look, young lady. In one I have on a steel helmet and around my shoulder is flung a French gas mask. We are required to carry a mask whenever we go anywhere near the front.

For this time Dorothy I shall say good night. A candle is very poor light. As I promised I shall soon write you a long letter on my typewriter. With love to all and a kiss for you.

Dad

Diary: Saturday April 6, 1918

Getting very tired of James. Bright enough kid but not house-broken. Went with him to Toul, Boucq and other places, stopping at Sebastopol to see young Archie Roosevelt* who refuses to talk to the newspapers. Got good story at Boucq of two Germans captured by Americans. Wrote story about it for New York and Paris. Learned from Colonel of Air Corps that not a single American airship is in France ready for operation.

No word from Bennett. Wired him yesterday I would not go with 1st Division till I hear from him. Most of the other men are going with the division but I shall not go till I get definite word from Bennett. Got letter from Dorothy saying they received my cable saying I was going to France.

Germans making continued slight advances on new line in Picardy.

Reasonably fine day.

Diary: Sunday April 7, 1918

Spent the entire day in Neufchateau. Roads so muddy didn't dare to go out. Met Bazin who is just back from the scene of the big battle. Wrote a story for mailing and packed up ready to go to Paris tomorrow to find out whether I am to stay at Neufchateau or go up to the front with one of the artillery regiments.

Weather very bad.

March 1918 - France

Correspondent N.Y. Herald

March 1918, France.
Correspondent N.Y. Herald.

* Son of President Theodore Roosevelt; served with US First Infantry Division.

Diary: Monday April 8, 1918

Came to Paris today. Left Neufchateau in auto with Bazin at 8 and took a train at Gondrecourt at 10:30. Train late arriving. So heavy movement of troops. Went to Crillon Hotel—got my hair cut and went to dinner with Price at the Chatham Grill. Got about a dozen letters including a note from the President [Wilson]. Stayed in the Paris office until 10:30 reading the papers.

The Commodore has been very ill with pneumonia which explains why I haven't heard from him.

Weather rainy but mild.

Regrettably, that note from President Woodrow Wilson to Don has not survived. One can only wonder what it was about.

This is the first record of Don Martin learning that James Gordon Bennett, owner of the New York and Paris Herald, was seriously ill at his villa in Beaulieu sur Mer. Bennett would live just two more months.

Diary: Tuesday April 9, 1918

Spent the day in Paris. Met Price in afternoon and went around to various offices to arrange for sending of cables to N.Y., if I go with the 1st division which I probably will. Commodore wired to use my own judgment, but he said he thought it inadvisable to detach myself from the main army. Commodore is wrong this time so I shall go with the 1st division if it can be fixed up.

Naboth Hedin

Met Bazin and went to Hedin's* office. Bazin, I find is very much of a four flusher. He sees the hole but not the doughnut. Hedin is a live one. Had dinner alone at Chatham Grill. The outfit there knows me now and I get the best there is.

Weather not pleasant.

Diary: Wednesday April 10, 1918

Went back to Neufchateau to get my typewriter, boots etc. for a trip to the front. Very uninteresting ride. Train an hour late at Gondrecourt. Auto waiting to take me to Neufchateau.

Sent short cable to N.Y. on American scrap near Toul. Spent the evening at the club.

Weather miserable.

* Naboth Hedin, correspondent for the Brooklyn Eagle

Don Martin wrote a letter to Dorothy dated April 10 from the Hotel de Crillon, in which he showed his itchiness to get to the front.

Hôtel de Crillon, Place de la Concorde, Paris
April 10, 1918

Dorothy

I came to Paris day before yesterday to see what could be done about getting up where the great big battle is being fought. I may be able to arrange it. I am going back to Neufchateau, which is a queer old place, about 5 hours ride from here, and tomorrow will come back to Paris. There is just a chance that I shall leave here Saturday to go to some place not a great way from Paris, to get a glimpse of a part of the big battle. Everything over here is done in a secret way. For instance, I shall not be able to buy a ticket for my destination until just before the train leaves because the authorities won't tell me what place I am going to.

There has been no bombardment of Paris by that big gun since my arrival and no air raid. However no one can tell when something will happen. I watch out as well as I can.

I got a great bunch of mail night before last. It was in the Paris office. There were letters from the office, from Alta, Rock and Mother. Then two days before I got a letter from you and from Rock, too. So, I am doing pretty well for letters. I am glad to know that you have been so well Dorothy. I guess you are the healthiest member of the whole family. I am learning to speak a little French. You will have to keep studying or I will be able to talk more French than you can.

I shall now pack a hold-all—that's a funny name isn't it?—and go to the Gare d'est—the Eastern station. It seems as if I spend about half my time packing and unpacking.

Oh yes—that cablegram you couldn't understand read (the last part of it) "Love, you Funny." I meant "I send you my love, you little funny girl." Now do you understand?

I shall write to you again before I go to the French front—if I do go. Tell John Knox I wrote him a letter four days ago.

With love + a kiss

Dad

Diary: Thursday April 11, 1918

Traveling. Traveling—all the time. Back to Paris today. Rode as far as Chaumont with Major Riggs and McKenna, a Canadian correspondent. Took the train at Chaumont. Got in Paris at 11 and went to the Hotel Crillon and to bed.

Sun shining.

Rue de Rivoli after the air raid on April 12, 1918. *(Agence Rol)*

Diary: Friday April 12, 1918

(Air raid in Paris. 9 killed – 60 injured.)

Spent the day in Paris. Saw Bazin at office of Hedin, Brooklyn Eagle correspondent. Both Bazin and Hedin have decided not to go with 1st division. Had dinner at Prunier's with Price and afterward went to the office. Then to the Crillon. Just as I had made myself comfortable in my room and was reading letter from Dorothy, heard cannonading. Lights then went out and I knew another air raid was on. Dressed hurriedly by candlelight and went down in the lobby for an hour and a half. Bomb hit gas main about a mile from the hotel on Rue [de] Rivoli and caused big fire which we could see from in front of the hotel.

German drive now directed at the British and looks quite serious.

Weather rainy.

Diary: Saturday April 13, 1918

Hung around the hotel most of the day. Undecided whether to go with 1st division or to return to Neufchateau. Think I will do the latter. Met Price at the hotel at 3 p.m. He interpreted during an interesting conversation I had with a French woman named Chaperon whom Bryan introduced me to.

Had dinner with Price at the Beef a la Mode. On way back with Price met Orr of International News. Walked in rain with him and Price up Champs Elysee but returned to hotel at 9:30. Called up Martin Green at the Hotel Lotti. He thinks he may go with the 1st division tomorrow and if he does I may go with him. Went to bed early. Commodore very ill yet. Apparently has relapse.

Germans fired shells into Paris from big gun.

Weather unpleasant. Rain at night.

Don Martin continued to struggle with how to get to the front of the 'big battle' and whether to accept an assignment with a regiment, where he would have to remain for a time. In the letter he wrote to Dorothy on April 13 from the Hotel de Crillon, he told her he would do that, but as the following diary entries show, he changed his mind.

Hôtel de Crillon, Place de la Concorde, Paris
April 13, 1918

(Yes, I received letters 1, 2, 3 + 4 + 14 yesterday.)

Dorothy,

Every time I come to Paris I find letters from all of you. Last evening I got here (just in time for an air raid too) and found a letter from you, one from Rock—a very long one—and one from Alta. They were all filled with news and yours in addition to news, contained some nonsense which just gave the whole bunch the proper balance. I had to laugh at the stomach "air raid" you had Dorothy.

It seems as if I am a sort of hoodoo. Every time I come here, or nearly every time, there is an air raid. Last night at a quarter to ten, I had made myself comfortable in my room here, with all the letters from you all in my lap when I heard the firing of cannon. I knew of course it was the guns in Paris firing at approaching aeroplanes. Then my lights went out, as the lights always do in Paris during air raids. I was half undressed and of course decided to go down in the lobby where there is much less danger. I lit a candle, provided for such emergencies, and went down in the lobby and stayed with about 300 other persons till the raid was over. From in front of the hotel, we could see a big glare from a fire one of the bombs had caused. Maybe there will be another one tonight. The Germans are using every possible resource they have to spread terror and fear, so they can win the war this Summer. They are a pretty dangerous foe, but France can hold them off if England can do her share; and then United States will do the rest.

Tomorrow morning I expect I shall go to a town not a great way from here to join the Americans who are already participating in the big battle. I shall have considerable difficulty getting around because of my inability to speak French fluently, and the fact that going to the front is not like going to a circus. One must have all kinds of credentials and wait around, sometimes for hours. However, if I manage to get to the point I am aiming at tomorrow, I shall be attached to the staff of an artillery regiment and may see one of the vital phases of the big battle which may decide the war. I must present an amusing picture Dorothy—a typewriter, a big portmanteau and a helmet, French + British gas masks over my shoulder. Quite a job carrying all this junk too, and there are no porters during wartime.

That was a great burglar epidemic you had, wasn't it? It's a good thing the police caught the gangsters. Much obliged for the clipping.

I shall write to you again after a bit. I don't know what facilities I shall have for writing for a while. The agreement the correspondents had to make was that they would "bury themselves" (that doesn't mean literally bury themselves) and stay with whatever regiment they were assigned to until released. So I may be gone two or three weeks, and during that time be out of communication with everyone so far as getting word from outside is concerned, though I shall be able to cable, I hope.

With love + a kiss Dorothy,
From Dad

Diary: Sunday April 14, 1918

Having decided not to leave Paris till tomorrow, took it easy. Went for long walk through Tuileries, meeting Bingham of N.Y. on way back. At 12:30 went to [New York] World office and met Martin Green, Joe Griggs and some others and then went to the New York bar where we sat for three hours with Perceval Gibbon, war correspondent of the London Chronicle and Myrtle Williams of Colliers. Gibbon, one of the best English correspondents, told many good stories. Went from there (alone) to the Chatham Grill and had a good steak. Then to the hotel. Have decided to go back to Neufchateau.

German drive against British continues serious. Good many persons pessimistic now but I'm not. It is pitiable though how helpless U.S. is. France is the only formidable ally.

Weather cold and rain.

Diary: Monday April 15, 1918

Left Paris for Gondrecourt at noon. Found auto waiting which took me to Neufchateau. Found there had been quite an engagement between U.S. troops and Germans on the Meuse couple days ago. Got details from [Stanley] Prenosil of the AP and sent pretty good story to Paris. Most of the correspondents are with the 1st division. Went early to my cold, smelly, candle-lighted room in the Hotel Agriculture.

Germans continuing their drive against the British. Are driving them back slowly with tremendous German losses.

Weather miserable. Rainy and cold.

Diary: Tuesday April 16, 1918

Went out in auto today with Franklin P. Adams who is a captain but a reporter for the Stars & Stripes, the government weekly. Went to Boucq, Ansauville and the French-American aviation field near Toul.

Saw [John N.] Reynolds and [Douglas] Campbell, Americans who have the Croix de Guerre for bringing down four Boche planes on Sunday. Had luncheon with them and other American aviators, including [Raoul] Lufbery, the best of them all. Wrote column story on the Croix de Guerre fliers for Paris, and about ½ col for N.Y.

[Joseph] Gregg of the World arrived today.

Germans continue to advance slowly against British.

Weather miserable. Mud terrible.

Letter from Rose Martin

Dated Apr 16, 1918; postmarked Apr 16, 5PM New York Herald Bureau, 38 Rue du Louvre, Paris, France

April 16th

Dear Don,

When I think every one else has written, then I think it's my turn. This is a beautiful morning, really spring is here, and how beautiful it must be in Paris (poor Paris). No one in France can enjoy themselves or be happy with so much carnage about them. I am glad you have been there and had some of their cookery. You certainly will have all kinds of eating before you get home, and we will all be glad to have you back in the United States. You certainly are traveling some. We got a letter yesterday, it was dated March 17, you were packing up to go to the front. And now, perhaps you are back somewhere else. Then we got one Friday dated March 12 telling us you were a Hoodoo about those air-raids, and that French maid (poor thing). I think myself it's some thing to be excited over, it's terrible. I do wish you did know how to talk French. Try to pick up a little, if it's possible. I always thought that would be the best place to learn it, where it was spoken. You will get used to the sounds, then it will come easy.

That was a fine French letter you sent. You would not have fooled me, but it did Dorothy for a little while. Then she laughed. At first, she looked so surprised, she read it nearly all without any trouble. The French with her seems to be the one thing that is neglected. She has a good feel to-day, so it is not her fault, but we will do some anyway.

I am glad you meet a good many Americans. Do you meet that Mr. Russell, he is the one you met on the ship?

Mel Spencer called here Saturday eve—just after Dorothy had gone to bed, but I got her up and dressed before he got here. (You see he called up Roscoe on the phone, telling him that he was at the garage and would be here in a ½ hour. So, Roscoe went to meet him. He seemed very much pleased to see Dorothy, and to hear her play. Roscoe wrote Sunday P.M. to you, and probably told you about it.

If you go back to Paris, I hope you will go back to that Hotel de Crillon. I am glad you can go to such lovely Hotels. We have the card you sent with the pictures of it. And also those Easter Cards, they are funny, but nice. Will have them framed. By the way, all your articles are signed now. Have been cutting out some this forenoon. We are all well, and hope you keep well too.

With much love, Good bye,

Mother

P.S. I must not forget to tell you that Dorothy wrote to you Saturday in French, and one on the typewriter at Alta's office Friday in English.

Diary: Wednesday April 17, 1918

Went to Baccarat today with Ford of International News and Taylor of U.P.—all good fellows but rather under-grade men for a job like this.

Got story of Dr. Patton of N.Y. who gets Croix de Guerre for taking off his gas mask to save 20 of his men. Cabled it to N.Y. and wrote good story for Paris. Had dinner with Gregg and Kenamore of St. Louis [World]. Spent most of evening at the club. Room too clammy to stay in except to sleep.

Weather rainy and raw. Sunny France!

Diary: Thursday April 18, 1918

Had Gregg and [Franklin] Adams for companions in trip to Boucq and the aviation field where we saw a French general present the medals to Winslow and Campbell*. Got no big news. Sent considerable to Paris and short cable to N.Y.

Got wire from Bennett through Price saying steps have been taken to have me accredited. Also suggests I stay with main army which I have done. Find only way to be accredited is through war department in Washington. So wired Commodore [Bennett] tonight.
Sunshine most of day. Wonderful.

Diary: Friday April 19, 1918

Gregg, Adams and I went to Verdun. Left at 9:30 a.m., returned at 6. Got pretty close to Verdun. Went well over to the 2nd [Division] line to see the 5th and 6th [Brigades] Marines. Adams is very much a bore. He, Gregg and I had luncheon in a French officers' club in Touilly. Opened especially for us after hours. Spent evening in the club at Neufchateau talking with American fliers, one of them young [Oscar G.] Gude of N.Y. who also plays the piano very well.

French holding well against Germans. British falling back a little.

Weather cold and raw.

Diary: Saturday April 20, 1918

Storm troops make attack on New England troops.

Went to Baccarat with Gregg—a long ride. [Baccarat is northeast of Epinal.] Got no news but on return to Neufchateau found Germans had made a strong attack with C2 or storm troops on two companies 26 (New England division) [at Seicheprey]. Cabled about 500 words to N.Y. Sent same to Paris. Censors cut out nearly everything worthwhile in both dispatches. Won't pass anything praising Americans for fear it will offend French. It is very annoying. I think I told Lieut. Conger* one of censors almost what I think of him. Had dinner at club with all the reporters. All are sore on the censors.

Weather clear but cold.

* Lt Arthur L Conger, chief of staff, Intelligence, 2nd Division

Where the Americans Fought in France

— Front Line of March 20, 1918   —·—·— International Boundary

As Don travels daily to locations near the front lines, it is helpful to have a map showing where the American expeditionary Force fought. James H. Hallas prepared this map, which is in his book, "Doughboy War, The American Expeditionary Force in WWI" (Stackpole Military History Series (2000), page vi). Neufchateau, where Don is based at this point, is south of Toul in the direction of Chaumont.

Letter from Dorothy (No.18)

Dated Apr 20, 1918; postmarked Apr 22, 9:30AM; no 'received' notation

Silver Creek, N.Y.
Apr 20, 1918

Dear Dad

I just finished dinner, and now I am going to write letter No. 18. I did not write this morning, as I usually do, because I went up in the woods after flowers. I got a large bunch of adder-tongues — those flowers some-times called yellow lilies — a large bunch of may-flowers, a large bunch of flowers called Crinkle Root, a _very_ large bunch of "Spring Beauties" and a few Dutchman's Breeches. I also found a birds nest — sparrows I think — which I am going to take to school to put with our collection of cocoons, nests, etc.

Yesterday when we got home from Buffalo, there was a letter from you here for me. It was from the front. You certainly got pretty close to the war that time with the Chicago man, didn't you? Grandmother says to tell you that you better be careful, and I say so too. But I guess you know how to take care of yourself, don't you? The letter which we got yesterday was dated _____, Well it is Sunday, Apr 21st now — that probably sounds funny, don't it? But it's true just the same. You see yesterday morning I went up in the woods after flowers — (which I _really_ hadn't ought to have done, as I have work to do — practicing — dusting, etc) — but I _really_ am _real_ glad that I did not miss going. I may go again to-day with Aunt Inez. Then in the afternoon, I started this letter — then Uncle Rock and

Aunt Inez came over to plant their garden, and of course I went out to help or watch them, as I love to work in a garden. After that I came in and did my practicing – during which I had 4 telephone calls – 2 from one girl and 2 from another, right along in succession. One wanted me to come out and play, and the other first asked me sumpin 'bout a dress pattern, and the 2nd time she said she was coming up in five minutes and she did. Then we (Jane Christy + I) went up to see Carrie Sanford, a minute, then went for Miss Butler, our gym' teacher, then went down to Grace Montzgomery's and came back with something for her, then we all went down to school to practice dancing.

We are going to have some sort of thing for the Red Cross, down at the Park Theater, Wednesday night. It is called "Hiawatha's Childhood" and I am in an Indian Dance and a Wind and Wave Dance. We may have to learn another dance. Well, so you see I was pretty busy all day, so I left this letter for to-day. Now, back to where I left off yesterday – as I was sayin' – The letter we received yesterday (Friday) was dated Mch. 21st and it reached here Apr. 18th. We also received a letter from the front last Thursday, but we took it down to Aunt Alta Friday, so I can not tell you when it was dated, but I will tell you in next week's letter.

All of your letters are passed around to all of the family to read, so there's hardly any use in writing to us all separately, although I guess we're all glad to have a letter of our very own.

We went to Buffalo in the auto Friday, but I was not sick this time. I took my music lesson and went to the dentist's. We didn't have any punctures or anything like that.

Are you going to bring your gas mask and steel helmet home? I hope you can. I want to see 'em. While you were in Paris, did you see or hear of a man by the name of Jack Butler? He is there doing some sort of work for the U.S. government. He is from Boston. He is Miss Butler, our gym' teacher's brother. She knew where you were and wondered if you had happened to run across him.

Did you see the Notre Dame Cathedral while you were in Paris? If you did, was it destroyed? Or how was it? We were talking about it in school Thursday and everybody thought something different.

They are selling Thrift Stamps in school now, and I am buying some. I have 2 now and am going to buy another Monday.

I guess I better close now, and get ready for dinner.

Lots o' love an' hugs an' kisses,

Dorothy

P.S. Did you get my French letter? Could you read it? Bet yuh couldn't! Ha! Ha!

Diary: Sunday April 21, 1918

Left early with Gregg and pest Adams for Boucq to get story of the battle of the Americans. Told by army authorities we had won big victory but later learned Germans captured 178 of our men prisoners and killed a good many. French apparently came to aid of the New Englanders who look pretty good but who certainly are nothing like their ancestors. Looks like a rather sad blow for our prestige.

Returned early and wrote column each for New York and Paris. More trouble with the censors. Got telegram from Commodore saying he had taken steps to have me accredited and that after that he wants me to go wherever I think best.

Weather cold and raw. Rainy in forenoon.

Diary: Monday April 22, 1918

Went to Chaumont with Gregg. Had heart to heart talk with Colonel Sweeney, head censor, who agreed to post a bulletin each evening at the censor's office, Neufchateau, telling us what has happened during the day. Returned at 4 p.m. Had dinner at the club. Got corking letter from Dorothy.

Quiet on the British and French fronts. Apparently the Germans are getting ready to make a new offensive.

Weather rainy and raw.

An extract of Don's report of the April 20 attack at Seicheprey shows his story-telling talent. It was published in the New York Herald on Tuesday April 23, 1918.

AMERICANS WITH BACKS TO WALL, OUTNUMBERED 12 TO 1, OUTFIGHT, THEN WHIP, GERMANS TO A FINISH

ENDURE VERITABLE HURRICANE OF EXPLOSIVES, MUSTARD GAS AND POISONOUS VAPORS

By DON MARTIN
[Special cable to the Herald]

WITH THE AMERICAN ARMY IN FRANCE, Monday

Facts gathered from Saturday's attack on the American sector near Toul show the Germans struck only after the most careful preparation with the expectation of dealing a demoralizing blow to the Americans.

It was a costly venture. Three hundred Germans dead were piled in one part of the square mile where the engagement raged for twenty hours. To-day the Germans are back in the same position as before the attack.

Twelve hundred picked shock troops, which were part of a large force used for several weeks to harry the Allies, especially the Americans, all along the line, had been rehearsing behind lines, but it was believed they would strike elsewhere. They swept out of the mists of dawn against four hundred Americans, and in some spots the Americans were outnumbered twelve to one, but fought gallantly, while German artillery sent a veritable hurricane of high explosives, mustard and other poison vapors.

The scenes in the village of Seicheprey were like those in famous battle paintings. The Germans advanced in mass formation until the American artillery scattered them. There were many bayonet clashes in Seicheprey, as the Americans often were fighting with their backs to the wall, surrounded in many instances by three to one of the Boches. No Americans were found with bayonet wounds.

In one scene of the liveliest fighting to-day I saw many Americans, representative of many cities, and heard stories which the soldiers told reluctantly, saying they have done nothing which the French and British have not done a thousand times. Nevertheless this is the first real baptism of fire for the Americans who until few months ago were clerks and workers of all classes, with no idea of ever fighting in the great war. Valor and modesty are their distinguishing qualities.

Bodies of Germans Everywhere

Bodies of Germans are visible everywhere, all vigorous and well dressed, also some officers of the Boches.

According to stories of prisoners, they intended holding Seicheprey, which, however, was retained only a few hours. The Americans had retired from the town because of the merciless shelling and blanketing by gas in the four hour bombardment from the heaviest guns and the infantry.

A shadow creeping barrage burst on the American patrols, then upon the first line. Subsequent happenings put the Americans through the test.

They clung to the trenches until the shells wiped them out. They clung to two patches of woods until thousands of gas shells filled with oily poison saturated the overhanging mist. Though struck with the full force of the enemy's artillery and his picked troops, the Americans insisted on recapturing Seicheprey, which they did by brilliant work in the open, using hand grenades, bayonets, pistols and rifle butts.

Diary: Tuesday April 23, 1918

Went to Epinal, Baccarat and Nancy. Got nothing much. At Baccarat saw the 69th New York regiment (now the 165th) starting for the trenches. Gregg and Adams and a lieutenant were in my car. Got back at 7. Met Bazin who had just come from Paris. Spent part of the evening at the club with Gregg. Got a letter from the Commodore saying he had cabled Ohl to have me accredited, and to go wherever I thought the news might be. The Commodore's signature doesn't indicate that he is nearing death as some reports have had it.

Weather miserable.

Diary: Wednesday April 24, 1918

Didn't go out today. Stayed in to write some mail stuff. Wrote 4 or 5 stories and took them to the censor preparatory to mailing them to New York. With Parkerson of A.P., Gregg and Lieut. Parks, called on [Major] General [Hunter] Liggett, the Corps [I] commander. He says he is an optimist but his talk didn't indicate it.

Weather rainy and wretched. Fine climate!

Don Martin wrote to Dorothy on April 24, 1918, on a rainy day in Neufchateau, mostly personal, but also about his situation regarding seeing the war.

Neufchateau, France
April 24, 1918

Dorothy

That was a great letter you wrote—No. 15. You certainly are a humorist, and I wouldn't be surprised if you became a writer too some day. That postscript, "Nothing," made me laugh. I guess you had told it all before you got to the postscript because the letter was a long one. I was glad to hear about the election and was glad to know about the hat, shoes and dress you have. Don't you forget, little Miss Funny, that you are to have some nice things this spring and if there is any question about it you just put your foot down and in- sist. Tell Grandmother to draw money out of the bank from my account. However I guess it isn't necessary for me to worry on this score. I imagine you will be rigged up pretty well.

I got your No. 15 letter day before yesterday and got one from Rock at the same time. I have had quite a few letters lately, more, I daresay than I have written. I haven't been writing much lately except to cable and that I do at the censor's office. My room is cold as the dickens. It is cold now and I have a sweater on. I am warm enough but the keys on my machine are cold and the air is so cold that I can blow my breath clear across the room.

It isn't so terribly cold outside but it is rainy and raw. It has been that way steadily now for two weeks wherever I have been and these stone buildings in France get very cold inside. There are no frame build- ings you know. Oh yes, before I forget it I must tell you that I had a good laugh over your remarks about being as proud of your Dad as the other girls are of theirs even though their fathers are deputy sheriffs, etc. Maybe I might have been a deputy sheriff if I had stayed in Silver Creek. That wouldn't have been quite so profitable as what I am doing but I would have been home more anyhow and that is quite a bit.

I wrote a long letter to John Knox so he has probably spoken to you about it before now. I shall write to him again after a bit. I shall probably write to a lot of people when the weather gets decent so there is some comfort inside. There are no stoves you see and no light at night. In the first place there are no electric lights in towns like this and anyhow on account of possible air raids all lights are out at night.

I haven't received any of the candy or sugar yet but am hoping it will reach me. If the maple sugar Rock wrote about gets here I will send a postal card to the man who made it. The London man wrote the other day that a box of candy had arrived there for me and that he had forwarded it to me here. That ought to be here pretty soon. I have been in quite a few places since I wrote to you in Paris. I went up North near where the great battle is being fought but no American correspondent is permitted to be with the French so, instead of staying with an artillery company, I came back here to be where things might happen. I go out somewhere every day, usually travelling from 75 to 150 miles in an auto. I go close to the front line now and then and see plenty of villages which have been shot all to pieces. I got a little glimpse of the battle in which the Americans were engaged a few days ago and wrote a piece about it which you probably read.

Today I remained in this town to write two or three mail stories and to write a few letters also. I imagine I shall be here for some time. Mr. Bennett has written that he has asked the New York office to have me formally accredited as a correspondent with the American army, and if that is done I may be here a good part of the summer. Maybe the weather will be decent in a little while. I never saw anything like the weather we have been having. The streets, or sidewalks, in the villages are always muddy and I don't blame people for wearing wooden shoes. There is never any hard rain but a continuous drizzle. That is not true of Southern and Central France but only of this part of the Vosges country. They say that May and June are nice. I couldn't live here permanently for a dollar a minute.

Rock wonders what my opinion is regarding the outcome of the war. I know practically no more about it than anyone else. That probably sounds strange, inasmuch as I am right on the ground, but it is true. My own opinion is that if Germany, by sacrificing hundreds of thousands more men, breaks through to the coast, separating the British and French armies, there will be peace. Most people don't think so but I do. I think so because England will not stand for the thing much longer if things look bad. But I don't think the Germans will break through. The French have taken over practically all the British line and the Germans cannot lick the French. They know it too. The Germans will never take Paris.

Now, tell Uncle Rock, if the Germans find they are unable to break through and are able a little later to resist any offensive the French and British make, I look for peace overtures from the Germans. Whether or not these overtures will be the basis of peace depends altogether on the attitude of the civil populations of England, France and United States. If England and France are willing to go on, as I confidently believe they will be, the United States will probably tell Germany that Germany will be officially notified when the time for peace comes. The Germans, I figure, will make peace overtures because it will be in the same position as the highway robber who has his pockets filled with loot and sees inevitable capture even though for the time being he is able to evade capture. Personally, everything considered I believe the war will last another year, and maybe two more and that Germany will be licked good and proper before it is all over. The wish may be the father to the thought but I hope not.

I shall write to you again in a few days young lady and meantime I shall hope to get some of that candy. Sugar, however, is not so scarce here as in London and Paris. I bought two pounds of chocolate in Nancy the other day. It cost $2 a pound, but was very good. Give my love to the whole family including yourself.

With love,
Dad

P.S. Why not go to Buffalo to a high class photographer and get some fine pictures taken? Why bother with the local photographer? That seems foolish to me.

Don Martin wrote a "good one" about ministering angels serving doughnuts on April 24 that was published in the New York Herald on Thursday April 25.

'MOTHER BURDICK OF TRENCHES' IS MINISTERING ANGEL TO MEN IN FRANCE, FROM TEXAS TO MAINE

By DON MARTIN

[Special cable to the Herald]

WITH THE AMERICAN ARMY IN FRANCE, Wednesday

From one end of the line to the other she is known as "Mother Burdick." When the boys come back from the land of the shivery patrols they drop in to say "Hello." When they are resting after their shift in the trenches they hang around to help her or to do the heavy work for her understudies, Miss Myrtle Turkington and Miss Gladys McIntyre.

Miss Gladys McIntyre serving doughnuts

"Hello, Mother!" said a rough raw-boned, red haired private nicknamed Texas. "How are the doughnuts?"

From head to toe he bore the grime of the trenches. His rough exterior camouflaged a rugged character.

"You don't want a doughnut—a great, big man like you. You want a meal. Now sit down—do's I tell you."

Texas sat down. Mother Burdick's wish is a first line command.

"You'll have to excuse me if I keep on with my work," she said apologetically. "We're sending a thousand doughnuts over to the trenches to-day, and there's no one to make them but me and Miss McIntyre here. The boys like them better than anything else we can give them except"---

She gave a half dozen brawny soldiers an opportunity to finish the sentence and they all did, in chorus: "Except apple pie."

Pie Only on Sundays

"But you can't have apple pie only Sundays," said Mother Burdick firmly. "It's a luxury. I'll stuff you so full of apple pie you'd bust if I had the apples and the sugar and the time to make it. You're lucky to get doughnuts."

"Lucky! Say, Mother, the war'd be lost without your doughnuts!"

All this and more you could hear any day in Mother Burdick's camp. She and her husband, Floyd O. Burdick, both from Texas, are verily among the ministering angels of the war. Not a soldier among the thousands who come to their shack for dainties and kind words but would go over the top for them any time.

She pointed rather apologetically to four cots in a tented corner of the shattered building, the floor wet and earthy, the roof tent leaky and black.

"It was a little cold in the winter. You see there is no way of keeping the wind out, although the boys here did the best they could to make us comfortable. But now the sum shines sometimes and we shall be perfectly contented. And anyhow it's no worse than the boys have to put up with, is it, Sam?"

Sam and the others made no reply.

"We're glad to help a little," continued this Samaritan, dropping coil after coil of dough into the vat of grease. "I figured it out this way:– Our children are grown up. They don't need us. There are thousands of women in the United States who would be here if they could, to do for the boys, but they are needed at home.

"We decided we'd come over here and do the very things the boys' mothers would do if they were here. They like doughnuts, the poor boys, and so we make doughnuts, and make 'em and make 'em and make 'em, and if I had the flour and the lard I'd make tens of thousands more and send 'em up in those trenches you can see from the top of the hill yonder. But if the officers would only let me

"Salvation Army Girls, Gladys and Irene McIntyre, Myrtle Turkington and Stella Young, serving doughnuts and coffee to soldiers."

(National Archives photo SC–10445, Ansauville, April 9, 1918)

'MOTHER BURDICK OF TRENCHES' IS MINISTERING ANGEL...

and the girls here go up in the trenches! We want to carry the doughnuts and chocolate up there ourselves, but the officers say we can't."

"That's 'cause they're taking no chance on losing you," said Texas.

When you see the whiskered old Santa with kettle and bell who stamps his feet to keep warm as he watches the human currents swirl around him in Herald square or wherever else it may be, give him something.

When the Salvation Army lassie comes around with her modest appeal to help the boys at the front, don't turn her away, for the Salvation Army is a ministering angel to the boys in the fighting ranks.

Diary: Thursday April 25, 1918

Visited Ansauville with Gregg. It has been shelled since my last visit and is by no means a safe place. Saw the old church which went untouched through all bombardments till this last which left several holes in it. Had luncheon at Toul with Gregg, Parkerson and Ford. Got back to Neufchateau at 5. Had dinner at club. Gregg is a nice chap but certainly has a great admiration for the Germans. I tell him his right name usually

once a day. Told him today the American who criticises England or France and sees virtue in anything German is by far the most dangerous propagandist of all.

German offensive against British growing in violence. Is making headway.

Rainy + raw.

The war correspondents stood for a group photo in Neufchateau on April 25, 1918. Don Martin is in the front row, second from left.

Newspaper correspondents with Allied Expeditionary Force, Neufchateau, April 25, 1918.
Back row, left to right: Joseph Griggs, *New York World*; Frank J Taylor, *United Press*; Capt. Franklin Adams, *Stars and Stripes*; Bert Ford, *International News Service.* Front, left to right: Clair Kenamore, *St Louis Post–Dispatch*; Don Martin, *New York Herald*; Frank P Sibley, *Boston Globe*; Henri Bazin, *Philadelphia Public Ledger*; John T Parkerson, *Associated Press. Source: National Archives, 111-SC-11337.*

Diary: Friday April 26, 1918

Didn't feel very well today. Had a sort of acute hay-fever attack which is certainly unusual for this time of year. At 3 p.m. went to Boucq. Very quiet on that sector. Had more hot talk with Gregg who is not exactly my idea of a hard and fast American. Dinner at the club. Sat around club in the evening for a short time.

Germans capture Mt. Kimmel overlooking Ypres. British not holding as the French did. Looks just a little to me as if this battle may hasten the end of the war.

Sunshine till 4 p.m., then rain of course.

Diary: Saturday April 27, 1918

Censor's office told us the Boche has made a raid on the Americans. Gregg, Lieut. [C.] Reynolds (chief censor) and I went to Boucq and to a hospital well up toward the German lines but found the raid was only a barrage.

Got back at 4. Made a 700-word cable for New York on what Hun prisoners have said about conditions. Am somewhat discouraged with the news situation. Can't write anything that is not helpful to Allied cause. I wouldn't anyhow but the restriction is too rigid.

German offensive grows in intensity. French holding; British yielding. Americans not in the fight.

At last a good day! Warm and sun shining.

Diary: Sunday April 28, 1918

Almost within sight of German lines and within hearing of guns, I saw on a plateau overlooking Boucq and a wide valley, a French General decorate the 104 Regiment [Massachusetts] and give Croix de Guerre to 117 members of the regiment for gallantry at Apremont on April 10, 11 and 12. It was a splendid spectacle. Cabled short story to N.Y.; sent long story to Paris. First American regiment to be thus decorated. Had about a two-mile uphill walk to scene but it was worth it. Went over with Gregg and Taylor.

German Picardy offensive lessening in intensity.

Weather warm but wet.

Diary: Monday April 29, 1918

Went to Chaumont and another place 25 miles from there to see first of the draft men to arrive in France. Got much good material for story. Cabled 600 words to New York. Also heard for first time that soldiers are calling themselves Buddies. Cabled short story about it and sent longer story to Paris. I drew this story out of some of the privates and Gregg and Taylor jumped at it of course. Maybe this is the name by which American soldiers are to be known. They don't like "Sammies" or "Amexes." Got back at 5 p.m. Dinner at club.

Germans meeting setbacks in big offensive. Looks as if French have stopped them. If Germans fail now their defeat is inevitable.

Weather clear part of the day—then rain.

Don Martin wrote a story about "Buddies" on Monday night, April 29, and dated it Tuesday. It was published in the New York Herald on Wednesday May 1, 1918. It seems to have been instrumental in its general adoption.

GOODBY, "SAMMIES!" AMERICANS IN FRANCE NOW ARE 'BUDDIES'

Newest of General Pershing's Forces Bring Over Familiar American Slang Sobriquet —They Like It and So Do the French and English

By DON MARTIN

[Special cable to the Herald]

WITH THE AMERICAN ARMY IN FRANCE, Tuesday

Not the "Amexes" or "Sammies," but "Buddies." That's the new sobriquet for the members of the American National Army in France. While the entire allied world has been hunting around for a suitable name for Uncle Sam's Liberty forces the men fresh from America took the task upon themselves and "Buddies" is the result.

No more euphonic emblem of fraternity, good will and downright devotion could have been seized upon, in the opinion of the latest recruits to General Pershing's forces, who soon will be in the thick of the Flanders fight.

From east to west, from north to south, "Buddies" is the accepted brand of comradeship. It means "pal," "comrade"—a sure-fire pledge "Buddie" will share his last "makings," his rations and risk his life for the company mate he honors with the familiar American slang term.

French and British soldiers already have begun to apply the word in salutation when they meet with their American comrades in arms. The British "Tommy" likes the tang of it, the French poilus find it an effective and easy designation and Anglo-British forces are predicting to-day the word will become familiar throughout France.

It is safe to say the American forces will take to it with alacrity. "Amexes" and "Sammies" were distasteful to the men.

Diary: Tuesday April 30, 1918

Boucq today with Ford, who seems to be a very decent chap. Went to American aviation field near Toul and got good story about two American fliers bringing down a German plane. Some of the correspondents who hurried to the other front with the 1st division are returning. Americans there have done nothing yet and correspondents were unable to send anything.

Bought a wrist watch in Nancy for 320 francs [~$75 then]—will give it to Dorothy when I return home.

French make slight gains against Germans. Germans drive has temporarily at least been checked.

Weather threatening and rainy.

Letter from Rose Martin

Dated April 30, 1918; postmarked May 1, 18 7AM New York Herald Bureau, 38 Rue Du Louvre, Paris, France

April 30th, 1918

Dear Don

Two letters (and best of all) your pictures came last Friday afternoon. I was so glad to get them, and we all were. It almost seems as if you were a Soldier and you almost look as if you were a Foreigner. If I didn't know you, I would say you were English. Well, they are you, Don Martin—and they are splendid and lots have seen them and they all think they are fine, especially that one in uniform. And now don't go to near where there is danger. I am glad you are where you can get some thing good to eat again but don't get too close to the Huns—or Sausages, that is what they are. I imagine you will know pretty well what war is before you leave there. I shall be very glad when you get back in America.

I hope you don't get too tired out and worn out with work. You certainly have much to do. We often speak of your candlelight. How I wish you had a good oil lamp, to do your writing by. Why not use two or three at once. But then, Don, there are lots and lots of others even worse off. N'est pas? Je espére que vous pouvez parler un petit peu de francais, et aussie le comprendre. Táchér de apprendre seulement un peu, enough for this time. I wish you could, though. Well, I wonder where you are today, probably way, way off in an automobile. Be sure to be careful of yourself, and don't go too near the Huns.

Dorothy is very well. I took her up to Kahabka's to have another sitting. Dorothy will bring the proofs this afternoon from school. I hope they will be good, as I know you want some pictures of her; will wait a little while as its almost time for her to come. Then I will know if they are good.

Well, she brought the proofs, and I think I will have Mrs. Kahabka finish two and send them off across the Ocean to you. And some time when we go to Buffalo, we will try there.

You certainly do a lot of writing. In today's paper there is a long article on the front page with your name at the heading. Its about the French pinning war medals on 122 of Pershing's war heroes. Your articles are always the first reading I do. You must be awful busy. I wish you could have a few days vacation.

With love and good wishes — Mother

Diary: Wednesday May 1, 1918

Out with Ford again. Had luncheon in Nancy. Then went to Boucq. Fronts very quiet. Got back to Neufchateau to find Draper and some of the other 1st division men back to cover this front. Spent the evening at the club.

Visited with Eyre of the World. He says the French, by wonderful fighting, prevented a German victory in Picardy after the 5th British army had gone back.

First decent day in a long time.

Diary: Thursday May 2, 1918

Wrote a few mail stories. At 2, with Taylor and Lieut. Reynolds, motored to aviation field near Toul and got story of German plane brought down by young [James A.] Meissner of Brooklyn. Got back at 6:30. Wrote good story for Paris. Cabled 250 words to New York. Spent evening at the club. Gregg, Parkerson and Ford leaving for the French front. Most of the other correspondents are back here.

Wrote to Mr. Bennett.

My 320 franc watch has refused to run.

Quiet in the North. Germans apparently preparing for another assault.

First good day in weeks.

Martin wrote on May 2 to James Gordon Bennett with complaints about the censorship and insights on the competition between the American war correspondents to "beat" the others.

 Dear Sir,

... I have remained here with the main army, believing that to be the best thing for the Herald. I have had several beats for the European edition, notably the engagement at Seicheprey, the bringing down of German planes by Americans and the decoration of the 104th Regiment. I cabled something on each to New York. It does not seem practicable to send the same dispatches to New York and Paris. The censors permit considerable leeway in cables to America but won't let anything go to Paris which might seem like boasting or glorification of American troops. The theory is that modesty must characterize everything printed in Paris so as not to offend the French and that we must also be careful not to reveal any information to the enemy which gets in a day or two everything printed in Paris. This censorship rule will explain why I am not able to put more punch in the stories in the European edition.

I have fought out the censorship matter with the authorities here and in headquarters, insisting that the Herald, in its European edition, must be permitted to have exactly the same privileges the Stars and Stripes has. The Stars and Stripes is an official government newspaper, printed weekly on the Mail presses in Paris and cannot be called a competitor of the Herald. I complained on several occasions that this official paper was allowed to print stories which the Herald could not publish and that it was distinctly unfair. The matter was taken up carefully and from now on the Herald will have precisely the same privileges given to the Stars and Stripes.

... Every American officer in France practically gets the Herald. I see it in the front line, in the clubs, in the dugouts, everywhere. ... In Neufchateau at seven every evening there is a crowd about the one newsstand waiting for the Herald. All the officers and a great many of the privates buy it. With the number of Americans in France constantly and rapidly increasing the Herald circulation should gain steadily.

... On Sunday I took the liberty of sending about 70 words to New York at full rate (25 cents a word) to provide a newsy lead to the story about the decoration of the 104th Regiment, Massachusetts. The A.P. man was late getting in and I saw a possibility of getting a beat in New York and in any event a different and newsy introduction. ...

All the correspondents who went to the other front, to the North, have returned here. The censorship was so rigid the three weeks put in there were lost. I shall remain here unless, in my opinion, it is better for the Herald for me to go to the other front for a brief stay. ... When the big battle in Picardy settles down I should like to make a try for a complete story on, and good interview with, General Foch. He is probably a hard man to reach but if it could be done, in my opinion, it would be one of the big stories of the war.

Respectfully,
Don Martin

Diary: Friday May 3, 1918

Went out with Taylor again. Visited Boucq and the aviation field near Toul. Some of the American fliers told us about young Chapman of Iowa losing his life in fight with Boche over the German lines. The others feel sorry—that's all. "Got to happen now and then," said young O.G. Gude of N.Y. Called earlier in day at French prison and saw a lot of Boche prisoners.

Situation on Picardy front quiet.

Weather delightful. Fine day but showers at night.

Diary: Saturday May 4, 1918

Had interesting trip. Went first to Ligny [-en-Barrois] where Taylor and I had lunch with the Salvation Army. Then drove—taking two Salvation Army girls who wanted to go to Menil [-sur-Saulx]—through [Commerage]: over a road in plain sight of the Boche, only two kilometers from the German trenches, to Aulneis to see "Machine Gun" Parker*. He is a good fighter maybe, but a bit crazy.

Got home at 6:30. In evening went to the office of the gas experts and saw the newest models of gas masks. Our experts say the war, beginning in a few months, will be fought in gas masks. We are using gas just as effectively as the Huns.

Fine day but showers at night.

* Colonel John Parker, 102nd Infantry Regiment, 26th Division

Letter from Dorothy

Dated May 4, 1918; postmark illegible; no 'received' notation New York Herald Bureau, 38 Rue Du Louvre, Paris

Silver Creek, N.Y.
May 4, 1918

Dear Dad

Well, I have not only an early start in my letter this morning, but everything; because I have evry bit o' my practicing done and I have eaten my breakfast and it is only half past eight. I can do my work as fast as I want to, when I happen to want to. But I wanted to this morning because I am going to get a dear little kitten, and I want to get it as early as I can. It is not going to run away either, because it is all trained and eveythin'! Mrs. Ferrington is going to give it to me. It's a little boy kitten, and is real frisky. Joseph is going to have a dear little girl kitten, too. He wanted a girl and I wanted a boy. I didn't want the girl, because if it had some little kittens, I would not give them away. I am going to try and teach mine tricks.

Aunt Julie took me to Buffalo yesterday. I took my music lesson, and went to the dentist's as usual. Aunt Julie bought a lot of new pieces for their new piano yesterday, too. Did she tell you about the piano? Well, they've got a new one anyway.

Wednesday morning I got a letter from you, in Paris, dated Apr. 10, and Wednesday afternoon I got another one from Paris, dated Apr. 13. Both of them were mainly about trying to get to the big battle. Wednesday was the first of May, so that's when they got here.

Wednesday afternoon I had a little club of eight girls here, that I belong to, and Wednesday evening I had to go down to the picture show and be in a dumb bell drill. It was a patriotic show, and we all had to wear red, white and blue. It seems as if we practice for something all the time, in gym' class. Now we are practicing for a May Festival. And we have to have all sorts of clothes and everything. It seems almost as if we were a travelling show, things come so often.

The weather is getting somewhat warmer; and the lilacs are budded and the tulips are out. We are cleaning house and everything.

Grandmother bought me a $100 dollar Liberty Loan.

You never could guess what I have bran' new – I got a letter from Aunt Lou the other day, and she said that my Uncle Charlie in Philadelphia had a baby boy, who will be 3 months old the 6th of May.

Well, I guess I have said about all there is to say now, and as I am anxious to get that cat, I guess I will close.

Lots o' love an' hugs an' kisses,

Dorothy

P.S. I just received a card from you showing a ruined village, which you had recently passed through.

Diary: Sunday May 5, 1918

Slept late for a change. Had breakfast at the club and went with Taylor to Chaumont and had a talk with Col. Surrey about censorship. Saw part of a baseball game at Chaumont. Spent the evening at the club with Percy Noel of the Chicago News.

Weather retired again—rainy.

Diary: Monday May 6, 1918

Went with James to the aviation field near Toul: saw some of the American fliers who are now organized as the Squadron of the Hat in the Ring. James unpleasant to be around with. Got word today that I have been properly accredited. Moved into a room at 32 Rue St. Jean [Neufchateau].

Quiet in Picardy. Germans evidently preparing to launch another big offensive.

Weather pleasant—some sunshine.

Finally, it happened. Don Martin was accredited as a war correspondent. He had been in Europe over four months, and in France for eight weeks.

Diary: Tuesday May 7, 1918

Spent the day with [Lt.] Parks, chiefly sightseeing. Went to Epinal where we met Eyre of the World. Had lunch together. Then went to Vittel where we stayed for an hour on account of a terrific rainstorm, reaching Neufchateau at 6:30. Found story about Capt. [Norman] Hall, author and flier, who was forced to descend inside the German lines. Wrote 700 words for Paris and 350 for N.Y. giving an interview I had had with Hall. Spent evening at club with crowd which sang army songs.

Weather wretched.

Diary: Wednesday May 8, 1918

Went to Boucq with James. Got nothing. Whole front quiet. Got some oil today and now I have a lamp instead of a candle to write and read by. It is a big improvement. Spent part of the evening at the club with Percy Noel of the Chicago News.

Weather rainy and raw.

Diary: Thursday May 9, 1918

Had a car to myself today. Went to Nancy to do some errands but found practically all the stores closed. Got a pair of heavy shoes. Went to aviation field and to Boucq but got little. Cabled 400 words to N.Y. for sort of feature story. Was at the club for short time in the evening reading.

Weather overcast but not rainy.

Now that he was accredited, he could take an auto by himself!

Letter to Dorothy on May 9, 1918, from Neufchateau describing the life of the American correspondents.

With the American Army, France
May 9 – 1918

Dorothy

Before I go over to the censor's office I shall write you a short letter in reply to your No. 16 which reached me two days ago—practically a month after you wrote it. You see your letters go to Paris and there is some delay there but so long as I get them some time it doesn't matter so much. That was a good picture you drew of a German. I guess you hate them about as much as I do. They are no good. I should like to have seen you dance at the Park Theatre. When I finally get back to United States you will have to teach me to dance. I don't think it would be very difficult and then we could dance together.

I haven't received a letter from Mother recently but with yours came a long one from Alta. You tell her that I am ashamed at not having written more often to her but the truth is I don't have a great deal of time. And anyhow, as I have often explained, my letters to you are intended for the whole family. The automobile trips we make are so long that they take up a great deal of time. For instance today I started out at eight o'clock in the morning, went 70 miles over to a point close to the front and then returned visiting several other points. I didn't get back till seven in the evening and was riding most of the time. Then I have to get dinner—and at the officer's club we have a very good dinner—and then write a cable or two in addition to some dispatches for Paris and wait around the censor's office till they are read. That takes time. The censor reads and re-reads them and nearly always makes some changes. After that I have to walk to the telegraph office about a third of a mile away and explain what I want done. By that time it is ten o'clock and until yesterday I had no facilities for night letter writing. I lived in that old hotel where the only light was by candle. Yesterday I moved into a private house where I have a nice front room—they call them billets in the army—with a fine bed, a settee, a center table almost as big as the dining room table we used to have before you were born, and an oil lamp. ONLY I have to furnish the oil. There is very little oil to be had in France so I managed to get enough from the American army headquarters. Last night I had a lamp to read by and tonight I am writing this with the lamp beside me. It seems rather queer but it is not bad.

The house I live in is the home of the leading city barber or coiffeur as the French call them. The shop is downstairs and the dwelling in the rear of the ground floor and the second story. The room costs me one franc (20 cents) a day but I pay one franc extra for service furnishing my own towels and soap. The low rates are due to the fact that the French government confiscates or seizes all the available rooms in all houses in villages and cities where soldiers are quartered and fixes the rents. So I am paying the government rate plus one franc extra which I donate. But that is only 40 cents a day. Just think of that! At the hotel it cost me $1 a day and the room was nowhere nearly so nice as this one. The French people are immaculate housekeepers. It seems as if they are scrubbing all the time.

I was up in Picardy where the big battle is going on but all the American correspondents returned so I came back also. I stayed only a few days. To remain there I had to be stationed with a regiment; had to sleep in a stable or on the ground or wherever it was necessary to be; ran the same risk as the other soldiers and stood a chance very day and every night of being hit by a shell. It wasn't worth while. Later when it is possible to see more and hear less I shall go back. I have seen enough to know something about what war is like. I shall for the time being at least remain here with the main American army and visit the principal points or sectors held by the Americans. I see a great deal of the soldiers; see them in the trenches, see a barrage now and then at night; see wounded men brought into hospitals and see about every phase of the business. It is very interesting and very terrible. United States no doubt realizes fully by this time that she is engaged in a terrible war but if she is not fully alive to it she will be before a great while. We haven't done much yet and are not in a position to do much but the time will come when we will be in a position to put the finishing touches on the German if he does not force the world to peace through terror.

I see Americans every day whom I knew somewhere in United States. The officer's club here looks as if it might be in Buffalo or Cleveland, only this place is a great deal smaller of course.

I understand the Herald signs my name to some of my cables. I haven't written anything very great yet because there has been nothing great to write—perhaps I should say nothing big. The only happenings have been small except of course on the Picardy front and no American correspondent can get away up to that front. We shall do so later.

I wish I had a camera. I would take pictures of some of the funny little boys and girls I see in the tiny villages. They are pretty as pictures and although they live in tumble down looking places sometimes they are as spick and span as the Dingle sisters. About half of them wear wooden shoes. They would make you laugh. I am going to get hold of a camera somehow and take a few pictures to send you.

Now my young lady I shall go over to the censor's office and then back to my new room. I shall write to you more often now unless I get out again where there are no conveniences. Tell Alta I shall write to her very soon. And say young lady you get some nice photographs taken and don't wait too long either. I hear you have a fine hat and that your fine coat looks nice but that you are growing so fast it is inclined to be a little small.

Here's a hug and a kiss Dorothy,
Dad

P.S. Nothing also, or rather are you going to have a cottage at Dahn's Beach this year?

Martin did not stay a few days in Picardy, as he wrote in that letter. One can only wonder why he would write that.

Diary: Friday May 10, 1918

Went out with Percy Noel. First to Boucq, then Nancy for luncheon and then Toul aviation field. Saw Gen. Edwards [Commander 26th Division] near Toul making a test with high explosives to break through wire. At aviation field had quite a visit with Gude, Campbell and Taylor, all fine fliers who some day "won't come back". Some sunshine but rain also.

Diary: Saturday May 11, 1918

Stayed in Neufchateau and wrote 4 stories for mailing. Also made arrangements to go to British front for a week if permission to cable is furnished. Spent hour or so around the club in the afternoon and in the evening sat around for 3 hours with a crowd of about a dozen, one being Wilson of the International News [Service]. Bazin has resigned from the Evening Ledger.
10 Americans killed and 100 in bad shape from gas attack in Toul sector.

Sunshine for 3 hours—then heavy rain.

Diary: Sunday May 12, 1918

Invitation from American censors to N.Y. correspondents to go to British front presumably to see the 77th division American Army which has been brigaded with the British. Undecided what to do. Went to Boucq alone. Got nothing. Spent part of the evening at the club but went to bed early so to get up early and start for Paris.

Weather pleasant; then showery.

Diary: Monday May 13, 1918

Left Neufchateau at 8 for Paris. On train met Judge Wadhams of N.Y. one of the procession of sightseers U.S. sending over. Arrived Paris 2 p.m. Tried taking pair military breeches to replace pair (my only pair) which has hole in the seat. Couldn't get them. Put on civilian clothes.

They feel very comfortable. Had dinner alone at Chatham Grill (cost $4.50) [$84 August 2020] and went to Crillon and to bed at 9. Received 5 boxes candy (including maple sugar) from folks at home.

Quiet on all fronts. German offensive soon to start.

Weather miserable. Downpour in Paris.

Diary: Tuesday May 14, 1918

Mr. Bennett died today—at 5 a.m. in Beaulieu. Result of pneumonia attack. I didn't know until 4 p.m. when on returning to my hotel I met a Stars and Stripes reporter who very bluntly told me the Commodore was dead. It was considerable of a shock although I knew he had been dangerously ill for long time. Is the last of the old "giants of Journalism." I am glad I saw so much of him. Great speculation now is—what will become of the Herald?

Saw Martin Green, Irvin Cobb, Lincoln Eyre and several other men I know. Had dinner with Price at the Chatham Grill. Then walked around until dark—9:30—when I came to the hotel. Sent telegram of condolence to Mrs. Bennett.

Weather clear and fairly pleasant.

Diary: Wednesday May 15, 1918

Got up at 9 and went to the American Consul's office to get my passports renewed. Was detained there 2 hours. Met Price in afternoon; went with him back to Consul's where I got my passports extended till July 2. Everyone talking about Bennett death. Herald devoted front page to it. No doubt his death removed a great and picturesque figure. Had dinner at the Chatham. Air raid alarm at 10. I was in my room reading. Remained there. Raid didn't amount to much.

Little activity on Picardy front but big attack soon to come. Weather fine.

Diary: Thursday May 16, 1918

Went to American Embassy and got nice tribute to Bennett from Ambassador [William Graves] Sharp.

Spent part of the afternoon at office. Staff wondering what will happen now to the Herald. My notion is it will be sold by the widow. I intended to go back to Neufchateau but have decided to wait to attend the funeral if it is to be held soon. Weather like Summer.

Diary: Friday May 17, 1918

Stayed in bed till 9. Went to Herald office Rue de l'Opera and read the New York edition for April. Found my name is being signed in big letters to all my stories. Went to the office Rue du Louvre. No news yet about time of funeral. Went with Price to florists and ordered flowers for New York employees for Cooper, Flaherty, for the staff here and the Publishers' Association. Chatham for dinner. Air raid alarm about 10:30. Was in my room. Went down and out in the Champs Elysees but nothing happened. Got nice letter from Dorothy. Weather beautiful.

Diary: Saturday May 18, 1918

Spent an hour trying to find Howard Dean but find he is in Toul. I shall no doubt see him there. Went to office in evening and wrote a thousand-word cable for New York on the approaching new German offensive.

Sat around the hotel in the evening waiting for an air raid that didn't come.

Weather like July at home.

The death of Commodore J. Gordon Bennett, owner of the Herald, in Beaulieu-sur-Mer, was big news for Don. Bennett, prior to his passing, had given his go-ahead for Don to serve as accredited war correspondent for The Herald. But the death added a note of uncertainty about the future of The Herald.

Don decided to stay in Paris to attend the funeral which took place some days later in Paris.

J.G.
"Commodore"
Bennett
1841–1918

Diary: Sunday May 19, 1918

Am staying over in Paris to attend the Bennett funeral. Went to the office for couple hours in afternoon. Had dinner alone at Prunier's. Walked around during the early evening. Got some letters from home.

Weather very hot.

Diary: Monday May 20, 1918

Went to the Gare d'Lyon at 8:30 to meet body Mr. Bennett. It arrived on time. Cohick (looking like an undertaker) and Price there also. Met Percy Mitchell, Bennett's secretary, for first time. Spent couple hours reading Heralds for April. The office certainly is "keeping me up".

Weather terribly hot.

Diary: Tuesday May 21, 1918

Just "hung around" hotel and the office. Too hot to do much of anything. Wrote a 350 word cable on Lufbery's death. Knew him slightly. It certainly seems as if our airmen are going fast.

Air raid alarm given at 10:30. Terrific barrage for an hour. I stood in front of the hotel and saw shrapnel bursting all over the sky but nothing else. No planes get into the city. Also, early in day, posed for photograph to send to Dorothy. Sent a cable to Dorothy.

Weather stifling.

Diary: Wednesday May 22, 1918

Just marking time till the funeral tomorrow. Spent most of the afternoon at the office reading. Had dinner at Prunier's. Then during evening walked through Tuilleries, along the Seine etc. Paris is no doubt a wonderful city. Then spent the evening sitting around the hotel waiting for an air raid which hasn't come.

Weather continues very hot.

Diary: Thursday May 23, 1918

Attended Mr. Bennett's funeral. Walked from the church to the cemetery with Miss [Laura E.] Birkhead who was one of Mr. Bennett's favorites. She is a good newspaper woman. Went to the Herald office afterward but did no work. The funeral was a big "success".

Diary: Friday May 24, 1918

Returned to Gondrecourt and Neufchateau.

Diary: Saturday May 25, 1918

Went alone to the aviation field near Toul. Met Taylor of the U.P. there and returned with him.

Letter from Dorothy

Dated May 25, 1918; postmarked May 27, 8AM; no 'received' notation; c/o New York Herald Bureau, 38 Rue Du Louvre, Paris

Silver Creek, N.Y.
May 25, 1918

Dear Dad A La Mode

I am very, very, very silly and excited this morning and I guess it's the same way with nearly everybody. As you know today is the great big day, as I have told you in my last 2 or 3 letters. You know – that big auction on ev'rything. I'll have sompin' to tell you about next week all right. I'm so excited I can hardly do anything – I guess you will notice it by the writing. You know – Katsy Barbeau, the Dickie Birds, (Ha! Ha! Ha! Ha!) and myself are going to sell popcorn, and Howard Webster said he'd pop all the corn for us, and Johnny Knox gave us 100 bags. We're lucky! I could tell you a million and 1 other things, but I'll wait till next Sat. when I have more time.

- - - - - - - - - - - -

Well it is Sunday now, and I am going to finish this crazy letter. Yesterday I was busy every minute – this is what I did – got this letter about half finished or to where I left off, then, had to go down to Joe's to get his wagon. Got back and had to take a lot of stuff down to one of the booths in the Park. Went over to Iola Dick's to see about the popcorn we were going to sell, came home – got some money for popcorn, took a basket of canned stuff, and some potatoes and went off again. Left canned goods at one of the booths, then saw Aunt Julie. She asked me if I'd go down for her potatoes too, went down and got those – Kathleen Barbeau was with me all the time – came back, and went to the church, then up Buffalo St. to a store to get the popcorn, then came down footbridge, went over to Webster's, then to Iola's, then Florice Dick came down, then we all traveled up to my house. Then I put my white dress on, also my Red Cross Set, and then I intended to do a little practicing or write a little more of my letter, but we wanted to be down to have the corn popped at 11:00 o'clock so I said I'd just have to wait, and do my work to-day. Then we stopped at Florice's, and she got ready, then over to Kathleen's while she got ready, and had to look all over the house for a pair of stockings, and then it began to pour!!

You know there was a dinner at the Presbyterian Church and we were all going. Well, Iola and I got under a raincoat while the other two got under a little umbrella, and in that way we got as far as Coquell's, then we let loose and ran over to the church. The 3 of us waited there, while Iola went over to her house to get fixed, and then when she came back, the rain had about let up, and we walked over to Webster's to have our corn popped. Iola and I put it in bags, salted it, etc. while the other two were kept busy throwing bags to us, and taking the full bags from us. When we finished that, it was twelve o-clock, so we left the corn there until after dinner. We had a good dinner, then we were off to sell pop-corn. I made $1.25, and in all we made $4.90.

Well, after that we wanted to sell something else, so we took tobacco and cigarette holders, but we didn't have much luck. So we took a grab-bag around and, oh! – such fun! We went over on the corner of Shofner + Parkin's or where the Barber shop is, with a bag full, stood there about 5 min, and our bag was empty. Iola and I made $5.48 with the grab-bag. All along with this we had lemonade, hot dogs, and so forth. Well, it got to be 6:00 o'clock, and we were resting in a tent, when Grandmother came after me to take me home. Well, I got another hot "Dawg" then, we came home, and got here just before a big fat storm (we have been having one all the time so far this morning too) – regular flood around here. You know the sewers stop up and the water runs all over. Last night the side walk on the other side of the street was covered with water.

Well, in about half an hour, it grew just lovely again! The sun came out and ev'ry thin' was fine – That reminds me of a schoolroom: when teacher's out of a room everybody's a lil' _____. But when she gits back – oh! Everybody's just as angelic! Well, o' course when it got so nice again, we had to go down town again. Everything was goin' on just the same – band playing – auctionin' still, and everythin' goin' jus' as if nothin' 'ad 'appened hat hall. Well, I guess that's about all about that. Some Rigmarole! Huh? I say so!

We went to Buffalo Friday, and ev'rything went just the same as usual, so I won't bother and tell all about it. Well, it is still raining, and we have a gas-light lighted it is so dark, but I guess that's better than candlelight, like you have, or do you have a better light now?

183

I must close now, and anyway I guess this letter's about long enough.

Lots o' love an' hugs an' kisses,
Dorothy

Dorothy included this drawing in her May 25 letter to Don, captioned: "You with I don't know what."

Diary: Sunday May 26, 1918

Went to Toul, taking Lieutenant Baird of the Secret Service along with me. Had luncheon in Nancy; then went to the Aviation field, Boucq and home. Spent the evening at the Lafayette Club.

Diary: Monday May 27, 1918

Went with James to Boucq. Heard of a raid on the Americans near Bernecourt so I went there over a road said to be very dangerous. No danger while I was on it. Came back by way of Ansauville over a still more dangerous road.

Wrote a cable which was mercilessly censored. Stopped at the aviation field and had luncheon with the observation fliers at Ourche. Took Remain as far as Domremy[-la-Pucelle], Joan of Arc's birthplace, and left him there with the understanding he would write me a story about the people there.

Diary: Tuesday May 28, 1918

Stayed in Neufchateau and wrote letters and some mail stories. Spent the evening at the club.

Diary: Wednesday May 29, 1918

Wrote a ten page letter to Dorothy, much of it about the children of France. Went with James to Nancy. Wandered around. No news. On return wrote an advance cable on Decoration Day in France. Also wrote a cable on Campbell, the first American flying ace. The German offensive continues. Is very formidable.

In the May 29 10-page letter addressed to 11-year old Dorothy, but obviously intended for the whole family, Don Martin included his experience in covering the war, his expectations for how it might continue, and he vented his feelings about the German use of gas.

Neufchateau, May 29, 1918

Dorothy

The very first thing I shall do now that I have a decent ribbon in my typewriter is to write to you. It seems a terribly long time since I wrote last and I guess it is a long time. I shall try not to let it happen again. You see I was in Paris for a week, first to see about going to the Rheims front and then to attend Mr. Bennett's funeral. I did some work while there. There was an air raid every night so the lights were turned out in the hotel and there was hardly a chance to write. Today I am staying in to write a mail story or two and also to write to you and to the office. Maybe this afternoon I shall take an automobile ride out to one of the aviation stations to see if anything has happened there. We each have an automobile but very often go in groups of two or three for the sake of company. The rides are very long but the country now is very beautiful and the weather good so I don't mind.

There was one stretch of 26 days during which it rained on 24 days. Now it has been sunshiny every day for two weeks. The weather is about like June back home but the sky somehow is never quite so clear as we have it. Clouds are always floating around—this is in the Vosges country you know, which is the approach to the Alps—and storms come up very suddenly. The nights are cool.

Just now the big new offensive has started and it is possible that I may get up there. Our troops are scattered around so much now that it is hard to be where they all are—in fact it is impossible. The Herald gets the war stories of Percival Phillips of the London Express so that we are covered on the British front. Then from the French front we get the Associated Press reports. Phillips is the dean of the war correspondents and one of the best. He works for the London Express and the same articles he sends to the Express are cabled each night to New York. I roam around where the bulk of the American troops are and some day if I remain here will have stories just as big as those coming from the Picardy-Flanders front now. If I do not go up North I shall probably put in a couple of days down in Alsace, returning here. The trip down there is beautiful. It will take me to Belfort and through a piece of the Alps on the very edge of Switzerland. It is German held territory there but the Allies occupy it.

About the big offensive—this, young lady, will I daresay not interest you so much, being a kid yet, as it will Rock and the rest of the family. The offensive is serious of course. Germany is throwing her full weight into it, sacrificing men like sheep in the expectation that she will emerge from the present test apparently the stronger of the two forces—so strong that the Allies will not dare to make an offensive themselves this year or next either; in fact not till United States comes into her full strength here. Should Germany be successful she would expect the unrest in France and England, or at least what she figures would become unrest, to force a peace which would be satisfactory to Germany.

Of course no one knows what the result of the present offensive will be. The worst storm will be over by the time this letter reaches you and my personal opinion is that the Germans, after going ahead a good way and seeming like victors, will find themselves against some genuine Foch (pronounced as if Fosh with the same o sound as gosh) strategy and tactics which will give them the same kind of dose they got at the Marne. In a way it is the critical battle of the war because it is Germany's last chance of mpressing her will upon the world. A complete victory for her troops now would be a very serious if not disastrous affair but at the same time Germany might break the Allied line and then be licked in two years. She has troubles at home which are likely to break out. They are certain to make trouble for her military leaders if the present battle does not bring a great victory for Germany.

France has a wonderful army yet. She has reserves who have never yet been in the line. When Germany goes up against these men, whose whereabouts is known only to French generals, there will be some dead Huns. The French are everywhere. They are backing up the line from end to end and they say there is no more chance of the Huns getting to Paris than there is of Germany capturing Philadelphia.

If the battle now going on ends in what amounts in a draw then there will be a different story to tell. Germany will find herself gradually facing an army larger than her own and she will have to get back herself or draw back under constant attack. But that may not be till next spring and summer. It is bound to be a long war unless something cracks during the next six weeks and I do not think anything will crack. The Germans are desperate. I have seen examples of their barbarity which would not be believed unless actually seen. They are beasts. They don't belong in a civilized world.

They may seem like, and be, good citizens in times of peace. They may pay their bills, take part in public functions and help their respective communities, but they are all of the same material. They are the Vandals and Huns reincarnated and worse than their ancestors because education and scientific perfection make them more dangerous. I wouldn't trust a German anywhere, no matter where he is. But they are in for a licking in my opinion and my only fear is that when peace seems in sight the sentimentalists and mollycoddles of the world will begin to weep because of the suffering of the poor German women and children and urge a peace which is too fair for Germany.

The thing for the world to do if it can ever do it, is to go straight into Germany and devastate their country the same as they have devastated France, killing people wherever they find them and making the whole nation cry for mercy. Then after it begins to cry go on to Berlin and tell the Germans how they must conduct themselves in the future. If some of the people in Silver Creek could see what I saw the other day—150 fine young Americans from out West, suffering from gas poisoning—they would never speak to a German as long as they live. I never saw anything to compare with the tortures of these youngsters many of whom are dead of course. The Germans threw a thousand huge gas shells into their line while the boys were asleep and there was not time even to get gas masks on. They are constantly inventing new gasses, each more deadly than the other, and they are all frightful. Of course the Allies are using gas. It is necessary. They would lose the war if they didn't. But the Allies would never have resorted to such a fiendish method of warfare if the barbarians over the Rhine hadn't started it.

There, I guess that is enough about the war. Maybe I better write something to you now young lady. In the first place I received five parcels from you folks. Four were candy and one Maple sugar. I gave two boxes away here and am slowly eating the others. The maple sugar is splendid. The candy is the real thing and I can tell you it tastes good. Every evening two or three of the correspondents drift into my room and intimate that they could eat a piece of candy. The parcels went to London and then were forwarded to Paris where I got them.

Tell Joseph I will buy a pair of wooden shoes for him and send them along with yours. But I am afraid his won't have his name on as yours have, because the French soldier who did the carving went to the front during the last big offensive and probably is dead by this time. However the shoes will be good. Joseph's letter was very funny. I was glad to get it and hope he will write another some day. He writes very well. He is certainly a bright youngster. The French phrases in your letters and Mother's I was able to translate. I can speak a little French but the verbs are what bother most. Maybe I will learn them after I have been here long enough. I had a lady here in Neufchateau go out the other day and buy me some fancy things for all the folks—Mother, Jule, Alta, Inez and you. I hope there's enough. I shall mail them some day and you may divide them as you think best. Don't get in a fight over them. The lady who bought them is the wife of a lawyer here. She has two officers living in her house and bought for them also. If I had gone to the store the pieces would have cost me twice what she paid and I might have got inferior stuff anyhow. She says what she got is the best. It is Luneville material. Luneville is not a great way from here—I have been there—and is famous for its lace and embroideries.

Now I suppose you want to know about Mr. Bennett's death and funeral. I knew he was very ill and expected he would die. I was in Paris when it happened and remained for the funeral. I never saw a funeral like it. There were enough flowers for all the hospitals in the city and many of the most distinguished people of Paris at the church and the grave. Everyone walked from the church to the cemetery. The distance is about a third of a mile. I walked with the rest. I saw his widow and her two sons. Then I returned here.

I don't know whether the death will have any effect on the work I am doing or not. The last instructions I got were direct from Mr. Bennett and it is likely that, unless the paper is sold or completely reorganized, I shall remain here or go to London. I am not particular which. As a matter of fact I'd just as soon return to United States but probably that will not be right away. The future of the Herald is uncertain. I would not be surprised if the widow should inherit the property, and sold the whole thing. I would probably remain if I wished to do so, but whether I did or not, I need not worry. There are plenty of places to go.

I imagine people in New York will know about the Bennett will long before I hear of it. I received a letter from Mr. Bennett only a short time before his death and got telegrams up to within ten days of his death. I had considerable correspondence, by letter and telegram, with him in five months and it is quite interesting. It is all business of course. Apparently I satisfied him in every way, so perhaps it is too bad for me that he died. I imagine if he had lived a couple of years he would have had me all over Europe.

You ought to see the little girls over here Dorothy. They all let their hair grow and girls of three and four have hair down around their shoulders. They are very cute, too. I pass through a great many villages during my trips around the eastern part of France and it is fun to see the children salute. They wave or give the military salute and smile. They are very pretty too. In some of the smaller towns the little girls trudge around in the mud—there is no mud now though—in wooden shoes and a funny little three cornered hat. But they are always neatly dressed. On Sundays they have on a particular dress and have their hair done up like young ladies. The other day I saw a half dozen little girls in a tent beside a house, just outside Nancy. I had the automobile stop and went to see what it was all about. The girls were about six or seven years old and were having a doll's party, just about like your doll parties I suppose. They had quaint looking dolls. They had them on tiny chairs, in improvised beds and sitting at a small table. I couldn't help thinking that little girls are just alike all over the world.

I suggested to the office that it send me a camera and if it does I shall take some snapshots of little things like this and send them to you. The expressions the little children pick up—English expressions—are amusing. An American general was in a little village one day when a sweet faced little girl about seven stopped in front of him and said "Hello kid." She thought she was saying something quite proper. She had heard some of the American soldiers use the phrase. I wrote a little piece about this incident.

I would like to have you along on some of my automobile rides Dorothy. You would enjoy them. The scenery is wonderful now. The fields are green everywhere and the panorama wherever one looks suggests that some wonderful landscape gardener had laid out the countryside. The farms are oblong and of varying shades of green with an occasional patch of yellow where mustard is being raised or buttercups have grown in a pasture. There are no fences. There are no houses. I could take you where you could gaze at a gently sloping hillside three miles long and a mile in depth, with the farms marked out as distinctly and accurately as if done by a surveyor. These hillsides look for all the world like a crazy quilt only vastly more beautiful. The people who own the farms live in the villages and go out to work every morning, returning in the evening. Women, old men and children are the only people seen in the fields now. But they have done and are doing a good job. One never sees a foot of wasted land; no stumps, no swamps, no marshland, no scrubby woods. Everything is regular and occupied. There are now and then patches of pasture fenced off but they are rare.

The villages have community pastures both for cows and sheep. Children tend the cows. Each village has its shepherd. In the morning he goes through the town and collects the family sheep, each stable, pen or back yard, having one, two, three or four. He drives them out to the country and at night brings them back. As they reach the town the sheep turn into their proper abodes, each knowing where he belongs and never making a mistake.

The forests here are uniform. They were all planted. No one dares cut a tree on his own land without permission of the local forester and when one is cut another has to be planted. France has beautiful forests and plenty of them. I had an idea the country was denuded but it is just as woody as any part of New York state except the Adirondacks. I was in a forest of about 2,000 acres the other day where the trees were all the same size and placed at regular intervals. Look any direction and there was a straight line ahead as far as the eye could see. This forest is of oak and is very valuable. When I say the trees are all the same size I am wrong. They are of four sizes. Some day the largest will be cut and in each place a new tree will be planted. Then, some time the weeding out process will be resumed but there will always be a forest of fine trees. France is dependent on her forests. The people of the entire country except in a few of the larger cities, burn wood for cooking and heating. The old ladies and men go into the woods and make up bundles of fagots and in front of every house at this time of year one may see piles of these fagots all tied in bundles. Just now United States has 20,000 men working in the French forests cutting timber for use on railways, and for corduroy roads etc. But not a tree is being cut which is not ripe and when the war is over France will still have her forests, with just a few exceptions. I saw one the other day which is being completely cut off. The growth is fir and tamarack and the poles are being used for a telephone line for United States.

My goodness but this letter is a long one. I must stop anyhow because I have some things to do. I received letters from you all in Paris but have received none since. I notice they are signing my name to my dispatches. That is all right. I haven't been sending so much lately but will soon resume. Remember me to the whole family and the neighbors too Dorothy. I am glad Lee Brand is going into the war because it will give him a new view of things. However I wouldn't go into the Y.M.C.A. for any price. Paris is just overrun with great big fat, smug Americans strutting around, or rolling around in expensive automobiles, all having the Y.M.C.A. mark on their uniform. It gets sickening. I counted 130 passing the Hotel Crillon one afternoon. There are more slackers in the Y.M.C.A. than anywhere else and a lot of them will not get their passports renewed.

The organization undoubtedly does some good but it is unpopular everywhere with the army men. It provides good accommodations for officers and some accommodations for the privates. It charges exorbitant prices for everything and ought to pay a splendid dividend on the money people have given to it. It got cigarettes from the United States government at seven and a half cents a package, with the understanding it would sell at cost to the soldiers. Then it charged 15 a package. It got chocolate at a minimum price and sold it at a franc (20 cents) a cup to the boys. It got ham and bread at rock bottom and charged a high price for sandwiches. There will be a scandal connected with it if the war lasts long enough. The soldiers say, "Give us the Salvation Army." They are right about that. The Salvation Army sells way below the Y.M.C.A.; trusts the boys if they are broke, a thing the Y.M.C.A. never does; gives them gum and cigarettes when the boys are up against it; and makes doughnuts and apple pies at its own expense and sends them up to the front line trenches. So, tell Uncle Rock that when the Y.M.C.A. comes along appealing for aid and telling how indispensable it is to the soldiers at the front, to keep his money in his pocket and mention the Salvation Army. This is not intended to knock at Lee. He is doing what he thinks is a splendid thing and I know he will do something worth while but the organization as an organization is most unpopular, is filled with men who ought to be home or at the front, and rather nauseates the fighting men over here. The American soldier doesn't need to be coddled. He is here to fight not to have all the luxuries of home. The Red Cross is ready to care for him if he is sick or injured and the Salvation Army will attend to his little wants up in the line. Just where the Y.M.C.A. gets off, people over here don't exactly understand.

Now I'm really going to stop. Just one thing more. In Paris I bought a couple of funny dolls and left instructions for them to be mailed to you. Perhaps they will go astray but I imagine you will get them some day. I shall be glad to know how long they were in transit.

I hear the nicest things about your music Dorothy! You will come along rapidly now. How about your school? It will be about out when this reaches you, won't it? I got some new photographs taken the other day and will send you one. Now I am going to quit for sure, sending a kiss first.

With love

Dad

P.S. No, Notre Dame has not been hit by shells, bombs or anything else yet. I was in some air raids in Paris but as you are of course aware was not hurt.

Diary: Thursday May 30, 1918

With James (whom I am getting to like a bit) went to Baccarat by way of Epinal. Had motor trouble which delayed us considerably. Returned by way of Nancy. Arrived Neufchateau at 8 p.m. Wrote cable for New York about [Leslie] Kirk and [William] Richards, English airmen who landed in German territory and made their way back to their own lines.

Don Martin finally got the kind of story he was looking for — the miraculous escape of Kirk and Richards after their plane was downed. Finished after midnight on Thursday and dated Friday, it was featured on page 1 of the Saturday, June 1, edition of the New York Herald. It is a great example of the storytelling skill that made his war dispatches so well received by readers back home in America.

2 FLYERS FALL 10 MILES INSIDE HUN LINE, ESCAPE

Swim Ninety Foot River in No Man's Land Under Heavy Machine Gun Fire

DIG UNDER ELECTRIFIED WIRE, CLIMB TRENCHES

Lieutenant and Aid Lie in Rushes for Hours with Only Heads Out of Water

By DON MARTIN
Special Correspondent to the Herald with the American Armies in France

NEUFCHATEAU, Friday

Swimming a ninety foot river in No Man's Land in a hail of machine gun fire; crawling under heavy barbed wire entanglements of the enemy; hiding in a hedge all day with the Boches hunting and sometimes getting within a few yards; being mourned as dead by their comrades, who already had packed their personal belongings to send to their folks, are only a part of the wonderful and thrilling experiences of Lieutenant Leslie Kirk and Observer William Richards, both British bombers.

I saw Lieutenant Kirk today among his comrades and heard the full details of this amazing tale of the pair. The hero who perhaps is the most picturesque of all airmen is a Scotchman from Glasgow, twenty-three, who has been in many of the most successful raids of the British reprisal squad.

He said in a modest way, *"Oh, it's just a piece of luck, that's all."*

Machine Smashed in Fall

Lieutenant Kirk and his companion escaped death when the machine in which they were on a bombing trip was damaged by the German barrage and forced to descend from a height of four thousand feet, ten miles inside the German lines. The machine was smashed to bits and both men were badly bruised and shocked. The crash attracted the Germans within a few seconds, but the airmen, rallying all their remaining strength, dashed to cover in the woods. They heard voices all about them and finally stole from cover and walked until dawn was breaking. Then hid in a hedge, with nothing to eat but half a bar of chocolate.

At nightfall they resumed their journey toward their own line. As they neared the German first line they made a noise which instantly drew a savage machine gun fire. The bullets spattered all over and about them in a torrent until they thought their finish had come. In vain they shouted "Kamerade!" The shooting continued, but doing no damage.

Being unable to surrender, they ran as fast as possible and finally reached the advanced wire entanglements, having skipped over the German trenches by sheer good luck and with great difficulty.

Dig Under Electric Wire

Here the wire was a dense as rabbit netting and was supposed to be charged with electricity, as is the custom of the Germans. Having no nippers, they finally dug beneath the wire with their knives and hands and forced their heads and shoulders under it and lifted it up.

2 FLYERS FALL 10 MILES INSIDE HUN LINE, ESCAPE...

They were three hours at this terrific task before they got through.

Then after crawling some distance they reached the river's edge in No Man's Land. The river is deep, but the current is not swift. The fear that probably wire was stretched under the surface of the water forced them to decide that their only chance was to swim.

Observer Richards went first and in five minutes reached the other side. He then shouted in a hoarse whisper that he was all right. Lieutenant Kirk started and made it, though he was a bad swimmer.

The swim was made all the more thrilling and perilous, as the Germans, hearing suspicious sounds, trained machine guns in that direction. The bullets spattered the water in a stream, while Lieutenant Kirk was cros-sing. One struck within a few inches of his head.

Lights also flared up, but too late to reveal the airmen, who were able by this time to take cover in the rushes on the edge of the stream.

Only Heads Above Water

They lay there for several hours with only their heads above the water, the rushes concealing their heads and knowing death lurked on both sides. Then the men crawled on their bellies for several hundred yards until they came to the French-American first line, drenched to the skin, but warmly welcomed by the startled French-Americans.

At daybreak Lieutenant Kirk telephoned to Captain Lindsay, the commandant, only to be told word had been sent that he was lost.

Today Lieutenant Kirk and his companion appeared at the headquarters of the squadron and became the centre of a great celebration. They were in the midst of it when I saw him. He said: --

"We hadn't gotten rid of our bombs – in fact, we were just getting to our objective – when shrapnel hit the engine and put it out of business. The shells were breaking all around us as we came down, but the machine was messed up so badly that nothing was left of it, in fact.

"I don't know how we escaped death. It was just luck and nothing else. Oh, yes, they fired at us with machine guns twice and I don't know how we escaped. Only luck again, and I guess I am a lucky Scotchman. It was mighty unpleasant lying in the water among the rushes, but better than being killed. The swimming was bad, too; I do all right when the wind is good, but I always was a bad swimmer.

Cry "Kamerade" in Vain

"While we were lying in the rushes we heard our own squadron pass over us on a bombing trip. I wished I'd been with them. They are queer people — the Huns. When they turned their machine guns on us at first the only thing we could do was surrender or be killed. So we called it quits and cried "Kamerade!"

"But that did not change the situation. They kept peppering just the same, so we shouted, 'All right, go to hell!' and we started off. It is funny how close bullets can hit all round, yet miss. Luck again, I imagine. The river we swam is the only river in No Man's Land. The boy with me is the bravest kind of kid.

"We thought the wire stretched under the surface, but he stepped in and struck off, taking a chance. You see I was anxious to get back, as I have leave beginning on Sunday, and don't want to miss it. There is nothing else I can think of."

Lieutenant Kirk is a man of few words. When he paused, Captain Lindsay, with a glow of pride in his eyes at Lieutenant's achievement, said, *"Kirk, show him your hands where the wire got you."*

Lieutenant Kirk hesitatingly held up his hands which were deeply cut.

"Kirk is sore at only one thing; that is that he had to spend two days among the Germans," said Captain Lindsay with a laugh.

Diary: Friday May 31, 1918

Went to [AEF General Headquarters at] Chaumont with James. Arranged to go tomorrow to real battlefront.

Diary: Saturday June 1, 1918

Started with James and Lieutenant Wilson for the Chateau-Thierry section. Went by way of Ligny, Vitry, Sezanne and Montmirail. Rode about 180 miles. Passed miles and miles of soldiers, both American and French on their way to the front to resist the onward push of the Germans. Saw the third division in line. Slept at Montmirail.

Letter from Dorothy (No. 24)

Dated June 1, 1918; postmarked June 1, 5PM; no 'received' notation

Silver Creek, N.Y.
June 1, 1918

Dear Dad

Here goes for letter No. 24. I have anything <u>but</u> an early start to-day, as this is afternoon. This morning I did not feel like working at all, t'all, so I just didn't. I played around all morning on almost nothing. I went to Joseph's for dinner, and we played around there for a while, then came up-town, got an ice cream soda, and then came home. I then took my bath, (which I needed very badly, as I had been barefooted all morning) and then started writing this letter.

It is terribly hot here, 86 out now, and I have my short socks on, and oh, everything. Grandmother took me to Buffalo Friday and Joseph went along, just for instance. Everything happened the same, but you know, I didn't have to go to the dentist's this week.

Have you received any of the candy, sugar, etc, which we have sent you? I have my little kitten now, and I wish you could see it go through some of its crazy performances. It takes a big fall and rolls on it, just like an elephant at a circus, and turns somersaults by the million, and then it will get way over near Week's, then when an auto or anything like that goes past, it starts and runs like the wind, way over into our house, then back and forth 4 or 5 times without stopping, then it comes up and looks at you.

I always have plenty of clothes so do not think I don't, as I have all I _need_, besides all I _want_. And I also have all the _money_ I want. Grandmother is going to get me some slippers next week.

We haven't heard from you in quite a while, and we hope we will soon. I must close now, and go for a ride with Jane Christy in "Red" Osbornes's "jitney bus", as he is up here fixing curtains.

Lots o' Love an' hugs an' kisses,

Dorothy

Diary: Sunday June 2, 1918

Got up early and motored up near Chateau-Thierry. Saw the French shelling the city. Was within a kilometer and a half of the city. Heard twenty shells a minute pass over! Airplanes were constantly overhead. It was soldiers, soldiers, soldiers! The French are moving by tens of thousands to check the sweep of the Huns. Things look bad just now. I was within sound of the guns all day. Saw thousands of refugees getting out; saw cattle being herded and driven back out of the threatened zone.

Started back for Neufchateau at 7 p.m., there being no other place where I could file cable dispatches. Bearing broke near Ligny. Spent the night there. Managed to get telephone connection with Neufchateau through the kindness of a Croix de Guerre man who came down in his night clothes and opened the telephone station.

Don Martin does not record it, but he met Martin Green at Château-Thierry on June 2; the meeting was mentioned in Green's tribute to Don.

The Paris Herald was deciding how to publish Don Martin's dispatches, which were now arriving daily. In the June 4 edition they dedicated a whole page 1 column to his short dispatches, with his name at the end, as was their custom.

Diary: Monday June 3, 1918

Waited in Ligny till noon before a car arrived to tow us in. Got to Neuf-chateau at 2 p.m. Wrote a 1500-word cable. Arranged to start up to the line again tomorrow.

Diary: Tuesday June 4, 1918

Waited all day around Neufchateau for an auto to go to the Chateau-Thierry sector. Wrote three mail stories, one on how a city looks under bombardment; one on the Red Cross women doing such noble work at Montmirail and one on France rallying for her greatest test of all.

Don Martin's report showed he was learning what the war really was in a mail story dated June 5, published in the June 30 Sunday edition of the New York Herald. Here is an excerpt.

WITH THE HERALD CORRESPONDENT, UNDER FIRE ON THE MARNE

Herald Correspondent Sits Between the Lines and Sees Struggle Along the Famous River and the Seizure of Château-Thierry—The Flight of Refugees

By DON MARTIN

Special Correspondent of the Herald with the American Armies in France

[Special Cable to the Herald]

WITH THE AMERICAN ARMIES IN FRANCE,
June 5, 1918

A hundred miles of soldiers, marching, packed in motor trucks, resting along the roadside, on horseback, mule back, on ammunition wagons, artillery trucks!

Dragging a difficult way in the opposite direction a steady stream of aged men, women and children, walking, riding on jarring farm wagons, their all packed along with them; bedding, chairs, cooking utensils – refugees making their second trip to land not threatened by the Hun.

It was a grim, sad, yet stirring picture of war, of France rallying her mighty strength for another battle of the Marne; her beautiful valleys just recovering from the devastation of 1914, again within reach of the onrushing Hun. The allied line between Soissons and Rheims and still further east has been attacked by the largest army Germany had amassed during the four year struggle. It had bent. It had bulged dangerously. The people of a hundred towns and a dozen small cities, recalling the terrors and horrors which came with the first German invasion of this beautiful region, were frightened. Dozens of villages were evacuated in a few hours.

In one region I saw ten miles of small carts pulled by horses, oxen, goats and even dogs trailing a picturesque way to the rear. On the faces of the old folks was an expression of grim endurance. They had been through the ordeal before. Their homes had been wrecked, their fields pillaged, and now after three and a half years of upbuilding they were expecting to see a repetition of the destruction. The children were pathetic pictures, snuggling close to their parents, or more grandparents, or struggling along afoot, being half dragged through the clouds of dust which at this time of the year literally sweep like sandstorms over everything.

The Trade of Fighting Men

But while feeling the deepest sympathy for the refugees – the greatest sufferers of the war perhaps – one could not help turning his thoughts to the mighty line of hardy French, British, Americans, who were rushing to the front to stop the tide of Germans that had for days been sweeping over French villages and farms.

I saw the French poilu as it had never before been my privilege to see him; hungry, dusty, tired, riding in ponderous trucks (camions) which jolted and bumped along the roads, marching with full equipment, head down, seeing nothing but the road directly in front of him, on the way, probably, to death or injury, yet happy.

For ten hours in an automobile I passed this picturesque stream of heroes and a thousand times received from poilus *[French infantry soldiers]* who were stuffed in

WITH THE HERALD CORRESPONDENT, UNDER FIRE ON THE MARNE...

the trucks a hearty salute and a pleasant "Américaine." Some were fine looking young French boys whose red cheeks glowed beneath the dust which whitened their ears and foreheads. Frequently they were singing some French song the strains of which were strange to me. I was told it was a college song and corresponds to this song in the United States. "For it's always fair weather when good fellows get together," etc.

Americans were in the line. One regiment was marching side by side with some French soldiers, and it was a splendid thing to see. The Americans, fresh, rugged, shoulders erect despite the pack of seventy-five pounds; the French smaller, weather stained, scarred, too, from four years' experience. For it was one of the finest French regiments, and it looked it.

Americans were camped along the road. The boys in brown swarmed over wheat fields to rest for an hour; they formed a terrace along two miles of road. Their guns were stacked up in rows, their packs strewn about and many were writing letters. British plodded along, artillery and infantry. Cingalese troops sprinkled through the spectacular line, and French colonials from Africa added a touch of color to the picture. At one point there is a straight stretch of road for twenty-three miles with undulating hills. This stretch seemed a solid mass of moving soldiers.

The Saviors of France

It was the army intended to save France. Perhaps it should be said, rather, that it was part of the army which was to save France from the last desperate attack of the desperate Hun, because along other roads, all leading toward the same region, were similar lines of camions and soldiers. And the railway lines as well were transporting their tens of thousands in trains moving as rapidly as possible.

France was doing again what she did at the first battle of the Marne. She was preparing to deal the Hun a crushing blow at the point where his ambitions and his army were shattered in the first months of the war.

The difference was that now, instead of being practically alone, she had the British with her in full strength, and in addition had the active cooperation of a great army of virile, eager Americans, and furthermore she had learned something of the methods of transporting troops by trucks and trains.

> " In one region I saw ten miles of small carts pulled by horses, oxen, goats and even dogs trailing a picturesque way to the rear. On the faces of the old folks was an expression of grim endurance. They had been through the ordeal before. Their homes had been wrecked, their fields pillaged, and now after three and a half years of upbuilding they were expecting to see a repetition of the destruction. "
>
> Don Martin, Herald, June 5, 1918

Two stories reporting on what Don Martin saw, dated Wednesday, June 5, were featured on the front page, Part Two, of the New York Herald on Thursday, June 6, 1918.

Diary: Wednesday June 5, 1918

With Floyd Gibbons of the Chicago Tribune, Lieutenant Hartzell and James, left Neufchateau for Paris by way of the front. Visited various division headquarters on the way. Arrived in Paris at 9 p.m. wrote a story for Paris.

Diary: Thursday June 6, 1918

Stayed around the Hotel Crillon all day with a sore throat. Gibbons went out to cover the story for me. Went to the office in the evening and wrote a long cable story for New York and a story for Paris. Air raid tonight.

Diary: Friday June 7, 1918

Floyd Gibbons

Was awakened at 8 a.m. by a telephone message from Lieutenant Hartzell who said Gibbons was shot by a machine bullet and badly hurt. His left eye probably destroyed.

Diary: Saturday June 8, 1918

Throat very sore. Unable to leave the hotel. James went out and said he would give me what news there was of the front. He gave me some but held out most of the good stuff for himself. That was very evident to me at once. However I wrote 400 words for New York and 1,000 words for Paris. Was a rather hard job but I managed to get away with it. Americans are fighting splendidly. Wrote a good letter to Dorothy.

That 'good letter', which was dated June 7, described his experiences in covering the war in a way that seems a bit too mature for an eleven-year-old, but he meant his letters to Dorothy for the whole family.

Paris, June 7, 1918

Dorothy

To begin with I received your typewritten letter of April 12 and it was funny with the "scribbles" scattered through it, etc. Your typewriting is very good though and I really believe you are going to be a first class writer some day. Anyhow you have a good sense of humor and life isn't worth while without that. There are two big boxes or packages at the Paris post office for me. I haven't opened them yet but probably will tonight. They are part of the cargo of candy, sugar, maple syrup etc. the family has been sending me, and it is none too large a cargo either. The packages are slow in coming, although they have been at the Paris post office nearly two weeks. Your letter was one of a dozen which went astray and finally reached me by way of Beauvais, Neufchateau and Paris. It is all due to the fact that I have not been in one place all the time lately. There was a letter from Alta and one from Mother. Now, no doubt, there are some more in Neufchateau.

I shall probably make headquarters in Paris for a while. The American troops are now in the real battle line and it is impossible to cover them from Neufchateau, so the correspondents have moved their headquarters temporarily to Paris and each morning we go out in automobiles, look over the line— that is from some distance back—and return here at night. It keeps us travelling most of the time and working when we are not travelling but it doesn't matter because we are seeing part, perhaps a vital part, of the greatest battle of all time. Last Saturday morning I left Neufchateau with another man in an automobile and rode 220 miles before night. The following morning I was in Chateau-Thierry when the Germans began to enter the city. I saw them come in and saw the Americans help drive them back. Then I got out. Later I stood on a hill just a kilometer from the city and watched the French, from behind where I stood, bombard the city. It was about as if you were standing on top of that hill away across the creek and watching a village up at the end of Burges Street. Shells whistled over my head all the time and with a glass I could see exactly where most of them struck.

I stayed till the Germans began to throw shells back; then I got out of danger. I returned to Neufchateau but the automobile broke down at ten o'clock outside a little place called Ligny en Barros and we had to wake up a hotel keeper and stay there overnight. We left the next noon for Neufchateau, towed by an automobile which had come for us. I spent the next day writing long stories about my experiences, to be sent by mail, and the following day, started for Paris by way of Chateau-Thierry and the Rheims, Soissons front.

Thursday I decided to stay in and Floyd Gibbons of the Chicago Tribune said he would cover the story for me. Now Gibbons is in a hospital with his left eye shot away and a hole through his left arm. He probably will live but will lose an eye and be incapacitated for several weeks if not months. However, that doesn't mean that if I had gone I would have been shot. He was a daredevil and paid the penalty.

He was following a regiment of American marines almost into battle, which is no sensible thing to do. I wrote a story last night to be sent to the Chicago Tribune under his name. There is no danger of a correspondent being hurt if he uses ordinary precautions, and your Dad uses extraordinary precautions.

I have seen considerable of the big battle up to date and expect to see considerable more. No doubt you have seen some of my stories in the Herald. The European edition publishes them with my name at the head of the column. I must be careful or I will become notorious.

And say Miss Dorothy, what do you think I received yesterday? Five pictures of a rapidly growing young lady with hair hanging over her shoulders and clad in a very, very pretty dress which I never saw. I could hardly tell at first whom it was, she has changed so, but I decided it is Dorothy Martin. The pictures are pretty good Dorothy but they serve the purpose of showing how splendid your photographs would be if they were taken by some real artist. You must have some taken in Buffalo. I have four of them stuck up in the side of a mirror in my room here in the Crillon Hotel and the fifth, which I don't like so well, is on the mantle over the fireplace. The fifth is one which shows just

Dorothy, 11 years old

your head. It is good but not terribly good, according to my notion. There was also your letter written in French, some of which I shall have to have translated, and Joseph's letter in which he says he would like to hear from me again. Tell him I shall write to him some day but you see I don't have a great deal of time to write to anyone. You explain that to him Dorothy.

Last night I received a nice letter from Lester Colberg, written from a military camp in France. He says he and his brother "Red" are both here but he doesn't know just where Red is. Lester Colberg said he has been reading my articles in the Paris Herald and decided to write to me. I shall drop him a note some day. He wrote a very nice letter indeed.

The weather here has been like midsummer and still is. I have been automobiling so much that my face is red as a brick. It is a new experience for me but an interesting one. The Germans will soon start a new offensive but I don't think it will result in the capture either of Paris or of the Channel ports. If it doesn't the Germans are finished. I have been in a couple of air raids and heard shells from the big gun strike a half dozen times since I returned to Paris. No one has a tranquil time in France, or at least in Paris, during these trying days but the real perils lie in the front line and Americans are taking their places there and fighting splendidly.

Give my love to the family and my regards to the neighbors. A hug and a kiss for you young lady.

(signed) Dad

P.S. Don't get the impression your Dad is taking undue chances or is liable to be killed. He is just about as safe as you are and looks after himself pretty well.   Dad

On June 8, back in Silver Creek, Dorothy wrote her letter No. 25 to Dad.

Letter from Dorothy (No.25)

Dated June 8, 1918; postmarked June 8, 4PM; no 'received' notation

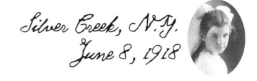

Silver Creek, N.Y.
June 8, 1918

Dear Dad

Here goes for letter No. 25. I did not feel like writing this letter this morning, either, so I waited until afternoon again. But I have all of my practicing done, so when I finish this letter, I am going out to play with some girls.

This week has been a very busy week, with me. Next week is also going to be a very busy one. I will tell you about last week – Monday – just regular school – Tuesday – gym', had to practice for a May, or rather June Festival, which was coming Friday. Wednesday – Had to go over in the baseball grounds to practice. Thursday – gym' again, had to practice for Fri. Friday – Busy day, busy day, busy day. I was in four dances, and a dumb bell drill. Luckily, we had to wear the same clothes (cheesecloth) all the time.

Well, that all went off pretty well and then came something in the evening. There was going to be a lady here, who has three sons in the war, who was going to speak in the Methodist Church. Miss Montgomery asked all of the school children to come and sing, as there wasn't any Community Chorus, so o' course I went.

Well, we didn't get out until almost ten o'clock, so you can bet I was pretty tired. I sure was, because I never got up until 15 after 8 this morning. We postponed the trip to Buffalo, and we're going Saturday, but as Dr. Hoffman and Miss Juergens could not see me, we did not go. But all of next week, we have exams, so I may not be able to go this coming Fri., but if I don't, we will go the following Mon. Then just think! – school is out for 2 whole mths. It will seem funny – I would almost rather go to school.

Your letter dated May 9 reached here day before yesterday – June 6. I do not wonder that you did not like to stay out on the Picardy Front. You have to live just about the way the soldiers do. We also got a card from you this morning saying that you had gone to Paris for some-thing about passports. The card was from Neufchateau. You call me young lady – but you wouldn't think I was one, if you could catch me at some of my performances. By the way, my yellow coat is plenty large enough, if not almost too large. Must close now.

Lots o' Love an' hugs an' kisses,

Dorothy

Diary: Sunday June 9, 1918

Went to Montreuil, 2d division headquarters, with Eyre and James. Got a good story. Returned to Paris at 6 p.m. Wrote 400 words for New York and 700 words for Paris. At 9 p.m. at the censor's office attended a protest meeting of the correspondents who are disturbed about being ordered to go to Meaux as a headquarters. I also got a notice that I was criticized because of my attempted cable censure of the censors. We certainly are under iron rule. James is worse off than I am.

My stories in Paris seem to be attracting much attention. They are widely commented on and copied in the French press. Got letter from Dorothy. We are figuring on moving to Meaux tomorrow.

Letter to Dorothy written in Paris on June 10, 1918 (only the first part survived).

Hotel de Crillon
Place de la Concorde, Paris
June 10, 1918

My dear Dorothy

The big battle going on now has made some rather abrupt changes in the arrangements of the correspondents. First we all came in from Neufchateau, expecting to have our headquarters here, and go each day in automobiles to the important places along the front. Today we get word that we must all go to a place some distance out from Paris and stay there. We don't like it but that makes no difference; we must go anyhow. I have just finished packing up and have about a half hour in which to get lunch after which I shall start out in an automobile.
I expect to see considerable of the big battle, which at one point is only 43 miles from Paris but, as I have often assured you, I shall keep out of danger.

Last night I got a long letter from Rock telling about the Liberty Loan slackers etc. Your letter, with a picture of the family hats, is a very funny one Dorothy. Aunt Alta tells me you are rapidly getting to be a fine musician.

I am mailing some Paris Heralds with some of my ...[rest of letter lost].

PART 5

Covering the Big Battles from Meaux — June to September 10, 1918

For three months from June 10 to September 10, Don Martin was housed with the American war correspondents in Meaux, a town 34 miles (54 kilometers) from Paris. It was possible to go to Paris by train, and he took advantage of that. Don Martin stayed overnight in Paris or made day trips to Paris ten times in this three-month period.

Getting to the front line from Meaux still required a long daily journey by car, although it was shorter than from Neufchateau. During this period, Don wrote that he got to see *"many of the horrors"* of the war *"at close range"* — the dead and wounded, the prisoners, the *"scores of wrecked villages"* — and he was often in the midst of shelling, including with gas. *"Got a story!"* was the main theme of his diary entries in these months, in which he recorded that he cabled 64,000 words (and many more were not enumerated). And what stories he was getting!

His stories about the doughboys at the front in the major battles in these three months were eagerly read back home. A highlight was his visit on August 26 to Quentin Roosevelt's grave, where a widely published photo was taken.

Diary: Monday June 10, 1918

Went to Meaux with James and took rooms at the Hotel Sirene. Sent a short cable to New York and wrote a story for Paris. The censors have moved out here and we have courier service to Paris.

Diary: Tuesday June 11, 1918

With James motored to the First Division headquarters in the vicinity of Beauvais. Saw hundreds of French camions [military trucks] on the roads. Had luncheon with American machine gun officers—a fine lot of chaps. Got a good story. Returned to Meaux and wrote a cable story of 500 words on German prisoners. During the evening Johnson, Eyre and several others came into my room to talk things over.

Diary: Wednesday June 12, 1918

With James went to the headquarters of the Second division. Saw 200 German prisoners captured by the Americans. Wrote a 500-word cable and a long story for Paris. At night had a long argument with [Ray] Carroll, Jimmy Hopper and Junius Wood on how best to increase the American hatred of the Germans.

Diary: Thursday June 13, 1918

Went to the 2nd and 3rd divisions. Had a narrow escape from a big shell which ripped up the road just before our auto got to the spot. Another struck even closer. We speeded up our auto and got by without difficulty. While we were at the headquarters of the Marines on the Chateau-Thierry road shells struck all around. This is about 5 or 6 miles from Chateau-Thierry which the Germans occupy. We got back at 4:30 p.m. Saw a new division of Americans—the 4th. They have been in France but a month but are on their way to the front line. They are fine looking boys. I feel sorry for them. They have no idea what an inferno they will soon be in. Wrote 700 words for New York on the Marines.

Diary: Friday June 14, 1918

Went to the 2nd division with Wales and James. Also went to brigade headquarters not far from where the shells struck yesterday. Returned early and cabled 500 words about letters found on German prisoners saying the Germans will be in Paris on June 28. Fine chance! Ford, Ferguson, Hopper and Parkerson in an auto accident. None badly hurt. Had a walk along the Marne in the evening with James. There is a new censor chief now—Major Bozeman Bulger, formerly baseball reporter on the Evening World. He was a good baseball reporter.

Diary: Saturday June 15, 1918

Had a car to myself today. Went to the Second division. It had 900 casualties last night. Its headquarters are in a farm house just outside of Bezu. I returned early and wrote 1,000 words for New York. Wrote a five-page letter to Dorothy. I wish it could be published.

I saw 10,000 Americans marching toward the front today. Many of them will never return. They are being used to check the German offensive. The French are hard pressed for men. The French are beginning to realize that America is now a real factor. The French soldiers now salute the Americans. It is about time they showed real appreciation. I am seeing more of war preparation than I ever saw before.

A really long letter to Dorothy from Meaux, written on June 15, 1918.

France, June 15, 1918

Dorothy,

Your Dad has been pretty steadily on the go ever since he wrote that long letter to you. As you all know of course the war is now in one of its vital stages and covering the operations of the Americans who are scattered all about is a somewhat difficult and formidable task. We are now quartered in a place not a great way from Paris and not a terrible distance from the scene of the big battle which is going on intermittently day and night along a front of 30 miles. The scene may shift any moment and then we shall be changed again. The automobile rides are not so long as they were when I was at Neufchateau because we are closer to the front but there are many points to be visited and the riding is tiresome just the same. I know very little more about the general situation than can be learned from reading the newspapers. Even if I did I could not expect to write it as the censorship is very rigid and justly so.

I was in Paris, with the other correspondents, for a few days but then we were all ordered over night to the place where I am now writing. The Germans are making their greatest effort of the war. The soldiers have postal cards, souvenirs, showing pictures of Germans, Turks and Austrians, arms around one another, saying "Our last great drive." They expected to sweep straight through to Paris, though did not figure in reaching there before the middle of the summer. They still believe they will do so but the Americans are proving a very serious obstacle on which they had not counted. And the Americans are coming along very swiftly and taking their place in the line. They are wonderful soldiers. The French speak most highly of them and there is no doubt that after they have been in the game a short time, they will outshine all the others. One American now can lick any three Germans in Europe and whenever they meet hand to hand the Americans do it. They have flabbergasted the Germans, who actually believed that the Americans would not fight or at least would not know how to fight. The Germans tried to blast the Americans out of one strong position in the Belleau woods. They used their heaviest artillery and some of their best troops but the Americans licked them to a standstill. The Kaiser himself—and I was told this by two German officers who were taken prisoner—sent his pet division, the 28th, to smash the Americans and give them a lesson. The 28th ran into a snag the first thing. Many of them are now prisoners and a new German division is pitted against them now with no successful results for the Germans. Failing to drive the Americans back with artillery and infantry attacks, the Huns have for four days been sending tens of thousands of gas shells over on them. They are using every fiendish method they can think of to beat the Americans at this point in the line but they will not succeed. The Americans are at this very moment—and it will keep up for a day more—giving the Germans a much worse dose of gas then they sent. If the Germans want to be barbarians, they will find the Americans fight fire with fire.

As a matter of fact the Germans are furious because of the resistance of the Americans and they will do everything possible to annihilate them. The valor of the Americans is proved by the fact that at the Belleau woods salient the Americans have captured more than 1,000 German prisoners and not a single American has been captured. They refuse to surrender. We can't publish too much about the Americans because it sounds boastful but the truth is they are opening the eyes of Europe by their fighting qualities and they haven't got started yet.

I have seen quite a bit of the war so far but will see much more. I have been in many of the American hospitals just after engagements and gas attacks and have seen some things which form a grim tragic contrast to the glamor of war. It is a terrible thing and is growing more frightful because of the Germans determination to fight the war with gas of the most frightful character. Any German in Silver Creek who still cherishes any love for the German government or the Kaiser or for that matter for the German people themselves, ought to be taken out and shot. Be sure to tell John Knox about this. They do the most unspeakable things and have not a shadow of humanity or mercy in their makeup. They are determined to win the war this summer because they know if they don't, and America is able to throw her full strength into the contest, Germany is doomed. They will begin long before this letter reaches you to start again for Paris, slaughtering and blasting their way and they will make some headway. It would be foolish to say they have no chance of winning this goal, but I do not think they will get much nearer Paris than they are now. Today I saw two miles of marching Americans trudging along to the battlefront. They wore campaign hats and looked American every inch. They are larger than the French, British or German soldiers and the people in the French villages gaze at them with glaring eyes. They have never seen such men, they say.

The other day I saw 400 German prisoners captured by the Americans. I talked to many of them, through an interpreter. They don't know what to think. They say their officers tell them they will go to Paris and that the Americans are no good. Most of the privates I saw look more like beasts than human beings. They look about like the lowest class of alien in America. The officers are high class and very intelligent. Whenever you hear—I say you, Dorothy, I mean this for Rock and the rest of the grown ups in the family—people talking about that pleasant but dangerous illusion that we are fighting the German government and not the people, tell them it is time for Americans to realize that we are fighting the German people and all the German people and that the people and the government are one. Three officers with whom I was talking—German officers—resented the suggestion that the people and the government are different. "They are one," they said.

I have seen two or three aeroplane fights; have seen considerable bombarding; have seen some of the big German shells strike not far off leaving holes large enough to hide an automobile and have seen all the preparations for a gigantic offensive against perhaps the largest army in the world. Even now three aeroplanes are whirring over the village where I am staying. They are around all the time, watching. Fifty times I have seen shrapnel bursting around German planes which were seeking to make observations over our lines. I didn't think I would be so fortunate as to see the war in the way I have seen it. We have credentials which permit us to go anywhere we wish—to the first line trenches if we wish, but that we do not wish. The trenches however are not so dangerous as places back of the line because it is the places back which the big guns are constantly shelling. The other day I was up toward Montdidier, right near the worst point in the battle line and heard constant cannonading. It was like a continuous thunderstorm—only a very heavy, wavering roar. It was our big guns throwing shells at the German positions, the fainter reports from the German guns aiming at us, and the roar of shells bursting far away. The life of the men who are in the midst of this is a delirium. And some of the Silver Creek boys will no doubt be there before long. I sat in an automobile today and watched more than 5,000 soldiers march by. I thought possibly I might see one of the young lads from home but none was there.

One of the pathetic features of the situation is the exodus of people from the villages which are threatened by the Germans. They pack up all their earthly belongings which can be carried, pack them all on the big wagon with only two very large wheels, drawn by two or three horses one ahead of the other; with the old folks and the children loaded on the top of the wagon, and start for somewhere where perhaps they will find friends to take them in.

I saw one of these wagons go by here the other day and on it were seven little children, the oldest perhaps fourteen, the youngest a baby in arms. They made a most touching picture. They didn't know where they were going. They sleep beside the road and eat hard bread and a few cooked things they carry with them. I have seen miles of wagons like this. So it is no wonder that France, while still courageous and willing to fight, is weary of the war. Some of these refugees are being driven out for the second and third time.

In a little town about like Smith's Mills, the people had all gone but one family consisting of an elderly woman, her crippled son and her three little granddaughters, all smaller than you. They watched the soldiers come and go; heard the guns booming night and day, saw aeroplanes sailing over them almost constantly, and yet they were contented and determined to stay where they were. The little girls were playing with dolls; the old lady was working in a little flower garden. Another time I saw a Frenchman helping stretch barbed wire and keeping an eye on two little children, presumably his own.

The war affords some most picturesque, tragic and pathetic contrasts and after one has seen many of them, he realizes what a horrible thing war is and what a monster the Kaiser and his barbarous associates must be. One can hate the Germans by reading of their performances but after one has seen their work fresh from their hands and seen their offensive swaggering manner, softened by the knowledge, which they must possess, that they have outraged the entire world, he regards them much as one regards a poisonous snake.

This is a queer kind of letter to write to a little girl, isn't it Dorothy? But then you are not a little girl anymore. You have long hair and look like a young lady. I have just finished a long cablegram to the Herald which you probably will have seen when this reaches you. I have heard nothing from the Herald since Mr. Bennett's death but have no reason to believe my connection with it will change in any way. I read that Mr. Ohl is managing editor by direction of Mrs. Bennett. He is a very fine man and a very good friend of mine.

I will write to you again pretty soon Dorothy and will try to tell you all about the little girls I see in France. They are all very pretty as I told you before, and always smile and wave their hands at the Americans. Even those no more than two years old know the Americans when they see them and wave their hands to them. Usually they say Goodnight which they think means How do you do?

Remember me to the folks and the neighbors. Here's a hug and a kiss for you young lady.

With love, Dad

P.S. I have neither pen nor ink so will sign this letter with a pencil and address the envelope on my typewriter. The weather here is warm and pleasant. Tell Rock the farmers are now getting in their hay and cutting their wheat. They will plant another crop very soon.

(signed) Dad

Floyd Gibbons who was wounded was a friend of mine; was, in fact covering the story for me the day he was hit but I would not have been where he was.

(signed) Dad

And back home, Dorothy wrote to Dad on the same day.

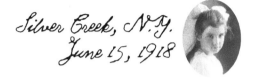

Silver Creek, N.Y.
June 15, 1918

Dear Dad

Here goes for letter No. 26. I have not much time to write to-day, because it is 1:15 now and I have some practicing to finish and I am going to Kathleen Barbeau's birthday party at four. I went down town this morning and bought a silk handkerchief for her present. When I came back I had my head washed, and then I went out on the back steps to get it dry. We had a late breakfast so Grandmother brought out some bread an' honey an' I had my lunch out there. Then when I finished, I came in and started this letter. Or rather I came out, for I am out on the veranda now.

We have not received any letters from you this week, so we hope we will get one next week.

We have had exams all week in school. But they weren't hard. Monday morning we have to go and take a Geography Exam, and Wednesday morning comes the regents.

If it is nice to-morrow, and Uncle Charlie don't have to work, he is going to take us to Letchworth Park. I hope he can. We will take a lunch, and have lots of fun. I wish you were here to go along. But you probably have just as interesting auto rides every single day. I do not mean that Uncle Charlie works on

Sundays, but there is a traveling man here so he may have to do something.

John Knox had your picture and an article about you put in the Silver Creek News, and Uncle Rock cut one out and sent it to you. Grandmother wrote to you the first of the week. I can't seem to think of any thing more to say to-day, so I will close.

Lots o' Love an' hugs an' kisses,

P.S. Wrong again! I mean Uncle Rock sent you the whole paper instead of just the article. Maybe I'll get things right after a while.

Dorothy

Ha! Ha! Some fancys. Huh? Ha! Ha!

Diary: Sunday June 16, 1918

Went to the 2nd division with Corey and James. Had luncheon with doctors at the hospital in Bezu. I got a good story about the Marines who did the fighting at Bois de Belleau and Torcy. Saw many of them, in the hospital and out. Also saw an impressive funeral of an American soldier near Bezu. I cabled 500 words. I have a recurrence of my sore throat and a cold in the bargain.

Diary: Monday June 17, 1918

Woke up with a very bad throat and hoarseness which is worse than anything similar I have ever had. Went to a French hospital to have it looked at. The doctor said there seemed to be nothing wrong with it. Then went to an American physician who says I have tonsillitis but nothing serious. I certainly feel very rotten. James tries to help but he is impossible. The chances are he will try to scoop me. I stayed in all day.

Diary: Tuesday June 18, 1918

Stayed around Meaux and doctored my sore throat. It certainly is sore.

Diary: Wednesday June 19, 1918

Am worried about my throat. Took an automobile at 2:30 p.m. and went to Paris. Got my hair cut and went to bed early. Am at the Crillon.

Diary: Thursday June 20, 1918

Left Paris at 8:30 a.m. with Martin Green and James. Rode eight hours to Neufchateau. On the way I cut my finger on a brass shell. Seems as if there must be something wrong with me. Had dinner at the Lafayette Club in Neufchateau. Spent the evening with Green at the club. He is sick. So is James. Looks as if we need a hearse instead of an automobile.

Diary: Friday June 21, 1918

Went to Baccarat, Comtoil where the 77th division is in camp preparing to go to the front line around Baccarat to relieve the 42. Part of it went in line Wednesday night. 77th is first draft division. Has everything in it from millionaires to oyster dredgers and barkeepers. Is from New York and Long Island. Returned 6 p.m. Martin Green and James were with me. Green has bad cold. James has one and I have bad throat. Can hardly make myself heard.

Diary: Saturday June 22, 1918

Returned to Neufchateau. First went to physician to have finger attended. Jammed it on a shell yesterday and now it has festered up, causing much pain. Had bad weather most of way back. Luncheon in St. Dizier. Two blow-outs on way. Arrived Meaux 7 p.m. Found everything quiet our sector.

Dorothy wrote her weekly letter, No. 27, to Dad on Saturday, June 22.

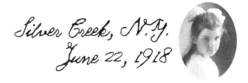

Silver Creek, N.Y.
June 22, 1918

Dear Dad

Here goes for letter No. 27. I feel very silly this morning, so I am writing this in pencil, so it won't look too terrible if I make half a million mistakes. I have quite an early start this morning, as I have eaten my breakfast, and have got all but fifteen minutes of my practicing done. You know school is out now, and when I get up in the morning, I think I have a letter to write etc. 'Course I have my practicing to do every day, but I think mebbe', I'll change my "letter day" around, mebbe (Ha!) 'cause we went to Buffalo yesterday, Grandmother an' I, an' Doc Hoffman is going to be in Farnham all the days but Tues., Wed, an' Thursday, so we'll have to arrange it with the music teacher, etc, etc. We said we'd try to arrange it for Wednesday. So you see, mebbe' (Ha!) (some letter, but you see I am silly) I might change my "letter day" around but I dont "guess" I will.

Although this is supposed to be the First Day O' Summer, one would think, rather, that it was supposed to be the first day of Winter, as it is cold and rainy. It rained hard all day in Buffalo yesterday too. We were going to have my pictures taken but it was such a bad day that we put it off 'till next week.

On the way home from Buffalo yesterday, we met a Mr. Peters, of Farnham, who knew us, and said he knows you. Do yuh' remember him? Grandmother said he was a little older than you, and used to go to school when you did. Oh, I almost forgot to tell you my exam marks – Physiology 88, Nature Study 97, English 94, and Regents in Geography 97, the highest in the Regents Class. We have not had any letters, etc. etc. from you lately, so we hope we will get one soon. Well, I guess I will close now, an' go an' play a while.

Lots o' Love an' hugs an' kisses
Dorothy

P.S. I am making a book of Dolly Dingles, or rather have been making it for the last mths, which I may get finished next year, to send to you. Ha! Ha!

Diary: Sunday June 23, 1918

Went with James to 2nd division headquarters. Stopped at La Ferte where the new American corps headquarters is. Saw American soldiers everywhere. Heard lots of dope from chief of staff which is rather discouraging. Says French won't let Americans fire artillery because they want to keep supply to meet new German drive. Says Americans getting badly treated by French. Hardly think Conger is right. Anyhow wouldn't write it even if the censor would permit it. Stopped at cemetery in Meaux. Saw new graves, 50 Americans killed last week. French putting flowers on them.

Diary: Monday June 24, 1918

Went to 2nd division headquarters with James. Got story of letters written by Germans captured by Americans. Stopped at American hospital at Bezu, had finger dressed. Was bruised and became infected. Had piece cut out. Think will get better now but incapacitates me for much typewriting. Certainly am having fine time. Throat still bad. Hardly able to talk. Sent cable 500 words New York. Sent long story to Paris on awards to soldiers for Bravery Cantigny fight. Sending stories to New York and Paris too, and putting up with James at the same time is a pretty tough job. Everyone kicking on censors. Am doing my share.

Diary: Tuesday June 25, 1918

Went to 2nd division again. Had my finger dressed at Bezu hospital. Is rather bad but probably will get well. Throat better but still have raucous voice. Returned early. Wrote cable taking broad line showing significance Italian victory, American stand, Austrian internal troubles. Also wrote long story for Paris on Pat Donohue, marine captured but returned to own lines. Saw German aeroplane brought down near 2nd division headquarters. Saw score aeroplanes flying over Meaux. In afternoon watched Marne fishermen who fish but never catch anything.

Diary: Wednesday June 26, 1918

Went to 2nd division headquarters with James. Got story about fight marines made against Germans in top of Bois de Belleau. Saw more than 200 prisoners, bestial looking men. Also saw many German injured in old church, used as hospital by Americans at Bezu. Returned before noon. Wrote 200 words full rate for New York, about 500 words regular press rate. Got them off by 1 o'clock courier. Returned to 2nd division headquarters. Got more details of marines' fight. Sent further story by cable. Wrote long story for Paris also. Finger bothering me somewhat yet. Voice still hoarse. Air raid in Paris tonight. Big barrage here.

Diary: Thursday June 27, 1918

Slept till 9:30. Need the sleep. At one o'clock with James went to 2nd division headquarters. On way stopped at Hospital (old church) Bezu to have finger dressed. It is still bothering me and makes it difficult to write, dress or do much of anything. While in hospital shells began falling in village. Germans apparently trying to hit hospital. One shell hit within 1,000 feet of hospital while I was there. Surgeons calm enough—calmer than I was probably. Took back road to division headquarters. Stopped and watched shells fall in village of Bezu and in fields close by. Were big ones. While at division headquarters saw many drop on village which only mile away. Took road never taken before by me to La Ferte. Road we had come over being badly shelled. This is a great war. No one safe anywhere. Air raid at night; shells falling everywhere. Just now guns begin booming; barrage at Meaux to catch airplanes passing on way to Paris. Electric lights have gone out. Am finishing this by candle light. Can't say I like this business a great deal.

Don Martin wrote to Dorothy again from Meaux on June 27. His comment that the danger to him is "small" contrasts with his diary entries.

Meaux, June 27, 1918

Dorothy,

Goodness but I've been lucky in getting letters lately! I have received from you letters dated May 27th, June 1st and June 8th. The June 1st letter was numbered 24. The others were not numbered. They were all nice letters Dorothy. They told me all about your selling things and the excitement of the occasion. They also told me a thousand and one things which were very interesting. That must be quite a kitten you have. I am glad you are entirely satisfied with the clothes you have. I always heard that girls were never satisfied. But Mother tells me you like bloomers and bare feet about the best of all and that is a good thing, only not very desirable in winter. You did very well with that grab bag I should say and taking in $4.90 cents for popcorn is also pretty good. Can you eat hot dogs without getting indigestion? I never could. You are a great girl. I can just see you hustling around with Iola, Kathleen and the rest of the girls.

The letter of yours dated June 8th tells about the festival and the dances you were in. You certainly have been a busy girl. And now school is out! I'll bet you are having a great old time. I think it is a good idea for you and Mother to go to Chautauqua this summer. It will be much better than Dahn's Beach. Only go to a good place—no cheap boarding house. I guess there is money enough and you tell Grandmother to use it.

Tell Uncle Rock I got his letters dated May 27th, June 3rd and June 8th. One enclosed a lot of clippings which I was glad to get. Another contained the News, which gives a list of the Red Cross subscribers. I looked over the list of contributors very carefully and was interested. I noticed some of those who might have given much gave little and some of the Germans gave almost nothing. Jule and Charlie apparently were very active in the work. His last letter was about the newsiest letter I have had in a long time. I guess he overlooked nothing. Tell him I will send him one of my pictures. He was going to tell me what Dan Reid said of me but I guess he forgot it. It doesn't matter anyhow only I was curious to know why Dan should say anything.

Mother's letter of June 6th came along with the others and furnished whatever news you and Rock had failed to send. Tell her she must not worry about me because if anything happened she would hear it within 24 hours and anyhow nothing will happen. I look out for myself pretty well. Of course there is more or less danger everywhere but it is so small where I go that it is no greater than it is in Silver Creek or New York. She tells me that you have everything you want or need. I know that of course and should not make suggestions at all; only I have the habit of doing it and continue notwithstanding that I know you would have everything if I never said a word about it.

Resnati, who is mentioned in the clipping she enclosed in her letter, is the man I made a flight with. Flying is pretty dangerous business. I have seen some air duels. Today I saw three different German airplanes in the midst of barrages being fired by our anti-aircraft guns. The Boches got away but they hurried. Flying is one of the great things in the war. Without machines an army would be helpless. The side which maintains air supremacy and backs it up with adequate artillery is certain to win. I wish United States would hurry along with some aeroplanes and do less talking about what it is going to do.

I haven't heard from Alta lately but she has been very good about writing and I have not written to her. It is only because I have been very busy. I write long cables for the Herald in New York then write

214

different stories for the Herald in Paris, which you can easily see is quite a job. Then it takes time to get around. I take automobile rides every day of from 100 to 200 miles. I recently made one trip which covered 675 miles in three days. I am quite sure I shall never care for automobile riding when I am finished here.

I got a letter from Lee Brand, written in Havre, just after he arrived. Then I received a card from him in Paris, giving me his address there. He is to have a very important job with the Y.M.C.A. and will be a big improvement on some of the Y.M.C.A. men I have seen here. The first time I go to Paris I shall look him up. He probably can tell me a lot about your antics young lady. Tell Josephine I shall see her husband without fail and will probably write to her and tell her how he is behaving.

I don't have so much time for letter writing as I would wish so you must not be disappointed if your letters are not so numerous as they were when I was in London. To add to the disadvantage I have a sore finger which makes writing a little difficult. I jammed the first knuckle on the middle finger of my left hand and the thing became slightly infected. That was ten days ago. I still wear a bandage on it but it is getting well. The American physicians say wounds are slow to heal here for some reason.

A funny thing happened. I had the thing dressed up at an American hospital in a quaint old church, used as a hospital, about eight miles back from the line. Yesterday I was having the bandage changed when there was a boom. A shell had struck about 1,000 feet away at the other end of the street. Then some more struck. In this old church we were safe because the walls are five feet thick and under the big thick ceilings there was no danger. However I got in my automobile and went back a distance and watched the shells fall just back of the village. No one knew what the Germans were aiming at—probably the hospital.

The chances are I shall go to Paris in a few days to get some clothes and have some laundry done up— also to have a bath. The town of Meaux has few facilities. It is about as old as any place in Europe and looks it. Every night there is a terrible roar of guns. The Germans' bombing planes on their way to Paris pass over here and the guns bang away at them. The bombers don't bother with a small place like this though, when they are so near Paris.

I guess I shall finish this letter now Miss Dorothy. Explain to all the family that it is intended for all. I shall not write about the war this time. The Americans are making a wonderful fight but everything to date shows that a soldier must be trained. With proper training the Americans can lick anyone. Without proper training the bravest and strongest man in the world is a pygmy. Anyhow gas and long-range artillery take all the glory and color out of war. It is a horrid thing.

Tell Alta, Rock, Mother and all the others that I shall write to them all some day soon.

Here's a kiss and a hug for you young lady.

With love,
Dad

Diary: Friday June 28, 1918

Went with James to the 2nd division. Stopped in Bezu. No shells falling. My finger is better and my throat is better also. Had a pleasant chat with Cameron Mackenzie of the London Chronicle, formerly editor of McClures. Wrote a long mail story on German prisoners. I mailed it, with sketches by a dough boy. I also sent by mail a short story of the soldier's funeral and a clipping on the Pat Donohue story.

Diary: Saturday June 29, 1918

Second division again. No news. Wrote 900 words for New York. Spent part of the evening with Wallace Morgan, the artist.

Dorothy wrote her weekly letter, No. 28, to Dad on Saturday, June 29.

Silver Creek, N.Y.
June 29, 1918

Dear Dad

Here goes for letter No. 28. I just finished my practicing and now I am going to write this letter, take it down and mail it, come back and eat a lunch, then raise the roof for a while. I am barefooted, and have my khaki suit on, so you see I am ready. Then I will have to go out and weed my war garden, an' buy a Thrift Stamp, an' then – oh – I don't know what next.

We went to Buffalo yesterday, and I had some pictures taken. Then Grandmother bought me a pretty white dress and two pairs of socks. She also bought a nice Gra-Houn-Glider, or one of those things that you just put one foot on – ok – you know. She bought it for me to give to Joseph on his birthday. He is giving a party on the 3rd, and I liked it so well that she is going to get

216

me one next time we go to Buffalo. I guess we won't go next week because of the 4th.

This morning in the mail, a lot of Paris Heralds came from you. I have been trying to read some of the French in them but I do not succeed very well. There are a lot of articles from you, all right! There are also some in yesterday's Herald. OK – I forgot – we bought a new scrap-book in Buffalo yesterday, as the first one is full. We also got two nice letters and some pictures from you the first of the week. One was a great long letter, and the other quite long. The pictures were good too. Is this the way you wanted them given out – to Aunt Inez, to Aunt Julie, to Aunt Alta and this house?

That was funny about "Hello kid", wasn't it? I am glad Joseph can have a pair of sabots too. Aunt Inez says to tell you that she's exercising a lot now, so when the fight comes with "those fancy things", she can get 'em all Ha! Ha!

Grandmother is making current jelly out in the kitchen and – um–yum–willyum but it smells good! Grandmother says to tell you that she will write next week.

Well, I guess I will close now, as it is about 12:00 o'clock.

Lots o' Love an' hugs an' kisses

Dorothy

P.S. Grandmother says she was very glad to get those papers.

Over...

Dorothy included this drawing on the back of the letter.

Diary: Sunday June 30, 1918

Went to the 2nd division. Very little going on.

Diary: Monday July 1, 1918

Went to 2nd division. Was told all the details of the assault to be made by our troops on the village of Vaux. Went to be Coulommiers, headquarters of our fliers. Saw the boys start on their first flight over the German lines. Returned to Meaux; then went to the Second division where I listened to reports from the 23rd and 9th infantry which were making the attack on Vaux. I saw part of the bombardment of the town. I returned after midnight with James and Mackenzie over a dark road. No light was permitted. Was a rather nerve racking ride. The boom of artillery was constant.

Arriving in Meaux at 2 a.m. were told we could not go down the main street as a bomb had just been dropped on a building which was now a mass of wreckage in the street. We motored all over the place before we finally got to the hotel and meanwhile bombs were being dropped and shrapnel was falling all over. It was a fierce experience. I sat in my room until 4:30 a.m. writing a story of the capture of Vaux. Our men did it in fine shape.

Diary: Tuesday July 2, 1918

Went to the 2nd division headquarters with James. Got a cleanup story on Vaux which was a brilliant victory for the Americans. Wrote a Fourth of July cable for New York and a follow on the Vaux affair.

Diary: Wednesday July 3, 1918

Went to La Ferte—corps headquarters—and to the air field near Touquin. Got a good story of fight between nine Americans and nine Germans. We lost no one, Germans lost four. Cabled two stories to New York. Waited for air raid tonight but none came.

Diary: Thursday July 4, 1918

With Lieut. Hartzell, James went to Paris to see the Fourth of July celebration. Saw the marines march down the Champs Elysees. Had luncheon at Cafe de Paris with James and Cameron Mackenzie.

Left Paris at 5 o'clock by automobile to return to Meaux. Was invited to motor up to Amiens to see Lloyd George review an American division but decided it was wiser to return to our own front.

Diary: Friday July 5, 1918

Went to airfield near Coulommiers. Got good story American fliers fighting with survivors Richthofen circus. Sent cable. Wrote two mail stories—one about the Marines, one on sidelights of the war.

Early in July the Buffalo Enquirer published an article with a cartoon about Don Martin's transformation from political reporter to war correspondent.

"THE STRAW MAN VOTE" ON THE FIRING LINE IN FRANCE

Don Martin, the New York Herald "straw vote man"—the editor who probably knows more politicians and inside political history than any other man in the United States—is now a full fledged war correspondent.

This is very interesting news to our readers, for all remember our publication of the New York Herald's political poll in 1916, compiled and managed by Don Martin. This remarkable forecast of Mr. Martin, showing Mr. Wilson's election, was only one of many polls conducted by the New York Herald that have been accurate in prediction.

However, it is not of past events we wish to write, but rather of the present. Mr. Martin a few months ago was assigned to the London office of the New York Herald.

In a few weeks we found him in Paris and within a short time he was in the front line trenches with Pershing's boys.

His pen picture of the battle of Seicheprey, where the Americans at Toul, outnumbered twelve to one, with their backs to the wall, fought the Germans to a standstill and whipped them, has been one of the most remarkable cables so far in this great war.

Because of Mr. Martin's wide acquaintance among the public men and officers of the army, and in view of his broad vision and experience, it is quite sure that his success as a war correspondent will measure up to that attained as "the straw vote man."

Charles E. Hughes during his Presidential campaign tour, addressing a vast throng at Silver Creek, N.Y., said: "An honest newspaperman is the noblest work of God, and this is Don Martin's home.

"I have great regard for Don Martin and am glad to come to his home town."

Dorothy wrote weekly letter No. 29 to Dad on Friday, July 5.

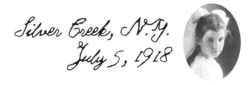

Silver Creek, N.Y.
July 5, 1918

Dear Dad

Here goes for letter No. 29. I am writing this on Friday, instead of Saturday, because I am going out to Frank Cockburn's to-morrow to pick currents. There are quite a few girls that have been looking for farm work for quite a while, and now they have found some. I am one of them. We use the money for W.S.S. Now do not think I don't have enough money to buy Thrift stamps, 'cause Grandmother would give me plenty, but I like to earn it. 'Course I don't earn it all, but out of my 25 cent allowance a week, and what Grandmother gives me just for instance (she gives me a lot of that) beside what I earn, why that's how I get money for Thrift stamps.

[W.S.S. – War savings stamps – were issued by the United States Treasury Department to help fund participation in World War I. Although these stamps were distinct from the postal savings stamps issued by the United States Post Office Department, the Post Office nevertheless played a major role in promoting and distributing war savings stamps. War savings stamps were principally aimed at common citizens. During World War I, 25-cent Thrift stamps were offered to allow individuals to accumulate enough over time to purchase the standard 5-dollar War Savings Certificate stamp .]

Then I like to work on a farm for two reasons, –1– because I love a farm, anyway, –2– because everybody at home is asked to work on the farms, and be patriotic, and when I find a new way of being patriotic, why, I want to be patriotic that new way right away. So that's why I am going to work on a farm, and that's also why I can not write my letter to-morrow. See? Or land? Ha! Ha!

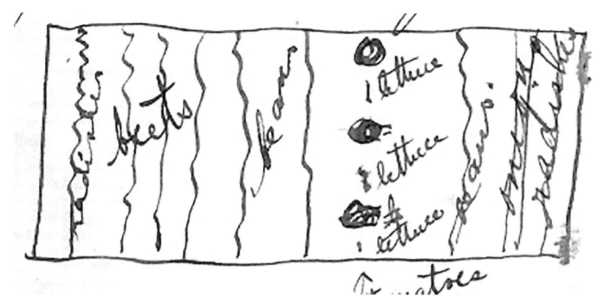

Dorothy's drawing of her war garden, with rows marked as radishes, beets, beans, tomatoes and lettuces, onions, radishes.

Last night there was a basket picnic and a dance at the Motor Boat Club, and Grandmother and I went. We had fireworks on the beach and, oh, everything. This afternoon at 1:00 I am going to take a lesson in theory, with a lot of the other children – Kathleen Barbeau, Dorothy Setter, and Dorothy Kahabka, Florence Dickenson, etc. Then at 3:00 Grandmother and I are going down to Dahn's Beach, at Hammond's cottage, and I am going in bathing, and, uh, everything.

We have the proofs to the pictures we had taken in Buffalo, and they are certainly a lot better than the others. I don't mean that I look better, but – oh – you know what I mean.

I have a dandy war garden – Here's a picture of it. Can you read what's in it? 1st – 1 row radishes, 2nd – 3 rows beets, 3rd – 2 rows beans, 4th – 3 tomato plants with head lettuce between them, 5th – 1 row beans, 6th – 2 rows onions, 7th – 1 row radishes.

I hope it don't rain to-day or to-morrow, because of going to the beach to-day and being on the farm to-morrow. I must close now, and get some clothes on, I mean a dress and some shoes and stockings. I am barefooted and have my khaki suit on now.

Lots o' Love an' hugs an' kisses

Dorothy

Diary: Saturday July 6, 1918

Went to second division. Very quiet everywhere. Sent no cable. Poker game at night but I didn't play. Looked for air raid but there was none.

Diary: Sunday July 7, 1918

Went to second division. Heard the 28th division had lent men to the French in battle for Hill 204 which the French failed to get. Went to headquarters of the 28th. Got good story. Cabled 900 words. Also saw Lieutenant [Benjamin] Harwood who narrowly escaped death in fight with German fliers. Cabled 500 words of this. Think James and I have scoop on both the 28th and the Harwood story.

Diary: Monday July 8, 1918

Went to second division. Very little going on. Got story in La Ferte, corps headquarters, of a document prepared by a German general praising the American soldier (this for circulation among Germans only) and returned to Meaux early in the afternoon. Sent 600 word cable to New York.

Letter to Dorothy from Meaux, written on July 8, 1918.

Meaux, July 8, 1918

My dear little Dorothy,

An old French woman who does the work in my room in the Hotel Sirene where I live looked at six photographs of you which I have around my room and said: "Is that your daughter?" I admitted such was the fact. Then she said she had admired the pictures many times and that I ought to be proud to have such a fine daughter. She said it partly in French and partly in English so I was able to understand. So you see, young lady, you are admired even here as well as at home.

I came in this afternoon about three o'clock after a trip up near the front and found a letter from you—No. 26 dated June 15. By this time you have taken your examinations and are finished with your school for a long time. I shall be glad to hear how you came out. When I took examinations, particularly Regents, I was always very anxious until I heard the results. Usually I passed but I believe a few times I failed. So if you fail don't worry. Your Dad failed too. But I imagine you will pass—or rather have passed—everything.

I haven't received the paper you say Rock sent, containing a picture of me and an article about me. You tell John Knox that I intend to write to him the first chance I get and I will see that I get a chance very soon. You have been able to tell from the paper I imagine, that your Dad has been pretty busy. I have been all over the front and have written a great deal. I could spend weeks writing special stories but I can't take the time. I wish I could spend time with you. On the Fourth I was thinking about the last Fourth, remember? When I had a sore toe and we had a fine display of fireworks at Dahn's Beach? We certainly had a good time and we shall have another one some time too. I have heard nothing from the office yet and don't know whether they want me to stay or return. I daresay they want me to stay. I am not so particular about it myself. I have seen a great deal now and the work certainly is no cinch. However, I wouldn't be surprised if I stayed until it is over.

I have certainly seen France at war. Today I passed a solid line of 30 miles of horse-drawn trucks carrying guns, supplies etc. I have frequently passed lines of 500 motor trucks—camions the French call them— loaded with men. Scenes like that may be seen anywhere along the line close to the front.

You see the Germans are soon to start another offensive and no one but the Germans knows when it will start. If the French knew exactly where it will be they could stop it without much trouble. The great problem is to learn what your enemy is doing. Tell Uncle Charlie—because I know he is deeply interested in such things—that the two great essentials (vitals) in modern war are airplanes and artillery. The army which is superior in both is a sure winner even though its army is vastly inferior in size. If United States had 100,000 aeroplanes over here—or even 25,000—the Allies would win quickly. I have seen several air fights and nearly every day see the fliers off on their patrols and observation trips and see them return too—not all of them sometimes. Frequently one or two don't return. I have luncheon quite frequently in a chateau with some of the leading American fliers and enjoy their talks. They are the greatest sportsmen in the world. Every time I go, someone's chair is vacant.

I don't know what will happen during the next month. No one does. I know the Germans are capable of striking a terrible blow. The belief is that they will begin in Champagne, in the region north of Chalons, with which I am very familiar by the way; and finish with an attack on the British in the North.

I am trying to keep in touch with developments so I can be close to the big drive and write about such Americans as are involved in it. Don't worry young lady, I will not get where there is danger. The Germans will probably push the Allies back—maybe a long way, but if they advance very far they will leave dead Germans three deep. I know that because I have seen the preparations being made for them. If Rock or Charlie could take one trip with me up toward the front he would see things which would startle him.

Americans are not a small factor now. They have shown that they are unquestionably the best soldiers in Europe. A French general told me that the other day. The Germans say so too. The Americans fight just as they do everything else. For instance a story is told of an American who met two Germans in No Man's Land and prepared to fight them. They immediately shouted Kamerade, which is the coward's cry. The American said: "Kamerade nothing, I came here to fight, not to engage in conversation." He didn't bring back any prisoners so you can imagine what happened.

The motto of the average American is, as the German reports, one of which I am cabling to New York today, says: "We kill or be killed." That's the only way to carry on a war. War these days is no afternoon tea. It is a game of murder and slaughter. That is the way the Americans intend to play it. They are losing many men, killed or injured. They will lose many more. If the war lasts two years they will lose hundreds of thousands. Which, I guess, is about enough of war. Let John Knox read part of this. I know it will interest him.

The other day I picked a couple of poppies and a corn flower from a spot in the Marne Valley where some of the bitterest fighting took place in 1914. You wouldn't know now that there had ever been a fight there except for the wooden crosses which mark graves everywhere of French-men who fell. I am enclosing the flowers which are all dried up but which you can regard as souvenirs of the Marne. Maybe, by the time they reach you, there will be more fighting at the very spot where I picked them.

My sore finger is about well. The weather is very hot and I am burned a dull red. You see I am out in the sun about half the time, in an automobile. I haven't seen Lee Brand yet. I was in Paris on the Fourth, to see the parade of Americans, but returned late in the afternoon. I am only 30 miles from Paris.

Here's a hug and kiss Dorothy,

(signed) With love From Dad

When the dried flowers sent by her father arrived, Dorothy and her grandmother pasted them on a sheet, framed it and displayed them on her wall. It has survived.

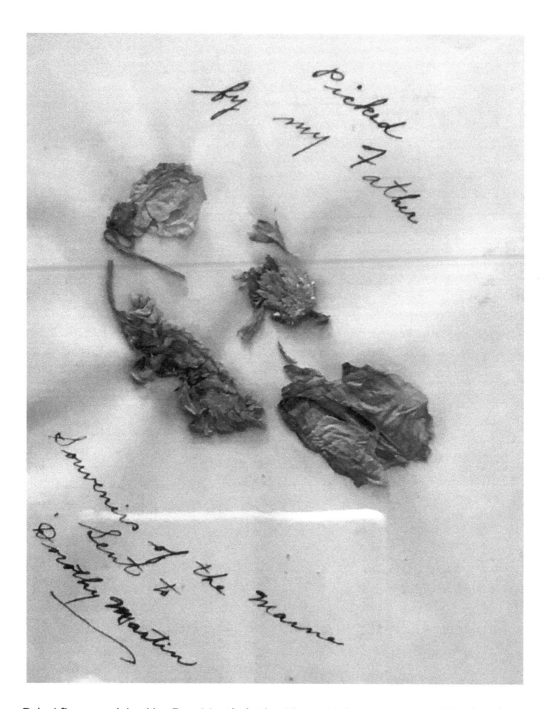

Dried flowers picked by Don Martin in the Marne Valley and sent to his daughter.

Diary: Tuesday July 9, 1918

Went out alone. Went to Second division, then to the Twenty-eighth division headquarters in a hunting chateau east of La Ferte. Got good story of what Americans did in a small battle. Wrote short cable.

Diary: Wednesday July 10, 1918

Went to Twenty-eighth division headquarters where James and I had luncheon with the officers—and a good luncheon too. Then came back to the chateau on the road to La Ferte to Bezu and saw General Pershing decorate 37 marines who earned their laurels at Bouresches and Bois de Belleau. Impressive picture. One thousand Marines in a review, a band playing southern melodies and patriotic songs and everything else distinctly European.

Returned to Meaux at 7:30 and rushed a story for Paris. Have just now finished a 600 word cable for New York on the decoration ceremony and a 250 word story on the first mustard gas attack by the Americans.

Diary: Thursday July 11, 1918

Roamed around all day with James looking for a copy of a German propaganda newspaper which says Hearst reflects real American opinion of the war. Had luncheon with Lieutenant Feland of the Marines. Wrote 200 word cable on the Hearst propaganda story. Everyone mystified at the delay in the renewed German offensive.

Diary: Friday July 12, 1918

Stayed in today to write mail stuff. Wrote 3,000 word story on the Marines; a 700 word story on German propaganda and about 1,000 calling America's attention to the fact that she has a big job on her hands in licking Germany.

Diary: Saturday July 13, 1918

Went out with Taylor of the U.P. Had luncheon with the gas experts of the 1st Corps. They say we are now supplied with a good deal of gas but not enough. They are able men but not competent, in my estimation, to cope with the German scientists and chemists who are devising or inventing new gasses. Visited 26th division headquarters and returned early to Meaux.

This morning while catching a basket ball thrown by Ray Carroll received a tough knock on the little finger of my right hand. It swelled up considerably so when I returned to Meaux went to a hospital. The doctors put it in splints saying I had a bad bruise which, if not properly cared for, might result in a stiff joint. I am having a fine time. My second finger is about well and I was just getting in condition to do some real typewriting when another finger is hurt. Guess I am a hoodoo.

German offensive has not yet started. Everyone expectant and worried. Everyone thinks it will be made north of Chalons. I don't. Think it will be made directly toward Paris. I was told today U.S. has 24 divisions of 30,000 men each ready for the front line.

Diary: Sunday July 14, 1918

Went with James to Twenty sixth division. Everything very quiet. Looks like calm before the storm. Wrote cable for New York indicating big offensive start tomorrow.

Letter from Rose Martin to her son, written on July 14.

July 14th

Dear Don

Your letter dated June 15, reached us about two weeks ago. We were very glad to get it. It is very nice and thoughtful of you to write us as often as you do, having so much writing to do for the Herald, and how much you do. I cut it all out and save it. I paste it in scrapbooks. And your letters are so interesting too. Your descriptions of the Germans makes me dislike all of them here in S.C. "Ce sont tout des Sauvage ses Allemand". That is what the French ought to call them, perhaps they do, still that is not half bad enough. I put our flag out this morning in remembrance of the 14th of July, a Holiday over there.

I wonder where you are now. Won't it be nice when you are back here, where everything is peaceful and quiet; that will be something new. But still war—war is everywhere. We know it's here too—the Boys leave every little while—it's very sad. Its Bands—Red Cross—and War Saving Stamps, and not much sugar, nor flour, but we have enough. It's the grip of war.

Well Don, I never thought your name would become so popular. I guess Don Martin will be known all over, but it won't change you one bit, not you. Dorothy is out on the veranda playing with her dolls. For a change it is good and warm today. Now she is taking their pictures.

Probably Alta wrote you that we had some taken of Dorothy and they are going to be very good. Just as soon as they are finished, I will send them to you, perhaps next week. I hope so as it takes so long to go over. By the way, yours were very, very good, especially the two last ones. I would know by the looks of them that you are well and healthy. You don't look as if you went hungry at all. I was very glad to get them, and I shall be glad when you get Dorothy's too. I am sorry. I tried Mrs. Kahobka, but I thought she would take them good, and you would get them so much quicker, and so did Julia, and Rosco and Inez. But she is not good, I know now.

All the little girls like Dorothy go berry-picking, and she is crazy to go too. Next week I may let her go for a day or two. She is a regular little Farmer. She passed her examinations fine, and she is doing splendid in her music. But I think we will have to stay home this summer, as we have to go to Buffalo every week, and of course she has to practice, that's what counts. But she is very happy and satisfied. Not many are at Dahn's Beach this summer. They came up with their cottage rents 15.00 a week, which is too much for those cottages. So people are not crazy to go at that price, and anyway everything is so high people can not afford it.

Every body is well in Silver Creek, and the same as always. There is a lot of fruit this summer—but very high in price. Peaches 30 cts a Doz; Red Raspberries, 28 a basket; Cherries, 20 a basket, and Eggs sell for 50 cts a Doz, they used to be 25 cts a Doz. But it did not make any difference with our old Pear tree, it's loaded and they are good and we will have all we want, and we won't let them go to waste.

Dorothy is very quiet. She is reading to her dolls, I guess. I wish we could win the war this fall. I close

With Love and good Luck,
Mother

Diary: Monday July 15, 1918

Big offensive started last night midnight as I predicted. Has been an exciting day. Big gun began sending shells into Meaux at half past six this morning. One struck close to the hotel Sirene and uprooted big tree and left great hole in street. Everyone excited. Correspondents particularly. Had breakfast while shells falling every ten minutes all around. People started at once to leave Meaux. James and I rushed out of town to corps headquarters, knowing big offensive had begun. Returned to Meaux despite big gun shelling and I wrote a hurried cable for New York. Then went away up to the Twenty eighth and Third division headquarters. Was within four miles of line. In midst big batteries sending shells over on Germans. Germans have advanced across Marne several points. Americans held two points. Looks not very good but have confidence in ability of French to hold. Think Germans will advance many kilometers. Drive is toward Chalons.

Diary: Tuesday July 16, 1918

German offensive in full swing. Germans shelling everything 30 miles back, dropping bombs all over. Destroyed railway station in La Ferte last night. I went to 3rd division headquarters also 28th. Saw hundreds airplanes; saw almost continuous firing from anti-aircraft guns at German fliers. Travelled about 150 miles by auto. Returned, wrote story for Paris and about 1,500 word cable on whole front and strategic situation for New York. Filed at 8:30 for Thursday's paper.

Bombers over Meaux last night, sent us all to the cellar. They were driven off. Expected them tonight but they didn't come. Floyd Gibbons with one eye gone arrived tonight for a short stay. Parkerson and Draper are being replaced. It is about time Draper was called back. Am seeing considerable of the war from very close range.

Diary: Wednesday July 17, 1918

Franco-American offensive started. Lieut. Delany called me at seven a.m., said all correspondents wanted for important announcement. Said Americans had attacked. Got an auto. Started with James for La Ferte from where we went to the 26th division headquarters. Got story. French with Americans attacked from south Soissons to west Chateau-Thierry. Won everywhere. Sent 400 words full rate.

In the afternoon went to the 1st division headquarters also 2nd. Returned to Meaux early evening. Wrote a long cable for New York.

Diary: Thursday July 18, 1918

Went out with Ferguson and James. Visited 1st and 2nd divisions. Saw many towns which have been almost wrecked with bombs. Americans advanced everywhere. Plan of Foch is to thwart scheme of Germans to straighten front for an attack on Paris. Is biggest thing of war for three years. Wrote long cable for New York. Lights went out so had to use candle. Air raid at three in the morning (Friday morning).

Diary: Friday July 19, 1918

Went to 1st division headquarters. Saw British Scots Canadians on way to Soissons front. Visited hospitals. Saw hundreds of Americans who had been waiting hours for treatment. All good natured. No complaints from any. Am amazed at the spirit of the Americans. I thought I knew them but I didn't. Wrote 1,000 words for Paris; 1,500 for New York.

Diary: Saturday, July 20, 1918

James, Johnson and I went to Second division; also visited hospital at Pierrefonds, shadow famous chateau. Saw many British soldiers on their way to the front. Franco-American offensive proceeding well. May not get very far but it will demoralize the Germans for the time being and put them in the position of having to wonder what the allies are doing.

In contrast to that low-key diary entry, Don Martin sent a 2000-word cable to the New York Herald which appeared in the Sunday, July 21 edition (First Section, Part Two, Page Two) with a major banner headline.

He reported on the "hideousness of modern warfare".

DON MARTIN DESCRIBES THE GREATEST WAR DRAMA IN HISTORY
Americans in Battle Likened Unto Demons

Don Martin Describes Fighting Hundred Times More Savage Than Civil War

MODE OF ATTACK DAZZLES GERMANS

Pershing Men Advance so Fast It Is Necessary to Reorganize Plans of Attack
[Special Cable to the Herald]

WITH THE AMERICAN ARMIES IN FRANCE, Saturday

Within the shadow of Paris is being enacted one of the most important military dramas of the world's history, and Americans, thousands of miles from home with the banner of the idealism of world freedom, are bearing a goodly part in the conflict, plunged in the seething maelstrom of flying steel, gas and bullets, a hundred times more savage than the civil war, showing to Europe that youths from a peaceful home country can be transformed, if necessary, into demons on the fields of battle.

They have been in the midst of madness for days, have lost many, but still are as plucky as ever, slaying the Huns by wholesale whenever they are able to meet them man to man.

The whole battle is so far open warfare, spectacular in the extreme. French cavalrymen, decked with paraphernalia putting the knight's of old to shame, are dashing into the fields, straight to the ranks of the Germans, who are trampled, speared and slain with their swords.

I saw the cavalry start on a spectacular gallop through the fields, take the road at a canter for a mile, then cross lots in a mad swoop, where they expected to crush the infantry seeking to advance in the face of the French troops.

This is one of several features giving a picturesque touch to the hideousness of modern warfare that is extending the line from Fontenoy to Chateau-Thierry in a gigantic battle, putting the Germans on the defensive, who were carrying on an offensive of their own from Chateau-Thierry to Rheims. It makes an interesting situation of the highest military importance and may bring about a crisis quickly.

General Foch's Master Move

The feeling is that it is Foch's master move, which is the first comprehensive step on a large scale attempted by the Allies since the Allied control came into being.

As I write the situation is highly satisfactory to the Allies, who expect fierce counter attacks, but are not worried about the result.

French and Americans have advanced far ahead of their tentative objectives, in some places as much as five kilometres.

This is advisable in view of the Germans terror at being attacked savagely with artillery.

They have surrendered by wholesale and have been slaughtered in large numbers.

Diary: Sunday July 21, 1918

Most interesting day. Visited Chateau-Thierry which the Germans evacuated last night. Captain Morgan accompanied James and me but had nothing to do with our visit. Wandered around the wrecked streets climbing over debris, etc. I was interested to see the effect of the shelling of the city which I had witnessed from a hill a short distance away on June 2nd. The city is badly shot up. Shells fell in the city (outskirts) while we were there. Wrote 700 word cable on my visit to Chateau-Thierry and a longer one on the general situation. The Franco-American offensive is progressing satisfactorily.

Dorothy wrote letter No. 31 to Dad on July 21, 1918.

Silver Creek, N.Y.
July 21, 1918

Dear Dad

Here goes for letter No. 31. I did not write this letter Friday, because I was so busy playing, etc. In the morning I was down at the playground with Miss Butler and the girls. In the afternoon I took my theory lesson, came home and put on old clothes, then went down to the playground again. Miss Butler took a lot of us in bathing, so I didn't get home 'till half past five, so I had to hurry up and get all dressed and washed up for the basket picnic and dance at the motor boat club. Kathleen and some other children were there, and I had lots of fun. Then Saturday morning Aunt Julie called up and wanted me to go to Buffalo in the auto with them.

Well, I went, and we had a dandy time. We went to the Shea's Hippodrome right after dinner, and after that to the zoo, then home. We all stopped in the 6+10, of course, and bought something. I bought a squirt gun.

We also — (Grandmother and I) — went to Buffalo Thursday, and everything happened the same as usual. We will send my pictures to you some time this week, I think. They were not ready Thursday. Grandmother said I was going berry picking for a few days you know, but I don't seem to find time for much of anything but play. Grandmother wrote you a long letter Sunday.

Tomorrow or Tuesday I am going to have about 8 girls here —

counting Eleanor and Virginia, Joseph's little cousins, just to have a little lunch and play with my dolls. It is for Eleanor and Virginia. I must close now, and get some good clothes on.

Lots o' Love an' hugs an' kisses,

Dorothy

Diary: Monday July 22, 1918

Another interesting day. Went practically up to the front line northwest of Chateau-Thierry. Passed through dozen villages which were shelled by the French and Americans before they drove the Germans out. Saw scenes of desolation which brought home very strongly the horrors of war. Went through Belleau woods, where I saw a great many German dead. Saw thousand relics of the terrific fighting at various places. Dugouts, trenches, many of them not yet rid of the dead. Bombs dropped in many places while I was there. Germans now making a stand on hills. They were dropping shells here and there, some of them near me, to register the hits, the idea being to get the proper range of villages and roads. Wrote 1,500 word cable and about the same for Paris. Got through early for a change. Brought back from my trip a German helmet which I took from a dead German and an automatic rifle which lay beside him. I might have got scores of ghastly relics but a few I thought would be sufficient.

Diary: Tuesday July 23, 1918

Didn't go out till afternoon. Taylor of the U.P. went along with James and me. Visited headquarters of the 6th French army in a chateau at Marigny which has been badly damaged by shell fire. Then went to the headquarters of the 26th division which are in a series of farm buildings on Picardy Farm. Were occupied as a regimental headquarters by the Germans three days ago. Roads congested with soldiers, wagons, camions, artillery, mostly Americans in this region which is northwest of Chateau Thierry. Rainy and muddy. Saw tons German foodstuffs, thousands German shells which were abandoned in the hasty German retreat to escape being caught by the pressing Franco-American-British lines. Never saw such wrecks as some of the villages hereabouts are, especially Vaux, Torcy, Belleau, Etripilly. Germans retreating rapidly. Americans and French chasing them. Germans sure to make a stand soon when there will be a smashing battle. Germans may give allies a hard blow but I think the allies will be able to hold.

This is one of the greatest crises of the war. It thwarts the plans of the Germans to start a gigantic attack on a front before Paris. Wrote 1,000 words for Paris and about 600 for New York. Censorship very strict. We can send nothing which can possibly give the Germans knowledge of French plans.

Diary: Wednesday July 24, 1918

Went out with James. Visited corps headquarters of the 1st corps which is not very far back of the line. Then went to the 26th division. Saw many towns which have been shot to pieces. Also went over some of the battlefields where I saw plenty of dead, German and American. Guns, graves, helmets, other ghastly relics everywhere. Spent couple hours in Chateau-Thierry to see what the Germans did in the fine residences they occupied. Found they had wantonly destroyed furniture and everything else in magnificent dwellings. No doubt the Huns are Huns. Wrote 300 word cable on the vandalism and 600 cable on the situation generally. Also wrote considerable for Paris. Germans still retreating from the Soissons-Marne Reims salient*.
I expect about tomorrow or on next day they will stop when a great battle will start. Americans are coming rapidly to the front and will be a big factor. Without them the war would be lost to the Germans.

At Château-Thierry, Don Martin visited a large number of looted and wrecked private residences. As indicative of the general looting and wanton destruction in that region, he reported the following list of what the Germans did in one single home.

Threw an inkbottle against a seven-foot mirror, afterward splashing ink on the walls and ceiling.

Jammed a bayonet through the works of five handsome marble clocks.

Tore covers and blocks of pages from costly volumes and strew more than 500 books about the floor, practically ruining a library which was very evidently the pride of a booklover.

Tore a Teddy bear in two; pulled arms and legs from large dolls; smashed a doll cradle and generally wrecked a child's nursery.

Smashed all the china in a cabinet and a cupboard and shattered expensive glassware.

Slit oil paintings and stamped holes in pictures, which had been torn from the walls and left on the floor.

Broke the keys on a costly piano.

Knocked tops off vases and fancy urns.

Slit tapestries and curtains to ribbons.

Threw bottles against handsomely decorated walls and poured various kinds of sauces and other liquids on expensive rugs and carpets.

Rifled every drawer in the house; blew open a small safe; threw trinkets and fancy articles of wearing apparel all over.

Wrecked beds, dressers, and mirrors in all the sleeping rooms.

Diary: Thursday July 25, 1918

With James went to Mont Pere, by way of Chateau-Thierry. Saw Major Spencer of Third Division. Not much going on on American front. Germans throwing shells at bridges which French are building over the Marne. American soldiers swimming in river nearby. Not worried. Wrote cable for New York.

*Salient: a battlefield feature, also known as a bulge, which projects into enemy territory.

Long letter to Dorothy from Meaux, written on July 25, 1918.

Meaux, France, July 25, 1918

Dorothy

Your Dad doesn't write very often now does he? Maybe he ought to be ashamed of himself but he has a good deal to do. Last night I was thinking that I had failed to write for a long time so I sent a short cablegram to let you know that everything is all right. I get your funny letters and now and then one from Rock, Mother and Alta. You all must know pretty well what I am doing from the cablegrams I send to the Herald. I have been sending quite a few lately—in fact since the middle of June there has been practically no let up.

In my last letter I told you that the Germans would probably make some advances in their big offensive and they did so, but now the tide has turned and it is gratifying to everyone. For the first time in a long, long period the French are going the right way—heretofore they have always been going back. The Germans were taken completely by surprise by the recent offensive and they have not yet recovered from it. They will find themselves however in a few days and then a great battle will start. I think the French with the Americans and British helping will be able to overcome any counter attack the Germans may make. The purpose of the allied strategy I imagine is to keep the Germans more or less on the defensive till winter when there will have to be quiet on both sides; and to build up a great army of Americans to make a final offensive against the Germans next spring. If the allies are able to keep the Germans back from Paris till winter there is no doubt that spring will see a steady, swift advance against the Germans. Let us hope the advance will not stop till the Germans are across the Rhine and German towns and cities have been devastated as so many French places have been.

I have been in a position to see a great deal of the war. When one is trailing in the wake of an advancing army he can go pretty close to the front without danger because the retreating forces do not have time to get their big guns in position for bombardment. I have been in dozens—I might say scores—of towns which have been practically wiped off the map by shell fire, chiefly from the French and Americans. I have been on battlefields five hours after the fighting was over and have seen ... I saw French cavalry start into action and have seen Americans "go over the top". I have been with men in the batteries firing the great guns and have stood far ahead of the guns and, with a telescope, watched the shells strike. Yesterday I saw the bodies of five Americans in a line, about twenty feet from each other. They were killed by German machine guns as they charged towards a woods. Every one of the Americans—and they were young chaps too—was headed the right way and the position of his gun showed he had his bayonet pointed straight for business. All over one field of about ten acres there are still remnants of the fight, packs, guns, cartridges, grenades, helmets, gas masks etc.

You will have read long before this a story I wrote about the mutilation by the Germans of the magnificent homes in Chateau-Thierry. I spent three hours in them yesterday and saw just what the Germans do. They are not human because no human being could do what they did. The homes there are beautiful—about like the finest in Buffalo—and they are wrecked. Everything inside is destroyed. German officers occupied the places.

But the Hun is getting a taste of real war now. The Americans have turned the tide. They looked the situation over, saw that the Germans are determined to terrify and slaughter so the Americans determined to fight fire with fire. In other words, the Germans started a rough war and they are getting it and they will continue to get it. The prisoners captured say that they never knew anything so savage as the artillery fire of the Americans. From what I have seen of the effects of the shelling by our guns I imagine the Germans are telling the truth. Some of the shell holes I have seen are at least ten feet across and seven feet deep. In my room now I have a German helmet with a bullet hole through it, showing that the German sniper who wore it was shot through the head. I saw him lying behind a rock, his rifle (which I also have here in my room) beside him. An American sharpshooter killed him.

The correspondents have been very busy since a week ago Monday when the Germans started their attack. We knew it had started because at half past … [some text missing] … everything in range when they start an offensive. It is part of the scheme to frighten people. We were all awakened by a terrific explosion at half past six and in a few moments everyone was dressing preparatory to going to the cellar. We all thought it was an air raid. But in precisely ten minutes there was another explosion and in precisely ten minutes more a third one and so it continued. Then we all knew the Germans had trained the big gun on Meaux. One shell struck in a boulevard about two blocks from our hotel and tore a tree two feet in diameter up by the roots. Pieces of dirt and pieces of stone flagging fell like a shower of hail all over, dropping on our hotel. Meantime there was great excitement in the hotel. We ate a hurried breakfast and dashed out of town in automobiles for the front. Hundreds of people in Meaux left the city. But at the end of five hours the shelling stopped and not a person was killed. There has been no shelling since.

Business goes on as usual now. The people know that the Germans can, if they deem it advisable, shell the city again but the streets are filled with people and shops are doing business the same as always.

American soldiers have certainly put ginger in the whole allied army. They don't know how to turn away from a fight. Everyone knows that the Americans who fought in the Civil War were great fighters but they couldn't have surpassed the boys of today for bravery and strength. War today is a terrible thing. It isn't a case of going into battle, fighting a few hours or a couple of days and then being through. Here the soldiers are never through. They are bombed in their quarters. They are shelled wherever they are. Their dugouts are threatened; shells are booming constantly day and night; and this goes on for days and weeks. A soldier goes into the trenches (there are few trenches now though; it is open fighting) or the front line and there he stays for a week, two weeks, perhaps three weeks and he is in a furnace all the time. To look over a battlefield after the thing is over one wonders how anyone could have been there and survived; yet a good many come out unhurt and a great many suffer only slight injuries.

Shrapnel and high explosives do the damage. The shrapnel wounds are terrible some times. I have seen bodies torn all to pieces. I have seen soldiers with half their heads shot away. There are comparatively few bullet …[text missing]… they come from, they are all alike. The English and French look like old men compared with the Americans. I saw an American grave yesterday—a mound of earth beside the road, a rifle stuck at the head of it with a helmet on top. In the middle of the grave was a stick about a foot high with a tiny American flag. Tacked on to the stick was a piece of paper saying "American Marine—unknown." There was also stuck to the stick the fragments of a letter the soldier had written to someone at home but had not mailed. I have the fragments of the letter and shall try to use them to identify the soldier who presumably was so terribly injured that all traces of his identity were gone.

After seeing what I have seen one can have no doubt that America is in the war and that she will have a heavy burden of woe and suffering to bear before it is through. I imagine the pro-Germans in the United States will have a hard time of it and they ought to have. Any German American who even acts friendly to Germany now ought to be taken out and hanged. The American soldier treats them the right way—treats the Germans. He kills them. They are cowards on the battlefields and shout Kamerade when they have killed as many Americans as they can and see that they are to be killed. The Americans know what to do in cases like this. Once in a while the Americans take a great many prisoners but that cannot be helped. If there are a hundred or more it is not easy to kill them all. The Germans call the Americans the American peril and the opinion generally in Europe is that the Americans are the most bloodthirsty fighters of all. I imagine that is true. The English started to fight on the theory that they were playing a game of football, where sportsmanship would count for something. They didn't understand the German character. The French did the same thing. The American is treating the German just as he ought to be treated. If a German and an American meet in No Man's Land it is a case of one being killed, and it is always the German.

Here I have given you a long treatise on the war again haven't I Dorothy? I guess you will think I don't write the kind of letters I used to write. I will though as soon as the pressure of the present crisis is over. I was glad to hear about your examinations. You passed splendidly. I see you are very good in English as well as other things. I am glad of that. You will be able to write all around your Dad after a few years. I am not so sure that you ...

I presume by this time you have had some pictures taken in Buffalo and I shall be very glad to get some of them. By the way, that was a great picture of me in the Silver Creek paper. I look as if I took the war rather seriously. Tell Rock he has told me everything except what Dan Reid said. I was curious about that. Probably by time I hear about it I will have forgotten the whole incident.

I have heard nothing from the office since the death of Bennett and don't know what is going on there. However, I don't care. I don't think the new situation will affect me. Maybe it might result in my returning to America after a while—though I doubt that—and in that case I would be very glad because I would get a chance to see you all. I haven't seen Lee Brand yet but shall look him up soon. Neither have I seen Jim Bennett. I got a letter from one of the Eoling boys who expects soon to be at the front. He is here in France now. Tell Rock he might mention this to his father. I wish you would let John Knox read part of this letter Dorothy. I know he would be glad to get some first hand news about the situation at the front. Give him my regards also. Are you and Mother going to Chautauqua? Probably you are there now. Love to all.

(signed) Dad

P.S. I enclose a clipping from the Intransigeant, a Paris paper. A good many of the Paris papers quote me from the Paris edition of the Herald. They don't have men of their own at the front and are glad I suppose to get information at no cost.

Love and a kiss from (signed) Dad

Diary: Friday July 26, 1918

Took 11 o'clock train for Paris. Ordered new tunic at Cook & Co. Bought a lot of stuff. Had dinner at the Chatham Grill; spent night at the Crillon. Rained most of the day in Paris. Read the papers part of the afternoon. Found the Herald is playing my stuff up pretty well.

Diary: Saturday July 27, 1918

Took train from Paris at 11 o'clock. Arrived in Meaux at half past twelve. Left at two for the front. With James went to headquarters of the 42nd division which is relieving the 26th. Got back to Meaux at 7. Wrote story for Paris and a cable of 600 words for New York. Had visit with Major Drouillard of the 2nd Division in the evening. James got the French communiqué at 10 o'clock; got quite excited over it. Indicates French making important advance.

Dorothy wrote weekly letter No. 32 to Dad on July 27, 1918.

Silver Creek, N.Y.
July 27, 1918

Dear Dad

Here goes for letter No. 32. I wonder how long it will be before you get this. Probably about 1 mth from now. We received your letter dated June 27, and it reached here last Wednesday (June 24)

— — — — — — — — — —

Well. I have been down town and 2 or three other places and now I am going to finish this letter. I took a nice leather case down town with 2 of my pictures in it and mailed it to you. It is the size of a pocket – an outside + inside view. Even though I am barefooted and haven't anything but my khaki suit on, I am terrible hot. Oui, oui, if fait tres chaud, vous comprenez? Ha! Ha!

It would be nice to go to Chautaqua [sic] for a week or so, but I really don't care a thing about it. Another thing, I have so much to do here – you know Miss Butler is down at the Baseball Park every day from 9:00 a.m. to 11:45 a.m. + from 1:00 p.m. to 4 p.m. They have teeters, swings, sandpiles, etc. and I am often there – ok, something is surely the matter with my typewriter fingers – look there, I meant there. Ha! Ha! I'm some writer. Well, as I was a-sayin' I'm down there nearly every a.m. from 9:30 to 11:30 or so. I do my practicing etc. before 9:00, then I'm off to play. Miss Butler is teaching me a lot of new stunts – turning a forward, also a backward somersault in a rope swing – that's easy – turning a backward somersault over her back, standing on my head – that's easy too – and standing and walking on my hands. Aunt Atta said she told you that in her letter. Well, now I can't do the walking part alone yet. I can stand on my hands alone, but not walk – alone. OK? I almost forgot to tell you, we just received a cablegram –(about 10 minutes ago)– from you which said – Love from Dad – Everything fine. Well, we are glad of that. It was mailed from Meaux.

I didn't tell you all the things I was so busy with – another thing is my war garden – then I have my practicing, and my theory. Then I am with girls playing most of the time, too. So you see, most of my time is occupied every day.

We went to Buffalo last Thursday and everything happened as usual except that I do not have to go to Doc Hoffman's for 3 weeks, so Grandmother thinks she will ask Miss Juergens if it will be all right for her to have my music vacation now too. We also went to the picture show to see Marguerite Clark. I am buying thrift Stamps right along. I bought a W.S.S. the other day and I am going to start a Thrift stamp book again today. I usually get a thrift Stamp whenever I mail you letters – that is every week, 'course not always.

Oh, something else – You know there is a basket picnic and dance at the Motor Boat Club evry 2 weeks on Friday, and we usually go. Kathleen and some other children are always there, and we have lots of fun. Then I go in bathing down at the motor boat club nearly evry day with the 2 Howson girls, Jane Christy, Joseph H. + Bob Christy and sometimes more. Aunt Julie takes me down sometimes but Miss Butler usually goes in with us. It's lots of fun to turn a somersault in the water. Ever try it?

Grandmother made a "awful" good apple pie to-day – umm. I wish you could have some.

Well, I must close now, and eat my dinner.

Lot o' Love an' hugs an' kisses.

Dorothy

P.S. We will send you some more pictures next week.

Diary: Sunday July 28, 1918

Got up at 7:30 o'clock. Went to Third division headquarters at Mont Pere; then to the 42nd headquarters and Trugny; then to the 1st corps in a chateau near Epieds. Got a good story about the Americans crossing the Ourcq. Returned at 6 p.m. Had a chicken dinner. Bought the chicken myself for 14 francs. Wrote 1,200 words for Paris and 1,500 words cable for New York about the crossing of the Ourcq.

Diary: Monday July 29, 1918

Spent most of the day motoring all over the country close to the line trying to find various headquarters which move nearly every day. Got a splendid story at the 42nd headquarters about Americans from New York City and elsewhere—the Rainbow Division—meeting the Prussian Fourth Guard in the vicinity of Sergy and capturing the village from them. The village changed hands nine times but the Americans finally held it. I wrote about 1,200 words for New York and considerable for Paris. Germans seem much upset by the allied advance and especially by the wonderful showing made by the Americans.

Diary: Tuesday July 30, 1918

Had a busy, exciting and thrilling day. Saw an air fight; visited the Bois de Chatelet and saw the big steel emplacement of the German gun which was used for remote firing, perhaps the bombarding of Paris; saw a cloud of gas rise nearby which caused everyone to put on his gas mask. We, in an automobile (James and I), went at a 60-mile an hour clip and just missed the cloud by a few hundred feet; but we had our masks on anyhow. Got a good story about the Prussian resistance to the American advance. The Americans are going ahead, but more slowly. Wrote 4500 word cable for New York on the big gun and about 1,200 on the general situation.

Diary: Wednesday July 31, 1918

Did not start out today till noon. Went with James as usual. Went to Marigny where we and other correspondents saw General Degoutte, commander of Sixth French army. He told us he was proud to be general of an army in which are Americans. Said they make ultimate victory possible. Told us all plans of French for immediate future. Said Germans had planned to take both sides of the Marne and make that the path of their march to Paris. Saw him in a chateau which was built in the thirteenth century.

Afterwards went to the corps headquarters but Col. Williams was out. Returned at five in the afternoon. Wrote considerable for Paris and about 500 words for New York.

Diary: Thursday August 1, 1918

Went out with James and Cameron Mackenzie of the London Chronicle. Went to headquarters of the 32nd division in a chateau north of Jaulgonne. Then to the 42nd division, in the wrecked village of Beuvardes. Returned fairly early. Wrote a cable of 1,400 words and about 1,000 for Paris. Went for walk in the evening with Maximilian Foster and Mackenzie. Spent rest of the evening visiting with Jimmy Hopper, Mackenzie, Jim Kerney, Ray Carroll, Carroll McNutt of Colliers and several others of lesser importance.

American soldiers doing most wonderful fighting of all. Are amazing Europe. Many of our boys are being killed and a great many wounded but they keep going ahead. It is very evident that their spirit, freshness and recklessness if it can be called that are demoralizing the Germans. This spirit on the part of the Americans may result in large casualty lists for us but it will win the war, not this year and perhaps not next year but it will win in the end.

Diary: Friday August 2, 1918

Went to Paris today. Nearly all the correspondents went. It was a rainy day and indications were it would be quiet along the front. Tried on a new coat at Cook & Co.'s; it was too small. Went to the office and read the papers up to July 16. Returned on the 5:25 train.

Wrote about 400 words for Paris and a cable of about 700 words for New York. Germans still retreating. Are doing a good job. If we were writing about a retreat of our own we would call it one of the most skillful in history. They are almost back to the Vesle. Looks as if they would keep on going till they get to the Aisne.

Diary: Saturday August 3, 1918

Went out with Forrest of the Tribune. James was still in Paris. Went to the chateau where the 32nd division has been found but it had moved. It is now in Cierges which was captured by the Americans only three days ago. Went over the battleground near there—the Cierges woods etc. Saw more that a hundred dead Germans in trenches, machine gun pits and in the fields and woods. Saw quite a few Americans also.
Saw Americans digging graves for one group of

75 Americans near Cierges. Spent several hours looking over fields where some very hard fighting took place. There is no doubt that this is a very rough war. Wrote 600 words for New York and about 800 for Paris. Got a cablegram from Herald suggesting I cable full rate but reduce size of my dispatches by half. It is evident they are not getting my dispatches as early as they thought.

Diary: Sunday August 4, 1918

Bad day so I stayed in. Wasn't feeling very well anyhow—liver out of order due to missing luncheon so much and getting bad food in Meaux. Wrote nothing for New York. Allied advance temporarily held up at the Vesle although that tiny river has been crossed at many points.

Tonight next to my room they are having a riotous party—Robert Collier, two of his writers, James Hopper and McNutt; Cameron Mackenzie, Forrest of the Tribune and Ray Carroll. Correspondents trying to get the censors to move somewhere nearer the front. The censors will probably do so when they find a town which contains a magnificent chateau for their use.

Don Martin wrote a long letter to Dorothy on August 4 from Meaux, saying it was a "family letter" and "all that about the war is for grown-ups".

Meaux, Sunday, August 4, 1918

Dorothy

I suppose you are in Chautauqua or Dahn's Beach or some pleasant place by this time. I trust such is the case. I wish I were with you. It is quite easy to get enough of this war—to get "fed up" on it as the saying goes. I haven't been receiving many letters from home lately but I guess it is because the mails are slower than usual. Everyone is complaining. I haven't seen Lee Brand yet either. I have been so busy roaming around the front that I have been unable to get to Paris except for a few hours one day when I ordered a new uniform. You make me laugh in all your letters — "I am going to practice, write a letter and then raise the roof." I supposed you raised it surely enough. Well have a good time. Now's the time for you to do it. In a year or two or three you will have to be a little Miss Dignity. You won't be able to run around in bare feet and turn somersaults all over the place. There is no reason why you shouldn't except that it doesn't seem to be the proper thing for young ladies to do.

I am afraid that scrapbook business will get to be a pretty big and tiresome job. However it will be a good thing to look over long after the war is over. I have been sending considerable matter lately. I judge from letters I receive that it is being printed in many other cities too. You see the Herald has a syndicate and what it prints the papers belonging to the syndicate publish also. I get letters from people asking about their sons or brothers and from old friends whom I had almost forgotten saying that they enjoy reading my articles. Then I get letters also from people in France—French people whom I do not know— congratulating me on what I write. The things I print in the Paris Herald are frequently copied by many Parisian papers and by papers published all over France.

I am wondering if Nenette and Rintintin have reached you. I'll bet you don't know who Nenette and Rintintin are. I don't exactly know either. They are supposed to be guardians of safety against air bombs. They are no good if one buys them for himself or herself but if someone presents them to you and you carry them, or hang them over your bed, bombs will never get you. Of course it is just a superstition but it is remarkable how seriously the people of France take it. The woman who runs this hotel where I live gave each of the correspondents a pair. Then someone else whom I do not know mailed me a pair. You see them—tiny little silk things—hanging to the coat sleeve of French officers—not all of them of course—and dangling from the back of camions (automobile trucks) or swinging from the roof of automobiles. They are all sizes and colors. I don't suppose anyone in Sliver Creek has any so I decided to have some sent to you. I went to the same store where I bought those funny dolls and told the lady there that as soon as some came to send them to you. There is such a big demand for them that the supply does not last long, she said.

Well now you know all about Nenette and Rintintin. I bought a pair of fancy dolls—small ones—which are very popular in Paris and ordered them sent to you also. They are just fancy dolls supposed to be the leading clown and clowness of France. You will have dolls enough I daresay after a while. I enjoy seeing the French children play with their dolls. I saw a little girl, very poorly dressed, sitting in front of her little stone home the other day holding a very ragged doll in her arms and rocking a much worn tiny cradle in which was another soiled doll, singing away just about as you used to when you thought no one was around.

The war is going along pretty well just now for the allies. We were all surprised at the extent of the German retreat and the vigor of the allied attack. The great importance of the present situation is, not the territory regained, but the placing of the Germans on the defensive. Now the allies have the initiative. The Germans must be guessing all the time at the next move. It has always been the other way. General Foch's and General Petain's skill as strategists, backed by the American troops made the allied offensive possible. The German now has been outgeneraled and out fought. The French did the outgeneraling; the Americans most strikingly did the outfighting.

But it must not be thought that the Americans did the brunt of it. Here is about the way the force was divided. Eighty percent of the entire attacking army are French and the other twenty percent British and American. So you see it is still the French fighting for everyone. She could not have done so however were it not for the constantly increasing number of Americans arriving at the front. Had she made an offensive and been successful, which she could possibly have done, she would have used up her reserves and made herself easy prey for Germany in a few months. But Americans take the place of the reserves.

The Americans are by far the most wonderful fighters in Europe. No exception need be made. They are all young men who don't know what it means to turn back. They may be reckless. We may suffer heavy losses because of the impetuosity of the Americans; but it is that "get there or die" spirit and the utter lack of fear, which has temporarily stunned the Germans and which will win the war. Europe never saw fighting such as the Americans are putting up. Perhaps Napoleon's Old Guard was good but certainly no better than the Americans. Now Germany stands no more chance of winning the war than I do of being President of France. Her teeth have been pulled. On the defensive she can fight for years if necessary, and fight a desperate war, but the crest of her wave has been passed. She is bound to slip, slip, slip until she is defeated. And America has made it possible!

We have a vast army here now and a vast army ready to fight. Along the roads in a part of the front now there are more Americans to be seen than anything else. I ask many of them where they are from. One says Alabama, one Arizona, Missouri, Michigan, Florida, New York, Ohio, Wyoming—or they come from every state and all look alike somehow.

Yesterday afternoon, on a hill overlooking the town of Cierges, I saw 56 Americans buried in a big grave. Strangely enough a German clergyman from Milwaukee conducted the ceremony. Of course, he is an American and I judge from what he said, a very good one. These men were killed by machine gun while capturing a woods where the Germans were strongly entrenched.

I wrote quite a story about the fight for the woods. On the field adjoining I saw dead Huns all over; in the woods there were scores of them. Around a little farm of ten acres, known as Bellevue Farm, I counted 72 dead Germans in a trench and could have counted more than a hundred in a quarry nearby if I had cared to do so. I was there the day after the battle occurred. The farm house was banged all to pieces but the old couple (I mentioned them in a story I wrote last night) were back trying to do something with the ruin. I could not help but feel that it is a fine thing to have someone come in and use your house and farm for a battlefield. I went along the entire wake of the retreating Germans; saw the fires at night, caused by burning ammunition dumps, and heard the constant booming of our guns which were dropping shells on the roads over which the fleeing Germans were going. The scene along these roads is not a pleasant one.

We are still located at Meaux but must move. It is possible we shall go to Chateau-Thierry but more likely to Epernay. Now it takes a three-hour automobile ride to get to the division headquarters (they are always four or five miles back from the actual front) and that is too far. There are difficulties in the way of going to Chateau-Thierry because the telephone and telegraph wires are all down and the water supply is bad. Also, it is hard to get food. Chateau-Thierry is pretty much of a wreck. I go through it in an automobile every day. But we shall move soon to some new place. It won't make any difference in the addressing of your letters though Dorothy.

That was a great picture in your last letter—which hand?

This is a family letter. You all understand that of course. Some of it is entirely for you but all that about the war is for the grown-ups. It isn't necessary for you to know too much about the war. I hope the people at home are reconciled to the fact that United States will pay a heavy price in lives to win the war. It can't be helped. It seems a terrible thing but the blame must be put on Germany. And how the Americans hate the Germans! The spirit runs all through the army.

The Germans are tricky and unfair, as the newspapers have told you. The men at machine guns keep shooting at the enemy until they see they are bound to be captured, when they put up their hands and cry "Kamarade", meaning they want to surrender. One man with a machine gun can kill or wound from 200 to 1,000 soldiers and the theory of the Americans is that a German who has done everything he could to murder and then asks for mercy, should be treated with a bayonet or a rifle bullet—and that is precisely what happens. The Americans however never disregard any cry of Kamarade when the soldiers give up in an honorable way. The truth of the whole situation is the Germans have found a foe that can lick them every time they meet, and Germany is worried.

I shall write to you again in a few days, young lady and meantime I shall look for one of those funny letters from you. Here's a kiss and a hug.

From Dad

P.S. Quite a coincidence. When I brought this over to be censored I found two letters from you—No. 30, dated July 12 and No. 29 dated July 5. Both nice letters but terrible pictures.

Dad

Diary: Monday August 5, 1918

Went out with James. Had a very long trip. Meaux is now about 80 kilometers from the nearest point we have to reach. Visited Fere-en-Tardenois, got some details of the fighting along the Vesle which is not progressing very well. Americans command Fismes and have a few men in the place but are afraid to occupy it because the Germans will shell them. Went to a place a short distance northwest of Tardenois and saw any number of French and German dead. Germans were all in their machine gun nests and the French dead were for the most part close up showing they had tried to take the places. No doubt the French are brave soldiers. Saw 1,000 Americans having luncheon in a field in the rain. They have been in France only 20 days but seem eager to get to the front although they must know it is a terrible place to be. Wrote about 1,000 words cable for New York which I file press rate. Got two nice letters from Dorothy. In one she says she is picking currants to earn money for patriotic purposes She is a real daughter!

Diary: Tuesday August 6, 1918

Went out with Forrest of the Tribune. Went through many villages which have been practically destroyed by shell fire from the French and Americans. German debris everywhere. Saw miles of abandoned ammunition, machinery, etc. Forrest a little timid about getting near the front. Insisted on taking back roads which was rather disappointing to me. Got caught in fierce rain and wind storm. Rode eight hours in an automobile. Had luncheon in an officers' mess in Tardenois. Got back to Meaux at 6:30 p.m. Wrote a column story for Paris and about 1,000 words cable for New York. Am getting a bit weary of the work. It requires constant application and endless travelling. This in addition to the dangers of being hours on roads which the Germans shell. Went

to a chateau which the Germans had defiled and practically ruined. They are a fine lot of vandals.

Diary: Wednesday August 7, 1918

Stayed in today and wrote one long mail story—about 4,000 words which I headed "In the Ugly Wake of Victory." In it I described many of the horrors I have seen in the last two weeks and gave a picture of the scores and scores of wrecked villages through which I have passed. Also wrote long letter to Ohl, managing editor of the Herald, and letters to John McDonald and John F. O'Brien, both of whom have written to compliment me on my cables.

Diary: Thursday August 8, 1918

Stayed in again today. Wrote another long mail story of about 3,000 words on the Huns as vandals. I told about the chateaux the Germans have mutilated and of the private homes in Chateau-Thierry and other places which the Germans defiled. At half past six in the evening took an automobile with James, Bailey of the London Mail, Ferguson of the U.P. and went to Paris to attend a dinner given to Floyd Gibbons and Martin Green who are leaving for America. I stayed but a short time because I saw that the crowd was a cheap one and furthermore they had given me a seat which was about the worst in the place. Went to the Hotel de Crillon and went to bed early. Franco-British offensive started today southeast of Amiens and is progressing satisfactorily.

Diary: Friday August 9, 1918

Did some shopping in Paris and started back for Meaux at 1:10. Junius Wood was on the same train.

Diary: Saturday August 10, 1918

Went out with Ruhl of Colliers. Took pictures etc. Went to Fere-en-Tardenois by way of Lizy, Coincy etc. Talked with some of the lumbermen and Indians in the 32nd division. They did some wonderful fighting. Cabled about 300 words.

Diary: Sunday August 11, 1918

Went out with Smith of the Chicago Tribune—a very fine fellow. Went to Fere-en-Tardenois, Coulanges etc. Had luncheon in a chateau north of Tardenois with two artillery officers from the state of Washington. Cabled 300 words on our lack of airplanes and 450 words on the formation of the first American army. James ill yesterday and today; didn't go out.

Don Martin learns of the enormous increase in the Paris Herald circulation, certainly aided by his reports.

Diary: Monday August 12, 1918

Went to Paris chiefly to buy a camera. Had a talk with Mitchell, manager of the Paris Herald. He says the circulation of the Paris edition is 165,000. A year ago it was 8,000. I bought a camera for 240 francs, including films and a leather case. Had luncheon at the Cafe de la Paix. Returned on the 4:25 train. Wrote a 600 words cable for New York on stories told by escaped British prisoners.

Diary: Tuesday August 13, 1918

Went out alone. Took my camera and took 20 pictures. Had luncheon with Major Stebbins of the 3rd Corps about a mile outside Coulanges. Got back early. Wrote nothing. Everyone now talking about moving from Meaux. The Americans expect soon to put on a big operation in the St. Mihiel region and I expect we will all be moving to Nancy very soon. The front here is very quiet. The Germans are resisting and neither the French nor the Americans are making any great attempt to push on farther north.

Diary: Wednesday August 14, 1918

Stayed in and wrote mail stories. Wrote one of 3,000 words on the importance of air supremacy; 3,000 on the way army headquarters move etc.; about 600 on Quentin Roosevelt's grave and about 1,500 on sidelights etc. Cabled nothing. Got five letters from family including Dorothy—a pretty good batch for one day.

Diary: Thursday August 15, 1918

Went out with James. Visited the 1st corps headquarters at Coulanges; got no luncheon and came back by a road south of the Marne. Wrote about 500 word cable for New York. Correspondents now told they must keep writing from here so the Germans will not suspect that we are liable to break out somewhere else. We are to stay here for ten days and then go to Nancy. Word came this afternoon for the correspondents to go to Chaumont tomorrow to attend an important conference at G.H.Q. General Pershing wants to talk to us.

Diary: Friday August 16, 1918

Rode more than 350 miles in a motor car today. Went to Chaumont by request to see General Pershing. Drove to Chaumont by way of Troyes. Went out to Langres also to see a tank demonstration. Saw Pershing at 5 with about twelve other correspondents. He said war m-a-y end next year but he apparently does not expect it will. He says the scheme is to keep the Boche guessing all the time. Says also we have 31 divisions in France now. He did not impress me as being much. Left for Paris at half past six. Delayed so decided to go to Meaux instead. Air raid on Coulommiers as we went through the place. Arrived at Meaux at midnight just after a raid there was over.

Diary: Saturday August 17, 1918

Went to Paris on train. Many of the other correspondents went also. Did some shopping and spent the night at the Hotel Crillon. Had two good meals. The censor's office is soon to move away from Meaux. The understanding is it will go to Nancy because the Americans intend soon to start a big operation in that region.

Diary: Sunday August 18, 1918

Left Paris at 1:10 o'clock. Did not go to the front. It is very quiet. Wrote 350 words for New York and a short piece for Paris.

Contrary to what Martin wrote in his diary, Phase III of the Second Battle of the Marne began on August 18 with the French 10th Army launching a major offensive near Soissons.

Diary: Monday August 19, 1918

Went to the front today. James went with me. Went to the Chateau Fere north of Fere-en-Tardenois; afterwards to Coulanges and up to Bellevue Farm to see the old man, Publier, whose home was wrecked during the fighting. Had luncheon with the Military Police outfit near Coulanges and a very good meal it was. Got back in Meaux at 4 o'clock. Wrote 200 words cable for New York. Sent cable to Dorothy—yesterday.

Diary: Tuesday August 20, 1918

Stayed in today. Wrote a long letter to Dorothy, one to Helene and one to McEwan. With McNutt, Ferguson, Smith and James we went to a new place for dinner and found some good food. Sat around and talked and sang till ten. Everyone expected an air raid because of the full moon but there was none.

Letter from Rose Martin postmarked August 19, 1918. It had not been opened.

August

Dear Don,

Two letters came from you today, after I have read them again, I shall pass them on to the rest. They are very interesting. How awful it must be to see so many men killed, even though they are Germans, but it is what they deserve, those wild animals, but the way they are killed, and taken prisoners, makes me feel as if the war can't last so terrible much longer. Well I am mighty glad we are getting the best of them and I do hope they won't hold out much longer. It is to [sic] bad our boys are getting killed the way they are. Last week when the Herald sent my check, they enclosed a little clipping. How nice it was of them to do that. John Knauf is always interested, about everything that comes from you. He watches all the papers. He is good and true all right.

That French article you sent in your letter was good. I recognized it as I had read it in English. O dear, it makes me feel as if I would like to kill some of those Huns too. "Ces Chien la."

Those little flowers you sent I mounted, and they look so pretty. The dolls and other things have not come yet. It certainly takes time. We sent you some pictures of Dorothy about a month ago. I am sure they ought to be there by now, will send two more tomorrow so to make sure you get some. We are all going to Dahn's Beach for about two weeks. Dorothy would rather go there then any where else, so it will be there. Am glad your finger is well. What awful sights you are seeing. Dorothy has written to you too, and I wonder if you will get them both at once.

With Love from Mother

In his letter from Meaux of August 20 to Dorothy, Don Martin made a prediction about the end of the war, and showed that his 'opinion' was not infallible. He also bemoaned the absence of America coming up with a new weapon to end the war—a premonition of the atom bomb that ended the next big war?

Meaux, Aug 20, 1918

Dorothy and the rest of the family,

Goodness, I ought to write a dozen letters—one to Mother, to Rock, to Julie, to Alta and to a lot of other persons in whom I am not so much interested. I get scores of letters from people who read my articles in the Herald—and in other papers which buy the Herald's service—and I just don't have time to reply to them all. The other day I got a nice long letter from Julie, a long letter from Mother, a long letter from Alta and a characteristic letter from young Miss Dorothy—and then, two days later I received a handsome leather case with two pictures of you in it. They are fine. I have them on my mantle now with the others which have been there for a long time.

You tell the folks now that we ought to have some large pictures of you—some like those taken in Albany a long time ago. I think you were four then. They will cost about $25 I suppose or maybe more, but if I have that much to my credit at home, tell Mother to have the large pictures taken. And go to the best photographer in Buffalo. Don't think that I am criticizing those you have just had taken. I am not. They are very excellent but I wish we had some larger ones.

You did well in all your examinations Dorothy and I understand are making splendid progress with your music. I also understand that you can stand on your head and walk around town on your hands and do a lot of other things which you will probably discontinue when you are a bit older. It's all right. You have all the fun you can. I'd like to be over there having fun with you. Just a little more than a year ago I was with you at Dahn's Beach—remember?

I heard a sort of rumor, emanating from New York, that the Herald wanted me back in New York for the Governorship campaign but I have heard nothing from the office about it so I guess it is not true. I almost wish it were. I would certainly like to see you young lady. Still the work here is very interesting though hard.

It is almost like living in an automobile. Last Friday for instance, I left here at half past seven in the morning and motored to Chaumont by way of Troyes. I reached there at a quarter to one in the afternoon. At 2 o'clock I went to Langres to see a tank demonstration; at five o'clock with other correspondents had a half hour talk with Pershing; at 6 started for Paris. We were delayed on the way so decided to go to Meaux instead of Paris. At a place about ten miles from Coulommiers we were halted by soldiers who said we must put out our lights as bombing planes were then raiding Coulommiers. We then rode in the dark—although the moon was partly up—all the way to Meaux, about 30 miles. The raiders had gone when we got to Coulommiers but people were on the streets and there were evidences of the raid on two or three streets. Then when we got in Meaux we found people on the streets, although it was nearly one o'clock in the morning. There had been a raid there also. So you see the life of a war correspondent, whether he is at the front or not, is likely to be exciting. I always keep out of real danger though Dorothy, so you need not worry. I suppose sometimes when you do not see dispatches by me in the papers, or do not hear from me, you begin to be uneasy but there is no need for that. Sometimes I do not send cables to the Herald for two, three or four days at a time. That is when there is not much news. If anything went wrong you would hear right away.

I have been writing a good deal lately and much of it will not be published for some time. I wrote several long stories and sent them by mail. One was labelled "In the Ugly Wake of Victory" and the other deals with Hun vandalism.

The Germans are receiving their first real setback since the first battle of the Marne. They are not licked yet though—not by any means. People at home are likely to get the idea from the glowing accounts they read of our troops that we have already started the Hun back home and that victory is in sight. That is far from true. We have been able to turn the tide against the Hun but he is still powerful and on the defensive will be able to fight for a long time. The war will not end this year. That is certain. It m-a-y end next year. My notion is that it will end next fall, but that is only opinion. America has done wonders but the hoped for device or invention has not yet appeared. The Edisons, Henry Fords, Teslas and other geniuses have not come through with a single thing which excels the Germans. The only thing in which United States excels is in the fighting qualities of the individual soldier. The doughboy as they call him — the infantryman — has done more than anyone expected of him. If the airplane makers and the wizards of industry and invention had done one tenth as much as the fighter in the ranks, the war would be over this year.

I am staying in today. The front is quiet and is likely to remain so for a few days. In four or five days all the correspondents will move from here but we don't know where yet. It probably will be some distance from Paris. I will let you know as soon as I am located. I sent a cable the other day because I suddenly realized that I hadn't written in quite a while. Now I shall write a letter to the office; one to Charles E. Hughes and one to the editor of the Paris edition. Here's a hug and kiss Dorothy.

(signed) From Dad

Diary: Wednesday August 21, 1918

Stayed in again. Little bowel trouble so did not get up (to stay) till noon. Hung around the hotel all day. Front very quiet. Most of the correspondents either having a holiday or loafing.

Diary: Thursday August 22, 1918

Stayed in again. Hottest day I have known in France. Had luncheon at a new place across the Marne. Not very good. Wrote a story for Paris but nothing for New York. Things quiet along the Vesle where the Americans are holding the line. The 77th division is doing the fighting and it is not quite up to the others. It is a draft division from N.Y. City, Westchester and Long Island. Suffered from the heat. Everyone else did also.

Diary: Friday August 23, 1918

Started out at 10 a.m. despite the heat. Motored to Fresnes, the 3rd corps headquarters. Learned the Americans had recovered slight ground lost yesterday. Visited a hospital where I saw many serious cases of Americans wounded. All smile and want to get well so they can go back to the line. Am all packed up ready to move to Nancy or Neufchateau. Everyone seems to know that the Americans intend to make an offensive on the front nearest Metz so I suppose the plan will be changed. French and English continue to harass the Germans. Yesterday got a letter from Ohl. He seems very friendly but did not say whether he is pleased or dissatisfied with my work. I am quite sure he is satisfied. Cabled 600 words.

Diary: Saturday August 24, 1918

Stayed in Meaux today. James went to Paris. Wrote some letters and took a nap. Had dinner across the river with McNutt and several other correspondents.

Diary: Sunday August 25, 1918

Stayed in today. Very warm so hung around the hotel most of the time. Had dinner across the river again with Eyre, Wales, McNutt and a lieutenant named Langstaff who has just come out of the line.

Diary: Monday August 26, 1918

Went out today with James. Went to Fere-en-Tardenois; then to the headquarters of the 28th division; then to corps headquarters and to Quentin Roosevelt's grave which has been newly decorated by the French. Got back at 5. Wrote short cable on Roosevelt's grave and longer one on Lieutenant Langstaff and various other things.

Diary: Tuesday August 27, 1918

Took the 11 o'clock train for Paris. Had a good luncheon at the Weber cafe. Spent night at the Crillon.

Diary: Wednesday August 28, 1918

Left Paris at 4:25 o'clock. Arrived in Meaux at 6:30. Found the 32nd division had been in the fight northwest of Soissons. James and Smith told me about it. Wrote about 500 words for New York. Spent two hours in the Censor's office with the other correspondents trying to get our stories through. Castiel, the French censor, objected to anything which seemed to glorify the achievements of the Americans, which I thought was right considering the smallness of what we had done compared with the bigger things constantly done by the French. Smith was sore. He kicked so much that Morgan, chief censor, ordered him out of the office. Talked with James for an hour before going to bed. Decided to get up at five in the morning and start for Soissons.

On Thursday, September 12, the New York Herald published on page 1 a photo titled:

'FAMOUS CORRESPONDENT AT HERO'S GRAVE'

with the following text:

"The photograph shows Don Martin, New York Herald correspondent with the American armies, at the grave of Lieutenant Quentin Roosevelt, near the tiny village of Chamery. The lieutenant was buried within a few yards of his wrecked machine and, as Mr. Martin cabled, the Germans placed a wooden cross over the mound of earth, reading, "Buried by the Germans". As soon as the Americans and French regained the terrain they enclosed the sacred spot with white birch saplings, the Salvation Army sent a floral wreath and soldiers quartered in the neighborhood went by thousands to pay their respects to the young hero's resting place. A photograph and a diagram, made by American engineers, were sent to Colonel Roosevelt, in Oyster Bay."

Picture of Don Martin at the gravesite of Lt Quentin Roosevelt, published in the Herald on September 12.

Diary: Thursday August 29, 1918

Got up at 5:30. Found Delany had put McFall of the A.P. in car I had engaged. Refused to go. Waited till 9 when James and I started out with Fowle. Went to a quarry which is the headquarters of the 32nd division. It is a weird place—40 feet underground, wired and lighted with electricity—more than 200 men working as efficiently as if they were in a Wall Street office building. While there, lights were turned off and message brought that gas shells were dropping nearby. Looked bad for a few minutes. I had my gas mask so I didn't worry much. Got story about the Americans—the boys from Wisconsin and Michigan making slight progress. Germans are resisting vigorously here. Returned by way of Fresnes and there saw the staff of the 3rd corps. Quiet on the Vesle. Got back to Meaux—100 kilometers—at 6. Had dinner with Battersby of Reuters. Wrote 700 word cable and a column story for Paris.

Weather getting cooler.

Diary: Friday August 30, 1918

Went to the 32nd division headquarters with Smith who is a very fine chap. Hung around the headquarters for a couple of hours. Stopped at a hospital near the Foret Villers-Cotterets on the way back. Took lunch with us. Returned at 6:30. Wrote a cable of about 500 words.

Dorothy wrote letter No. 37 to Dad on August 30, 1918. It was unopened.

Silver Creek, N.Y.
Aug. 30, 1918

Dear Dad

Here goes for letter No. 37. I feel quite silly this morning so this probably will be a crazy letter. Crazy, yes'm. You guessed it Hee Haw Hee Hatto.

We went to Buffalo yesterday. I took my music lesson and went to the dentist's as usual. And now to wait for tomorrow and Dahn's Beach! Oh, Boy! I can hardly wait. Oh, I'll have a grand time! And then some!

I am quite busy this morning. I have done my practicing and after I finish this letter, I have to write a note to Miss Juergens, my music teacher, and then go down town and mail both letters, and buy 4 Thrift Stamps, and get some things for Grandmother, and oh – everything. Then I have to go over to the playground + have my picture taken, standing on my head, shoulders, hands, etc.

Grandmother gives me so much money that I can't keep track of it. I had just counted out 1 dollar 44 (Ha!) Thrift Stamps. Then I took out a quarter for a camera film. Then I have 60 cents left to take to Dahn's beach. I was looking in my drawer and what did I find but 10 cents more she had stuck in. So, I have plenty of money all right.

We are having grand weather now. Not too hot nor too cool, but just right. I will be glad when school starts. I do not know whether I told you about Nenette and Rintintin. If I did, I have forgotten it. Well, they came and they are awfully cute. I wear the large ones quite often, and the little ones we keep in the house.

Well I guess I better close now and go down town.

Lots of love and hugs an' kisses,

Dorothy

P.S. My Import License came, and as soon as Uncle Rock can fill it out, we will send it after the dolls. They ran away! Ha! Ha! Ha!

Diary: Saturday August 31, 1918

With Smith and James went to the 32nd headquarters. There was not much of a story. The Americans advanced and took the village of Juvigny. I stopped at the hospital and talked with some of the men who had been in the Juvigny fight. They are all from northern Wisconsin and Michigan. Wrote about 900 words cable.

Diary: Sunday September 1, 1918

Stayed in today. Nearly all the other correspondents did the same thing. Battersby of London and Captain Morgan returned from the front at 3 p.m. and said that the Americans had gone ahead farther and had taken 550 prisoners. I told James and Eyre. James sneaked off and wrote a story about it which he filed at the telegraph office. He has queer notions of fair dealing. However I wrote a story myself.

Got letters from Dorothy (in French and very clever), from Rock and Alta. Had dinner at the Golden Bull with Eyre, Johnson and Corey. Spent the evening around the hotel.

The story Don Martin wrote and cabled to New York on September 1 was another masterpiece — almost 2900 words long. The New York Herald placed it on page 1 of its September 2 edition with a headline emphasizing how near to fighting he had been.

DON MARTIN, HID IN SHELL HOLE 500 YARDS FROM GERMAN LINE, WATCHES BATTLE AT JUVIGNY

Herald Correspondent Sees Americans Under Rain of Lead Creep Upon Foe

ADVANCE BY SERIES OF BURROWED HOLES

Heads Bob Up and Scoot Down Like Prairie Dogs in Their Short Dashes

Today on the outskirts of Juvigny I saw a remarkable panorama of modern war. East of me German machine guns were attempting to hold off the advancing Americans.

I was with some of our officers in a shell hole within five hundred yards of the front line, which extends along the edge of the railroad skirting Juvigny.

Looking over the slope which extends to the railroad track, not a soldier was visible. With only the distant roar of the guns audible, the very silence seemed weird — uncanny to find here in the very lap of war such seeming tranquility.

Officers had been advised not to show their heads above the shell hole. The reason for this order soon was understood by all. I glanced through a peephole and for a second I saw acres of the sloping field in front of me transformed suddenly into life when our men there lifted up their heads.

Immediately it was the signal for the staccato-like sputter of enemy machine guns on a hill a quarter of a mile distant. Quickly the heads disappeared, but the sputter continued for ten minutes. Then hundreds of heads popped up again, like prairie dogs, and again the machine guns opened on them. These tactics continued, but every time the heads of our men were lifted it meant a short dash forward toward the Huns. When the machine guns would begin firing at them they would spring like foxes into holes which they had burrowed into the side of the hill. To dash up this hillside was certain death. They had dug their holes the night before — methodically, determinedly, for they were after the Huns.

Waves Burrow Like Beavers

I saw them dart forward twice, while there were short lulls in the enemy's machine gun fire, and they used their shovels like beavers burrowing new holes and working in the very shadow of death, but always advancing slowly and surely. They knew that enemy observers were watching them and that these observers were giving the firing orders to the Huns in the machine gun nests.

---[Paragraphs deleted]---

Fighting at Juvigny Savage

The fighting in the village of Juvigny was savage. When the Germans found the Americans getting around the town on two sides they tried to escape, but our men swept through the streets

255

DON MARTIN HID IN SHELL HOLE 500 YARDS FROM GERMAN LINE...

like demons, bayonetting, hurling grenades and using their rifles and pistols. Many of the Germans tried to hide in cellars and caves, but our men knew their locations and rooted them out.

Sometimes they would come across sullen groups of the enemy who attempted to fight. In such cases the Americans showered them with grenades, killing all.

To get into the village the Americans had to pass through a strip of territory which was heavily saturated with gas.

They traversed this safely, however, by the use of their masks, at the handling of which they are now adept.

In one cave in the village they found a battalion. Fifty Germans surrendered.

The others were either killed or wounded.

During the mopping up process in Juvigny the Americans were harassed by the fire of an enemy sniper, who seemed to be everywhere at once.

A detachment of our men was sent out to kill him. In ten minutes the detachment returned, each man in it having put a bullet into the sniper.

Diary: Monday September 2, 1918

Went to the 32nd division with James. Brought McNutt back in our car. Came back through Soissons which is in ruins. Only front wall of the cathedral is standing. While we were there about 50 guns in and around Soissons began a barrage to blaze a way for the advance by the Moroccans who have gone in the line in place of the Americans. Wrote cable for N.Y.

Diary: Tuesday September 3, 1918

Went to Paris. Met Mitchell at luncheon and talked things over generally with him. Stayed at the Crillon. Paris feeling much different than it did a few months ago.

Diary: Wednesday September 4, 1918

Arrived in Meaux at 2 p.m. Learned that Huns had begun retreat from the Vesle. Ferguson of the U.P. was good enough to tell me the story which I wrote for Paris. Sent about 300 words to New York forecasting retirement to Aisne or Chemin des Dames. Got cable from office saying cable received Sunday night was repetition of message received before. Can't understand it.

On September 4, the Second Battle of the Marne came toward its end. The initiative on the Western Front had passed to Allied hands, where it would remain. American Expeditionary Forces Divisions started to shift from the Marne to the Verdun sector. The pause gave Don Martin a little time to visit Paris and relax.

Diary: Thursday September 5, 1918

Went out with Ferguson and McNutt. Had luncheon with some doctors at Cohan—a good luncheon too. Visited Fismes which the Germans had recently. While there gas shells dropped so we got out. Visited observation post close to the line and saw the effect of our shelling on the heights between Vesle and the Aisne.

Diary: Friday September 6, 1918

Visited headquarters 3rd corps and 28th division with James; went up to observation post; saw German plane bring down two observation balloons; had lunch with some doughboys; ride 175 miles; had dinner with Sam Blythe and Arthur Sinnott and wrote 700 word cable for New York.

Diary: Saturday September 7, 1918

Stayed in today. Wrote a long letter to Dorothy. Sent 500 word cable to New York on bravery of the 32nd division on the defensive. All the correspondents are restless because of the distance to the battlefront and the prospects of an American offensive soon over on the Toul front.

Dorothy wrote letter No. 38 to Dad on September 7, 1918. It had been opened.

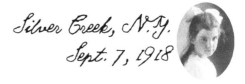

Silver Creek, N.Y.
Sept. 7, 1918

Dear Dad

Here goes for letter No. 38. I feel very silly this morning, so this will probably be a crazy letter. Quite crazy. uh-huh. I am sitting in front of the fire (and it is lighted), writing on the little white stand. Ok, I forgot to tell you – We are not at Dahn's Beach now. It rained so hard that we couldn't go out doors most of the time, so Thursday we came home. And, of course, the next day (Friday) the sun came out and everything was lovely, except that it was cold in the morning. But we are going back this P.M., and stay the rest of our time. That is, until Monday P.M. It is very cold this morning, but the sun is shining, and I think it will get warmer this afternoon like it did yesterday morning. Ok, I guess I'm surely crazy – I mean yesterday afternoon. We walked down to West Irving on one of the 2 days when it was nice and got some grand whitefish. I ate your share of them, I guess. Ok, they were terrible good. I did not get a chance to see Old Wallace, but I probably will go down to-morrow. I have a pound of sugar, and some other things for him.

We did not go to Buffalo last week on account of being at Dahn's Beach, and also because of the first day of school. I like school real well this year. It seems good to be back with all the kids again. And I'm going to like gym' all the better this year, because I can do some stunts. Uncle Charlie took my picture standing on ma tete at Dahn's Beach and we are going to send it to you. Have you the other pictures yet? Not the ones in the case, but the others? Oh, I see. Uh huh. No. No, I don't either. Uh huh. Good-bye. Ha! Don't get inquisitive. I was just talking with this paper.

We have not had any letters from you this week, but from the number of things in the paper, why it looks as if you must be pretty busy. But even if we didn't get any letters, I got something from you. My French Dolls came! And, OK, I just love 'em! I had to laugh when I saw the Red headed one. She's got pretty bright red hair. Oh, but I just love 'em, and their dresses are of real French silk. And it's so soft and nice. Even if people are going to have Nenette + Rintintins, they aren't going to be straight from France and I bet nobody'll have dolls like those. Oh, I just love 'em! Now about Nenette and Rintintin, they are goin' to make 'em over here, now, and they are going to be "good luckers". I saw it in the Herald.

Well, I think I will close now and go down town and mail this letter, and buy some bread for Aunt Josephine. She told me to tell you that she and Mrs. Grasho were giving a picnic to-day for Grace Dean, Helen Gaston, (and they are all here) and oh — all the rest of the old "gals".

Lots of love an' hugs an' kisses.

Dorothy

P.S. We just got a letter from you, from Meaux, dated Aug 20.

Dorothy included this drawing with her letter.

Don Martin's lengthy letter to Dorothy from Meaux dated September 7 was about family things, but he did include stories about the wheat harvest and about viewing the war at close range. Dorothy's letter of August 10 that he mentioned has not survived.

Meaux, Sept. 7, 1918

Dorothy

That was a great French letter you write on August 10. I am wondering if it took you as long to write it as it took me to translate it. I could make out what it meant without a dictionary but in order to make a complete job of it I looked up some of the words. It was very evident that you were "joue, joue, joue." What a shame that there has to be so much fussing about getting some dolls to Silver Creek! Anyhow they got there and I'm quite sure you will like them; but no better than those which are on their way now and which I hope will reach you before very long. There are two more dolls, as I have already written—and the Nenette and Rintintin which should have reached you before this. I would get more things for you if it were not such a terrible job getting them packed up, appraised etc.

In this letter were the bachelor buttons, the larkspur and the other flower with the remarkably-hard-spelling name. They are very pretty. Now you have a poppy from the Marne and I have some flowers from your garden. That is a fair exchange. I notice young lady that you are using some pretty long words—"extraordinarily happy". That is a big one.

Summer has about gone here. There is a touch of autumn in the air and the days are over about 7 in the evening. The days are hot for a few hours but when riding in an automobile one needs an overcoat. The wheat crop has all been stacked in great piles with thatched tops. They are about 40 feet high, on an average 30 feet in diameter and are shaped about like this *[handwritten diagram]*. In going to La Ferte on a main road—a distance of fourteen miles—I could count probably 1,000 of these stacks. They are symmetrically perfect, except in the case of a few, and the farmers seem to take pride in having them artistic. They thatch them with straw of a hue which is quite a contrast with the body of the stack, and it makes a pretty effect. In fact these stacks, dotting the horizon all over at this time of year, give the landscape a touch never seen in America. The wheat stays there until the thresher comes along.

It is interesting also to see the gleaners of whom you have read. When the mowers have cleaned the fields, the women and children go out and pick up every stray sprig of wheat. They go over a ten acre field and get armfuls of grain. When they have finished, there is nothing left. One day I saw a school teacher coming along a road with about 40 little girls your age. They had been off on a holiday and had been working as gleaners. Each had her bundle of wheat and I could see that each was very proud of what she had done. That is all part of the French system of wasting nothing. It is true that not a single thing goes to waste. That is why the French are so prosperous and in times of stress, always have money enough.

The trees do not turn here as they do at home. There are no hard maple. There are beech, ash and poplar in abundance—and considerable oak—not to mention fir, spruce and pine but the leaves of none of these trees change color much so the gorgeous color schemes we have at home beginning about now are not to be seen in France.

I got Rock's letter and Aunt Alta's also, the first dated Aug. 11 and the other Aug. 8. Tell Alta that that man Scott exaggerates a good deal. I don't know where he got all that weird information about me going over the top and sitting down with mud-caked boots writing with tears streaming down my eyes. It is barely possible that on a few occasions my boots have been mud caked but I have yet to shed a tear. That is something I am not given to. Don't let anyone, Dorothy, make you believe that your Dad is taking chances. He is staying well back in the safety zone. I see a good deal but it is possible to do that and still not to get in any particular danger. For instance day before yesterday I went up on a hill just south of the Vesle River and watched the Americans start up on the slopes leading to the Vesle heights. I was about a mile away and perfectly safe. I was in an observation post; that is a little house built in a tree where two soldiers sit day and night watching for airplanes; watching developments on the enemy side; ascertaining as nearly as possible the effect of our shell fire on the enemy and observing movements of men and vehicles across the line. These observers have the most powerful field glasses made. With it they can detect a man ten miles away. I looked through this glass and saw a great deal. Of course if the Germans knew where we were they could have trained field guns on us but in the first place they didn't know an observation post was there and furthermore they have better use for their shells than to send them at a target they might never hit.

I have been all the way from Noyon to Reims and have been in about every town the Allies have retaken from the Germans. I was in Soissons the other day. I was in Fismes the day after the Germans got out. I saw a wounded American—just slightly wounded though—sitting on a pile of debris and he was from Canandaigua. He had been shot on the hills north and was walking to a hospital. I put him in the automobile I was riding in and took him to a hospital about two miles away.

Yesterday I saw more war than I ever expected I would see. I was in another observation post north of the Vesle. I saw a German flier swoop down out of the clouds and attack a string of about eight French observation balloons. The observers—one to each balloon—dropped through the bottom of their baskets and came down gently in their parachutes which are always attached to them. The crews aground began to haul in the balloons but before they could get them out of danger the Boche had fired two which descended a whirling mass of flame and smoke. Meantime antiaircraft guns were spotting the sky with puffs of smoke—bursting shrapnel—hoping to injure the Boche and damage his machine but to see him pass through the cloud of shrapnel one would have thought his machine was armor-clad. He disappeared a few moments later. No one was hurt. Then I saw several German ammunition dumps up toward the Aisne explode and send up huge volumes of smoke. Meantime three miles to the south I could see the constant flash of our guns which were bellowing away at the Germans north of the Aisne. The gun flashes seem about like the flash of a mirror turned for an instant to the sun, only it was as if there were fifty of these mirrors.

I have been expecting to move from here any day. When the move comes it will be a considerable one I imagine. It will however make no difference in the addressing of your letters.

The war looks pretty good now, as you of course know. The people at home however must not get the idea that the Hun is licked. He has suffered a stinging reverse but he has much fight left in him yet. When the Allied summer campaign is over the German will be back a little—but not much—farther than he was before he started his big offensive on March 21. So you see there is much yet to be done.

The Americans continue to fight with the same spirit as at first. They are wonders. The other day I saw a bunch of negro laborers burying 250 Americans on the side of a hill near the village of Sergy. They had been buried all over the region and the Americans have decided to put all the dead in groups. The chaps who died here were all from northern Wisconsin and Michigan. They fought the Fourth [.......] to a finish but paid a high price.

Recently I have been making a daily visit to an American [...] headquarters which is in a cave within a kilometer of the front line yet just as safe as Paris because it is so deep. Shells strike once in a while above it but the noise is hardly heard.

I was very sorry to hear of Mrs. Van Wormer's death. I could see last summer that she was failing. Give Carrie and Wally my kindest regards and tell them I regret I could not have seen Mrs. Van Wormer before she died. I always thought a great deal of her. Rock's letter was full of news and I should answer it in detail. But as you know this letter is for you all. I will send a card to W. J. Fender, as Rock suggests. Alta's letter was full of information too. She intimates that you have worn a path from the veranda to the mill lane turning somersaults forward one way and backward the other. That's all right Dorothy. Have all the fun you can because you know it will be only a few years now before you will be working in a laundry or waiting on table somewhere. I think that was it, wasn't it? Maybe though you will be an acrobat in a circus. How about that?

Your Dad is staying in today. To cover the front now I have to start at 8 in the morning; travel 175 miles; return and write some matter for Paris; eat dinner and then write whatever cable there is. It is by long odds the hardest-working job I ever saw and I can't say I am crazy about it. Here's a hug and kiss young lady and best wishes to the whole family. Tell Joseph I'm surely going to write to him soon.

With love,
Dad

Diary: Sunday September 8, 1918

Stayed in again today. Went for a long walk along the Marne in the afternoon despite rain. Also watched the celebration of the 4th anniversary of the Marne victory.

Had long visit with Sam Blythe. In the evening attended a conference of all the correspondents with Major James of the Press division. He says we shall move soon to Nancy and that before any American operation is started we will have the entire thing explained to us.

Diary: Monday September 9, 1918

Went to Paris to attend to the transfer of my bank account from London to Paris. Came right back. Nothing to do in the evening. The 77th division made two attacks last night and today but apparently did not make a success of them so we are writing nothing.

Sat around in the evening with Henry N. Hall of the London Times.

Diary: Tuesday September 10, 1918

Slept late today. Was awakened about eleven by Lieutenants Hartzell and Light who said to be prepared to move tomorrow morning at 10 o'clock. Packed up and wrote a few letters. Most of the correspondents are in Paris but will be back tonight.

It is now assured that the Americans intend to make a big offensive around Nancy. Everyone knows about it so it presumably will be no surprise for the Boche. My idea is that there will be something new and terrible in the way of artillery and gas which will startle the Hun.

Diary: Wednesday September 11, 1918

Great doings around Hotel Sirene, Meaux this morning. The correspondents sang songs and drank champagne with the owner of the hotel. We had been awakened at seven and told that we would start by auto for Nancy at ten. We all left, probably forever, about noon. I rode with Wales of the [International News Service] and James, also Lieutenant [Arthur E.] Hartzell. It was a very uncomfortable ride. Rain all the way. Arrived in Nancy at 5. Had dinner. All correspondents then went to Gen. Nolan's* room. He had maps etc. and explained how the Americans intended at 1 a.m. Thursday to begin an offensive to close the St. Mihiel salient which has been sticking out like a sore thumb for four years.

Stayed up and listened to the barrage. Then went to bed at 1:30.

Before the Battle of St Mihiel, France. From left: Ray G. Carroll, Philadelphia Ledger, Lt. Arthur Delaney, Napoleon, Henry N. Hall, London Times, Lt. Freeman Light, Don Martin, New York Herald, Tom Johnson, New York Sun, Capt. Arthur E. Hartzell, New York Sun. The photo of the correspondents before leaving their hotel in Meaux has been preserved by the Overseas Press Club of America.

Source: Press Club of America, World War I Journalists: Before the Battle of St. Mihiel, www.opcofamerica.org/content/world-war-i-journalists-battle-st-mihiel

* General Dennis Nolan, Chief of Army Intelligence

PART 6

Covering St. Mihiel Salient, Argonne Forest Battles and Struck by Spanish Influenza – September to October 1918

For the next week, Don Martin covered the taking of the St. Mihiel salient, the successful first offensive under command of the American Expeditionary Forces.

Diary: Thursday September 12, 1918

Got up at 3:30. With James and McNutt went out to see the barrage. Had wonderful view of it. It was still going at daylight. Visited various headquarters. Returned at 11 to write a story for New York. Went out again at 3 and returned at six.

Wrote long cable for New York. Has been busiest day I can remember. Americans took the Huns by surprise. Are driving them back.

Diary: Friday September 13, 1918

With James went to various headquarters. Wrote considerable of a cable for New York. Censor's office in famous Stanislaus Square where we have club rooms, etc. Alert given for air raid tonight. No raid but everyone excited. Germans withdrawing from salient Americans decided to close. Not heavy fighting.

Diary: Saturday September 14, 1918

Tried to get to Thiaucourt which was evacuated by Germans yesterday but got caught in congested traffic and had to turn back. Rode through fields for considerable distance. All our men and supplies are moving north on heels of Germans. Rode with Battersby of Reuters and James. Wrote 1,200 words for N.Y. Dined with Bailey of the Daily Mail at the Stanislaus. Had splendid dinner. Air Alert.

Diary: Sunday September 15, 1918

Visited various corps and division headquarters. Went to Thiaucourt. Shells fell while there. Several struck within hundred feet of us. Decided best thing to do was to leave. Every one getting into shelters. Risky running through town in auto. Chauffeur who is one of the toughest of the whole outfit turned pale and didn't want to take chance. We made him go. Afterward went to corps headquarters and returned to Nancy at 5. In evening was an alert. Sat around with Carroll, Wood and Mackenzie.

Back at the New York Herald office in New York, the name 'Don Martin' had become a "by-word", according to a colleague in a letter dated September 15. Here is an excerpt.

Dear Mr. Martin,

... I want to tell you we are all reading your cable and mail stories with a great deal of interest. It is making a big hit everywhere and Don Martin is a by-word throughout the office. As you know, I come in contact with the men of the composing room, where ... the expression of appreciation of your stuff is universal, "Gee," one of them said the other day, "did you read Don Martin's story this morning—that's great stuff." And that is the opinion of all. It is great stuff. In my humble opinion, it is the best matter that is reaching this side of the globe. There is a human interest touch to everything you send which makes it different from the stereotyped reports of other correspondents ... Last night I ... [saw] Jack Regan, of the St. Lois Republic, who is now up at the Times. He gave me his unsolicited opinion that Don Martin's stuff is superb—that is the word he used....

Sincerely yours,
Phil Dietz Jr., Syndicate Desk

Diary: Monday September 16, 1918

Had interesting trip. Went to Essey; then to Nonsard and on through Heudicourt to Saint Mihiel. Talked to several persons who lived in villages during German occupation of four years. Saw German cemetery in Saint Mihiel—fully 6,000 Germans buried there. Monuments elaborate as anything in Europe. German efficiency has a counterpart in German effrontery. Americans here about cleaned out the salient. Germans never stopped to give a fight. Our casualties are very small, but we have about 20,000 prisoners.

Met Jack Wheeler tonight.

Another air raid alert.

Diary: Tuesday September 17, 1918

Stayed in Nancy. Had luncheon with Tom Johnson. Had trouble finding a place to eat. The city is packed with Americans. Wrote 1,000 words for New York. Had dinner at Angleterre. Later sat around with Jimmy Hopper, McNutt waiting for the air raid alert but there was none. The operation in the Saint Mihiel salient is now completed. We have established a new line and the Germans have also.

In his dispatches on September 17, 1918, Don Martin reported being under shelling in Thiaucourt.

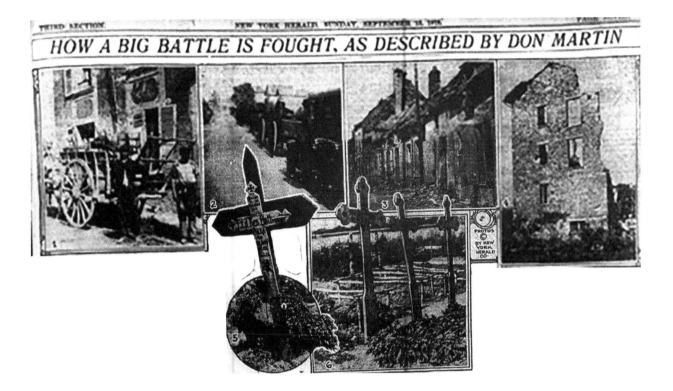

One of the feature spreads featuring
photos taken by Don Martin.

"Six photos by Don Martin

No. 1—These two Frenchmen are moving back to their wrecked home. They left it in June and it was badly damaged by shells.

No. 2—A movement toward the front.

No. 3—A village street on the outskirts of Fere-en-Tardenois.

No, 4—An aerial bomb struck this house. On June 1 it was a fine new dwelling owned by a wealthy manufacturer of Chateau-Thierry.

No. 5—Typical grave of a German lieutenant, holder of the Iron Cross

No. 6—In the village of Beuvardes, recaptured by the Americans and French, the French cemetery has been despoiled by the Germans. There are twenty German markers, some of which are shown in the photograph over spots where French citizens of Beuvardes, dead many years, had been buried."

Diary: Wednesday September 18, 1918

Stayed in Nancy. Our front very quiet. Preparations being made for attack at new point probably west Verdun. Walked around the city for exercise. At night hotel filled with aviators who drank far too much.

In his dispatches on September 18, 1918, Martin reported on bombing of the Rhine valley.

Diary: Thursday September 19, 1918

Went to Ligny, headquarters America's first army. Got story about documents found in German headquarters etc. Met Herbert Parsons, former political leader of New York and had luncheon with him in Ligny. He is a major of intelligence now and a very fine man.

Sent 500 words to New York. Got telegram from Mitchell in Paris congratulating me on my work. No raid alert tonight which seemed good. Quiet on our front.

Diary: Friday September 20, 1918

Stayed in Nancy. Took long walk. Had dinner at Angleterre with James and Corey. Sent about 400 words to New York. All marking time till new operation by Americans is started.

Diary: Saturday September 21, 1918

Stayed in again. Spent most of the day in the Censor's office. Was introduced to the French widow in black who is on her way to visit her husband's grave in Luneville. She is a very charming woman.

Diary: Sunday September 22, 1918

Went to Menil la Tour with James, also to Saizerais. Wrote short cable. Little going on on our front. [Ray] Carroll has sent cable to his paper saying that most of the correspondents are of draft age.

Had dinner at Angleterre with the widow who is a very fine woman with homes in many places.

No raid alert.

Diary: Monday September 23, 1918

Stayed in again today. Orders to correspondents are they cannot leave the war zone, meaning something is soon to happen. Played billiards for couple of hours with Battersby of Reuters [London], a very able man who was a great friend of Tolstoy.

Had dinner at the Angleterre. Wrote nothing for New York. At night sat in Carroll's room and listened to Junius Wood abuse Cameron Mackenzie and Mackenzie good naturedly abuse Wood. Carroll abused everyone. Bailey, James, Forrest and several others came in and talked till two in the morning when we all went to bed. Indications are we will leave here for a few days very soon.

Don Martin's last diary entry was written on Tuesday, September 24, 1918, in Nancy. Why he stopped and whether he wrote more that didn't survive, we do not know. It was then less than two weeks until his death.

Diary: Tuesday September 24, 1918

Stayed in again. Wrote about 600 words cable on the doughboy as a fighting man. Major Bulger, chief of press section, at six this afternoon told all the correspondents to be ready to start off on a three or four day trip at short notice. We cannot leave Nancy tonight or tomorrow. This means the Americans are to start an offensive somewhere probably west of Verdun. My opinion is it will be a big French offensive with the Americans co-operating. We have a vast army ready for business.

Had dinner at Angleterre with Claire Kenamore of St. Louis, McNutt of Colliers and Boothboy of the Y.M.C.A.

Wednesday September 25, 1918

The time had come for Marshal Foch to launch his grand counteroffensive, the battle to break the Hindenberg line. In preparation, over ten days, some 428,000 men, 90,000 horses and mules, 3,980 guns, and 900,000 tons of supplies and ammunition were moved in secrecy from the St. Mihiel sector to the Meuse-Argonne sector.

On September 25, the war correspondents were moved from Nancy to Bar Le Duc. Don Martin stayed the first night at the simple Rose d'Or hotel. A comprehensive briefing was given to the American correspondents on the Meuse-Argonne offensive "in a small store up a cobbled side street" by Captain Arthur E. Hartzell and Major General Fox Connor.

Thursday September 26, 1918

The American Meuse-Argonne offensive roared to a start on Thursday, September 26. Don Martin cabled a triumphant story to the New York Herald, and also sent to Paris a triumphant message, which was published in bold in the Paris Herald on Friday, September 27.

FOE DESPERATELY TRIES TO REPULSE ONRUSHING "AMEX"

Doughboys Again Prove Mettle, However, and, With Tanks, Sweep All Before Them

(Special Telegram to the Herald)

By DON MARTIN

WITH THE AMERICAN ARMIES, Thursday

Credit the Americans with another brilliant victory.

The offensive started at daybreak, following a savage barrage which lighted up the heavens for miles. They advanced seven miles on a front of thirty-two kilomètres, from Verdun west to the Argonne.

Five thousand prisoners at least have been taken.

The Germans sought desperately to prepare new defenses when their first were destroyed by the American artillery, but the Americans swept on relentlessly, killing the machine-gunners and mowing down all obstacles with tanks, pausing only when destroyed roads and mined bridges compelled delay while the engineers, with their customary bravery, reconstructed them.

Many towns were retaken by the Americans, the hard spots being captured by encircling movements, all of which have been successful to date.

As I write the Germans are striving to rearrange and reinforce their line with combat troops.

It has been one of the big operations of the war, the Doughboys redemonstrating their mettle, as shown at the Marne and at Saint-Mihiel and elsewhere.

270

Friday September 27, 1918

On Friday, September 27, Don Martin was able to move to a more comfortable hotel, the Metz, best hotel in Bar Le Duc.

He reported on the Americans' victorious onward sweep. In his report sent to Paris he mentioned things not included in his New York dispatch—steady downpour of rain; strong resistance and desperate fighting in the Argonne—early indicators that the Argonne was going to be tough going for the Americans.

Saturday September 28, 1918

On Saturday, September 28, Don Martin visited the battle in the Argonne forest from Bar Le Duc. His cable sent to the New York Herald reported the Americans meeting stiff resistance in the Argonne.

Sunday September 29, 1918

On Sunday, September 29, Don Martin was again at the front in the Argonne Forest. He reported that the Argonne would furnish an epic of the American fighting men.

That day Don Martin wrote from Bar Le Duc what would be his last letter to his daughter Dorothy in Silver Creek, New York.

Bar Le Duc, France, September 29, 1918

My Dear Dorothy

I have been chasing from place to place during the last three weeks and have done nothing much but write, travel and sleep—and of all the writing not a single letter to you. Well, no one else got any letter from me during that time either. I haven't received any mail from anyone for quite a while, but it is due to the fact that my address has constantly changed and mail has difficulty in finding me. I went from Meaux to Nancy where we had fine headquarters and where the correspondents all had good rooms. I knew it was too nice to last. First thing we knew we were notified to be ready to leave at once for 'somewhere west'. We packed up enough belongings to carry us through four or five days and at night we put off here—one of the quaintest old towns in France. Rooms had been engaged and such rooms as they were!

The town is packed full of officers and soldiers and most of the houses are closed because of the frequent air raids of a few month ago. I slept one night in a quaint, dingy hotel called the Rose d'Or, but it was too dismal for me. The next day I managed to get a room in the leading hotel of the town—the Metz—which is not such a bad place. I have electric light in my room, but no heat. You have read about the American offensive west of Verdun. That is what we came over here for. I have been all along the line; have seen our boys in action and have seen thousands of German prisoners. Yesterday, I went through part of the Argonne Forest, which is one of the best known forests in France. Germans and Americans are fighting there now.

I have been out every day since I arrived here—a week ago—and expect in a little while to start out in an automobile for Montfaucon, a town captured from the Germans day before yesterday. You can look it up on your map. It was a place about as large as Fredonia. The Americans are still fighting all along the line, but it is a queer kind of fighting. The two armies can't see each other. The Germans hide themselves in woods and villages and use machine guns. The Americans sneak up on them the best they can.

The war is coming along pretty well. Tell Uncle Rock that. The Germans are on their way home. There is no doubt of it. They will go slow, but they will never make another advance. America has done it by giving the Allies the preponderance of men. Just now, the interest centers in Bulgaria. If Bulgaria really gets out of the way it means that Turkey will have to get out also and that Germany's end will be brought much nearer. I have seen thousands of German prisoners lately and know that their morale has lowered. In fact, I think there is just a possibility that the war may end this winter.

Love, Dad

> "
> I have seen thousands of German prisoners lately and know that their morale has lowered. In fact, I think there is just a possibility that the war may end this winter.
> "
>
> – Don Martin,
> September 1918

Monday September 30, 1918

On September 30, Don Martin visited recaptured Varennes-en-Argonne.

Tuesday October 1, 1918

Don Martin spent Tuesday, October 1, at the front and visiting the wounded at a field hospital. His dispatches reported the 'heaviest resistance' in the Argonne forest.

Wednesday October 2, 1918

October 2 was Don Martin's last busy day on the front, reporting on the difficult battle in the Argonne Forest. And he also gave his own newspaper some publicity in a dispatch published in the Paris Herald on Thursday, October 3.

Fliers Shower "Heralds" Among Fighting Yanks

(Special Telegram to the Herald)
By DON MARTIN
WITH THE AMERICAN ARMIES, Wednesday

In order that the American troops in the front lines have their favorite newspaper giving the latest news from all parts of the world, American aviators yesterday showered one thousand copies of the current issue of the Herald over the trenches. They were quickly gobbled up.

Thursday October 3, 1918

On October 3, Don was on his way to Paris, a very sick man. Somehow, he wrote a dispatch for the Paris Herald, perhaps while in transit to Paris.

Germans Attack Americans After Crying 'Kamerad!'

(Special Telegram to the Herald)
By DON MARTIN
WITH THE AMERICAN ARMIES, Thursday

Scores of instances of alleged German atrocities on the field of battle are heard but it is seldom that one is printed because the United States authorities have ruled that no atrocity story may be published until it is verified. Here is one which has been verified.

During the fighting in the Argonne forest the Americans attacked the abri [dugout] of St. Louis, one of the strongest local entrenchments in the forest. The Germans waited till the Americans were about 100 feet from the abri and then one hundred of them came out and offered to surrender. They threw up their hands and the Americans accepted their plea, and as the Germans advanced the Americans paid little attention to them.

Presently the Huns put down their hands and hurled a deluge of hand-grenades on the Americans, inflicting severe casualties.

The Americans thereupon attacked the Germans still resisting in the abri....

Don Martin sent his last dispatch to the Paris Herald on Wednesday night, October 2.

Don Martin arrived in Paris on Friday, October 4, checked in at his 'home' in Paris, the Hotel Crillon, where he was seen by a doctor, who said he needed rest. The Crillon invoice for this stay shows him having only cake and port.

Saturday October 5, 1918

The Crillon invoice for October 5, shows Don Martin having a last full and good meal, with a fish course, turbot, followed by veal cutlet and sautéed potatoes and dessert. But his fever rose to a high point.

No dispatches were written; his reporting on the Great War had come to an end.

Sunday October 6, 1918

On Sunday, October 6, Don Martin left the Hotel Crillon and was taken to an American hospital at Neuilly.

Monday October 7, 1918

Don Martin died on Monday, October 7 at twenty minutes past nine from the Spanish influenza. On that day, his daughter Dorothy, back home in Silver Creek, New York, was having her twelfth birthday.

Tuesday October 8, 1918

Don Martin's sudden death came as a shock to his fellow war correspondents and to the world at large. It was a shock, even though it was the peak of the Spanish influenza epidemic. Around the world, the epidemic would eventually claim millions of lives.

What a shock it must have been in Silver Creek, to daughter Dorothy, Mother Rose, the aunts and uncles and all Don Martin's friends and acquaintances. Their sorrow remains untold.

But the New York Herald European Edition in Paris placed a big story in the prime location at the center of page 1 on Tuesday, October 8, 1918, headlined:

"Don Martin, the Herald's Correspondent at Front, Dies Suddenly of Pneumonia in the American Hospital"

"Passes Away After Few Days' Illness Following Chill Caught on Battlefield"

"For Many Years New York Herald's 'Straw Man' – Dies at Forty-Five"

The New York Herald ran a big story, which started on page 1 in its edition of Tuesday, October 8.

Don Martin, Herald War correspondent, Dies in France, of Influenza

Ill Only Two Days, Career of Widely Known Newspaper Man Closes

DEEPLY MOURNED BY PROMINENT MEN

Gained a Nationwide Reputation as a Political Editor and Foremost Election Analyst.

Paris, Monday – Don Martin, war correspondent of the New York Herald, died here today from Spanish influenza after a two day illness.

It was learned here that Mr. Martin contracted a severe cold, when with the troops fighting between the Argonne and the Meuse. At first he refused to abandon his work, but as his condition became worse he was forced to repair to Paris for expert medical attention.

Career As Political Editor And Analyst

Don Martin, for many years political editor of the Herald and since last December staff correspondent of the Herald with General Pershing's expeditionary army in France, is dead. The news, received late yesterday afternoon in a brief cable despatch from Paris, caused profound sorrow throughout the newspaper world in all parts of the country and among men in public life.

For fourteen years Don Martin had been a member of the Herald staff. Before that he was a writer for the Buffalo Express; but from one end of the country to the other he was known as a journalist, able, honest and fearless; a man of superb judgment, keen analytical powers and possessed to an extraordinary degree with common sense, a sense of proportion and a sense of humor.

In his personal life he was a man of unusual charm, his natural magnetism bringing to his circle of friends men in all walks of life.

He knew and was known to bankers, business men, politicians, national and State legislators, Governors, Presidents, men high in statecraft – in fact, included in the intimacy of his life were almost all of the men of all political parties who have lived and done the big things in this country during the last fifteen years.

Keen Observer; Virile Writer

A keen observer, a virile writer, with all the enthusiasm of his trade, he nevertheless maintained to the highest degree the ethics of journalism and was trusted with secrets that were passed to few men whose livelihoods are gained by writing the news of the day.

To HERALD readers Don Martin was best known for his political writings and for his amazing success in forecasting the result of local, State and national elections through the eyes of the Straw Man.

Don Martin was the Straw man and through some of the closest and most perplexing political situations that ever developed in this country he saw the truth

275

with amazing clarity, always taking HERALD readers into his confidence on the Sunday before elections.

When Don Martin went to Europe last December to join General Pershing's forces he was absolutely new to war correspondence.

With that adaptability for which he was famous, however, he rapidly adjusted himself to new conditions, new experiences and new environment, and for the last few months HERALD readers have had many rare treats from his pen.

That he died in the performance of his duty will cause no surprise to those who knew Don Martin. Plunging into the fray with the American forces when Foch started the great allied drive at Chateau-Thierry, he remained in the field, tireless in his labors until he was stricken down a week ago.

One of his last personal messages from abroad was a letter to Theodore Roosevelt, an old friend, in which he gave that stricken father the last details of the death of his gallant son, Quentin, and enclosed a photograph of the rough grave in which lies the body of the young aviator.

Tidings of His Courage

When Floyd Gibbons, of the Chicago Tribune, who won the Croix de Guerre for his gallantry in action, although himself technically a non-combatant, reached

New York several weeks ago, he called at the HERALD office to tell of the work of Don Martin in the field.

Dozens of such tributes have come to the HERALD during the last few months, but never a word from Don Martin himself of the hardships, perils and difficulties of his task, of the sleepless nights spent in mud holes, with little food or water, and continuously under fire, during which he must observe, note and promptly dispatch from the front the news of the day so that the readers of the HERALD would have it without fail when they picked up their papers in the morning.

Here are the words of Joseph Scott, overseas commissioner of the Knights of Columbus, when he returned from Europe in August and called at the HERALD office to tell how he has seen Don Martin sit at a typewriter in a quiet little village, his boots mud caked and tears in his eyes from the memory of what he had seen during the day in the trenches:

"No more valorous man fights on the battlefields today than this man. I could tell you enough to fill a book about the hardships he endures to furnish the news to the HERALD readers.

"When the Americans go over the top, over goes Don Martin with them. When they are under barrage fire he

does not hesitate, but goes forward grinning like the rest of the American soldiers. The men of the army in France respect and admire Mr. Martin for his gallantry and his eagerness to get the news and forward it accurately to his newspaper.

"Sometimes as I have watched him buckle on his brug bag and walk out beside the swinging columns of American soldiers on their way to the places where the bullets are thickest, I have felt a very deep desire to come back to America and go from one end of the country to the other telling of the bravery shown by men such as he, about whom nothing is said, but about whom volumes could be written."

Don Martin was as well known in Albany, Washington, Philadelphia and other large American cities as he was in New York.

He began his newspaper career in Buffalo, to which city he went as a boy from his birthplace, the village of Silver Creek. There he worked side by side with such men as Samuel G. Blythe and Byron R. Newton, now Collector of the Port of New York. He early developed a taste for political writing, although in handling news of any character he was a reporter and writer of the highest type. One of his early successes was his graphic description of the assassination of President McKinley at Buffalo.

His stories at that time attracted attention in parts of the country and resulted in his being brought to New York, where he became a member of the staff of the HERALD.

During his service on the HERALD, he was day city editor, political editor and reporter. For the last few years he had been Albany correspondent during the sessions of the Legislature.

In 1912 and 1916 he was in charge of the reporting of the republican and democratic conventions at Chicago, Baltimore and St. Louis. One of his greatest personal triumphs was in 1916, when he predicted the re-election of President Wilson because that result was indicated by the HERALD's straw vote, which he personally conducted.

Presidents His Friends

Don Martin numbered among his friends such men as Theodore Roosevelt, William H. Taft, President Wilson and Charles E. Hughes.

In October 1916, when Mr. Hughes was travelling through the country in his campaign for the Presidency his train stopped for a few minutes at Silver Creek, N.Y.

Recalling that this was the birthplace of Don Martin, he paid this remarkable tribute to him:

"I am glad to have come to Silver Creek and greet you because of the many pleasant recollections and for another reason. An honest newspaper man is the holiest work of God. And this is Don Martin's home. I have a great regard for Don Martin and am glad to come to his home town."

> ❝ ...from one end of the country to the other he was known as a journalist, able, honest and fearless... ❞
>
> – New York Herald obituary
> October 8, 1918

Wednesday October 9, 1918

Tributes to Don came from leading public men. One of the first was from former President Theodore Roosevelt. It was sent special to the New York Herald the day after his death, and published on October 9.

Chicago, Ill, Tuesday – Theodore Roosevelt, just before leaving for New York today, was informed of the death of Don Martin. Mr. Roosevelt was affected visibly. He said:

"Martin was one of the best and the truest men with whom I have had a close relationship in my experience with the active working men in the newspaper business. I am truly, very truly, sorry to hear of this. He was of that sort that makes it quite worth while for a real man to do his best, efficiently, honestly and thoroughly.

Just before I departed from New York on this trip I received a letter from Martin, written from the western front. Martin had made it his personal business to have seen to it that the grave of my boy, Quentin, had been cared for. He enclosed a photograph that he had made himself of the spot and his own story of all that had happened. I am very, very saddened to have such news."

The esteem with which Don Martin was held by the leaders of the American Expeditionary Forces is shown in the letter dated October 31. 1918, sent to Don's mother by the Commander-in-Chief General Pershing,* included in the Introduction to this book.

A school girl friend wrote a letter, which was published by the New York Herald on October 9.

To the Editor of the Herald

It is with a sharp pang I read in the morning papers of the death of my old friend and schoolmate, Don Martin. I have known Don since I've been old enough to know anything. At six years of age we were in our children's parties together – all through school together and in our school pranks. I remember these particularly well, for Don was politic and escaped, while I – but that's another story.

The boy was well loved in his home town, Silver Creek. His musical abilities won him many friends, when but a very tiny little fellow he played in public, his feet dangling from the piano stool. Poor Don was always most sensitive as to his stature. But like most little men he meant to measure big in other ways and this he has done. Since we have to lose him I'm glad he could go in this greatest of struggles. This is as he would have wished it – noble little fellow, and I'm so proud of one of my home boys.

HELEN G. FISH
New York City, Oct. 8, 1918

* History of Buffalo & Erie County, 1914-1918, Ch. LXXIV, 267-269

Further tributes to Don from eminent men came to the New York Herald and were published, including the Honorable Charles E. Hughes, New York Governor Charles S. Whitman, and Alfred E. Smith, Democratic nominee for Governor.

Saturday October 12, 1918

Editors of New York newspapers expressed their deep regret on the death of Don Martin in editorial comment published on October 12:

New York Tribune: "It is a distinct shock to hear of the death of Don Martin, of the Herald, at his post on the western front. He was universally respected as a man and as a news gatherer. Of attractive personality, he had a host of friends, none of whom will mourn him more sincerely than the newspaper men with whom he came in contact. He was in the front rank in a profession where character and reliability mean everything."

Brooklyn Eagle: "The death of Don Martin, the New York Herald's correspondent with the American troops in France, will be a loss to the readers of that paper, and to newspaper men, among whom Mr. Martin was widely known and highly respected. Mr. Martin went everywhere that the soldiers on the American front went, and he sent home some of the most interesting accounts of their achievements, particularly those of the soldiers of this city, to whom he devoted special attention. His was a fine life given in a good cause."

Tributes were also published by John T. Curtis, managing editor of the Philadelphia Inquirer:
"Don Martin was the kingpin of American correspondents at the front. While other writers witnessed battles, he was a part of them, and the soul of the soldier unconsciously revealed itself in his virile paragraphs. The Philadelphia Inquirer shares with the New York Herald the keen sense of regret at the death which has removed him from his accustomed post—at the edge of the front line."...

... and by the St. Louis Globe-Democrat and the Hartford Courant newspapers.

Sunday October 13, 1918

The New York Herald published tributes to Don Martin from his two noted companion war correspondents, Martin Green and Floyd Gibbons, in its Sunday edition of October 13, 1918, with an introduction and a photo of the three comrades.

Don Martin's Comrades at Front
Pay Touching Tribute to His Memory

There were three of them who went out to war last year — Don Martin of the New York Herald; Floyd Gibbons, of the Chicago Tribune, and Martin Green of the New York Evening World.

Only two came back—Gibbons, wounded three times at Bois de Belleau and one eye gone, but proudly wearing the Croix de Guerre, bestowed by the French government for gallantry in action [and] Green, broken in health but now fully restored and about to return to the battlefields of France.

Don Martin is dead—dead of disease brought on by overwork, exposure and privation endured patiently and uncomplainingly in the service of the Herald and its readers.

Herewith are touching tributes to the memory of Don Martin from two of the three brave spirits who went to the front a year ago.

THREE COMRADES SEPARATED.

Left to Right.— FLOYD GIBBONS, DON MARTIN and MARTIN GREEN.

"My Girl in the United States" Was Don Martin's Little Daughter

Martin Green Tells of His Comrade's Devotion to Daughter, Twelve Years Old, as an Indication of His Character – Tribute to His Honor as a Journalist

By **Martin Green**, *War Correspondent of the New York Evening World*

A gray mist hung like a pall over Neufchateau. The hour was eight in the morning; the month was March. Into the headquarters of the press division of the Intelligence Department of the American Expeditionary Force in France came the correspondents of the American newspapers, wrapped in heavy overcoats and slickers, carrying gas masks and steel helmets, sleepy eyed, because they had reached the camp from the front late the night before – but eager to get back to activities with American fighting forces nearly one hundred miles away.

In the dark narrow street half a dozen automobiles assigned by the army to men reporting the war for the press at home were lined up, awaiting their journalistic cargoes.

The first man to enter the kerosene lamp lighted office of the army censor was Don Martin — Martin of the Herald — not the almost slight, always well groomed Don Martin of Albany and Washington and New York and the United States in general, but a bulky khaki colored Don Martin, almost as broad as he was high, what with his heavy uniform and his thick outer covering against snow and rain and his hobnailed boots and his field accoutrements. Good little, old Don Martin, always on the job — generally first on the job.

"Any mail?" inquired the round little man, backing up against the alleged stove in the middle of the room.

"No mail until ten o'clock," replied the officer in charge. "The mailboat arrived two days ago and I understand from Paris that we'll get a mess of letters."

"There's a letter coming from my girl in the United States," said Don Martin. "If I remain out at the front I wish you would send it to me by one of the boys coming out tomorrow morning. Is 'Jimmy' James here?"

"Jimmy" James – otherwise Edwin L. James of the New York Times, Don Martin's touring partner, as it were, along our battle front — had not arrived. He came in a minute later with other correspondents who had breakfasted at the Officers' Club. Don Martin gave "Jimmy" James a complete calling down for being late and away they went, their automobile leading the way to a long line of correspondents' automobiles bound for the Luneville sector by way of Nancy.

Don Martin might have remained in Neufchateau to get the mail and the letter from his girl in the United States, but his programme was "the paper first," and it so happened that he didn't get his mail until three days later. He pounced on the packet of letters, picked out two and opened one of the two and his face set into a smile and his eyes moistened.

"She's some girl," said Don Martin to me, who was fortunate enough to be with him when he received his belated communications. "Only twelve years old and look at the French she springs on me!"

Don Martin's girl was his only daughter and he used

"My Girl in the United States" Was Don Martin's Little Daughter...

to read to me in France the sparkling communications he received from her most regularly, and I can bear witness that no matter how bulky his mail and no matter how many envelopes there were, indicating from the green tinted envelopes that they bore messages from the New York Herald, the first letters he read were those from a little girl in Silver Creek, New York. The correspondence between Don Martin and his twelve-year-old daughter, in mixed English and French, was a beautiful exemplar of the household tie between France and the United States, which this war has created. I think of him now crouched back in the seat of an automobile, whizzing along a poplar lined road in France, reaching into his pocket for a letter and saying: -- "I want to read you something my girl told me in her last letter."

And he was never too busy or tired to write to his girl. He was always picking up remembrances for her. I shall never forget what a row he raised when, on a trip with a unit of our forces, he lost a pair of little wood-en shoes he had bought for her, with her name artistically cut into the sole of each shoe. He almost tore up the United States army in France.

An angle on the sentimental side of Don Martin, and a big side it was, too. Now for another side.

On the afternoon of Sunday, June 2, I met Don Martin at Montreuil, a town a little to the eastward of Chateau Thierry. The Germans had taken the north side of Chateau Thierry and American troops were swarming by us into the Belleau Wood, to stop the German advance on Paris. American troops had played an important part in preventing the Germans from crossing the Marne and taking the entire town of Chateau Thierry. Montreuil was the headquarters of one of our divisions.

Only three American reporters were near Chateau Thierry that Sunday afternoon – Don Martin, "Jimmy" James and I. I had ridden out from Paris in two hours. Martin and James had come from Neufchateau, 150 miles away. The skin of Martin's face was peeling off from the effect of sunburn and windburn. He had a good story – the first story of the presence of American soldiers in the Chateau Thierry defense.

"Come back to Paris with me," I urged. "You can file there tonight and beat New York. This American intervention is a big thing."

"I know," said Don Martin, "but Jimmy and I promised Major McCabe, who gave us a pass to come up here, that we would go back to Neufchateau and file. You go back to Paris and file your story and beat me if you want to, and be damned to you, but I'm going to keep my word."

And he did. He went back that 150 miles to file his story because he had pledged his honor as a journalist, and to Don Martin his honor as a journalist was a sacred thing.

A clean, sweet character. I worked in association with him for sixteen years in New York City, at national and State conventions and at the front in France, and I have never known or heard of an action of his of which a man could be ashamed.

Don Martin Did More Than Write About The War
– He Lived It and Fought It

By **Floyd Gibbons**, War Correspondent of the Chicago Tribune, Sioux City, Iowa, Saturday, October 12, 1918

It is one of the unexplainable tricks of fate that a man of the fearless spirit of Don Martin should die in France in this year of the Great War as a victim of disease.

Don Martin, when marked for death this year, deserved a soldier's grave on the field of battle. In his death American newspapers lose a capable, conscientious informant, and American journalism suffers the loss of one of its finest exponents.

I have ridden the front of France with Don Martin. I have been with him under shell fire and have observed his coolness in advance positions when withering barrages of indirect machine gun fire speckled the ground close by.

One day last May I was in a dugout in a front line playing checkers with Don Martin, when suddenly a terrific concentration of enemy shells landed near by. The ground shook. Loose earth tumbled down from the roof of the shelter, the air trembled and the candle — our only illumination — was extinguished by the blast.

Floyd Gibbons, who wrote this tribute.

By the time I had recovered my breath Don, sitting on a box on the other side of the table, had relighted the candle and I heard him say in his cool, even voice: — 'It's your move.'

In the first days of June, Don Martin was the last American correspondent to leave Chateau-Thierry as the Germans entered the north side of the town. On July 21st, when the Germans were forced to evacuate Chateau-Thierry and subjected it to a terrific long-range bombard-ment, Don Martin rode back into the town with the first American troops. In the fighting along the Marne, the Ourcq and the Vesle, Don Martin daily and nightly followed the American advance, close on the heels of the retreating enemy. He visited the front lines every day and more dangerous than that, he

had to run the double risk of transportation on the roads up to the front lines and back. Twice his automobile was damaged beyond repair by shellfire, but these incidents never seemed to prevent him from getting another car and going over the same ground the next day.

During the cold and rainy season and the heat of summer this intrepid journalist braved all kinds of weather to serve his readers. He competed physically with men who possessed much younger bodies, but none that had a younger mind. I have seen him returning at night to the correspondents' headquarters, sometimes with his face pinched with cold, sometimes soaked to the skin with rain, sometimes covered with the mud of the trenches, sometimes with his face blistered from the sun and the wind and covered with the gray dust of the road. I have seen him return dog weary and tired and forswear his dinner hour in order that he might transmute into despatches, the human news stories

Don Martin Did More Than Write About The War...

that he had gained at first hand along the fronts that day.

Don Martin above all was human. His pockets were always full of cigarettes when he went to the front line, and always empty when he came out. He liked to talk to our young American soldiers like a daddy or a big uncle. In addition to his own work he wrote many times to their fathers and mothers telling them that their sons were alive and in good health. In action he used to take care of our wounded, giving them water or making them more comfortable on the stretchers. When ambulances were scarce he used to transport them in his automobile.

Don Martin did more than write about the war, he was living the war and fighting the war every day and minute.

When I was wounded at the front Don Martin was among the correspondents who offered to "carry on" in my place and protect my publications until a relief could arrive. Although far from being a well man himself at that time, he was among the first to visit me at the hospital.

He was a real fellow. Of the eighteen original accredited cor-respondents at the American front, Don Martin, Green and I are the only three who are not on the job today. As certainly as I expect to return, so surely do I feel that Don Martin from the spirit land will observe and report from above the triumphant entry of our troops into Berlin. The men who wear the green brassard in France feel deeply the loss of a true comrade.

Sunday October 13, 1918: Don Martin's funeral service in Paris

A funeral service was held in Paris on Sunday, October 13, 1918, at the American Church, Rue de Berri. The New York Herald published this report on Monday, October 14, 1918.

MANY FRIENDS AT CHURCH SERVICE FOR DON MARTIN

Simplicity and Sincerity of Character of "Herald" Writer, Theme of Dr. Goodrich's Sermon

Funeral services for Don Martin were held yesterday afternoon in the American Church in the rue de Berri. They were simple and impressive. Before the pulpit rested the coffin, over which was spread the American flag. Floral offerings were arranged around it. Flat against the wall behind the pulpit were two American flags and the tricolor, and on either side were standards of these two emblems.

Uniforms of the United States army predominated in the gathering of 200 persons composed of friends Mr. Martin had known for years at home and friends he had made in France. The depth and beauty of character which drew these old and new friends to Mr. Martin formed the theme of the sermon delivered by the Rev. Chauncey W. Goodrich, pastor of the church.

Simplicity, sincerity and the power to give fully of himself were the foundations of this character, said Dr. Goodrich. These traits, long known to his intimates, were revealed to the general public by Mr. Martin in his daily dispatches to the Herald chronicling events on the American front of battle.

His knowledge and his ability made these articles of high value to the world, said Dr. Goodrich, and they will be missed greatly. It was his devotion to his duty which made Mr. Martin remain at his post too long.

Dr. Goodrich spoke of the swiftness and tragedy of the death of a man so far from his home and considered it a sacred duty and privilege for those able to be present to represent Mr. Martin's loved ones and old-time associates on such an occasion.

Singing of "America"

The service was opened by the Dead March from Saul and was closed by Chopin's Funeral March, after which the first and last verses of "America" were sung. Between the prayers the organist and soloist of the church rendered "Lead, Kindly Light," and "Nearer, My God, To Thee."

Among the floral offerings were wreaths from the war correspondents at the front, "In Affectionate Memory"; from the New York and European staffs of the Herald, from the New York Herald, from the "Amen Corner," an organization of New York political writers, of which Mr. Martin had long been a director and leading spirit; from the Associated Press, from "G-2 D, G.H.Q." (the Censorship Division of the Army), from Miss Evangeline Booth, commander of the Salvation Army and from M.H. Dequis, director of the Hotel de Crillon, where Mr. Martin stopped when in Paris.

American and English correspondents in Paris and at the front were present in large numbers, a delegation coming down from Press Headquarters in the field. Major A. L. James, Jr., Chief of the Censorship Division, represented the Army, and Captain Wickes was present with many of the other censors stationed in Paris. There were also present representatives of the big relief organizations in France, army officers and soldiers with whom Mr. Martin had made friends at the front.

The body will rest in the church vault until such time as it can be sent home.

The New York Herald featured on the front page of its Magazine section in the Sunday edition of October 13, 1918, perhaps the best Don Martin war story.

The Ride of Baldwin of Albany
Don Martin's Great Story of a Gallant Soldier

"*RAT-TAT-TAT! RAT-TAT-TAT-TAT*!" sang the German machine guns. The Yankee soldier who had been peering over the top of the American trench across the Vesle River tumbled back into the arms of his comrades. Just above the brim of his helmet was a tiny hole.

"*Rat-tat tat! Rat-tat-tat!*" chuckled the Hun machine guns.

The company commander swore; the soldiers muttered curses against those carefully hidden machine gun nests. Some of them gathered in the doorway of the dugout into which had been carried the soldier's body. They were brushed aside by a physician, who took one look at the khaki clad young figure stretched on a rude table. He hardly examined the form. What was the use? In the centre of the white forehead of that upturned young face was a blot of scarlet.

One of the soldier lads, looking down into the dugout from its doorway, was weeping. He was quite a young soldier, that American, and war was very new to him. The dead man had been his closest friend. Other soldiers, although more calloused to death, respect-

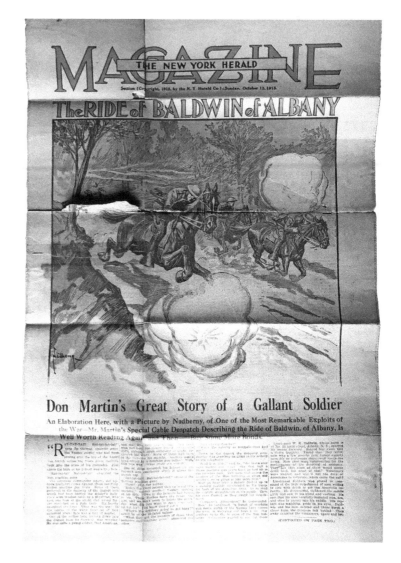

ed his tears. Some of them had been in the trenches for months. Another man's head drilled by a machine gun bullet? Well, this was war. What could one expect?

One of them mounted his helmet on his bayonet and cautiously stuck it above the trench top.

"*Rat-tat-tat! Rat-tat-tat-tat!*" chanted the German machine gun.

"*Darn*" said the soldier.

"*Makes the third helmet they've bored this morning,*"

nodded another Yankee, leaning on his rifle. *"Two of the helmets had heads in 'em. Those boches have the range, the aim, and we can't seem to locate the nests. Say, what did you want to spoil your new tin hat for? You knew they'd get it."*

"When's the artillery going to get busy?" asked he of the ill-fated helmet.

"When they get the location of those Hun batteries and machine guns," answered the other.

"And when'll that be?"

"When the cavalry or sharpshooters find out."

Down in the dugout the company commander was growling an order to his orderly at the telephone.

"Send it in code," he said, *"the Huns may have tapped our wires. Say that half a dozen machine gun nests have us tied up in the trenches here. Tell them that unless the location of the Hun batteries is given our artillery, we're going to lose more men."*

Half an hour later a runner dashed up to a cavalry captain surrounded by his troop, far back of the American lines. As he read the captain straightened in his saddle. Then his eyes flashed as they swept his detachment.

"Companeee, Atten-shun!" he commanded. *"Men,"* he continued, *"a bunch of machine gun nests, north of the Yankee lines across the river, is worrying our boys a lot. Our artillery lacks the location of the Hun batteries. Volunteers wanted to spy out those nests."*

Lieutenant W. R. Baldwin, whose home is at No. 291 Lark street, Albany, N.Y., spurred his mount forward. Behind him came half a dozen troopers. Young men they were, men who a few months past looked eagerly upon life as a glorious thing, well worth the living. Now they were volunteering for the performance of the deadliest of missions. They felt that some of them would never come back, but what of that? Volunteers were wanted, and was it not the duty of Americans to volunteer when came the call?

Lieutenant Baldwin was placed in command of the little detachment of men willing to ride with death to aid the American infantry. He dismounted, tightened his saddle girth and saw to his pistol and carbine. He saw that his men carefully imitated him, too, and then he swung into his saddle. His captain was watching, pride in his eyes.

Baldwin and his men saluted and there burst a cheer from the troopers left behind. Then away cantered the volunteers, spurs and bridles jingling, saddles creaking, the morning sunlight flashing, glinting from rifles and sabers.

The American and German forces had grimly settled down to machine gun and artillery duels across the Vesle River.

The enemy had been steadily gathering his forces, and it was partly due to this that the Yankees were making no efforts to push their lines any considerable distance north of the river.

[Don Martin, the Herald's special correspondent with the American armies in France, true to his post, was right where the guns bellowed loudest; right there where he could see for himself the news in the breaking and making.

It was to the Herald correspondent that Baldwin told the story of his daredevil gallop, and it was Martin who gathered the tale of how the monotonous rattle of hidden Hun machine guns had been taking venomous toll of American lives. Fresh from the front, where he had penetrated further north than any of the allied officers or enlisted men, Baldwin was interviewed. Graphic was his description of his ride with his detachment into the German lines north of the Vesle, opposite Fismes, for the purpose of learning the location of enemy machine gun nests and batteries. Here is the story, and for sheer nerve, gallantry and daring it deserves a place on the lists of all famous rides, including those of Paul Revere and Sheridan. The charge of the Light Brigade, as told by Tennyson, was not more heroic – Herald editorial staff.]

"Are you ready, boys?" cried the lieutenant, turning in his saddle when he and his men reached a spot where they were to break into a road full in view of the enemy and swept by German guns.

"We're ready!" came the answer. *"Then ride like hell!"* cried Baldwin, and clapping spurs to his mount he swung down into the road and up

The Ride of Baldwin of Albany...

the thoroughfare, leading the field like the favorite horse leaping away from the pack at the post. After him galloped his men, hard riders all, strung out like a whip lash, each man straining forward his mount. Whip and spur and loose rein it was, every man bent over his saddle bow, some of them coaxing on their horses; others silent, grim of face, hoping by some miraculous chance to escape unhit from the horizontal hail of German machine gun lead.

Shells ripped open the road. One huge missile shrieked and whined its Hunnish rage before it shattered to earth fifty feet behind the rear horse. The animal reared and plunged, but its rider clung to the saddle and yanked the reins until his beast was again racing forward, head outstretched, tail streaming behind. Whips and spurs, spurs and whips, and still they galloped on, not a man even scratched by a Hun ball. Shrapnel burst above them, a machine gun bullet stung a horse like the flick of a hundred lashes, and one Trooper was nearly thrown when his steed plunged and shied at the edge of a shell made crater.

Close to the German lines the Yankee troopers jumped from their panting, steaming horses, pulling them into a small wood, where the animals were tethered to trees. Then on their bellies the Americans crawled until two hundred yards from the first line of the Huns. They were instantly spotted.

"Rat-tat-tat! rat-tat-tat!" sang the German machine guns. German bullets moaned and whined futilely, ricocheting from the few trees about the Americans.

But Baldwin and his companions stayed until they had learned all they wanted to know, and then, still scorning the leaden rain, they turned back to their horses. They were there, trembling, nervous, eager to be off and away from the bullets splintering the trees about them. Somehow not a horse had been injured.

Then it was a race for life against death, and race they did. Back over the shell ploughed road they had to ride, back through all the terror of shell fire.

Spur rowels deep in their horses flanks, galloped the troopers, leaning forward under cover of the necks of their mounts. They coursed as if they bore charmed lives, and, reaching American headquarters, they reported the location of the Germans and their batteries and machine guns.

Formation of Don Martin's posts of American Legion

The American Legion was chartered by Congress in 1919 as a patriotic veterans organization. On March 15-17, 1919, members of the American Expeditionary Force convened in Paris for the first American Legion caucus. At the St. Louis Caucus on May 8-10, 1919, "The American Legion" is adopted as the organization's official name. On Sept. 16, 1919, Congress chartered The American Legion.

In Fall 1919 servicemen in Don Martin's hometown, Silver Creek, N.Y., formed an American Legion *"Don Martin Post of Silver Creek"* Post No. 148 named in his honour. Several months later, the world war veterans on the staff of the New York Herald and Evening Telegram organized the *"Don Martin Post of New York,"* Post No. 666 of the American Legion.*

In only one other instance had the American Legion permitted the use of the same name by two posts. That was the "Quentin Roosevelt Post of Oyster Bay," New York, and the "Quentin Roosevelt Post of the Bronx," New York.

January 1920: Don Martin goes home to Silver Creek, New York.

It took until January 1920 for Don Martin's remains to be transported across the ocean to New York. With the assistance of the two Don Martin Posts of the American Legion, his body was brought to his hometown of Silver Creek, New York, and a funeral took place on January 29, 1920. This was reported in the Silver Creek News of January 29, 1920, as follows.

FUNERAL OF DON MARTIN WAS HELD THIS AFTERNOON

Services in Charge of Don Martin Post No. 148 American Legion
—Tribute from George R. McIntyre

The body of Don Martin, New York Herald correspondent, who died in France, October 7, 1918, arrived here Wednesday accompanied by Wellington Wright of the Herald staff, Commander of Don Martin New York Herald Post, American Legion. Mr. Wright was in France at the time of Don Martin's death.

Mr. Martin's body was brought home on the steam-ship La Savoie which sailed from Havre January 17 and arrived in New York on Tuesday. On the steamer a stateroom was arranged as a mortuary chapel and was under guard of two sailors day and night throughout the voyage.

On arriving in New York Don Martin New York Herald Post took charge and brought the body to this vil-lage. Here, Don Martin Post, the second to be named in honor of Mr. Martin, took charge. Members of the Post met the Pennsylvania train and escorted the body to the Presbyterian Church where a guard of honor was stationed until the hour of the funeral.

The funeral of Mr. Martin was held at the Presbyterian Church at 2 o'clock this

* The Fourth Estate, November 22, 1919

Funeral of Don Martin Was Held This Afternoon...

afternoon. Rev. C. H. Dudley conducted the services which consisted of reading of several selections of Scripture, a brief address, the reading of a tribute of George R. McIntyre of the Chicago American, a boyhood friend of Mr. Martin, prayer and benediction.

The Honor Roll of the Presbyterian Church, containing between 50 and 60 names of which the only gold star represents Mr. Martin's name, was read. The casket was draped with the American flag and surrounded with a large number of beautiful floral tributes.

The active bearers were selected from the Navy Men of the Don Martin Post. The honorary bearers were John Knox, J. O. Bennett, Henry Martin, Bert Barnes, Bert Brooks, George H. Shofner, M. L. Barbeau, Leon H. Brand, W. J. Brand, C. G. Jackle, Wal-lace Imus.

The burial service was conducted at the grave in Glenwood cemetery by Don Martin Post No. 148.

Mr. McIntyre's Tribute

The following tribute to the memory of Don Martin was received a few days ago by George V. Barbour, and was read today at Mr. Martin's funeral:

"Don Martin was of the type of newspaper men that make one glad that he is a member of the profession.

He was more than a newspaper man. He was a man, and when I have said that it seems to me that I have paid him the highest tribute that can be paid to any man, for he possessed to the full every manly quality.

My earliest remembrance of Don Martin was on a sunny morning when my mother went next door to see his mother, Mrs. Martin. I waited in the living room and presently my mother came out of a bedroom with a little bundle on her arms. She partially opened it and I looked down on the baby face of Don Martin. As a boy it did not interest me until the baby, looking up at me wrinkled his face into a smile. That smile seemed to just transform little Don's face. It was the same kind of a smile that I remembered years afterward; it was the index of the sunny, optimistic nature of Don Martin.

He was never afraid to tackle any task. Nothing was too great for him to try, and he always went at it with that same cheerful smile of his. I can imagine that smile spreading over his face when the managing editor of the New York Herald assigned him to go to France as a war correspondent.

We know the history of his work over there. He faced it with the same indefatigable energy with which he prosecuted all his newspaper work. He left nothing to guesswork—he was always sure of his facts. He always knew whereof he wrote, and when an article appeared in the Herald under his name the reader could be sure that every word was true.

Systematic, careful, unsparing of himself he was a man who had every consideration for those who worked under him, and throughout his arduous work at the front he had time always to remember the loved ones at home and to write to them.

Don Martin was as truly a soldier as any of the men who shouldered guns to drive back the German hosts, and I am sure he was just as truly a loving son, a kind and loving husband and father.

All honor to him. I have heard that two American Legion Posts are named after him. I have read the eulogies written by his co-workers and those who were close to him in the arduous work of recording the daily progress of the greatest war in the world's history.

I ask only the privilege of adding my humble praise, my laurel wreath to the memory of Don Martin.

When the real history of the Great War is written, I am sure that Don Martin's name and the work he did will find a place in it.

Short though his life was, we who knew him knew that he did not live in vain.

To those of his family who survive I would give the comforting thought that Don Martin has truly died for his country as the men who faced the bullets, and though he is dead his name will live.

Sincerely,
GEORGE R. McINTYRE"

During the funeral service conducted by Reverend Dudley on January 29, the poem 'Crossing the Bar' by Alfred, Lord Tennyson, was read:

"Sunset and evening star, and one clear call for me!
And may there be no moaning of the bar when I put out to sea.
But such a tide as moving seems asleep, too full for sound and foam,
When that which drew from out the boundless deep turns again home.

Twilight and evening bell, and after that the dark!
And may there be no sadness of farewell when I embark;
For though from out our bourne of Time and Place the flood may bear me far,
I hope to see my Pilot face to face, when I have crost the bar."

[Crossing the Bar
Alfred, Lord Tennyson, 1890]

| 1901 | 1917 | 1918 |

Don Martin

Final Salute to Don Martin, Soldier of the Pen, and Dorothy

We have reached the end of the story of Don Martin, World War I war correspondent, and his "girl", daughter Dorothy.

This book has chronicled my grandfather's relationship with Dorothy and the remarkable story of his contribution to the Great War.

What better way to end than by recalling Minna Irving's poem, published shortly after his death:

Dorothy Elizabeth Martin, 1918
11 years old.

A SOLDIER OF THE PEN

He took the simple words we use
And shaped them with his art
In wondrous imag'ry to show
Poor France's bleeding heart.
He made us hear beyond the sea
The roar of flaming guns,
And feel the nameless agonies
Inflicted by the Huns.

Enfold him with the starry flag:
He died in uniform,
A stormy petrel of the press
Who loved the battle storm.
Salute him with your lifted swords,
Ye Allied fighting men,
Don Martin was a soldier, too—
A soldier of the pen.
—Minna Irving.

Yes, let us salute Don Martin, Soldier of the Pen! And his daughter Dorothy.

Dorothy Martin continued growing up with her family in Silver Creek, New York.

A scholarship from the newspaper men of New York in memory of her father funded her attendance at Vassar College, from which she graduated with honors.

She then went to Don Martin's favorite city, New York, and started a career in book publishing with Doubleday.

CPSIA information can be obtained
at www.ICGtesting.com
Printed in the USA
BVHW020603170322
631521BV00024B/716